A History of
Trinity Church in Newport
1698–2000

Looking up Frank Street from the corner of Thames Street to Trinity Church, showing the church as it looked for nearly 250 years, crowded in by small houses. A pencil sketch by Richard Grosvenor, 1973.

Semper Eadem

A History of Trinity Church in Newport
1698–2000

by

John B. Hattendorf

Revised and Expanded
Second Edition

Volume I

Trinity Church
Newport, Rhode Island

MMXVIII

LIBRARY OF CONGRESS CATALOGUING-IN-PUBLICATION DATA
Hattendorf, John B.
        Semper Eadem: a history of Trinity Church in Newport 1698–2000

Library of Congress Control Number: 2018951187

ISBN: 978-1720608240

I. Hattendorf, John B., 1941- II. Title 1. Trinity Church (Newport, R.I.: Episcopal) - History
2. Newport (R.I.) - Church History 3. Episcopal Church - Rhode Island - Newport - History
4. Anglican Communion - Rhode Island - Newport - History

Book design: Jane Carey
Photographs: John Corbett

Table of Contents

Letter from the Presiding Bishop

THE MOST REVEREND FRANK T. GRISWOLD
PRESIDING BISHOP AND PRIMATE, THE EPISCOPAL CHURCH

THE EPISCOPAL CHURCH CENTER
815 SECOND AVENUE · NEW YORK NY 10017-4594

(212) 922-5322   (212) 490-3298 FAX
1-800-334-7626

September 21, 1998

Trinity Episcopal Church
Newport, Rhode Island

My dear Brothers and Sisters in Christ:

Congratulations on the 300th Anniversary of the founding of your congregation.
Tragically, so few people realize that in the United States there are churches that have
worshipped God and served the people of God for this length of time.

What a different day and age it was in church and state when Trinity was founded. The
Prayer Book was 1662 and the Queen was Anne, the last monarch before the coming of
the House of Hanover. Now we have the 1979 Prayer Book and Trinity is part of a
Republic.

What an extraordinary sweep of time your congregation has experienced. The Church of
England in the colonies has now become the Episcopal Church of the United States.
Episcopacy has come to this country. We are now a national church. Rather than a few
huddled communities along the East Coast, we are a country of fifty states.

Now Trinity is ready for another 300 years. God will be worshipped. The Word of God
will be read and preached. The sacraments will be celebrated. There will be ministry to
the people of God.

I give thanks for the past life of Trinity and pray for its witness in the years ahead.

Faithfully yours,

Frank T. Griswold
Presiding Bishop and Primate

FTG:awb

Preface to the Second Edition

Trinity Church originally published *Semper Eadem* in September 2001 as part of the extended commemoration of the three hundredth anniversary of the parish's establishment between 1698 and 1700. The first edition appeared in a print run of about eight hundred copies, of which the last copy sold several years ago. Since then, new members of the parish, visitors to the church, people researching their genealogy, and others interested in the preservation of Trinity's historic structure and its connections to the history of Newport and Rhode Island, have created a demand for a new edition. This second edition is printed in two volumes with the first containing the narrative history without substantial change from the 2001 edition, other than correcting typographical and small errors. Many will be pleased to learn that the original appendixes, now contained in Volume II, have been revised and expanded to include detailed information on grave inscriptions, along with updated churchyard drawings, plus additional pew drawings and lists. Volume II also includes a new fourth appendix containing comprehensive lists of clergy associated with the parish between 1700 and 2018.

Trinity Church continues to be the spiritual home and place of worship within the Episcopal Church of the United States for its active and engaged parishioners. Much has happened within the parish since 2001 for which we do not yet have enough distance and perspective to explain in historical terms. One can, however, point to key events that highlight some of the trends in recent years. In May 2010, The Reverend Canon Anne-Marie Richards became the first woman selected to be the parish's rector in its three-hundred-year history. She is the fifth woman member of the parish clergy in a series that began only in 1984 when The Reverend Mary Johnstone arrived at Trinity as a deacon and rose to become priest in charge in 1992–94. In November 2012, The Right Reverend W. Nicholas Knisley, Jr. became the thirteenth Bishop of the Diocese of Rhode Island, succeeding The Right Reverend Geralyn Wolf. In 2015, The Most Reverend Michael B. Curry became the first African American to serve as the 27th Presiding Bishop and Primate of The Episcopal Church. In 2016, the Carr-Rice House was demolished in anticipation of constructing a new parish house for a wider range of parish activities on Trinity's campus. In December 2017, the parish had its first parish Christmas pageant in more than a decade. The parish's community outreach has expanded with free meals offered three times each month to those in need. In recent years, holiday outreach programs have included Stockings for Soldiers, Christmas Giving Tree, and Gifts for Teens. After a period of decline over the past ten years, the parish has grown with participation in Sunday worship services rising from an average of 123 in 2010 to 197 in 2018.

Today, Trinity parishioners cherish the parish's history at the same time they relate to the present and look to the future. Through the occasional use of appropriate and inspiring contemporary religious art used from time to time on service leaflets, and significant art installations in both Honyman Hall and the sanctuary, the parish has looked for ways to connect historic roots to 21st century expression. Music, too, provides a way to connect past and present as Trinity continues its commitment to preserving the Church's musical tradition and exploring new repertoires. The parish rightfully boasts about the high quality of its music program, including an accomplished choir and the leadership of a series of talented organists and choirmasters.

The parish's historic wooden church building from 1725-26, influenced by Sir Christopher Wren's designs for London parish churches in the late seventeenth century, remains one of the most beautiful structures from the American colonial period. Its landmark white spire survives, as it has for centuries, as an inspiring beacon to all who arrive in Newport by land or by sea.

Acknowledgments

Printing, editing and publishing this second edition is made possible by donations from the leaders of Trinity's Guiding Ministry, Charlotte Johnson and Harle Tinney, who, along with myself and other committee members—Barbara Roos, Cassandra Dias, The Reverend Canon Anne Marie Richards, and The Reverend Alan Neale—agreed a second edition was necessary. Scans of the 2001 edition were converted to MS Word in order to make necessary corrections. This painstaking copy editing process was led by Charlotte Johnson with conscientious proofreading by Terry Commodore and The Reverend Alan Neale. Volume II has been revised and expanded with new drawings of the churchyard and pews by retired architect Robert J. Wilson, who is also one of our dedicated tour guides, or "sitting saints." A newly-discovered manuscript of churchyard grave inscriptions is included in its entirety, thanks to Special Collections Librarian Michelle Farias, and Patrick Crowley, Director of Library Services at the Redwood Library. The new fourth appendix listing clergy involved a research effort that was greatly facilitated by Joan Bartram's recent reorganization of the church archives at the Newport Historical Society.

October 2018 J.B.H

Acknowledgments (First Edition)

"Semper Eadem" was the personal motto of Queen Anne. Only nine months after she had succeeded to the throne of England, and two days before Christmas, in 1702, she directed that any representation of her royal arms carry these words, the same motto that her great predecessor, Elizabeth I, had used. In translation, the motto means "always the same" and, in taking it, Anne was particularly expressing her unswerving devotion to the principles of the Church of England. In her understanding, the motto was a reminder to guide her, as temporal head of the church, in a course of moderation between the rival camps within church politics and practice.

This same motto was prominently carved as part of the reproduction of the royal arms that Norman Isham designed to hang over Trinity's altar during his restoration of Trinity Church. Removed from the altarpiece in the church in early 1931, it was unearthed from storage in 1956, at the time of the construction of the new parish house, Honyman Hall, where it hangs prominently today. At that time, Canon Lockett F. Ballard quite rightly suggested that that same phrase also characterized the parish of Trinity in Newport, Rhode Island. In following the story of this parish, I have been inspired by the words of Anne's motto, which not only reminds us of the early days of our parish but also characterizes the enduring nature of its members over the past three hundred years. Through many changes, Trinity Church still remains very much the same in its devotion to principles.

I am grateful for the support and encouragement of many people in bringing this history to fruition. Since I first became a member of the Trinity family in 1964, many people have shared their knowledge with me, including Trinity's clergy, staff, and parishioners. I am particularly grateful to Bobby Wright, who first convinced the leadership of the parish to proceed with a full-scale history; to Herb Lawton and Marie Maguire, who graciously made material available from the office files when I needed it; and to the Tercentenary Celebration Committee under the chairmanship of Cora Lee Gibbs, with Sam Barker, Bob Connelly, and Anne Livingston, who have patiently overseen the project as it progressed to fruition.

In addition, I am grateful to the many volunteers, who have helped to organize and to preserve the parish archives on permanent deposit at the Newport Historical Society, where Dan Snydacker, Joan Youngken, Ron Potvin, and Bert Lippincott provide the proper storage and research facilities as well as personally serve as friendly and invaluable sources of information and advice. In preparing the volume, Jane Carey has done her characteristically excellent job in illustrating and designing the volume, while Pelham Boyer has done the copyediting, and John Corbett has been particularly helpful in taking new photographs to complement those in the archives. The Redwood Library and its staff in Newport have been a particularly valuable resource at all stages of researching, writing, and illustrating this book. Many other institutions and their staffs have also provided valuable assistance: the Bodleian and Rhodes House Libraries of Oxford University; the Episcopal Diocese of Massachusetts Diocesan Library and Archives; Holy Trinity Church, Marylebone

Road, London, England; the Records of the Society for Promoting Christian Knowledge; the John Carter Brown Library, Providence, Rhode Island; Lambeth Palace Library, London, England; Massachusetts Historical Society, Boston, Massachusetts; New Haven Colony the Historical Society, New Haven, Connecticut; Public Record Office, Kew, London, England; Rhode Island Historical Society, Providence, Rhode Island; Society for the Preservation of New England Antiquities, Boston, Massachusetts; and the University of Rhode Island, Kingston, Rhode Island, where the records of the Episcopal diocese are located.

I am grateful to Professor Stanley J. Lemons of Rhode Island College for his constructive comments on the early drafts of the first chapters, and to former clergy at Trinity who provided me with their recollections and photocopies of information from their own files: The Reverend A. Royston Cochran, The Reverend Lorne Coyle, The Reverend Mary Johnstone, The Reverend Alan D. Maynard, and The Reverend James R. MacColl III. For the final three chapters, former senior warden Dr. B. Mitchell Simpson III made valuable constructive comments for improvement.

The printing and publication of this history have been made possible by a generous donation from Ann Fletcher in memory of Carolyn Skelly and by donations to the Tercentenary Fund of Trinity Church in memory of my mother, Dorothy Collom Jarvis, who was a member of the parish during the last two and a half years of her life, received from Maxwell D. Bardeen, Jr., Captain and Mrs. Frank H. Barker, Mrs. Mary S. Baskerville, Mrs. Dorothy T. Donnersberger, Mrs. Joseph H. Hartmann, the Hattendorf family, Mr. and Mrs. Cassard Kaesemeyer, Mrs. Alice J. Lundberg, Mrs. Elizabeth S. MacMillan, the Naval War College Wardroom, Mrs. Harriet S. Norgren, Mr. Donald Parker, Mrs. Barbara A. Prisk, Mrs. Beatrice Spencer, Dr. and Mrs. Hâkan Sundell, Mr. and Mrs. Donald E. Swanson, Wim and Evert Vandermeer, and Vice Admiral and Mrs. Thomas R. Weschler.

March 2001 J.B.H.

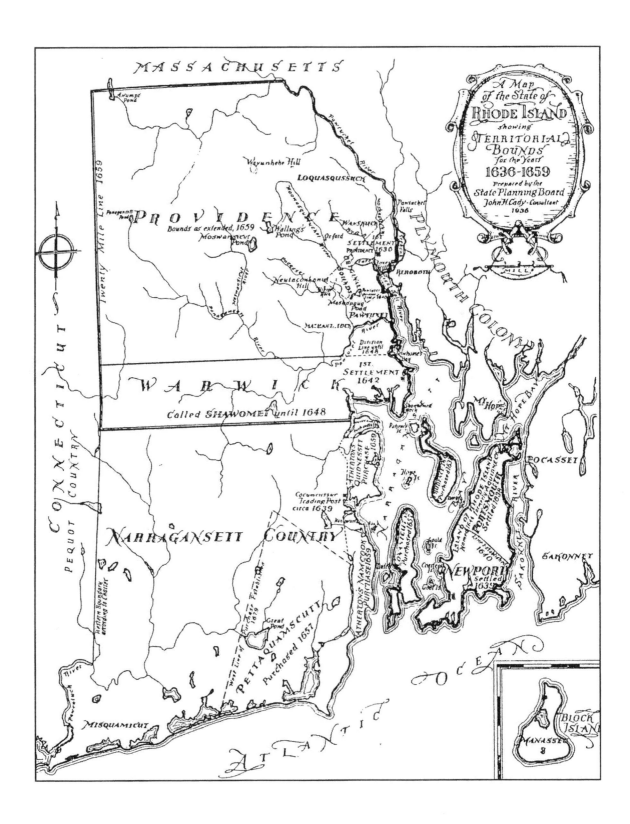

1

Colony and Town, Empire and Church:

The Context of the New Anglican Parish, 1698–99

As the 1690s brought the seventeenth century to a close, Newport was the largest port and most important town in the English colony of Rhode Island and Providence Plantations. The colony was not very old, and Newport was not very large. Only sixty years before, in 1639, the first settlers had laid out Newport. The town's first settlers had come from England via Massachusetts. They had left England to get away from the Church of England, and soon after, they had left Massachusetts when its leaders enforced another type of strict religious conformity.

From the outset, the Anglican Church was not welcome in New England, but several ordained clergymen came for short periods to the Pilgrim and Puritan colonies in Massachusetts, although few stayed long. Among the earliest was The Reverend William Blaxton or (Blackstone), a 1617 graduate of Emmanuel College, Cambridge, who came to the site of Boston in 1624. He never practiced his ministry in America, and his ideas were similar to those of the Puritans, but in 1634 he left Massachusetts for the isolated forests at "Study Hill," near present-day Lonsdale, Rhode Island. As the first European inhabitant of what would eventually become Rhode Island, as well as its first Anglican clergyman, he is remembered in the name of a river in the northern part of the state. Explaining his need to begin again, Blackstone wrote that he had "left England to escape the power of the Lords Bishops, but found himself in the hands of the Lords Brethren."[1]

Blackstone was the precursor of many another who settled in Rhode Island after repeated searches for a place where they and their ideas could live in relative peace. The large islands of Narragansett Bay and the surrounding mainland soon became a haven for people who were having to make second, even third, attempts to live in the American colonies. They came in separate, independent groups to settle these areas, then seemingly distant from the English colonies in Plymouth and Boston and from their similarly rigid offshoots being founded along the Connecticut River and in New Haven. One such independent-minded person was Roger Williams, who obtained an Indian deed to his "providential place" on the banks of the Great Salt Cove in 1636. Two years later, an ecclesiastical court in Massachusetts banished Anne Hutchinson for her "antinomian" views on personal grace and revelation, views that diminished the importance of the clergy. She joined the rest of the exiles from Boston, including William Coddington. Hutchinson became their spiritual leader in a new settlement at Pocasset at the northern tip of Aquidneck Island, which Roger Williams called "Rode Island," which he said meant "Isle of Roses" in Greek.[2]

In 1638, Coddington, Dr. John Clarke, Nicholas Easton, and others separated from Mrs. Hutchinson's group and moved to the southern end of the island, where they established the village of Newport in 1639. There they set up the basis for the small, idyllic agricultural community that they wished to create. However, it was neither their particular beliefs nor their agrarian society but the place they had chosen for their settlement, with its good harbor and ready access to the sea, that were to be the key factors that determined its future. While its independent-minded people attracted others of a similar bent—and even those who were so independent minded as to be lawless—the natural characteristics of the place, similar to those of Boston and New Amsterdam, soon brought commerce, trade, and direct connections to the wider English Atlantic world.[3] These created additional influences on the growing community at Newport, influences that would soon impel it into the league of the nascent urban centers of England's North American colonies.

In one sense it was natural for the leaders of independent Newport to reach out to nearby English settlements, even though they were all communities of outcasts who had temporarily resolved their disputes over religion by founding towns distant from one another. In 1640, Newport took its first tentative step and asserted control over the group from which it had sprung, Anne Hutchinson's colony in present-day Portsmouth. Meanwhile, in Massachusetts and Connecticut, the memory of the difficulties the colonists had experienced in trying to coordinate their responses to defend themselves during the Pequot War in 1636–37 joined with a new threat, that the Dutch might expand their colony at New Amsterdam in a northeasterly direction. Representatives of the four colonies of Massachusetts Bay, Plymouth, Connecticut, and New Haven met in Boston in 1643 and established the United Colonies of New England as a means to protect themselves more efficiently. However, the independent-minded people who had recently settled around Narragansett Bay were excluded from this arrangement; for their part, they immediately saw this initiative as a threat, the very thing they had originally left Massachusetts Bay to avoid. It was in fact no idle threat, as Massachusetts Bay now claimed jurisdiction over the area of present-day Cranston and Warwick. When Plymouth Colony attempted to extend a claim to Aquidneck Island, Anne Hutchinson was so fearful that she left as soon as possible for New Amsterdam.

In the face of this threat, Roger Williams went to England and sought a charter that would unite the villages of Portsmouth, Providence, Newport, and Samuel Gorton's newly established settlement called Shawmut (Warwick, after 1648). At the time, England was wracked by its Civil War; the royalist forces of King Charles I were on the way to defeat by the armies of the Puritan-dominated Parliament. In this conflict Williams naturally sided with the Puritans and, through those connections, obtained in 1644 a charter from the parliamentary committee on colonial affairs, which included his friend Sir Henry Vane, who had been governor of Massachusetts in 1635–37. In England, Vane, who had as governor been sympathetic to Anne Hutchinson's views, welcomed Williams into his home as a guest. With Oliver Cromwell in the field, Vane was the key civil leader in England during the years 1643–53 and a key member of the parliamentary committee that dealt with colonial affairs. Other members of that committee included Cromwell and the Lord High Admiral of England, Robert Rich, Earl of Warwick. The patent that Williams obtained from this committee granted the powers of civil government to "Providence Plantations in the Narragansett Bay in New England," comprising all the settlements in the area.

This, however, did not meet with everyone's approval. In March 1644, Coddington and the government of the two towns on Aquidneck Island formally declared that their island "shall be henceforth called the Isle of Rhodes or Rhode-Island."[4] Coddington in particular loathed the thought of having to join any government that included Gorton's Warwick, and he sought to keep Rhode Island an independent commonwealth, separate from Providence Plantations. Despite much wrangling and political maneuvering—Coddington managed at one point to obtain a separate charter for Rhode Island that made him governor for life—the arrangement created by the 1644 patent remained in effect. This was largely due to the need to manage the rivalry that had developed among the towns over expansion into the Narragansett country, and to the strong local sentiment against the United Colonies.

A general assembly of freemen from the four towns established the laws of the colony on a basis that allowed the towns to remain dominant, established freedom of conscience, and separated church and state. Increasingly, Newport acted as the capital; it was the host to the agencies of government and supplied many officials to it. The 1644 patent remained in effect until the restoration of the monarchy under King Charles II in 1660, when the king voided all independent acts of Parliament and of the Protectorate that had existed during the Civil War and the interregnum.

Because only the authority of a parliamentary committee had sanctioned the Rhode Island colonial government, the colonists quickly realized that the Restoration was a direct threat to the local political stability that they had achieved. Three months after they received news of the Restoration, on 18 October 1660, the colonial government took advantage of the moment and proclaimed Charles II, the first of the New England colonies to do so. It was many months before the Puritan colonies of Connecticut and Massachusetts followed its example. Both had been sympathetic to Cromwell, and the New Haven Colony had harbored some of the regicide judges who had executed Charles I. Notwithstanding the Rhode Islanders' profession of loyalty, the move was in fact more to protect their own interests than to embrace the political consequences it involved. The Rhode Island colonists were slow to revise their laws to invoke the king's name, and they did not hurry to seek a new charter.[5]

The delay led to a boundary dispute with the New Haven Colony, which had obtained its charter first and had defined its eastern boundary as Narragansett Bay. After obtaining funds and instructions from home, Rhode Island's agent in London, Dr. John Clarke of Newport, drafted a new charter, to which he finally obtained the king's assent in July 1663. Addressing himself to the "Governor and Company of the English Colony of Rhode Island and Providence Plantations, in New England, in America," the king granted the right to maintain a self-perpetuating corporation. This corporation had the power to elect its own officers and to admit new freemen, thereby establishing a form of government by which the colonists would govern themselves under their own laws. In addition, the king granted to Rhode Islanders all the rights of natural-born Englishmen living in Britain. The charter noted in particular Rhode Islanders' right to be released from conformity to the Church of England, "because some of the people and inhabitants...cannot, in their private opinions, conform to the public exercise of religion, according to the liturgy of the Church of England, or take or subscribe the oaths and articles made and established in that behalf."[6] With this in mind, all people in Rhode Island were [to] "freely and fully have and enjoy his and their own judgements and consciences in matters of religious concernments,...they behaving themselves peacefully and quietly and not using this liberty to licentiousness and profaneness, nor the civil injury or outward disturbance of others."[7]

In making such a grant, for the first time in English history, Charles II acknowledged that it was meant "to hold forth a lively experiment that a most flourishing civil state may stand and best be maintained, and that among our English subjects, with a full liberty in religious concernments."[8] In this, they were to abide by English law, "as near as may be,...considering the nature and constitution of the place and the people there."[9]

It was clear that Rhode Islanders were dedicated to a civil society that separated church from state and that tolerated a religiously diverse community. In Newport, the earliest settlers had developed a variety of sects. Many became Baptists, but they soon began to split up into specific groups of their own: The Five Principle (or Calvinist) Baptists in 1644, the General Six Principle Baptists in 1654, and the Seventh Day (or Sabbatarian) Baptists in 1671. Others became Quakers and developed that form of worship. Quickly attracting additional members, the Quakers soon became the dominant group and provided several key leaders in the colony. Meanwhile, the colony's unusual religious freedom attracted other groups, including Jews and Moravian Brethren. In short, it was quite clear that the early settlers of Rhode Island placed the highest value on individual conscience, personal insight, and particular understandings of religion. The last thing they wished to be directly associated with was a state church, headed by a ruling monarch, supported by a government, and formally established in law, with a hierarchy of priests and bishops interpreting theology. Rhode Island seemed a very unproductive place for the Anglican Church. Given their origins and their values, Rhode Islanders had good reason to suspect Anglicans.

The basic outlook of Anglicans in England and in the overseas colonies was quite different, and it stressed other values than those in the Rhode Island charter. Anglicans shared the belief that God was the ultimate sovereign, but the Anglicans placed great value on traditions, sacraments, and government, through which they believed He had always revealed His goodness and promises, in an orderly way. They felt that it was inappropriate to speculate about one's personal salvation, as that was something to be revealed in due course. For Anglicans, as one historian has put it, "novel and unpleasant surprises were not to be anticipated in either heaven or earth."[10] The typical Anglican was attracted neither to the firm doctrine of the New England Puritans nor to the emotion of revivalism. Anglicans stressed that government was good and necessary. "Religion and law went hand in hand. Classes and stations in the mystical body of Christ on earth provided men and women with their identities as well as their purposes. Society with its national traditions preceded individuals. Support of the institutions of government and community by those individuals became a mandatory good work through which the faith might become manifest."[11] Therefore, they used the Book of Common Prayer, emphasizing that it was indeed held in common, and they stressed the importance of bishops, who could maintain uniformity of belief and religious practices among the clergy and different parishes, enforcing conformity through their own ecclesiastical courts.

For an Anglican in the seventeenth and eighteenth centuries, the Church of England was the spiritual and ecclesiastical counterpart of the state. The church and the state, the religious and the temporal, were both embodied in the person of the monarch, who, in theory, had the privilege and also the obligation to rule. In practice, however, tension developed during the seventeenth century between individual monarchs, whose personal religious beliefs tended to be those of the Church of Rome, and Parliament, which often reflected the ideas of the Puritans. In this situation Parliament came to play an increasingly important role, taking some of the responsibility that had initially lain within the king's prerogative. Thus, Anglican clergy developed dual connections; on the one hand with the Crown, as the symbolic head of the church, and on the other with Parliament, which regulated the church.

There were other colonies in America and the West Indies, where, unlike in Rhode Island, the Anglican Church had always played a leadership role. In many cases Anglican services had come with the first English explorers. The first Anglican service in North America may well have been held in San Francisco Bay, under the aegis of Sir Francis Drake, in 1579. However, before 1680 the first sustained work of the Anglican Church in North America was carried out in the Chesapeake Bay area, particularly in Virginia. In 1619, Virginia had been the first of six of the original thirteen colonies to "establish" the Anglican Church. In the technical meaning of the word, this was not just to found a parish but to grant the Anglican Church official status, with government support as well as certain privileges and immunities. About half the other North American colonies eventually followed Virginia's example. New York City and its adjacent counties were the first to follow suit, in 1693. In the eighteenth century, other colonies did the same: North Carolina in 1701, Maryland in 1702, South Carolina in 1706, Nova Scotia and Georgia in 1758. In those places where the Anglican Church was formally established as a state-supported church, Anglicans had a certain social status and some definite privileges in education, public office, and political power, privileges that were not open to others. For example, only Anglicans were readily allowed admission at the great universities of Oxford and Cambridge. Parliamentary laws restricted the holding of public office to communicants in the Church of England. This applied to Crown officials, such as royal governors, customs collectors, and officers in the army and navy. Where the church was established in law, public taxes paid for a portion (though by no means all) of its expenses. In return, the colonial governments supervised appointments in the church and had a strong influence on internal church policies.

In the 1680s and 1690s, some new factors began to alter the original basis upon which several of the American colonies had been founded. The first signs appeared in Boston, as it began to develop into the most important commercial center in North America. The royal officials appointed to enforce the Navigation Acts began to suspect that local merchants were smuggling goods and evading payment of the required customs duties. The failure of Massachusetts to take appropriate action led royal officials to bring suit against it, requiring the recall of its charter and making it into a royal colony. Although Massachusetts was the object of this enquiry, suspicions and charges led to merchants in Rhode Island and in Connecticut. Meeting in Newport, the Rhode Island General Assembly reacted by passing laws that required conformance with the Navigation Acts but kept enforcement of the laws a matter for the colony, through its own "Naval Officer" (responsible for taking bonds and issuing clearance certificates to merchant vessels leaving port). Closely associated with efforts to enforce the Navigation Acts were attempts in 1684 by Governor Joseph Dudley in Massachusetts and Lieutenant Governor Edward Cranfield in New Hampshire to introduce Anglican worship in their colonies. Both failed in the face of stiff local resistance.

Upon his accession to the throne in 1685, James II set out to create the Dominion of New England, under a governor appointed by himself. Its purpose was to combine under Governor Sir Edmund Andros of New York, and his lieutenant governor, Francis Nicholson, the governments of the colonies of Pennsylvania, New Jersey, New York, Massachusetts, Maine, and New Hampshire, so as more efficiently to enforce the Navigation Acts and organize defense in case of attack from New France. In 1686, the king's province in the Narragansett country was included, and in the following year all of Rhode Island and Providence Plantations, as well as Connecticut, were incorporated. Rhode Island's official seal was broken, but Governor Walter Clarke refused to deliver up the charter, a course that Connecticut followed when it successfully concealed its own document in the Charter Oak.

In June 1687, Rhode Island became a province within the Dominion, ruled by the Court of General Quarter Sessions and Inferior Court of Common Pleas, a panel of ten judges presided over by Francis Brinley of Newport. The Dominion was not popular, and it did not last long, but during its short life two things of importance occurred for our story: The Anglican Church and the French Huguenots arrived in New England.

First, Andros's government brought Anglican worship with it. He demanded that the Congregationalists share their South Meeting House with Anglicans, until King's Chapel could be built for the latters' own use. The Reverend Robert Ratcliffe first read the Anglican liturgy in Boston, on 30 May 1686; his supporters soon claimed that there were up to four hundred "daily frequenters" of Anglican services. In the latter half of his reign, King James—himself a Catholic—showed tolerance for other sects in the colonies, but the colonial governors were quite another matter. Many New England colonials remained suspicious of the governor's intentions, some seeing them as primarily aimed at destroying the rule of the Puritan saints. Others saw them as leading to Anglican imperial dominion, as a veiled means of eventually foisting papist practices on English Americans, or even as a lapse from grace by God's chosen people. Nevertheless, the Andros government successfully sustained Anglican worship in New England, but it was accompanied by the king's instructions for preserving liberty of conscience.[12] The instructions tacitly recognized that the Church of England faced a new and different situation in America, where, unlike England, theological diversity was already a fact of life.

Secondly, in 1685 King Louis XIV of France revoked the 1598 Edict of Nantes, by which the French Crown had granted liberty of worship to the Calvinist Huguenots. Thousands fled in fear of persecution and sought asylum in England, Switzerland, the Netherlands, and several of the German Protestant states, where they later typically excelled as fine craftsmen and prominent merchants. The English government's policy toward the refugee Huguenots was to resettle them in America, where some two thousand had come by the 1690s.

They included such famous families as the Faneuils of Boston, the Manigaults of South Carolina, and the Delaneys of New York. Under this policy, the Dominion of New England authorized several settlements, including one at Oxford, Massachusetts, and another at Frenchtown, near East Greenwich, Rhode Island.

American colonial society quickly assimilated these people, and they did not remain a distinct ethnic group for long. From the outset, a number of Huguenots in America intermarried with English settlers. Many Huguenots did not continue practicing their Calvinist religious beliefs in America but shifted instead to the Anglican Church, a move that expressed their appreciation and loyalty to the English Crown for its support of the Protestant cause. They used in some places a French translation of the Book of Common Prayer. One of the most attractive things they saw in the Anglican Church was its encouragement of lay participation in church affairs. The experiences of the Huguenots in France had led them to distrust the clergy, and they believed that government control over an established Protestant church would prevent the situation they had faced earlier.[13] As a result of English resettlement policy, several French Huguenot families arrived in Newport, where they added to the tiny percentage of foreign-born or non-English residents. Up to that time, the only non English elements in Newport had been the small group of Sephardic Jews from the Dutch Colony at Curaçao, a few Indian servants, and the first of the many black slaves who would eventually populate the town.

With the Glorious Revolution in 1688, in which James II fled to the protection of Catholic France and the Protestant William III and Mary II jointly ascended the English throne with the blessing of Parliament, the Dominion of New England collapsed. In Boston, an armed band attacked the newly founded King's Chapel to express the pent-up fury at the Andros government. Andros fled from Boston to Newport but found no sympathy, and he was held until men from Massachusetts came to take him to trial. In Newport, the Quaker Walter Clarke, who had been governor of Rhode Island before the Dominion, suddenly produced from hiding King Charles II's charter. On 1 May 1689, the freemen of the colony voted to restore to office those who had been removed on the establishment of the Dominion two years before. Thereupon Clarke issued a declaration justifying their resumption of the government of the colony under the charter, in view of the collapse of the Dominion. After authorizing a proclamation of the colony's loyalty to William and Mary, Clarke resigned his office rather than violate his Quaker beliefs by becoming involved in preparations for the war that immediately broke out in Europe.

William III, King of England, 1689–1702
Print from George Champlin Mason, *Extra Illustrated Reminiscences*, vol 5,
343-B. Collection of the Newport Historical Society.

For New Englanders in general, King William III represented something quite different from preceding English monarchs. Throughout New England many hailed his accession, noting in particular that he was a Protestant, brought up as a strict Dutch Calvinist. Because of this, many saw him as a man with views both akin to their own and very different from those of his immediate predecessors, who had leaned toward Rome. Despite the impression their personal backgrounds created, the reigns of William and Mary and of their immediate successor, Anne, were noted for the personal encouragement that the monarchs gave to the establishment of the Church of England in the American colonies. In 1689, Henry Compton, the bishop of London (1685–1713), began to appoint representatives, called commissaries, to assist in administering the church in distant places. The first of these was James Blair in Virginia; he was instrumental in establishing the College of William and Mary.

In 1694, the governor of Maryland, Francis Nicholson, who had a strong interest in promoting the Anglican Church in America, asked that the bishop appoint a commissary for his colony.[14] In response, Compton in 1695 appointed Thomas Bray as his second commissary in America. Unlike Blair in Virginia, Bray did not go immediately to his assigned pastoral work in Maryland but stayed in London, where he devoted himself to organizing means by which educational materials could be sent to the overseas colonies. In 1698, he founded his first organization, the Society for Promoting Christian Knowledge (S.P.C.K.), which immediately began to collect funds to purchase books for colonial libraries. Among the key donors were Gilbert Burnet, the latitudinarian bishop of Salisbury, and Princess Anne, who would succeed King William on the throne within four years.

In the same year, Bray also wrote an influential study, *A General View of the English Colonies in America with Respect to Religion*, in which he pointed out the weak position of the Anglican Church in America and the shortage of clergy there. Of the church's strongest districts in America, Bray reported, there were only thirty clergymen for fifty parishes in Virginia, sixteen clergymen for thirty parishes in Maryland, eight for fifteen parishes in Jamaica, and three for the nine parishes on Bermuda. Only one Anglican parish existed in each of the colonies of Pennsylvania, South Carolina, and Massachusetts, and there were none in the remaining colonies. In the course of his work, Bray began to come into contact with Anglican clergymen who might be interested in going, or persuaded to go, into pastoral work in America, and he soon became the main resource for information on the Anglican Church in America. During this period,

Bishop Compton made Bray personally responsible to him for finding appropriate clergymen.[15]

In 1700, Bray finally went to Maryland to take up his own assignment as commissary there, but when the Maryland legislature voted no stipend for him, he returned to London permanently, convinced that a missionary organization was needed to help support Anglican clergy in America. To fulfill this purpose, William III in 1701 granted a charter to the Society for the Propagation of the Gospel in Foreign Parts (S.P.G.).[16] Reflecting Anglican views, the author of a draft document in the papers of Bishop John Robinson from some twenty years later noted that before the establishment of the S.P.G.

> most of the inhabitants of these large provinces, who are now grown very numerous, and highly deserve the care of the Government had scarce so much as the face of any Religious worship establish'd amongst them, but did what was right in their own Eyes, had what Religion they pleased, or, if they pleased, no religion at all. But an attempt having been made towards reducing these poor bewildered people to a sense of virtue and Religion, the late King William was graciously pleased to form a Society. [17]

The S.P.G. soon became important to sustaining the parish in Rhode Island, but the move to create the parish predated it, having been developed more directly in the context of political, military, and imperial considerations.

In addition to its religious implications, William's accession to the throne had created a revolution in English foreign policy. There had begun a series of wars with France that were to last until 1815. The first of those, the Nine Years' War, was fought between 1688 and 1697 between France and the Grand Alliance, consisting of England, the Dutch Republic, and Austria. Called "King William's War" in America, the war raised a number of unresolved issues for the colonies, issues that New England, Rhode Island, and Newport in particular, shared.

First, the close proximity of New France, with its capital at Quebec, was an international security risk for all the colonies in New England. The northern New England colonies could be attacked over land, while the more southerly New England colonies had shipping and sea communications with England gravely exposed. The threat was real for Newport. French privateers successfully attacked Block Island three times during the war. They made one unsuccessful attempt to raid Newport, and another was thwarted only just before it took place.

Secondly, the war showed once again, as had been seen earlier in connection with the threats from both the Indians and the Dutch, that it was extremely difficult to raise and to organize defensive forces in the separate colonies. As officials in London faced the facts of fighting a war that involved putting armies in Ireland and on the continent of Europe, operating naval squadrons in European waters and the Mediterranean, and conducting overseas military and naval operations, they found their national resources stretched. In order to fight such wars, the London government increasingly needed support. In particular it needed the political, military, institutional, logistical, tax, and financial support of its colonies. All these things began to draw colonists out of their earlier isolation on the far side of the Atlantic and into closer cooperation and exchange with England and within the English Atlantic world. This created further tensions between the colonists' immediate needs to carry on their productive work and trade, and the needs of the imperial government in London to provide defense and to wage war.

In the context of these factors, Rhode Island was neither the only nor even the greatest problem to the government in London, but the colony did present a number of particular issues that are important to the subject at hand. In Newport, the dominant political influence of the Quakers, with their pacifist sentiments, presented a situation that was particularly difficult for London to manage. Additionally, since the overthrow of the Dominion of New England and the resurrection of the colony's prior government, Rhode Island had operated without confirmation of its royal charter, and would until 1694. Partly because of this, even when the Rhode Island General Assembly tried to assert its views, it could not make its citizens obey; it had been unable even to collect taxes. Moreover, though the militia organization was in disarray, Rhode Islanders resented the attempts of the governor of Massachusetts to take command of its militia and to put it in order, as his instructions from London repeatedly required.

As a growing seaport town, however, Newport had two assets that it could lend directly to the war effort: ships and seamen. Privateer commissions carried an attractive allure of profit for local merchants, and they had the dual advantage that such commissions authorized holders to arm and protect their own ships carrying cargo. From all this arose a serious controversy between

London and Rhode Island, a by-product of which was to be the call for the first Anglican clergyman to come to Newport. The origins of the dispute lie in Rhode Island's maritime history.

The first Rhode Island vessel to fight the French was the sloop *Loyal Stede*, which had been commandeered, armed, and manned by the colony during the privateer attacks of 1690. Assuming that the colony's charter was valid, this was an entirely legal act for a colonial government. However, a few years later, in about 1693, Deputy Governor John Greene issued letters of marque authorizing local Rhode Island merchants to arm their own ships and cruise as privateers to capture enemy shipping. When these and other vessels began to have success, they needed an admiralty court that could adjudicate the prizes, sell the ships and their cargoes, and distribute the proceeds. In the absence of specific authorization while awaiting confirmation of the charter, the General Assembly voted that this responsibility fell within the right of the governor and council, acting as the high court of the colony.

Shortly thereafter, when the charter was confirmed, the instructions accompanying it gave jurisdiction to a judge of a vice-admiralty court, with powers delegated from the High Court of Admiralty in London. The colony, denying any prior wrongdoing, protested that such instructions infringed its charter, and a legal battle ensued with London. Associated with the argument were charges that Rhode Island was lax in enforcing admiralty law and that the colony was harboring and encouraging piracy instead of controlling privately armed merchant ships in attacks on enemy shipping. Some local seamen in fact found the distinction a thin one and abused their commissions as privateers. Certainly, piracy was a widespread problem of the day, and Rhode Islanders were not alone in such profitable ventures.

As this problem was brewing, a general crisis in England's wartime economy brought political demands for action. King William III in 1696 established the Board of Trade, which eventually developed into the most enduring of the administrative organizations that supervised the British Empire before 1773. Its first years were devoted to its own organization and to immediate wartime demands. By the time peace was made at Rijswijk in 1697, ending the Nine Years' War, the board was ready to turn to the task of regulating colonial administration after a period of neglect and sometimes, as in the case of Rhode Island, confusion. In the renewed Navigation Act of 1696, Parliament provided the legal basis for suppressing illegal trade, and in 1698 the Customs Commissioners drafted royal instructions to governors establishing a broad policy for maritime trade.

With this basis, the board focused on the issue of piracy, which had become a widespread problem. The end of the war had released a large number of fighting seamen from naval service and privateering, but a number of them had continued to use their wartime skills plundering merchant vessels, particularly in the Indian Ocean. Officials found that numbers of American colonial vessels were outfitting at Madagascar and were attacking whatever vessels they could, developing a considerable and illegal direct trade in East Indian goods with the American colonies. This was a direct threat to the small and economical vessels that the East India Company was beginning to use and to the monopoly the company had on such trade. Moreover, the Board of Trade in London understood that since it was a well-known fact that the pirates were Englishmen, or at least pretending to be Englishmen, it was damaging to England's relations with the Mogul in India and to the trade privileges he had granted. Among all the pirates of the day, the most prominent figure was Capt. William Kidd, who had actually begun in operations against the pirates, fully supported by key political figures, before turning pirate himself. A number of others had engaged in such activity, such as William Mayes and Thomas Tew, who had Newport connections.[18]

By focusing on piracy, the board believed, it could deal with all the key problems facing colonial administration. Through this approach, the board hoped to gain parliamentary support to regulate more closely the administration of the proprietary and charter colonies. It could extend and standardize the practices of the colonial vice-admiralty courts. It could counteract the tendency of colonial governors to protect pirates in return for bribes from wealthy colonists, or for votes for greater salaries granted by colonial assemblies, to the same effect. All of these issues were reflected in the king's appointment in 1698 of Francis Nicholson to be governor of Virginia, and in 1697 of Richard Coote, Earl of Bellomont, to be simultaneously governor of New York, Massachusetts, and New Hampshire. These two became the key proponents of the board's effort to coordinate colonial policy and administration. Although the recently reconfirmed charters of Connecticut and Rhode Island exempted them from this revitalized attempt to combine colonial governments, Bellomont's instructions required that he should approve, in the king's name, the annually elected governors of those colonies and additionally, with his appointment as captain-general, command the militias of East and West Jersey, Connecticut, and Rhode Island in time of war.

In gathering intelligence on Rhode Island, the Board of Trade had obtained information from several sources. Francis Brinley, Peleg Sanford, and the other "royalists" who had controlled the colony's affairs while it was part of the Dominion of New England made up one set of sources. Another was Jahleel Brenton, a Congregationalist who had earned respect with officials when he had occasionally served as the colony's representative in London and had been the Crown-appointed collector of customs for New England from 1689 to 1699.

Reacting to the changing situation in 1698, the General Assembly elected Samuel Cranston as governor of the colony to succeed to his uncle, Walter Clarke. The Assembly repeatedly reelected Cranston to this post until his death in 1727, making him the longest serving of any governor of any of the colonies. Over this long period of time, Cranston succeeded in building the colony of Rhode Island into a flourishing place, with Newport as the center of its commercial development. Carefully protecting local rights and Rhode Island's independent charter, he skillfully maintained the colony's position and developed a working relationship with royal authorities. Throughout his tenure, his method was to acquiesce in the requests of royal officials by having Rhode Islanders carry out the official functions that were required, but to resist changes in the structure of Rhode Island's government or attempts of royal officials to interfere directly in local matters. Upon taking office as governor, Cranston faced a series of crises. The most serious was the arrival of Lord Bellomont in Rhode Island to investigate personally the suspicions and charges against Rhode Island.

In 1698, the Board of Trade had raised questions about the adequacy of Rhode Island's courts and laws to support the king's trade and colonial policy. Cranston had sent copies of official documents to London in support of his argument that the colony was properly organized and fully competent to carry out its responsibilities. Unconvinced, the Board had replied that the documents were neither complete, adequate, nor legible, and it had ordered Lord Bellomont to Newport to investigate the situation. Arriving at Boston from New York by sea, Bellomont first dealt with the issues posed by the larger colony of Massachusetts and then, on 18 September 1699, traveled over land from Boston to Bristol, then on to Newport, where he arrived on 20 September. Remaining in Newport for a week, Bellomont gathered a wide number of documents and interrogated colonial officials on all aspects of concern to the Board of Trade.[19]

Bellomont's visit confirmed all of the suspicions that he and the Board of Trade had shared about the people of Rhode Island. Much of the problem, Bellomont believed, derived from lack of education in personal and moral values. On returning to Boston, Bellomont prepared for the board an official report that listed twenty-five "irregularities and maladministrations," including smuggling, harboring and encouraging pirates, ignorant and biased judges, and inadequate laws. He first explained what he saw as the fundamental problem, the colony's lack of morality and religion. Referring back to the wording of the colony's charter, Bellomont established a legal reason why it should be revoked;

> They seem wholly to have neglected the Royal Intention and
> their own professed declaration recited in the Letters Patent of
> their Incorporation, of Godly edifying themselves and one an-
> other in the holy Christian Faith and Worship, and for the gain-
> ing over and conversion of the poor ignorant Indian natives to
> the sincere profession and observation of the Faith and Worship
> upon which grounds they were granted to have and to enjoy
> their judgements and conscience in matter of Religious con-
> cernments, they behaving themselves peacefully and quietly
> and not using their liberty to licentiousness and profaneness.
> In that they have never erected nor encouraged any schools of
> learning or made the means of instruction by a learned ortho-
> dox ministry. The government being elective has kept in the
> hands of such who have strenuously opposed the same, and the
> generality of the people are shamefully ignorant, and all manner
> of licentiousness and profaneness does greatly abound and is
> indulged with in that government.[20]

Bellomont's views were harsh, but in the light of the experience of the previous dozen years there was some justification to his criticisms about the colony's administration and organization. These things Cranston went far to improve in the next quarter-century. Bellomont's views on religion, however, showed no appreciation for the depth of faith that actually existed in Newport among the Baptists, Jews, Quakers, and recently arrived Congregationalists. His statement clearly reflected his own opinion, as well the king's instructions that the Angli-can Church be brought to Rhode Island, with "a learned and orthodox ministry."

On the fifth day of his visit to Newport, Lord Bellomont had interro-gated at length Robert Gardner, the colony's Naval Officer.[21] Bellomont was suspicious that the colony's officials were not diligently enforcing the law in this area. The main topic of the conversation must have been the overlapping interests of the Crown-appointed customs collector and the colony-appointed Naval Officer, who typically clashed. But the conversation may also have touched on the Church of England, for on the very next day, 26 September 1699, Gardner was one of sixteen people who presented a petition to Bellomont declaring that they had "agreed and concluded to erect a church for the worship of God according to the discipline of the Church of England." They asked Bellomont to write on their behalf to the Board of Trade and intercede with the king in favor of their effort to obtain "a pious and learned Minister, to settle and abide among us."[22]

Before Bellomont completed the official report on his visit to Rhode Island, he found an opportunity to send a letter to London. On 24 October he wrote to the Board of Trade relaying and strongly seconding the request that an ordained Anglican clergyman be sent to Newport. "It will be the means I hope to reform the lives of the people in that Island," Bellomont wrote, "and make good Christians of 'em, who are at present all in darkness."[23]

Three months later, Bellomont's letter arrived on the other side of the Atlantic. On 2 February 1700, the secretary of the board read it to the assembled members of the Board of Trade in London. Several other matters concerning Rhode Island were also raised at the meeting, and the board called the colony's representative, Jahleel Brenton, for his advice. The board decided to refer the matter of a minister for Newport to The Right Reverend Henry Compton, bishop of London. Three days later all the board members signed a letter to Compton forwarding Bellomont's letter with the petition.[24] Meanwhile, with their formal request in the hands of the bishop of London, a small group of Anglicans in Newport carried on with their independent efforts to create the first Anglican parish in Rhode Island.

Notes

1. Quoted in John Frederick Woolverton, *Colonial Anglicanism in North America* (Detroit: Wayne State Univ. Press, 1984), p. 108. See also, J. A. *Venn, Alumni Cantabridgiense* (Cambridge: Cambridge Univ. Press, 1922), vol. 1, p. 162, and Edgar Legare Pennington, *The First Hundred Years of the Church of England in Rhode Island*, publication number 47 (Hartford, CT: Church Mission, 1935), pp. 1–2.

2. The derivation of the name is uncertain. For an alternative explanation, see Samuel Eliot Morison, *The European Discovery of America: The Northern Voyage, AD 500–1600* (New York: Oxford Univ. Press, 1971), p. 303.

3. Carl Bridenbaugh, *Cities in the Wilderness: The First Century of Urban Life in America, 1625–1742* (New York: Alfred A. Knopf, 1964), pp. 1–5.

4. Morison, p. 302.

5. Sydney V. James, *Colonial Rhode Island: A History (New York: Charles Scribner's Sons, 1975), chap. 4. See also, Sydney V. James. John Clarke and His Legacies: Religion and Law in Colonial Rhode Island, 1638–1750,* ed. by Theodore Dwight Bozeman (University Park: Pennsylvania State Univ., 1999), chap. 4.

6. John Russell Bartlett, ed., *The Records of the Colony of Rhode Island and Providence Plantations in New England,* 7 vols. (Providence, RI: A. Crawford Greene and Brothers State Printers, 1856–62), vol. 2, pp. 3–5.

7. Ibid.

8. Ibid.

9. Ibid., p. 9

10. Woolverton, p. 16.

11. Ibid.

12. James, p. 108; Bridenbaugh, p. 103; Woolverton, pp. 112–13; Philip S. Haffenden, *New England in the English Nation, 1689–1713* (Oxford: Clarendon Press, 1974), p. 10.

13. Robert M. Kingdon, "Why Did the Huguenot Refugees in the American Colonies Become Episcopalians?" *Historical Magazine of the Protestant Episcopal Church,* vol. 49, co. 4, 9 December 1980, pp. 332–34.

14. H. P. Thompson, *Thomas Bray* (London: S.P.C.K., 1954), p. 14.

15. Ibid., p. 38.

16. Robert Prichard, *A History of the Episcopal Church* (Harrisburg, PA: Morehouse Publishing, 1991), pp. 27–33.

17. Bodleian Library, Oxford, MS Rawl. C 933, fo. 166: Undated Draft Memorial to King George I.

18. See I.K. Steele, *Politics of Colonial Policy: The Board of Trade in Colonial Administration, 1696–1720.* (Oxford: Clarendon Press, 1968), pp. 42–59, 66. See also, Robert C. Ritchie, *Captain Kidd and the War against the Pirates* (Cambridge, MA: Harvard Univ. Press, 1968), and Alexander Boyd Hawes, *Off Soundings: Aspects of the Maritime History of Rhode Island* (Chevy Chase, MD: Posterity Press, 1999).

19. Public Record Office, Kew; Colonial Office Papers: CO 5/1259, fo. 573: Lord Bellomont's "Journal of My Proceedings."

20. PRO, CO 5/1259, fo. 565: Lord Bellomont to the Board of Trade, 7 November 1699.

21. PRO, CO 5/1259, fo. 617.

22. The full text of the petition is printed in George Champlin Mason, comp., *Annals of Trinity Church, Newport, Rhode Island, 1698–1821* (Newport, RI: George C. Mason, 1890), p. 11.

23. Ibid., p. 12

24. *Calendar of State Papers, America and West Indies, 1700* (London: HMS, 1911), documents 84, 92, 94, pp. 54, 58: Journal of the Council of Trade, 2 and 5 February 1700.

Anne, Queen of England from 1702—1714.

2

A Tumultuous Beginning:
Forming the Parish, 1698–1709

Tradition has long held that the parish was first established in 1698, but from time to time 1694 has been inaccurately given as the date when Anglicans in Newport gathered for their first services from the Book of Common Prayer. It is impossible to date precisely how long before Lord Bellomont's visit to Newport in September 1699 Anglicans had been worshipping in Newport. It was probably no more than a year, if that. Until recently, the early history of the parish remained shrouded in mystery, but research in English archives has now explained something about that tumultuous decade of disputes and why the founders mutually agreed in 1709 that they would not save the record of their own recent activities.

Certainly, the main organizer of the Anglicans in Newport was Robert Gardner, Naval Officer of the colony. In 1709, Gardner would recall that a group of nine families had come to Gardner's own Newport home to hold the first Church of England services and to hear sermons. After a short time, interest grew, and more people wanted to come.[1] By the time Bellomont visited Newport, sixteen men had signed the petition asking for a clergyman: Pierre Ayrault, Gabriel Bernon, Anthony Blount, William Brinley, Edward Carter, George Cutter, Thomas Fox, Robert Gardner, Thomas Lillibridge, Thomas Mallett, Isaac Martindale, Richard Newland, Thomas Paine, William Pease, Francis Pope, and Robert Wrightingham.

Among these, several names stand out. Ayrault and Bernon were both Huguenots, the former a physician and the latter a successful merchant. William Brinley was a son of Francis Brinley, who had presided over Rhode Island's affairs when it was part of the Dominion of New England; William's brother, Robert, had been a founder of King's Chapel in Boston. Gardner was a key suspect in Bellomont's investigation of wrongdoing in the colony, while Isaac Martindale was in charge of the local militia. In 1702 he would become famous for defending the colony's rights by refusing to take orders from the royal governor of Massachusetts.

At the end of 1699, this group was trying a number of avenues to build its church, but it is not clear now in what order these occurred or on what dates the members took their different initiatives, using various family, business, and political connections. In addition to the petition presented to Lord Bellomont, the congregation also wrote to Governor Francis Nicholson in Williamsburg and to The Reverend Samuel Myles, an Oxford graduate who had been the rector of King's Chapel, Boston, since 1689. Myles was attracted to the idea; he wrote to Governor Nicholson a few months later, "I had a great mind to have a church settled at Rhode Island, knowing what witched, ignorant atheistical people there are there."[2] Myles decided that he and his newly arrived assistant, The Reverend Christopher Bridge, a 1693 Cambridge graduate who had been installed as "lecturer" at King's Chapel in March 1699, would share the duties and that they would take turns with the services in Newport.

Bridge appears to have left London at about the same time the news arrived there with Bellomont that a clergyman was needed in Rhode Island. The bishop of London had sent directions to Myles to make Bridge available for this purpose, but Myles specifically chose not to share with the vestry at King's Chapel the fact that he was assisting the Anglicans in Rhode Island.[3] The Newport congregation made a horse available for Myles's use in traveling to Newport, but when it arrived, Bridge decided that in accordance with Bishop Compton's orders, he would take his turn first. Bridge stayed about six or seven weeks, and Myles took his turn immediately thereafter, for another seven weeks.

When Bridge arrived to take the first service, Robert Gardner went to see Governor Cranston and the Newport Town Council, requesting them to allow the congregation to hold its services in the Town Hall, where more people could attend. This was permitted for a time, but when objections were made to using a government building for religious services, the congregation began to meet in the town's schoolhouse.[4]

Boston's Anglican clergy, then, had already inaugurated Anglican services in Rhode Island over twelve to fourteen weeks when, at the end of the first week of November 1699, the congregation received Nicholson's reply indicating his willingness to help. Nicholson had already been in contact with Samuel Myles on the question and had suggested a Mr. Ebuan for the position, but it soon became clear that finding the funds to pay a clergyman would be a problem.

On 18 December 1699, Robert Gardner wrote to Governor Nicholson that on the previous Saturday he had made a bargain with a carpenter to build a church for the parish; it would be forty feet long and thirty feet wide, with twenty-foot posts. Paralleling a second petition from the Rhode Island congregation for Nicholson's assistance, Gardner wrote, "We hope through the help and blessing of Almighty God and the aid of our friends and brethren to startle a great many who think that all our pretensions were only a flash."[5]

Samuel Myles was successful during his pastoral visit in Newport. The Newport Anglicans received him warmly, and when he returned to Boston he began to raise donations from the congregation at King's Chapel to help pay for the new church building at Newport. Shortly after Christmas one of the Newport parishioners, Anthony Blount, wrote to one of the two Boston clergymen that even without a clergyman, the services were going on as before in the Newport schoolhouse. "It is high time we had some good man among us.... I fear we do not walk or carry it so brotherly to each other as you left us charged in your last sermon or may expect we do," Blount wrote.[6]

By February 1700 Myles had gathered pledges totaling fifty to sixty pounds for the new building; "Only one man refused to give anything but hard words."[7] An undated account in the records at Fulham Palace, London, shows that the largest single donor was Governor Francis Nicholson, who gave five separate donations to the new parish, totaling ninety-one pounds. The list shows twenty-one donors from Boston, thirty-six from Newport, and eight "strangers." Of the donations from Newport, the largest was from a Major Wanton, who gave nineteen pounds, followed by Robert Gardner and Thomas Lillibridge, who gave eighteen each; Thomas Mallet, who gave ten pounds; and Robert Carr, whose gift of land was valued at ten pounds.[8]

Christopher Bridge, however, managed to antagonize immediately a number of people in the congregation by making it clear that the congregation should be able to provide a stipend of a hundred pounds for the clergy. William Brinley and others believed that Bridge demanded too much and had overestimated the congregation's resources. Brinley and other members of the congregation advised Bridge that they could barely manage thirty to thirty-five pounds, along with Thomas Mallet's generous offer to provide a visiting clergyman free lodging, food, and washing for a month. The urgency with which Bridge had represented his need for a substantial salary, and the unsympathetic ear that Newporters gave it, created ill will on both sides. On Myles's return to Boston, Bridge refused to go back to Newport, leaving the people in Newport to conclude that he was only an opportunist who was jealous because he had not assisted in sending the original petition to the bishop of London. Myles repeatedly asked

Bridge to take the services in Newport, but he stubbornly refused, creating a serious dispute between the two.[9] At the same time, Bridge had offended people in Newport. Brinley complained, "If Mr. Bridge should ever come up to preach here again, I will assure him I shall not be one of his hearers, and for aught I know shall make known to my Lord of London his carriage and behavior in denying his Lordship's commands."[10] In this situation, both Myles and Bridge returned to King's Chapel, and the nascent parish in Newport was left without a clergyman.

In the meantime, the new church building was being erected. Robert Carr had donated the land for the first church. He was the son and namesake of a Robert Carr who had died in 1681 and had owned a strip of land between Thames Street and present-day Spring Street. This strip was located on either side of a dead-end lane leading a few hundred yards up the hill from Thames Street, and it adjoined Francis Brinley's land to the south. This lane later became Church Lane, Honyman's Lane, and finally Church Street after it was put through to intersect with Spring Street. Carr had built a "mansion house," set back at the corner of the lane and Thames Street. On his death in 1681, the land had been divided into several lots. The young Robert Carr inherited the mansion house, where he raised his family. While some of the lots were distributed among other members of the family, the young Robert retained the lot just beyond the end of the lane at the southeastern corner of the original Carr land. The eastern boundary of this lot was not at the corner of present-day Spring and Church Streets but some thirty-five feet west of Spring Street, including the width of Church Street. Its southern boundary was at about the north wall of the present church.[11]

The new church building extended nearly across the lane leading up to it.[12] The south wall of the church began just to the north of Thomas Mallett's 1704 gravestone and extended to the west (see map page 26). There are no known illustrations or drawings of the first church, but by comparing other churches of the period, Norman Isham suggested in 1936 what it might have been like and how its thirty-five known pews might have been laid out on the ground floor (see Isham's suggested interior layout page 29). His suggested plan errs in that it followed the model of King's Chapel and measures twenty-eight by fifty-four feet, while new research shows that the first building actually measured as noted above, thirty by forty feet.

In the autumn of 1700, a "North Briton" named David Bethune appeared in Newport with a young boy in his care. The congregation welcomed

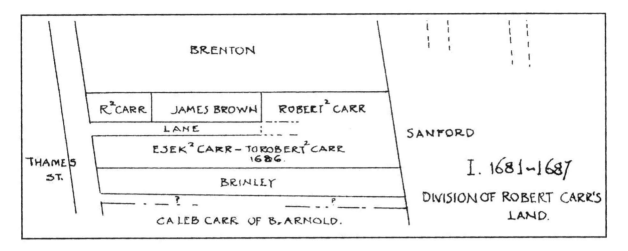

The division of the first Robert Carr's land between his death in 1681 and 1687,
on either side of what later became Church Lane and before present-day Spring
Street was extended to this point. His son, the second Robert Carr, donated the
land for the first church about 1699–1700; it included part of present-day
Church Street and the area south of the present-day church. Sketch map by
Norman Isham for his 1936 architectural study, Trinity Church in Newport,
Rhode Island.

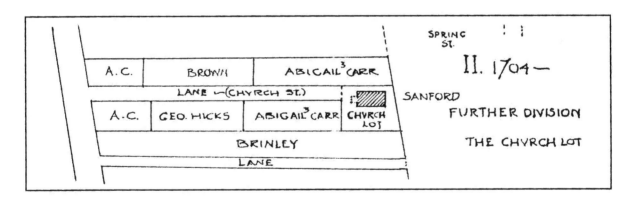

The further division of the Carr land, after the second Robert Carr's death in
1704. Sketch by Norman Isham.

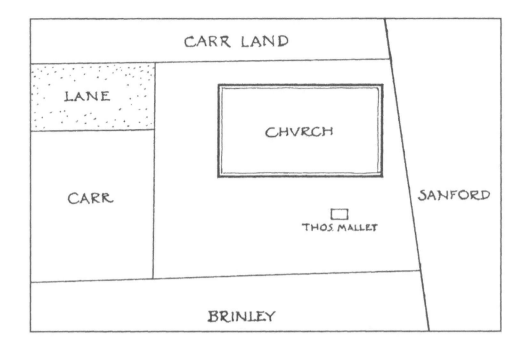

(Above) Location of the first church building, completed in 1700, at the end of Church Lane and north of Thomas Mallet's 1704 grave. Sketch by Norman Isham.

Isham Papers, Box A-12,
Newport Historical Society.

(Left) Thomas Mallet, an inn-keeper, who owned the property at 28 Clarke Street, was one of the founders of the parish. His 1704 gravestone is the oldest in the churchyard, and its location helps to locate the first church building.

him warmly, believing that he was the clergyman that they had requested from London through Lord Bellomont. In the only known document bearing his signature, he signed a receipt on 19 October 1700 for books sent out by the SPCK for the parish library at Newport, signing as "to be minister of that place."[13] Bethune did lead the little parish with some success for a number of months. Suddenly, scandal shattered the parish; Bethune fled town when it was discovered that his young boy was actually a young woman wearing boy's clothing. Bethune had brought a number of new families into the parish, but they immediately left, resenting "so ill a thing" and reducing the parish to its "primitive constitution again."[14] This incident nearly ruined the reputation of the Anglican Church in Newport and destroyed what progress had been made in gathering a parish. The small group of devoted laymen who founded the parish had to begin their work once again.

After nearly three centuries, Bethune's background remains a mystery. No record of an ordination of a person by that name has yet been found. Subsequently, his name appears only on the registers for St. Anne's parish, Sandy Point, on the island of St. Christopher's in the West Indies; no correspondence from or about him survives.[15] In London, Dr. Thomas Bray, who was just beginning to organize and coordinate the assignment of clergymen in America, paid a sum of money for a "List of the scandalous Ministers about the Town[,] that I might not be imposed upon in the choice of those whom I send into the plantations." Unfortunately for us, this fact is only mentioned among Bray's financial accounts, and one does not know whether Bethune's name might have been on it.[16]

However, a new opportunity for a clergyman to come to Newport occurred in May 1701, when the frigate HMS *Active*, Capt. William Caldwell, commander, returned to Boston Harbor. Just over a year earlier, the *Active* had been in Boston to pick up the pirate Captain Kidd and take him to London for trial. The Massachusetts authorities had placed Kidd and several others under close confinement on board the *Active* for three weeks before the ship sailed for London. The Royal Navy chaplain assigned to the *Active* was a Scot, The Reverend James Honyman. The son and namesake of a clergyman, the young chaplain had been born in Kineff, Kincardinshire, about 1675 and had become a naval chaplain in June 1699.[17] During his first visit to Boston, Honyman most probably made contact with The Reverend Samuel Myles at King's Chapel, but Honyman was too occupied with his ministry to the imprisoned pirates to think of any other duties at that point. On this second visit, however, the ship

Inscribed "Given to be lent in Rhode Island, 1700" this 1697 Course of Lectures Upon the Church Catechism *was among the first volumes in the parish's new lending library, sent by Dr. Bray from London. It was among those that The Reverend David Bethune signed for and brought with him to Newport in 1700.*

Collection of the Newport Historical Society.

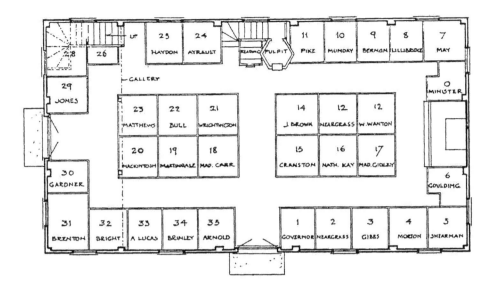

In the 1920s, restoration architect Norman Isham drew this conjectural plan of the interior layout of the 1700 church building, believing that it was similar in style to the original King's Chapel in Boston, which may have been modeled on the simplest of Wren's designs, St. Mildred's Church, Bread Street, London. Typical of that time, churches had an altar at the east end and a pulpit separated from it on the north wall. According to a 1719 list, there were thirty-five pews on the main floor, with one set aside for use of the governor, then Samuel Cranston, and there were eight pews in a gallery.

Isham Papers, Box A-12, Newport Historical Society.

remained in Boston from May through early July 1701 before sailing to New York. At some point when HMS *Active* was in Boston, Samuel Myles brought Chaplain Honyman to Newport, where Honyman temporarily took charge of the new church building until his ship was ready to sail. On 8 September 1701, HMS *Active* anchored briefly in Newport harbor, apparently picking up Honyman before she sailed for her other duties.[18] Honyman remained assigned to her until she returned to England in December 1702. Honyman had not made a good first impression on everyone in Newport: "His conversation was so light that most of the congregation was scandalized at it," William Brinley commented. He also noted with disapproval that that the young naval chaplain had been attracted to the daughter of one of the parish's benefactors, Robert Carr.[19]

Meanwhile, in London, Dr. Bray had not neglected the search for an appropriate man to be sent out to take up a permanent position in Newport.

His various informants repeatedly stressed the immediate need for Anglican influence to counteract the Quakers and Baptists in Newport. In the autumn of 1701, the governor of Massachusetts reported that the entire colony of Rhode Island and Providence Plantations consisted of "five thousands souls in seven towns, at present under a Quaker Government," but he felt that it might be appropriate to have eventually "two ministers and a schoolmaster in the colony, with one of them at first subsisted from hence."[20] Similarly, The Reverend George Keith, a former Quaker who had recently converted to Anglicanism, reported to the newly organized Society for the Propagation of the Gospel that he had visited Rhode Island many times and that it had "many Quakers and Anabaptists, but never had a Church of England until of late."[21] The way in which Anglicans mentioned the presence of Baptists and Quakers in Rhode Island underscores the importance and the urgent necessity they felt of creating an Anglican ministry to counter their influence. In promoting their own views, Thomas Bray and other Anglicans in this period stressed the importance of baptism by a priest in the apostolic succession. They believed that this was the most appropriate way to accept the covenant of the gospel, in which God promised forgiveness of sin and everlasting life, in return for which the believer promised repentance and belief in Christ.

The Society for the Propagation of the Gospel had not yet received its charter and was not authorized to begin its work. Nevertheless, Bray had proceeded on his own and selected The Reverend John Lockier, a young man in his twenties who just had been ordained in London, on 27 October 1701, to make a beginning in Newport.[22] Born in Beccles, Suffolk, Lockier had obtained his bachelor's degree at Trinity College, Cambridge, in 1698. The young clergyman left London for Rhode Island in mid-November 1701 and arrived about March 1702, armed with two sets of books provided by Society for the Propagation of Christian Knowledge. One set was the Society's "Parochial Library" and the other its "Layman's Library," valued at thirty pounds a set. Fifteen or sixteen people in Gloucestershire had donated money for the library and for an allowance of fifty pounds per year for the minister.[23] Lockier also carried with him similar sets of the Layman's Library for the parishes at Boston and Philadelphia. The set Lockier brought to Newport became the town's first library. It comprised books covering a wide variety of subjects, including the natural sciences as well as theology. While it had materials that the clergy could use, its main purpose was to circulate the books widely within each town. Bray and his society believed that through these books, both nonconformists and nonbelievers could learn of the reasonableness of the Anglican view.

One of the original bindings from the parish's lending library. These volumes were the first public library in the Colony of Rhode Island.
Newport Historical Society.

In June 1702, The Reverend George Keith began a tour of the colonies, traveling from Maine to South Carolina preaching the Anglican faith. Expressing himself with the zeal of a recent convert, he often found himself directly attacking others. He verbally dueled with Cotton Mather in Boston and attacked Harvard graduates for their views on predestination. In early August he came to Newport for a month, and Lockier invited him several times to preach at Trinity Church. In Newport, Keith reported that he found "a considerable number of persons of good Discretion and zeal, professed members of the Church of England and many others well effected."[24] In addition, he attended several other church meetings and arranged a public debate with the Quakers at the Town Hall.

Shortly after Keith's departure, Lockier made his first annual report to the Society for the Propagation of the Gospel, asking for direct assistance from the society in promoting the work of the parish. In his September 1702 letter Lockier reported, "Our Church is but young, it not being four years yet complete since we began to assemble ourselves together on that occasion."[25] Lockier reported that the church building was finished on the outside, with the exception of the steeple. Inside, it was "pewed well although not beautified." By this time the altar was in place—the same that is presently used in the church—and Lockier had already twice celebrated communion, "without those necessary conveniences that this table in England are furnished with."[26]

Lockier noted that Newport "is one of the chief nurseries of Quakerism in all America, but now we have some reason to hope that the Rev'd Mr. Keith, by God's assisting his skill in that disease, hath pretty well-curbed, if not quite stopped so dangerous a gangrene." Commenting on the continuing tension between the two groups in Newport, Lockier offered that the Quakers were civil, "although slyly and underhand we are sensible they would pinch us in the bud."[27]

In mid-January 1703, the governing body of the Society for the Propagation of the Gospel met in London. Among those present were the archbishop of Canterbury and the bishops of London and of Worcester. At that meeting, the society's secretary read aloud the letter from Newport. Particularly taken with Lockier's comments about his makeshift celebration of communion in Newport, those present agreed to spend up to fifteen pounds to supply the church with a chalice, patten, and "other necessities" for communion services.[28] The surviving records of the society suggest that this was the first instance in which the society gave communion silver to any church. In its February meeting, the society agreed on the inscription that was to be engraved on the chalice and patten for the church in Rhode Island:[29]

Deo et Sacris in Ecclesia Parochiali de Newport in Rode Island
ex dono Societitis de Propagando Evangelio apad Exteros in Anglia Stabilitatae,
Jan 15. AD 1702.

The engraved date recorded the day on which the society decided to send the silver, but the year was shown as 1702 rather than 1703, since at that time Englishmen marked the new year on Lady Day, [25] March, not on 1 January, as would be the custom after 1752. The London silversmith John Boddington completed the silver chalice and paten, marking it with his hallmarks, and at the society's March 1703 meeting a Mr. Hodges reported that the engraved pieces were complete and would be sent to Rhode Island at the first opportunity.[30]

The Society for the Propagation of the Gospel in Foreign Parts ordered this chalice and paten set for Trinity Church in January 1703 from the workshop of the London silversmith, John Boddington, who made the two gilt silver pieces for £15. This was the first of many other sets that the newly formed society would eventually furnish to parishes around the world.

By coincidence, the same meeting of the society approved the appointment of The Reverend James Honyman to take charge of the church at Jamaica, Long Island, New York. Some months earlier, Thomas Bray had convinced Honyman to resign from the navy to take up this particular appointment, replacing a Reverend Gordon, who had recently died. In April, Honyman embarked in the *Portsmouth Galley* for the voyage to America. He faced a long delay; his ship waited with other vessels more than four months for a naval escort to protect them from attack in crossing the Atlantic at that early phase in the War of the Spanish Succession. Honyman finally arrived in Boston at the end of October 1703, and he was in Newport at the end of November, preparing to move on to New York.[31]

A few days before Christmas, John Lockier wrote to London to thank the society for sending the silver and the furnishings for the communion table.[32] In his report he mentioned the continuing tension with the Quakers, who dominated the town. However, Lockier reported, the Quakers were declining in number at Newport, although they were building a number of new structures in the nearby towns of Providence and Narragansett. Governor Cranston remained courteous, "yet his religion which is Quakerism will not allow him to do us any kindness."[33] In order to minister to Anglicans, Lockier had traveled to Little Compton and Narragansett. At Portsmouth, at the far northerly end of Rhode Island, he reported setting up a lecture "to stop an inroad, which the Quakers were making."

At the end of 1703, the little parish in Newport was continuing to grow. "We are now building a steeple which will make our church much larger by reason of a Gallery," Lockier wrote, "so that it will be able to hold the congregation which hath many new converts frequenting it whose consciences as yet will not suffer them to hear the Gospel."[34] Lockier's own reputation grew, and one person reported, "The Quakers themselves as far as I can hear have no evil to say of that priest."[35] Aware of Lockier's growing stature and success in the community, Thomas Bray advised him that the original source of support for his mission, donors in Gloucestershire, could only be continued through the S.P.G., which had been founded explicitly for that purpose. In order to secure his position, Bray advised, Lockier had to apply to the society to continue his annual fifty-pound stipend. That Lockier did in early 1704, in order to bring the parish more fully under the cognizance of the S.P.G..

Meanwhile, Honyman had encountered unexpected difficulties with the congregation at Jamaica, even before his arrival there. When he had been the chaplain on board HMS *Active*, moored at New York for a long period, Honyman had rented a room in a home ashore. Before Honyman returned to America, one of the young women who worked as a servant in that house had been arrested for prostitution and the murder of a child. In the course of her trial she had accused Honyman of being scandalously intimate with the woman who owned the house and employed her. On hearing the news that the S.P.G. had appointed Honyman to Jamaica, the congregation strenuously objected to the governor of New York, Lord Cornbury, who had been appointed to that position in November 1701 following Lord Bellomont's death.

Cornbury contacted John Lockier at Newport, suggesting that the two clergymen exchange their posts. Apparently, Honyman heard of this directly from Lockier when Honyman stopped in Newport en route to his new post. Honyman would have gladly accepted the exchange. He felt that he had a good rapport with the Newport congregation, and he would soon marry Robert Carr's daughter, Elizabeth. However, Lockier was ill and did not feel that he could make such a move at that time.[36] Honyman continued on to Jamaica and,

The altar table shown in this modern picture of the chancel was certainly in use in 1702 and probably was used from the very first services in the church. It was transferred to the new building in 1726 and remained in use there until about 1837, when it was discarded. It was returned to the church in the early twentieth century and has remained in use as the altar since that time.

despite the public outcry, took up the difficult post. Later, several people who observed him closely would speak highly of his work for that parish.[37]

John Lockier died in April 1704, after a short period of illness, and the Newport parish was left without a clergyman. The wardens and vestry of Trinity Church applied directly to Lord Cornbury for his assistance. Hearing reports that a certain faction in the Jamaica parish was continuing in its opposition to Honyman, Cornbury told the church wardens at Newport in July that he would write on their behalf to the bishop of London asking for a permanent appointment. In the meantime, he wrote, so that "you might not be deprived of the light of the Gospel in the best form of Religion now extant in the habitable world, I recommend to you the Rev'd Mr. Honyman, who having served the church at Jamaica for some time has discharged his duty with zeal and application, and to the content of good men."[38] Honyman arrived in Newport shortly thereafter and by October 1704 had effectively been filling Lockier's place for several months.[39]

Nevertheless, scandal and dissension followed Honyman to Newport. Reports of the New York affair filtered to Newport. In addition, several leading members of Trinity's congregation remembered that they had not taken well to him when he had temporarily served at the church as a naval chaplain. In particular, warden and parish founder Robert Gardner was a strong opponent of Honyman, and officially reported his dissatisfaction to the S.P.G. in December 1705. Noting that Lord Cornbury had sent Honyman on a temporary basis, until a new appointment could be made from London, Gardner reported that Honyman "had disobliged most of our people who left Church at his coming here, but we having no other, and being in hopes that time and his good conduct for the future would bury all animosities in oblivion, but to our great grief they continue to the great decay of our congregation which still grows less and less."[40] The degree of tension within the parish can be measured by the letter of a Honyman supporter who wrote to the S.P.G. in London charging that Gardner was "the ringleader of a rabble of boys and debauchees who have impardonably dared to address the Bishop of London for another minister by what I understand the address is full of lies."[41]

The dispute soon thwarted a renewed attempt to have Christopher Bridge, in Boston, appointed to take Honyman's place on a permanent basis. In 1699, Bridge had refused to preach in Newport for the lack of a sufficient salary; this renewed attempt to appoint him to Newport was designed to remedy two conflicts: Bridge's long-standing dispute with Samuel Myles in Boston and the dispute about Honyman within the Newport parish. In February 1706, Bishop Compton had the situation in Boston uppermost in his mind when he wrote to Bridge urging him to go the new Rhode Island parish at Narragansett, as the best way to settle his differences with Myles.[42] The bishop's suggestion left the more important appointment at Newport unfilled. As one correspondent advised the S.P.G., "Newport is really the next flourishing place to Boston in that part of the world for trade, conversation and number of people."[43]

Nevertheless, the controversies smoldered on. Members of the Newport congregation, as well as members of the Anglican clergy in New York, wrote to London praising Honyman. One of them described Honyman as

> a Gentleman who by the goodness of his life, the innocencey of
> his Conversation, and pureness of his Doctrine has gained the
> love of all Sober and Considerate people, tho' indeed he has
> lain under the censure of some who only want to Protest of

disliking their minister to avoid going to Church and really of whom "tis a scandal to be well spoken of."[44]

By September 1706, the division between the two parties in Newport was so strong that the wardens and members of the congregation sent opposing reports to London on the same day. The wardens asked the S.P.G. to appoint Bridge, complaining that in Lockier's day the congregation had numbered forty to fifty but that under Honyman it had sunk to only fifteen or sixteen.[45] Opposing them, other members of the congregation wrote directly to Bishop Compton praising Honyman and requesting that the bishop send their parish church a bell, which "will be an excellent ornament for our charge and always sounding your Lordship's praises."[46]

The tension finally erupted in a series of lockouts and break-ins. Finding that the parish in Narragansett could not provide him a house, Christopher Bridge returned to Newport to take possession of Trinity. Unable to obtain the keys to the church, he broke the locks and declared himself the rector on 6 November 1706. Shortly afterward, the Narragansett church came to a temporary accommodation with Bridge and recalled him. Honyman took charge at Trinity again. Just a year later, on 6 February 1708, Bridge again returned to Newport and once more broke the locks to take possession of the Newport church. This time, a number of parishioners protested Bridge's action and refused to hear him preach. Seventeen communicants refused to receive the sacraments from him.[47] These incidents were reported to Governor Cranston as a series of illegal break-ins, but he declined to interfere in the matter as an ecclesiastical issue, beyond the limits of his authority.[48] The royal governor of Massachusetts, Joseph Dudley, had no such qualms and reported to the bishop of London his views on the broader political consequences of this squabble:

> They are both men of good learning and acceptance in the
> service of the Church, but for want of your Lordship's order
> they have interfered in the congregation at Rhode Island, who
> are a violent and earnest people on both sides to the degree
> that there is scarce any advising them, and thereby they give
> advantage to people of other persuasions (or of no religion) in
> the place to reproach them.[49]

Shortly after Bridge's second forcible seizure of Trinity, Honyman decided to sail for London and place his case directly before the Society for the Propagation of the Gospel. After consideration of the circumstances, the society referred

38

Oral tradition has it that this was the first bell used at Trinity Church, before the first large, 800-pound bell arrived in 1709. No record of this earlier 1702 bell has yet been found, although it was used until 1845 in the belfry of the parish's Kay School on School Street, and donated, at that time to the Chapel of Holy Cross in Middletown. It remained there until Ruth Ann Hall of Bristol, R.I., donated a larger bell. Returned to Trinity in 1901, it has been displayed in the tower room of the church since 1913. It has the appearance of a ship's bell and the broad arrow

suggests it was Crown property used in a naval vessel. However, one campanologist has identified the arrow as the maker's mark of the Bilbie Bell Foundry of Chew Stoke, Somerset.

Honyman's case to Bishop Compton and to the archbishop of Canterbury, Thomas Tenison.[50] In the meantime, following Honyman's departure, Bridge and the wardens garnered support from Governor Cranston. In November 1708 Cranston wrote to the S.P.G., arguing in a letter carrying the official seal of the colony that Honyman would destroy the Anglican parish, "giving my opinion freely of it and to assure you most sincerely his having been here so long already hath been the very cause [that] the Church of England in this place hath not found that encouragement and success it hath met with elsewhere in America.[51]

However, in the course of the ensuing investigation of what Bishop Compton called "that insolent riot upon the Church in Rhode Island," it became clear that the reports about Honyman were untrue.[52] The parish had not declined—he had baptized twenty-eight adults and thirty-five children in Newport. Bishop Compton and Archbishop Tenison considered advice from Francis

Nicholson.[53] They read strong letters supporting Honyman from Col. Caleb Heathcote of Scarsdale Manor, New York; The Reverend John Talbot of Burlington, New Jersey; The Reverend George Keith; The Reverend George Muirson of Rye, New York: and Capt. John Hamilton of Burlington, New York. After due consideration the bishop and archbishop exonerated Honyman and directed him to return to Newport to continue permanently in charge at Trinity Church.

Honyman's troubles were not yet over. Returning to Newport on 19 March 1709, Honyman found that deep resentment lingered. Bridge had left Newport before Honyman returned, having reportedly had only a dozen hearers and five communicants at Christmas.[54] Honyman's strongest opponents were the wardens, who still continued to support Bridge and deny Honyman access to the church. Two days after his arrival, Honyman appeared before Governor Cranston and demanded that the colony order the return of the church to him. The governor told him that he could not act without the approval of the General Assembly, scheduled to meet the following day. Honyman prepared a petition, but the Assembly declined to hear it, due to the press of other important business. Frustrated, Honyman went to the church on 24 March and broke open the door. After his departure the vestry immediately secured the church again, but Honyman broke it open once more, this time taking with him the pulpit cloth, the cloth around the reader's place, and the "carpet off the [altar] table."[55]

Even after Honyman succeeded in taking charge, Governor Cranston wrote again to London saying that he did not want Honyman restored to the pulpit at Trinity but wished to have Bridge in his place.[56] By the time this request reached London, however, the S.P.G. had already directed Bridge to take charge of the parish at Rye, New York, where he was to pursue a successful ministry.

By late June 1709, Honyman had managed to bring peace to the warring factions and assuage the bitterness within the parish. The bishop of London had answered the congregation's 1706 request with the gift of an eight-hundred-pound bell for the church steeple, and it had just arrived. Following a vestry meeting on 20 June 1709, Honyman and two new wardens, Nicholas Lange and Thomas Lillibridge, reported to Bishop Compton: "We being extremely sensible of the unhappy consequence of those divisions which have like to have prove so fatal to our infant Church have agreed that nothing relating to this Church shall be transacted nor representations made but by joint consent of the ministers, churchwardens and Vestry of this Church."[57]

The parish's June 1709 address to Queen Anne, in the midst of the War of the Spanish Succession, giving "most humble thanks for the design your Majesty has been pleased to encourage of adding the conquest of Canada to the glory of the British Empire." Vestry Minutes. Collection of the Newport Historical Society.

In a detailed document, all concerned agreed "that as far as possible both the names and nature of factions and parties be banished and forgotten."[58] Undoubtedly, this statement explains the sparseness of parish records before this date. Leaving only the vaguest hints of the tumultuous decade that had just passed, the parishioners of Trinity Church looked to the tasks ahead, emphasizing common and practical goals. They agreed that henceforth they would keep the vestry's correspondence in a common register; that they would immediately repair broken panes in church windows; that they would retrieve the funds donated by Governor Nicholson to Trinity Church and temporarily held by the colony and by The Reverend Samuel Myles in Boston; and, finally, that they would call in, and account for, all the books lent out from the parish library.

As the culminating mark of the happy conclusion of this difficult era, the parish sent a statement of loyalty and thankfulness to the head of the Anglican Church, Queen Anne. Addressed "To the Queen's Most Excellent Majesty the Humble Address of the Minister & People Belonging to the Church in Rhode Island in America," this document expressed several important themes for Trinity Church. First, it declared the congregation's shared belief in the Anglican understanding of the relationship between church and state, along with the value it placed on public service. The document contrasted starkly with earlier Quaker views in Rhode Island; at this stage in the War of the Spanish Succession, there was a newfound patriotism. Governor Cranston had worked for several years to improve the colony's militia and defenses.

Up to this point in the war, England had concentrated almost entirely on fighting France in the European theatre. A small contingent of Rhode Islanders had joined the Massachusetts militia in an unsuccessful attack on Canada in 1708. The following year, the Rhode Island General Assembly supported a new plan for an attack on New France, this time involving a major military and naval expedition from England, supported by ships and troops supplied by the northern English colonies. The commander of the land forces that were to undertake an attack on Montreal was Col. Francis Nicholson, who had returned to a military career after being recalled as governor of Virginia in 1705; he remained an active figure in the S.P.G.. Thus, the parish's address to the queen was designed to compliment Francis Nicholson and to bring to the attention of the highest authorities the parish's appreciation for his generosity and support.

Over its entire first decade, Nicholson had repeatedly provided assistance to Newport Anglicans, acting consistently as their key supporter. First, the parish had turned to Nicholson in its earliest attempts to find a clergyman. Soon,

Nicholson began donating small sums of money for the work of the parish. He invariably supported the parish's interests through his influence and recommendations to the Society for the Propagation of the Gospel, and most recently he had been a key figure supporting Honyman, who had used part of Nicholson's donations for the installation of the new bell.

In the event, the expedition against Canada did not take place in 1709. Hopes that France might agree to peace terms prevented the expedition that had been prepared from leaving England. However, those peace negotiations failed, and the war continued for several years. Eventually, in 1710, Nicholson commanded a similar and successful expedition, which included a Rhode Island contingent. The expedition acquired Acadia for Britain and renamed it Nova Scotia. On news of this great victory, the parish once again sent an address to Queen Anne "with exaltations of joy upon that uninterrupted series of Glorious success wherewith heaven has crowned your triumphant arms against the common enemy and oppressor."[59] As before, it particularly wished "also to acknowledge it the peculiar favour of divine Providence to that worthy gentleman who had the honor to command who has not only been the pious founder of our church, but the most generous and munificent patron that ever religion had in America."[60]

Notes

1. Lambeth Palace, Papers of the Society for the Propagation of the Gospel: S.P.G. 16, fo. 3: Letter from Robert Gardner to John Chamberlain, 24 January 1708.
2. Lambeth Palace, Fulham Papers 41, fo. 22v: Letter from Samuel Myles to Francis Nicholson, 29 February 1700.
3. Ibid. Myles's statement in this letter is also supported by the fact that the records of King's Chapel at the Massachusetts Historical Society make no reference whatsoever to the activities in Rhode Island.
4. For the similar experience of the Congregationalists, see Sydney V. James, *John Clarke and His Legacies: Religion and Law in Colonial Rhode Island, 1638–1750* (University Park: Pennsylvania State Univ. Press, 1999), pp. 111, 188 note 27.
5. Lambeth Palace, Fulham Papers 41, fo. 25: Letter from Robert Gardner to Francis Nicholson, 18 December 1699.
6. Loc. cit., Fulham Papers 41, fo. 25v: Letter from Anthony Blount, 28 December 1699.
7. Ibid.
8. Lambeth Palace, S.P.G. 16, fos. 74–75: Subscriptions for the Church in Rhode Island, undated c. 1701.
9. Lambeth Palace, Fulham papers XXXVI, fo. 30v: Copy of a Note sent to Mr. Bridge by Mr. Samuel Myles on his return from Rhode Island.
10. Ibid., Fulham Papers 41, fo. 24v: Letter from Robert Gardner to Francis Nicholson, 6 November 1699; Fulham Papers 41, fo. 5: Letter from William Brinley to Francis Nicholson, 7 November 1699.
11. Norman Morrison Isham, *Trinity Church in Newport, Rhode Island: A History of the Fabric* (Boston: Printed for the Subscribers, 1836), pp. 23–33.
12. Ibid., pp. 3–37.
13. J. F. Jameson, "The First Public Library in Rhode Island," *Proceedings of the Rhode Island Historical Society,* vol. 4 (1896), pp. 227–31. Charles T. Laugler, *Thomas Bray's Grand Design: Libraries of the Church of England in America, 1695–1785,* ACRL Publications in Librarianship, no. 35 (Chicago: American Library Association, 1973, pp. 47, 51, 54, 63.
14. Letter from Gardner to Chamberlain, 1708; see note 1.
15. Lambeth Palace, Fulham MS XIX, fo. 62, 174, lists for the years 1722 and 1728.
16. Rhodes House, Oxford: MS Bray, Dr Bray's Accounts, f. 11; p. 39.
17. PRO, ADM 6/6, fo. 3v and ADM 6/427, p. 65: "Warrant for Mr. James Honyman recommended by the Bishop of London to be chaplain of His Majesty's Ship the *Advice* (4th rate), Captain James Greenway, commander, dated 16th June 1699."
18. Gardner to Chamberlain, 1708; PRO, ADM 51/13: Captain's Log, HMS *Active,* 1700–1702 (No. 13, Part VI).
19. Gardner to Chamberlain, 1708.
20. Lambeth Palace, S.P.G. 10, fo. 257: Governor of New England, "State of the Plantations," 19 September 1701.
21. Loc. Cit., S.P.G. 10, fo. 7: George Keith, "State of Religion in North America."
22. The name was alternatively spelled "Lockyer"; I have used the spelling in J. A. Venn, *Alumni Cantabridiense* (Cambridge: Cambridge Univ. Press, 1922), vol. 3, p. 98.
23. Rhodes House Library, MS Bray's Associates, f 11: Dr Bray's Accounts, Part II. The surviving elements of this parish library are on deposit at the Newport Historical Society. On the terms of Lockier's appointment, see Rhodes House, Papers of the U.S.P.G., A1, letter 164: Bray to Secretary, S.P.G., 24 May 1704.

24. Rhodes House Library, Papers of the U.S.P.G. A1, letter 50; George Keith to the S.P.G., 29 November 1702. See also "A Journal of the Travels and Ministry of the Reverend George Keith, A.M." *Collections of the Protestant Episcopal Historical Society for the Year 1851* (New York: Stanford & Swords, 1851), pp. 13–26.

25. Lambeth Palace, S.P.G. 15, fo. 213: Lockier to S.P.G., 29 September 1702, and Rhodes House, Papers of the U.S.P.G. A1, letter 44: Minister and Churchwardens of Rhode Island to S.P.G., 29 September 1702. Similar phrases appear in both these letters, but there are some differences between them. See also Mason, *Annals,* pp. 13–16.

26. Ibid.

27. Ibid.

28. Bodleian Library, MS Rawlinson C 933, fo. 31; Minutes of the S.P.G., 15 January 1703.

29. Ibid., fo. 34: S.P.G. Minutes, 16 February 1703.

30. Ibid., fo. 38: S.P.G. Minutes, 19 March 1703.

31. Ibid.; Lambeth Palace, S.P.G. 13, fo. 25: Letter from James Honyman, Portsmouth, 10 May 1703; S.P.G. 12, fo. 85: Letter from James Honyman, 16 November 1703; S.P.G. 15, fo. 215: Letter from James Honyman to Rev. Dr. Beveridge, Rhode Island, 25 November 1702.

32. Lambeth Palace, S.P.G. 15, fo. 218, and Rhodes House, Papers of the U.S.P.G., A1, letter 157: Lockier to S.P.G., 23 December 1703. The coincidence in dates makes it intriguing to speculate whether Honyman may have brought the chalice and paten with him to Newport, but no explicit mention of it has been found in the documents.

33. Ibid.

34. Ibid.

35. Lambeth Palace, S.P.G. 12, fo. 188v: Letter from John Talbot, 7 April 1704.

36. Rhodes House, Papers of the U.S.P.G., A1, letter 186: Honyman to the S.P.G., 18 April 1704; A2, letter 27: Col. William Urquhart to Secretary, S.P.G., 1 November 1704; Lambeth Palace, Fulham Papers VI, fos. 126–27: Lewis Morris to John Chamberlain, June 1704.

37. Rhodes House; Papers of the U.S.P.G., A2, letter 3; Churchwardens, Jamaica, to Lord Cornbury,
9 October 1704.

38. Bodleian Library, MSS Clarendon 102, fo. 151r: Notes for Cornbury's letters; Rhodes House, Papers of the U.S.P.G., A2, letter 30: Cornbury to the Wardens of Rhode Island, 13 July 1704.

39. Lambeth Palace, S.P.G. 13, fo. 77: "A Summary Account of the Church," 5 October 1704; S.P.G. 15, fo. 220: Letter from the Church in Rhode Island to the S.P.G., 19 October 1704.

40. Loc. cit., S.P.G. 15, fo. 224: Church in Rhode Island to S.P.G., 11 December 1705.

41. Loc. cit., fo., 231, Letter dated 24 January 1706.

42. Loc. cit. S.P.G. 7, fo. 192: Letter from bishop of London to Christopher Bridge, 4 February 1706; S.P.G. Minutes 16, fo. 35: Extracts from minutes, 16 April 1706, 20 September 1706, 30 May 1707. See also Wilkins Updike, *A History of the Episcopal Church in Narragansett, Rhode Island.* Second edition edited, enlarged, and annotated by Rev. David Goodwin (Boston: Merrymount Press, 1907), vol. 1, pp 35–36 and notes on pp. 339–41.

43. Loc. cit., S.P.G. 12, fo. 110: Henry Newman to John Chamberlain, 19 August 1706.

44. Edgar Legare Pennington, *The First Hundred Years of the Church of England in Rhode Island* (Hartford, CT: Church Mission, Co., 1935), quoted on p. 9.

45. Loc. cit., S.P.G. 15, fo. 240: Church in Rhode Island to the S.P.G., 24 September 1706.

46. Loc. cit., S.P.G. 15, fo. 244: Petition to the bishop of London, 24 September 1706.

47. Loc. cit., S.P.G. 14, fo. 100: Letter from John Barbor to S.P.G., West Chester, NY, 28 February 1708.

48. Loc. cit., S.P.G. 16, fos. 11, 13: Statement of Governor Cranston, 6 November 1706, Letter from Cranston to Bridge and Honyman, 3 February 1708.

49. Loc. cit., S.P.G. 12, fo. 136: Letter from Governor Dudley to Bishop Compton, 27 May 1708.

50. Loc. cit., S.P.G. 16, fo. 30: Honyman's petition to the archbishop of Canterbury, 4 January 1709.

51. Loc. cit., S.P.G. 16, fo. 45, Letters from Governor Cranston, 18 November 1708.

52. Quoted in Updike, vol. 1, pp. 35–36 and note on pp. 340–41.

53. Loc. cit., S.P.G. 16, fo. 10: Vestry to the archbishop of Canterbury, 1 February 1708.

54. Loc. cit., S.P.G. 16, fo. 49: Letter from Honyman, 24 March 1709.

55. Loc. cit., S.P.G. 16, fo. 50: Vestry of Trinity Church to S.P.G., 28 March 1709.

56. Loc. cit., S.P.G. 16, fo. 46: Governor Cranston to S.P.G., 12 May 1709.

57. Mason, *Annals,* p. 19: Letter to the bishop of London, 20 June 1709.

58. Ibid., pp. 17–19: Resolution of the Vestry, 20 June 1709.

59. Mason*, Annals,* pp. 23–24: The Humble Address of the Minister and Vestry of the Church of England in Newport on Rhode Island in America, 12 December 1710.

60. Ibid.

The Reverend James Honyman served as a chaplain in the Royal Navy before becoming a missionary in America. On leave from his ship, HMS Active, *he spent the summer of 1701 at Trinity in Newport and later returned from 1704 until his death in 1750 to be the longest-serving clergyman at Trinity. He was a key figure not only for the development of the parish, but a major figure behind creating Anglican missions in New England. G. Gaines painted Honyman toward the end of his life. In 1774, Samuel Okey, an engraver working in Newport, published a mezzotint of the portrait. In 1816, one of Honyman's granddaughters, Mrs. Catherine Tweedy, bequeathed the original portrait to the parish.*

3

James Honyman and "the Most Beautiful Structure in America," 1709–50

F rom the church steeple, Trinity's new bell sounded through the town every day at sunrise, noon, and sunset, as well as at services and on public holidays.[1] With internal conflict no longer punctuating the parish scene, the rhythm of daily life marked a period of remarkable growth and development. By 1709, Trinity Church had provided a secure position for an ordained clergyman, and it was furnished with an altar, silver chalice, paten, altar cloth, and bell.

To meet the customary requirements of a typical Anglican parish church in that period, Trinity lacked only an altarpiece, with the Ten Commandments, the Lord's Prayer, the Apostle's Creed, and the royal arms. The parish had previously asked the society to furnish one, and in December 1710 Honyman mentioned this to Colonel Nicholson in sending the parish's address to the queen through him.[2] Six months later, in July 1711, with the arrival of the altarpiece, Honyman's wish was granted.[3]

As the congregation in Newport grew, Honyman was also reaching out and becoming a missionary to other towns in the area. In 1711, he was preaching in Narragansett and Tiverton as well as in Newport. In 1717–18, The Reverend William Guy briefly replaced him in Narragansett, but on Guy's departure for South Carolina, Honyman resumed visits there until The Reverend James MacSparran came to take up that post permanently in 1721. By 1717, he was also preaching in Portsmouth. "I have the greatest encouragement to continue it," Honyman wrote, "not that I receive six-pence from the people nor ever shall (the only way to lead them on being to preach the gospel freely) but I have the surprising and unexpected attendance of all persuasions upon it."[4] He had begun in 1720 to preach in Providence, where he found the people "quite rude and void of all knowledge of religion."[5] Two years later, he reported preaching there to "the greatest number of people that ever I had together since I came to America."[6]

His success in Providence led him to recommend the founding of a parish there and that the S.P.G. send a permanent minister for that work.

In 1723, Honyman apologized for not being able to meet all his commitments in the countryside as well as in Newport. In that year, he wrote, there was "an unusual and yet universal illness in this place," one that required "the constant exercise of my function at my church" as well as "my necessary attendance on a great number of pirates who were executed here, in assisting their preparations for Death."[7] In this, Honyman must certainly have been mindful of his earlier experience in ministering to Captain Kidd and his associates when they were returned to England for trial. In 1723, Honyman ministered to the condemned when a special court was established in Newport to try the notorious Charles Harris and his twenty-five-man crew for their sadistic practices as pirates. These men, with their ships *Ranger* and *Torture*, had engaged HMS *Greyhound*, mistakenly thinking her a likely prize, and had been overpowered by the warship. Following a sensational trial in Newport, they were publicly hanged at the end of Long Wharf and their bodies buried between the high and low-water marks on Goat Island.[8]

By 1719, the growing numbers of people attending services at Trinity were bringing misunderstandings over the use and ownership of the pews. Since no prior record had been kept, the vestry ordered that all the pews be numbered. They also established a record book, documenting the sale and ownership of the pews as personal property, and created a system by which pews were transferred and under what conditions they could revert to the church.[9] Interestingly, pew number 1 was allocated at this time for the use of the governor. Samuel Cranston came from Quaker stock and had been no friend of the parish or of Honyman in his early days, but he was not known to have formally joined any other church. However, Honyman baptized three of his children, John, Walter, and Mary, in July 1713.[10] In addition, Cranston's daughter Elizabeth became Honyman's second wife sometime after 1737.

The church proved attractive to many young merchants in Newport, while it was also attracting people who, for one reason or another, had fallen away from the rigid rules of their own family churches. In this period the moral control that New England churches had wielded was beginning to wane, at the same time that Anglican liturgy and latitudinarianism began to attract members from families that had previously stressed strict and formalized worship in simple, plain, and undecorated surroundings. Expanding trade and closer relationships among the various seaport towns in the American colonies created a

The original brass chandelier. The oldest is marked "Thomas Drew, Exon., 1728." The second may have accompanied it, or the parish may have commissioned a copy of Drew's work made in Exeter, England. A third was ordered in 1763 when the church was enlarged. The fourth, hanging over the altar, is a replica of the first and was made and installed in 1987.

In 1718, John Mulder and William Bright, a Trinity vestryman, donated this silver bowl by Newport silversmith Daniel Russell for use as the parish's first baptismal bowl. Its Latin inscription reads: "Donum D. Johannes Mulderi et D. Guilielmi Bright in Usum Ecclesiae Anglicanae in Novo Porto in Insula de Rhode Island."

growing secular spirit, particularly in the seaport towns. As an example of this reaction and the passionate attitudes it involved, tradition has it that when the Newport Quaker merchant William Wanton fell in love with Ruth Bryant, a daughter of a "presbyterian bigot," the objections were so strong from both sides that William told his fiancée, "Friend Ruth, let us break from this unreasonable bondage—I will give up my religion and thou shalt thine, and we will go over to the Church of England, and go to the devil together."[11]

While Newport Anglicans were in the midst of these changes, there were a number of other recurring issues for the parish. One was the matter of paying the clergy. By and large, the congregation was not wealthy in these years, and its resources remained limited to what incomes could provide. Honyman had complained in 1716 that the parish could only provide thirty-five pounds per year. From the beginning a fifty-pound stipend had come from London to augment what the parish could raise, first from donors in Gloucestershire and then from the S.P.G.. In 1718, Honyman had received an additional five pounds for his work in Portsmouth, and in 1719 the S.P.G. raised his stipend to seventy pounds in light of the work he was doing in looking after the people in Narragansett and Providence.[12]

The need for an Anglican school in Newport was another matter that concerned the parish. Unlike other Rhode Island towns, Newport had shown a great interest in education. The Reverend Robert Lenthall, an Oxford-educated teacher, had kept the town's first school in the early 1640s. In 1675, John Clarke had left a provision in his will for scholarships that still support Newport students to this day. By 1683, the first town schoolhouse had been built; a newer one was constructed in 1708. There were several private schools, including a Latin School, which opened in 1700. The Quakers maintained their own school, to avoid the corrupting ways that their youngsters learned at the public school, purchasing land from Walter Clarke in 1711 for a new building at the corner of present-day Mary and School Streets.[13] On September 1711, James Honyman joined with Governor Cranston and ten other townspeople as proprietors of the land and the schoolhouse.[14]

It has hard to know whether it was the constantly changing town schoolmasters, dissatisfaction with the teachers, or concerns about the religious aspects of the teaching that bothered the Trinity congregation most. In 1714, however, Honyman was particularly worried about the moral character of the town. There is "an open contempt of religious Ordinances, a profanation of the Sabbath, lewdness, and incest and such other immoral practices as would put a

A page from the church records for the parish's annual meetings in 1722 and 1723. Traditionally held on the Monday after Easter up until the twentieth century, the 1722 meeting voted in the new vestry as well as authorized that "there be posts and rails set up at the end of the lane leading up to the Church and a turn-stile made." The 1723 meeting voted in the housewright, Richard Munday, as a new vestryman and established a committee to get subscriptions for a new church. Parish Records. Collection of the Newport Historical Society.

Modest Heathen the Blush and which are avowedly committed with impunity and without Restraint," Honyman told Francis Nicholson.[15] Newport, Honyman concluded, needed a scholar of learning, licensed by the bishop, "to retrieve the rising generation from the rudeness and ignorance of their forefathers."[16] Although the town built additional schools to serve various parts of Newport, other church groups, including the Quakers, Baptists, and Congregationalists, also began to build their own schools in the 1720s and 1730s. In 1717, however, the S.P.G. was unable to provide Trinity with a schoolmaster, and it would be 1741 before Honyman could bring this initiative to full fruition.

The issue of education and schooling was closely tied, in Honyman's mind, to the need for a bishop to supervise the Anglican Church in America. This was a central issue that repeatedly arose in colonial Anglican churches and one that involved some central tenets of the Anglican viewpoint, but Honyman saw a particular issue in the unusual circumstances that Rhode Island presented.[17] In Rhode Island he found a fundamentally negative and anti-Anglican feeling. The Congregationalist Jahleel Brenton had written to the S.P.G. in 1710 that the only Anglican in the colonial government was "Mr. Lang, the Sheriff, who is a Churchman, but a perfect Quaker tool."[18] Honyman found that the Quakers and Baptists felt that they had a greater right and liberty to exercise their religion than any others, because they had settled the place first and for that particular reason. In local politics, attending the Church of England "was looked upon as a Just reason to be overlooked in the election, and Professing an aversion to it, is esteemed a meritorious step to Preferment."[19] Honyman believed this situation was due to the lack of a regular and settled Anglican ministry in Rhode Island under the inspiration of a bishop. To rectify the situation, he believed each of the colony's eight towns needed a minister as well as an Anglican school and schoolmaster, all under the guidance of bishop. However, none of these remedies could be quickly or easily met, and this issue remained a problem for some time. "Nothing here hinders the propagation of religion in the way of our Church," Honyman wrote to the new bishop of London, Edmund Gibson, "as the frowns of the charter government whose members are its professed enemies and nothing could be of greater service than removing those discouragements that oppress our people."[20]

In November 1713, the parish addressed its third message to Queen Anne. In it, Newport's Anglicans made their first formal request for a bishop, declaring that "religion and Virtue seems [sic] to languish in these countries, for want of Bishops."[21] Honyman had observed several problems that had arisen.

For example, in trying to attract former Baptists to the Anglican Church, some Anglican clergy had been led to practice baptism by immersion without sponsors. Because of this and other non-Anglicans practices, Honyman saw a need to regulate the clergy as they became influenced by other groups in the process of their own Anglican work in reaching out toward New Englanders. A bishop was important "not only by the necessary exercise of their sacred functions in conferring Holy Orders, confirming our children, settling of churches and blessing us all in their master's name & by His Authority," Honyman and the vestry wrote, "but by their presence influencing the Several Governments into the faithful discharge of that part of their office, the restraining of vice, & of encouraging virtue, awing the multitude into an observance of Religious duties and giving a check to those licentious practices that are so frequently abroad."[22] The government of the colony was certainly aware of Honyman's views and took exception to them. The General Assembly in 1716 passed a law that clearly reaffirmed religious liberty and the equality of all denominations within the colony, sharply forbidding the government from backing any religious group. In the following years, Honyman was more reticent in public about his views, discussing the need for a bishop only to keep order and maintain consistency of teaching among Anglicans.[23]

Honyman was concerned about the local government's prejudice against Anglicans, and it may have hindered somewhat the growth of the parish. A more serious problem, however was the small size of the church building, where crowded services discouraged newcomers from attending. This must have been an issue for some time. In October 1720, Francis Brinley of Boston sold for fifty pounds the adjoining lot of land, just to the south of the 1700 church building, to wardens Daniel Ayrault and Williams Gibbs. In April 1723, Honyman reported to London that the parish was going to build a new church.[24]

Through his connections with Samuel Myles in Boston, Honyman must certainly have been aware that, through Myles's initiative, a new parish had been formed in Boston's North End. Perhaps Honyman also knew as he wrote to London reporting his own initiative that the foundation stone for Christ Church, Boston, had already been laid and that the building would be completed at the end of December that year. With a similar vision in mind, Honyman had begun the fund-raising effort by announcing his own pledge of thirty pounds, but the project in Newport proved to be a much more time-consuming one than that in Boston. It was not until the vestry meeting on 10 September 1723 that the parish formally decided to go ahead with building the new church.

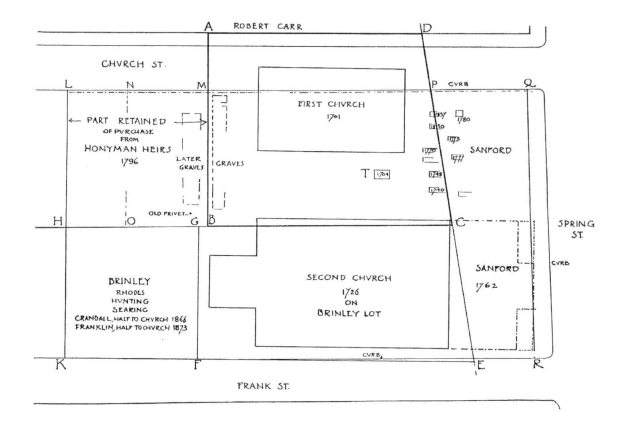

The original lot and the additions to it. Drawing by Norman Isham.

ABCD: the original lot donated by Robert Carr, c. 1700.

T: grave of Thomas Mallett

CEFG: the lot Francis Brinley sold to the churchwardens for £50,
       3 October 1720.

DE: the west side of the Sanford land.

PQRE: former Sanford land acquired by the church about 1758–62.

ML and GH: the north and south lines of the land purchased from the
       Honyman heirs, 1790–96.

NO: West line of the property voted to be retained by the church on sale of
       the Honyman lot to Simeon Martin, 1802.

LH: West line of the property actually retained by the church on sale of the
       Honyman lot to Simeon Martin, 1802.

HGFK: former Brinley land; Robert Crandall sold his half interest in the lot to
       the church in 1866; Robert Franklin sold the other half interest to the
       property to the church in 1873.

A committee was formed under warden Daniel Ayrault to oversee and superintend the construction work. It included William Wanton, William Coddington, Henry Bull, Godfrey Malbone, and John Chace.[25] By late November 1723 Honyman had raised nearly a thousand pounds, but he estimated that the cost would be nearly double that amount. Nonetheless, work began in Newport on construction of Trinity's new church in the spring of 1724.[26] No direct connection has been documented between the construction of the two buildings in Boston and in Newport, but the visual similarity in their Christopher Wren-inspired designs is unmistakable. Neither at Newport nor at Boston is there any direct documentation as to who the master builders or the workmen were. Clearly, they were different, even if inspired by a similar model. The Boston church, with its brick walls, seems slightly closer to the model of Wren's London parish churches than the all-wood church in Newport. In both cases, however, the model was a local builder's interpretation of Wren's mid-seventeenth-century designs, not the more modern designs that the Church of England's 1711 commission had adopted and later implemented, by Nicholas Hawkesmoor and other architects. In Newport, the similarities between Trinity Church, the Sabbatarian Meeting House, and the now-destroyed Ayrault House suggest that those three buildings were all built by Trinity parishioner Richard Munday. In the following years, the vestry regularly called upon Munday to make repairs to the church, adding evidence for this argument.[27]

In July 1725, most of the Anglican clergy in New England gathered at Trinity and saw the construction progress at first hand. During their meeting, they submitted petitions to both King George I and the S.P.G..[28] These petitions, along with the letters that accompany them, repeatedly juxtapose two points: the need for a bishop, and the handsome new church being built in Newport. Whether it was intended or not, the reader gets the clear impression that the new church would make a proper seat for a new bishop, should one be sent from England. Perhaps it was the Boston clergy's reticence on this point that led Samuel Myles to decline to attend the meeting, pointing out the impropriety of holding a meeting of the Anglican clergy in a "Quaker government."[29] Perhaps also it was the reason that The Reverend John Usher, the new missionary at Bristol, abruptly left in the midst of the meeting and did not sign the petition.[30]

The new building was under construction for two and a half years. During this period, the church continued to grow. In 1724, Honyman reported baptizing fifty-three people, including six "Negroes and Indians, and one Indian

Trinity's original "wine-glass" pulpit, with its long ten-step staircase in the back and fronted by both a clerk's desk and reading desk, is still in its original location and the only remaining free-standing, triple-decker in the United States.

One of the "warming boxes" for hot coals used in the pews before heating was installed.

In 1734, Daniel Russell of Newport crafted this six-inch-high and sixteen-inch-long silver baptismal bowl as part of Nathaniel Kay's legacy to the parish. One of the most distinctive pieces of American colonial silver, it continues to be used for the baptisms of many parishioners, as it was for the parish's two most famous naval officers, Oliver Hazard Perry and his brother, Matthew Calbraith Perry.

child."[31] The cost of the building must have been one major reason for its slow progress. In December 1725, the vestry arranged for a plasterer to come from Boston to complete the ceiling, but it is clear that in doing so the parish was reaching the bottom of its financial resources. The vestry agreed to sell the pews in the new building as the best means to find the funds necessary to complete construction. It declared that on 8 December everyone who wanted a pew should meet in the church, decide on the particular pews they wanted to purchase, and pay half the required amount at that point, with the remainder due two months later. At the same time, it assigned numbers to the pews and formulated rules for their future sale and disposition.[32]

On 18 September 1726, Honyman preached his first sermon from the pulpit of the new church. Ten days later he wrote to the bishop of London, "I now preach in our new Church, acknowledged by all the finest building in these parts."[33] More than a year before, the S.P.G. had promised to send furnishings for the new church, but they had not arrived when Honyman gave his first service in the building. Finally, in February 1727, they arrived: a "handsome plain purple communion cloth and also a pulpit cloth and cushion."[34] In September 1727, when the new church building had been in use for nearly a year, Honyman wrote a long letter to the S.P.G., mentioning his activities in preaching at Little Compton, Tiverton, and Freetown. Briefly recounting the history of the parish, Honyman explained that the first building, a structure of fifty by thirty feet (including the tower), had been built in 1700. It had proved too small and needed repairs, the congregation had agreed to build the new structure and had given "the old to the people of Warwick, who now have it."[35]

The fate of the old building is obscure. The parish in New London considered purchasing it, but it appears that it was taken across the bay and reconstructed at the settlement known as Cowesset, near Warwick, where it served for a time. When that community dispersed, it was disassembled again to be moved to Wickford. While it was disassembled and in transit, a severe storm, perhaps a hurricane, scattered the pieces, and the plan was abandoned.[36]

The new and larger building, Honyman described as

> 70 foot long and 46 foot wide, beside 6 foot more for the break
> of the altar and 16 for the belfry, in all 92 feet in length. Therein
> is two tier of windows. It is full of pews and galleries all around
> to the East End and the pulpit at the end of the Middle Alley
> near the communion table, and is owned by all to be the most
> beautiful structure in America made of timber.[37]

The Perkins and Kay flagons. In May 1733, the vestry voted to use the recently-received legacy of Capt. Richard Perkins to purchase a silver flagon for the communion table. At the same time, the customs collector, Nathaniel Kay, agreed to purchase a flagon of equal value. The Kay flagon was completed first and is dated 1733. Perkins's executor, senior warden John Gidley, carried out the legacy, and the second flagon was completed by July 1734. Both 12-1/2-inch tall, matching silver flagons have been attributed to the Newport silversmith Benjamin Brenton (1710–66), who owned land at the corner of Mary and Thames Streets.

In the new church, the parish's S.P.C.K. library was kept in the vestry, which at that time was probably a small room, adjoining the paneled church wardens' pew, under the stairs leading to the gallery on the south side of the church.[38] On Sundays, Honyman reported, the church was well filled, although fewer than four of the original promoters of the church attended. He preached "twice every Sunday and administer[ed] the sacraments once a month, observe[d] all fasts and festivals, [had] prayers twice a week in Lent, and publicly catechize[d] the children."

In addition to conducting all the services, Honyman remained concerned about education in the parish. He reported at that point there were two schools in town. One was a Quaker school, where pupils learned to read, write, and do arithmetic. Another, he reported, was kept by "an ingenious young man belonging to my Church, Edward Scott," a native of Newport who taught Latin, Greek, and mathematics as well as instructed about forty or fifty scholars in the catechism. Some fifty to seventy Indians and Negro slaves attended public worship on Sundays, of whom Honyman had baptized about thirteen. "When I have occasion," he wrote, "I instruct and teach them with patience and compassion and press upon their masters, both in public and in private, for their instruction."[39]

Stressing the differences from a town of similar size in England, Honyman pointed out there were four times the number of trades and types of employment that one would find in a comparable town in England. In addition, "I am perhaps in the most difficult as well as laborious situation of any missionary, surrounded with sectarians of all sorts with whom I am often obliged to converse in over to conviction." In addition, "the minister has no house, no glebe nor any fixed salary, but about £30 English in contribution."[40] To this, the assembled Anglican clergy of New England added another point when they met once again at Trinity in December 1727:

> The Church's chief discouragements in Rhode Island are from those in the Government who are always ready to oppose its settlement and frown on its progress, there being but one Baptized Christian among the whole bench of magistrates, unless we allow the Governor [Joseph Jencks, since May 1727] a rigid Anabaptist and one deeply hing'd with the original principle of his Sect to be another.[41]

To deal with this situation, Honyman in 1728 published a 150-page book addressed especially to Rhode Islanders and entitled *Faults on All Sides. The Case of Religion Consider'd.*[42] The colony's first printer, James Franklin (Benjamin Franklin's elder brother, who had come from Boston to Rhode Island in 1726 with a promise of a contract to print official documents), printed the volume in Newport. It was the first book ever printed in Rhode Island and was sold at both of Newport's bookshops, those of James Franklin and Mrs. E. Neargrass. Newport's Quakers quickly met this challenge with a locally printed edition of the standard theological work that presented their viewpoint: Robert Barclay's *Apology for the True Christian Divinity*, printed on Franklin's press in 1729 and sold through the same booksellers.

With the new church completed and a busy flock to tend, Honyman and Trinity's parishioners settled into the routine of their work. As the years passed, the parish continued to grow, despite the unaccustomed "frowns" of government on an Anglican parish. Honyman attracted rising Newport merchants to his congregation, with such well-known family names as Cranston, Wanton, Coddington, Sanford, Brenton, Bannister, Ayrault, Mumford, and Bours prominent among them.

It was in this situation that an Irish Anglican clergyman, Dean George Berkeley, found Newport and Trinity Church when he arrived at the entrance to Newport Harbor on 23 January 1729. Born near Kilkenny in 1685, Berkeley had attended Trinity College, Dublin, where he took his bachelor's degree in 1704. He had stayed on to be elected a Fellow of the College in 1707, also serving as Librarian of the College during the period that Thomas Burgh designed its famous library. Between 1709 and 1713, Berkeley was ordained and had published a series of books that established his reputation as one of the leading philosophers of his time. In October 1713, Berkeley had temporarily left Dublin when Lord Peterborough appointed him as his chaplain. In this capacity, Berkeley accompanied Peterborough on a diplomatic mission to France and Italy in the immediate aftermath of the War of the Spanish Succession.

Returning to Dublin in 1720, Berkeley took advanced degrees as bachelor and doctor of divinity and soon became lecturer in divinity at Trinity College. By 1724, he found preferment in an appointment as dean of the Anglican cathedral at Londonderry, or Derry, as it was known. At this point, he resigned his fellowship at Trinity College, but he did not take up residence in the seaport town of Derry, on the northwestern coast of Ireland. In this period, such assignments were sometimes regarded as means of support for clergymen who had another important function but no other income. In this case, however, the appointment was more a matter of prestige than great income. Berkeley

The Reverend George Berkeley, D.D. Alfred Hart's portrait after a painting from life by John Smibert. Collection of the Redwood Library and Athenaeum.

delegated his duties to others and moved on with an important project that already fascinated him.

Berkeley's earlier travels on the continent had convinced him that Europe was in a state of moral decay. Reflecting on what he had seen, he became convinced of the need to pay further attention to spiritual values. Like other thinkers in his time, Berkeley had also become influenced by the vision of America as a kind of unspoiled Eden, contrasting with Europe. With these thoughts in his mind, as early as 1722 Berkeley had developed a utopian plan to go to Bermuda and establish a college. In that idyllic place, away from the temptations of Europe and isolated from the corruption of commercial competition, Berkeley wanted to educate young men from the American colonies to become Anglican ministers and serve their own colonies, taking with them a fully-cultured appreciation of music, art, philosophy, and literature. In addition, he wanted to educate native Americans to become Anglican missionaries to their own people. In "America, or the Muse's Refuge, a Prophecy," Berkeley expressed his ideal vision of a cultured America, combining his understanding of theology and philosophy with his sense of the growing British empire:

> In happy Climes the seat of Innocence,
> > Where Nature guides and virtue rules,
> Where Men shall not impose for Truth and Sense
> > The Pedantry of Courts and Schools:
>
> There shall be sung another Golden Age,
> The rise of Empire and of Arts, . . .
>
> Not such as Europe breeds in her decay; [but]
> > Such as she bred when fresh and young,
> When heav'nly Flame did animate her Clay, . . .
>
> Westward the course of Empire takes its Way:
> > The four first Acts already past,
> A fifth shall close the Drama with the Day;
> Time's noblest Offspring is the last.[43]

Looking from afar, Berkeley and his friends thought that Bermuda was some sort of earthly paradise, ideally placed off the American coast, where it had equal access to all the colonies in English America, from the West Indies to Nova Scotia. In fact, the realities were quite different. The geographical advantages that Berkeley and his philosophically-minded friends imagined when they looked at a map were cancelled out by the prevailing winds and the ocean currents that controlled communication by sailing ships. Only later did they learn that the island was so barren as to lack food products and was inhabited by "the roughest and rudest sort of people, sailors."[44] Nevertheless, Berkeley pressed on with his plan and managed to gather powerful support from a variety of influential backers, ranging from London bankers to the bishop of London and the archbishop of Canterbury. He obtained £3,400 from individuals and applied to King George I for a royal charter for St. Paul's College in Bermuda. About the same time, Berkeley learned that under the provisions of the Treaty of Utrecht, which had ended the War of the Spanish Succession in 1713, France had been required to cede the West Indian island of St. Christopher's (St. Kitt's) to Britain. As a result of this, various lands on the island had reverted to the British crown, and the British government planned to sell them to individuals, at considerable profit. Berkeley proposed that in connection with this future sale the British government donate twenty thousand pounds to his college, arguing this would in effect be returning profits made from the colonies to the general good of the American colonists.

Based on promises that these financial arrangements could be brought to fruition, Berkeley sailed from Greenwich, England, on 6 September 1728, in the ship *Lucy*, Captain Cobb, master. Along with him he brought his wife, Anne, the daughter of John Forster, Speaker of the Irish House of Commons and Lord Chief Justice of Ireland. In addition to books and supplies for the new college, he brought several other associates, including John James, Richard Dalton, and John Smibert (who would become one of the most famous of America's early portrait painters). In the tedious, circuitous voyage that the prevailing winds at that time of year dictated, ships typically traveled south from England to the vicinity of the Azores, passing across to Barbados and the Caribbean toward Jamaica before heading north along the coast of North America. On some similar track, the *Lucy* arrived in Virginia after a voyage lasting four months and four days. It was advantageous for Berkeley to stop in Virginia, as that colony remained the center of Anglicanism in North America, as well as the seat of the College of William and Mary, which had been founded on Anglican principles. After a brief stay there, Berkeley, with his wife and associates, continued north to Rhode Island in a coastal trading vessel.

It was not happenstance that they came to Newport. On the one hand, Newport was a practical location from which to reach Bermuda under sail. Thus, it was a good place to establish a farm that could supply the future college. Additionally, Berkeley's arrival was closely tied to the repeated appeals the Trinity parish and the Anglican clergy throughout New England had made for a bishop. For James Honyman and other Anglicans in Rhode Island, Dean Berkeley represented the first solid step toward establishing a resident Anglican bishop in America.[45]

When the ship arrived off Narragansett Bay, Berkeley was able to get the pilot boat to take a letter ashore to Honyman. The pilot boat landed on the Jamestown side and passed the letter to two members of the parish. They brought it across the bay to Newport and had it delivered to Honyman at church, where a holy day service was in progress. Shortly afterward, Honyman and those present went to the ferry landing, where they arrived in time to greet Berkeley as he and his group stepped ashore in Newport.[46] A large group of people cordially ushered them into town. Honyman invited Berkeley and his wife to live with him in his home on the southwest corner of Thames and Church Streets. The Berkeleys remained with the Honymans for three months,

The Reverend James Honyman's house on Church Street, near the corner of Thames Street, c.1920. The Reverend George Berkeley lived here with the Honyman family and at the Honyman farm in Middletown until his own farmhouse was ready. Painting by Helena Sturtevant, (detail) collection of the City of Newport.

until they could move into a home of their own; they were to remain in Newport for a total of two and a half years. During these first three months, when Berkeley was living at the Honymans', the dean preached every Sunday in Trinity Church, beginning on 26 January and ending on Whitsunday of 1729.[47]

Berkeley was excited about what he saw in Newport. Writing to his friend and patron Lord Percival at the end of March, Berkeley exclaimed, "The climate is like that of Italy north of Rome, and in my opinion not quite so cold, though this has been reckoned colder than ordinary."[48]

> The town is prettily built, contains about five thousand souls
> and hath a fine harbour. The people, industrious, and less
> orthodox, I can say they have less virtue (I am sure they have
> more regularity) than those I left in Europe. They are, indeed,
> a strange medley of different persuasions, which nevertheless
> all agree on one point, viz. That the Church of England is
> second best. Mr. Honyman, the only eminent clergyman in
> this island in whose house I now am, is a person of good sense
> and merit on all accounts, much more than I expected to have
> found in this place.[49]

In another letter, Berkeley made a similar description of the religious life of Newport, pointing out that there were four types of Baptists, as well as Presbyterians, Quakers, Independents, and many who adhered to no faith at all. "Notwithstanding so many differences, here are fewer quarrels about religion than elsewhere, the people living peaceably with their neighbors of whatsoever persuasion."[50] With Honyman's assistance, Berkeley purchased a ninety-six-acre farm from Joseph Whipple and his wife, Anne, the daughter of Abraham Redwood. The site was adjacent to Honyman's own farm in present-day Middletown. Berkeley enlarged the dwelling on it and named it "Whitehall." From early May 1729, Berkeley and his wife settled into their life, making plans for the future college and tending the property. There his wife gave birth to their first two children, a son and a daughter.

To assist him with the work, Berkeley had purchased three slaves, whom he personally baptized on 11 June 1731 in Trinity Church as Philip, Anthony, and Agnes Berkeley. In baptizing black members of the Newport community, Berkeley followed Honyman's already established example, but Berkeley's action raised the issue to the level of an early-eighteenth-century philosophical debate. Odd as it may seem to us today, it was a serious question in his time

The Reverend James Honyman's farm in Middletown, as it looked in the early twentieth century. Honymans land adjoined the property that Joseph Whipple sold to Dean Berkeley in 1729 for "Whitehall." Newport Historical Society.

whether or not a person who was owned as property could also have an independent soul. In baptizing his own slaves in Trinity Church, Berkeley was making a radical statement and setting a clear and controversial example for Newport's other slave owners.

In his 1729 sermon at Pentecost, Berkeley departed from his earlier sermons from Trinity's pulpit. "Many Quakers and other sectaries heard my sermons in which I treated only those general points agreed by all Christians," Berkeley later wrote.

> But on Whit-Sunday (the occasion being so proper) I could not omit speaking against that spirit of delusion and enthusiasm which misleads those people: and though I did it in the softest manner and with the greatest caution, yet I found it gave some offense, so bigoted are they to their prejudices. Till then they almost took me for one of their own, to which my every-day dress, being only a strait-bodied black coat with out plaits on the sides, or superfluous buttons, did not a little contribute.[51]

From that time on, Berkeley took fewer services at Trinity, but he occasionally traveled to other Anglican churches in the area. He often preached

ALCIPHRON:

OR, THE

MINUTE PHILOSOPHER.

IN

SEVEN DIALOGUES.

Containing an APOLOGY *for the* Christian Religion, *against those who are called* Free-thinkers.

VOLUME *the* FIRST.

They have forsaken me the Fountain of living waters, and hewed them out cisterns, broken cisterns that can hold no water. Jerem. ii. 13.

Sin mortuus, ut quidam minuti Philosophi censent, nihil sentiam, non vereor ne hunc errorem meum mortui Philosophi irrideant. Cicero.

The SECOND EDITION.

LONDON:

Printed for J. TONSON in the *Strand.* 1732.

Tradition has it that Berkeley wrote much of his book, Alciphron, *while overlooking the sea and the salt ponds in Middletown from the hollow of "Hanging Rock" in today's Norman Bird Sanctuary. This book contains Berkeley's defense of natural and revealed religion. The vignette on the title page of the first volume is an allegorical representation of his failed project to establish a college, his forsaken "fountain" of learning that does not hold water.*
Newport Historical Society.

at the Narragansett church, whose rector, James MacSparran, had been born in 1693 at Dungiven, County Derry, Ireland. With him, he called on Col. Daniel Updike, the attorney general of the colony from 1722 to 1732, at his home, "Smith's Castle." He was also able to visit some of the Indian villages in western Rhode Island. These visits to the Indians provided Berkeley with information that he used after he returned to the British Isles.[53]

At this time, Berkeley also made contact with The Reverend Samuel Johnson, who became a figure in his own right in American philosophical development. Johnson often visited Berkeley at Whitehall. The two soon developed an important correspondence on philosophical matters, which carried on when Johnson became the first president of King's College (now Columbia University) in New York. Following his own philosophical pursuits, Berkeley had joined with Honyman to form a Literary and Philosophical Society in Newport. In addition, he spent a considerable amount of his Newport period writing a book. Eventually published in London in 1732, the book was entitled *Alciphron, or, The Minute Philosopher: In Seven Dialogues containing an Apology for the Christian Religion, against those who are called Free-Thinkers.* Some of the passages in his dialogue provide descriptions of recognizable local places, while some of his characters and their religious ideas are reputed to be based on Newporters that he met. The text certainly shows that he found inspiration by walking Second Beach, not far from "Whitehall," and as noted, tradition has it that he often visited nearby Hanging Rock.

Among the church services that Berkeley performed, there is only one wedding recorded, and that was the marriage for the Honymans' only daughter, Elizabeth, to William Mumford, at Trinity in May 1729. Toward the end of his stay, in July 1731, Berkeley also preached before the assembled New England clergy at Trinity. The Reverend Thomas Harwood of Boston reported to the bishop of London that he had not been able to attend, having had to attend to the duties of his colleagues while they were in Newport, but that he had heard from them that Berkeley's "discourse kept them two and an half hours, which to me is somewhat strange for such an hypochondriacal disposition. I hear he intends for England some time before Michelmas. He seems tired of this country, thô he has seen nothing of it."[53]

By that time, Berkeley knew that the financial plans for his college had failed. Eventually realizing that Bermuda was not the best choice for his college, he had considered Newport, but it soon became clear that any thought of establishing it anywhere other than where the royal charter provided would create a major political problem. At any rate, such an idea was moot if there was no money. It was clear that Walpole's government would never send the promised twenty thousand pounds. Accepting the failure of his project, Berkeley and his family packed their things and prepared to leave Newport. He gave "Whitehall" and the books that he had intended for St. Paul's College to Yale College, which he also provided funds for its first fellowships in Greek. In early September, only three days before the family was due to leave Newport for Boston, where they planned to take passage for England, the Berkeleys' infant daughter Lucia died. Her father had baptized her less than two weeks before. The customs collector, Nathaniel Kay, offered the family a portion of his own lot in the churchyard to bury the infant child.

Berkeley arrived in London in October 1732 and within two years was consecrated bishop of Cloyne in County Cork, Ireland. Before becoming a

The north side of "Whitehall," the home that Dean Berkeley designed in 1729, expanding on an existing structure on his ninety-six-acre farm in Middletown. With the help of the colony's attorney general and Trinity vestryman Daniel Updike, Berkeley purchased the property. Photograph by William James Stillman, 1874. P402. Newport Historical Society.

bishop, he took care to remember Newport. First, he wrote to the S.P.G. recommending that the society honor James Honyman, who, Berkeley wrote,

> is the oldest missionary in America, and he hath done long and excellent service in that station and is a person of very good qualification for life and learning, it would seem that both for his own and other encouragement he may well be distinguished, but how far or in what manner, the Society are proper judges.[54]

Next, Berkeley presented the church with an organ, making the gift through the Society for Promoting Christian Knowledge. The organ builder, Richard Bridge, completed the work in London in July 1733. By mid-October the society's secretary, Henry Newman, had made arrangements with Captain Draper of the ship *Godfrey*, a vessel owned by Trinity parishioner Godfrey Malbone, to carry it back to Newport. "It has been touched and approved by some of the most eminent Masters in London but not so many as I intended," Newman wrote to Honyman,

> being obliged to take it to pieces as soon as it was finished for fear of losing the opportunity of sending it in so good a ship as the *Godfrey*, which calling at Lisbon in her way to Rhode Island. I have with the Dean's leave insured 150 £ Sterling towards making good the miscarriage of it if that should happen and shall pay the freight of it here to ease your flock of any burthen on that score.[56]

A few days later, Newman enclosed another letter to Honyman with the organ, commenting that he had paid the insurance and

> paid nine Guineas freight here on account of the Captain's taking the utmost care of it notwithstanding he calls at Lisbon and may perhaps be obliged to go thence to Cadiz for a loading of salt. The Frontispiece of the Organ with the other Paper of the Disposition of the Pipes which as I remember are 508 will fully instruct any Body that has ever seen the inside of an Organ how to put it together.[56]

Organs were quite rare at that time in British America. While the French had used organs in Quebec since 1657, and they were widely used in the Spanish colonies, the first documented organ in British America was used by a German congregation near Philadelphia in 1694, followed by the small organ at

On Berkeley's return, he arranged for Trinity to have its first organ in 1733. The original keyboard with the maker's label in Latin, "Richard Bridge, London, maker, 1733," is on display at the Museum of Newport History.
Newport Historical Society.

King's Chapel, Boston, which had been installed in 1713. With this in mind, the society in London was concerned that it might be providing something that would not be used. Henry Newman cautiously raised the point when he wrote to Honyman, "I shall be very glad to hear that you are provided with an able performer to be your organist, or if that point be done, that you can find means to make it worth such as one's while to leave Boston or New York to serve you, but the Dean reckons you have a skillful man already."

Apparently Berkeley already was aware of Charles Theodore Pachelbel. The son of Johann Pachelbel, Carl (he later called himself Charles in America) had been born in Stuttgart in 1690. Shortly before, his father, well on the way to becoming the greatest and most productive German composer of his time, had become the organist to the court of Württemberg, under the patronage of

Duchess Magdalena Sibylla. His son immigrated to America about 1728. In Boston, during January 1729, the young Pachelbel staged the first colonial public "Concert of Musick on Sundry Instruments," and taught harpsichord and spinet to some of Boston's more elegantly raised children.[57] Immediately upon the *Godfrey*'s return to Newport with the organ in February 1734, the vestry sent to Boston to Pachelbel that it had arrived and ask him to come and assist in assembling it. For this service, he was paid one hundred pounds.

In connection with the installation, the vestry asked Richard Munday to modify the west gallery and remove several pews where the organ was to stand, with its tall wooden case, surmounted by a gilded royal crown and two mitres, symbolizing the archbishoprics of Canterbury and York.[58] Pachelbel remained in Newport as the organist in 1734 and into 1735, but he declined the parish's offer to stay for another full year. Typical of others in his itinerant profession, he moved on to New York and then to Charleston, South Carolina, where he also taught music and performed. Following Pachelbel's departure, the vestry applied to Henry Newman, the secretary of the S.P.C.K. in London, for a new organist. Newman, who had been born in Rehoboth, Massachusetts, and graduated from Harvard in 1687 before going to England in 1703, was acquainted with Newport. In the meantime, a member of the congregation, Capt. Charles Bardin, filled in as organist until Newman's choice for the position, John Owen Jacobi, could make the journey from England. Upon his arrival in June 1736, the parish paid Jacobi a salary of twenty-five pounds a year.

Honyman continued to be a strong leader of the Anglican clergy in the New England area, and his sermon at King's Chapel, Boston, before the assembled clergy of the region was published in 1733 and widely distributed.[59] These years also marked a series of rapid improvements to the church building. In 1733, Jahleel Brenton, the son of the Congregationalist customs collector of 1689-99, donated a large clock, built by the Newport clockmaker William Claggett, to be installed in the church tower as one of the earliest public clocks in America. In 1734, the vestry moved quickly with other improvements to the building. First, the wardens were authorized to purchase paints and to have the building painted as soon as possible, both inside and out, and to obtain a frame for the altarpiece. Shortly thereafter, the vestry authorized use of a legacy left to the church by Capt. Richard Perkins to purchase a silver flagon for the communion table. Nathaniel Kay agreed to donate a matching piece of the same value, both to be made by the Newport silversmith Benjamin Brenton.[60]

Kay died the next year, and his will provided a donation of suitably inscribed pieces of silver to three other parishes in the area: Bristol (then in

The loft over the plastered ceiling in the 1725 church, showing the roof beams and the tied ropes that hold the chandeliers.

Massachusetts) and the Rhode Island parishes at Narragansett and Providence. The inscription that Kay arranged, "An Oblation from Nathaniel Kay, a Publican," suggested that he was well aware of the opprobrium repeatedly assigned by the New Testament to his profession as a tax collector.[62] By calling himself a "publican" he reminds us of the ancient Jews who, having accepted positions as tax collectors under the Romans, were regarded as outcasts and traitors among their own people. In addition to the silver flagon matching the gift of Captain Perkins, Kay also left money for a baptismal bowl. Newport silversmith Daniel Russell, who had also made the parish's first, and smaller, baptismal bowl in 1718, made the bowl in 1734.[62] Kay also gave a legacy of two hundred pounds to Trinity, half of it to assist the poor of the parish and the other hall for the use of the church. He gave his house and land in Newport for the support of a school in Newport, making a similar gift of two hundred pounds to St. Michael's Church in Bristol, along with his farm on the south tip of Poppasquash Point.

It would take several years to put all of Kay's donations into effect. In the meantime, the parish in Newport was growing and developing rapidly. There was continual pressure to obtain more space for pews. In the first major attempt to accommodate more pews on the ground floor, the two facing doors on the north and south sides at the east end of the building were closed up, and windows were added above them.[63] In addition, pews were added along the east wall, on either side of the altar apse. In 1739, a walkway of flat stones was constructed from Church Street to the north door of the tower. In the following year, the vestry enclosed the churchyard with a fence and, when the eight-hundred-pound bell cracked, the vestry immediately acted to have it recast and replaced with a larger, thousand-pound bell.[64]

In the autumn of 1740, a number of Anglican churches in America were shocked to find among them a quite unusual missionary figure, The Reverend George Whitefield. As an undergraduate at Pembroke College, Oxford, Whitefield had met Charles Wesley and his brother John, becoming highly influenced by the Wesleyites and the early Methodist movement within the Anglican Church. Soon after his graduation from Oxford in 1736, Whitefield made his first trip to America, and in 1739 he returned, making a tour through all the colonies. At this point, Anglican churches had not spread inland; all were within reach of port cities, with their direct maritime connections to England. After some time in Savannah, Georgia, Whitefield began to work his way northward in September 1740, spending more than a year preaching in different Anglican churches along the way. His preaching tour laid the foundation for "the Great Awakening," his call for repentance and a confession of faith in the savior, Jesus Christ.

As he traveled, he began to draw enormous crowds, often forcing him to speak in the open fields. Although an ordained Anglican, he appealed to Congregationalists, Presbyterians, Baptists, and many others, including men and women, black and white, literate and illiterate. As he traveled he established ties with revivalist ministers from other churches, including the Congregationalist Jonathan Edwards, Presbyterian Joseph Tennant, and the Reformed pastor Theodore Freylinghuysen. Despite Whitefield's popularity, his colleagues among the Anglican clergy were disturbed with some of his practices. He did not confine himself to the Book of Common Prayer, used extemporaneous prayers, and clearly did not believe in the apostolic succession of the ordained clergy. The most serious weakness in his approach was its impulsiveness. In Philadelphia, the rector at Christ Church repeatedly interrupted his sermon to point out errors in his theology; at New York, the rector of Trinity refused to allow Whitefield to use

John Gidley was a prosperous merchant, who served as junior warden in 1734 and senior warden in 1735. His father, John Gidley, had come to Newport from Exeter, Devon, and served as judge of the vice-admiralty court in Rhode Island before his death in 1710. The son was serving temporarily as judge of the vice-admiralty court when he was killed in the explosion of a gun in 1744. Both are buried in the churchyard. Portrait by Robert Feke.

Collection of the Newport Historical Society

his church; in Boston, the Anglican clergy was so adamantly opposed to him that Whitefield did not even bother to ask to speak in their churches. Instead, he went to Boston Common, where he claimed that twenty thousand gathered to hear him.[65]

On 18 September 1740, James Honyman reported that on the previous Sunday, "the nosie Mr. Whitefield" had arrived in Newport by sea from Charleston.[66] "He came to church in the afternoon and behaved decently," Honyman reported to the S.P.G.. Later that day, he and some other Newport clergymen called on Whitefield. When Whitefield proposed that he use Trinity Church on the following Monday and Tuesday, Honyman expressed some reservations. Before Honyman would give permission, he asked Whitefield to explain "his call and commission from God, as man to go about as he did and told him of the unhappy consequences which did and would follow from his irregular conduct." Others present suggested that he use one of the other meeting houses in town. Summarizing the reports of these events, the minutes of an S.P.G. meeting in London record that "several of the chief of Mr. Honyman's own people being present, and vehemently importuning him to lend Mr. Whitefield the Church, he at last yielded to them, but will make it his own earnest endeavor to correct Mr. Whitefield's mistakes and errors and teach his Congregation how to distinguish between Christianity and Enthusiasm."[67]

Whitefield's tour of the colonies left its permanent mark on American religion. In some respects it was divisive, forcing people either to follow Whitefield or oppose him. Anglicans, in general, fundamentally disagreed with Whitefield but soon discovered that they benefited from his presence, as many who were uncomfortable with Whitefield's religious fervor found a refuge from it in the Anglican approach. The Anglican Church in Newport, as well as other churches all over New England, gathered new members in the wake of Whitefield's evangelizing. In a substantial increase, Honyman reported in 1743 that he had baptized 115 in the previous two years, including fifteen adults, five adult blacks, and two black children. There were eighty regular Anglican communicants and one hundred blacks who regularly attended services, of whom five were regular communicants.[68] Pressure for pews continued, and a few years later, in 1747, the vestry was forced to close off the aisle between the north and south doors at the west end of the church, and four more pews were added to the center section to take advantage of that space. About this time, the pew used for christening was converted to a warden's pew.[69]

Another reaction to Whitefield's work appeared in a renewal of the emphasis that Anglicans had consistently placed on education. In general,

Anglicans of the day believed that they could refute the errors of the "Great Awakening" through a sound and broad education. In higher education, this led Anglicans to found King's College (later Columbia) in New York and, in 1755, to obtain a charter for Benjamin Franklin's Public Academy of Philadelphia, later known as the University of Pennsylvania. On the parish level, basic schooling was also a major issue for Anglicans.

James Honyman had consistently maintained his interest in education and had done what he could to support it in Newport. By 1726, the schoolhouse, along with its adjacent small house for a schoolmaster, that Honyman and a group of proprietors had built in 1711 for the town had fallen into disrepair. Since a number of the original proprietors had refused to pay their shares of the maintenance costs of the buildings, the remaining proprietors had finally decided to sell at public auction the shares of those who had not paid, reimbursing the original owners and redistributing the shares among others who would actively agree to help. Under the new arrangement, nine Trinity Church parishioners joined together to buy up all the new shares. William Whiting, John Chace, George Goulding, John Dickinson, Joseph Whipple, Henry Bull, Jahleel Brenton, Jr., and Godfrey Malbone each bought one share, while Nathaniel Kay held two, taking up Honyman's share at this point."[70] At this point, the Latin School used the building. Honyman had repeatedly recommended that the S.P.G. support the Latin School's master, Edward Scott, as the parish's schoolmaster. George Berkeley had seconded this recommendation in 1733, when Scott became a member of the vestry.[71] The S.P.G. took no action on these recommendations, but later, as a warden, Scott served on several committees relating to the parish's school.

Six years later, Nathaniel Kay's 1734 bequest of his house and land, with the income from its rental, as well as four hundred pounds to build a new schoolhouse, finally began to come to fruition and to become a continuing story in the parish. In 1740, Kay's former home was rented out for £130 per year, and arrangements were made to use the four hundred pounds to build a new schoolhouse at the corner of Mary and School Streets.[72] In October 1741, Honyman offered a temporary position as schoolmaster to Cornelius Bennett, until such time as the S.P.G. could send an ordained schoolmaster. Honyman made this offer on the explicit condition that Bennett would teach ten poor children and, in addition, that "the gentlemen belonging to the Church will put their children to him for his further encouragement."[73] In 1746, the vestry increased Bennett's salary to sixty pounds, but a dispute with the vestry ensued. Soon thereafter,

Captain Philip Wilkinson served as junior warden in 1742–43 and senior warden in 1743–44. Later, he also served a number of terms as a vestryman between 1755 and 1771. A merchant who had immigrated from the north of Ireland, he was a business associate of Daniel Ayrault. In this portrait attributed to Robert Feke, he is depicted in a Newport-made chair with one of his own ships in the background. Collection of the Redwood Library and Athenaeum.

Nathan Coffin replaced Bennett at a salary of one hundred pounds, but it proved increasingly difficult to retain a lay schoolteacher on the terms offered, although several additional offers were made.[74]

Despite James Honyman's repeated reminders over a four-year period, the society in London had not acted on Trinity's request for an ordained schoolmaster and assistant to Honyman. During these years, Honyman's health had been slowly declining. In August 1745, he fell from his horse and was incapacitated for some weeks, during which time James MacSparran came from Narragansett to assist with the parish work. In a diary entry for August 1745, MacSparran noted some differences in the parish and wrote that despite Honyman's temporary absence, "all his People, roundly and without exception, went to several meetings." MacSparran went on to note, "His strange Conduct has given his People inconsistent Principles and lessened that Reverence, they were noted for, to the Clergy."[75]

Finally, at its November 1746 meeting, the society agreed to send an ordained clergyman to take up the position of schoolmaster under the arrangement left under Nathaniel Kay's will. The schoolmaster would be assigned to Trinity Church and teach ten poor boys grammar and mathematics free of tuition. The parish would provide a salary of twenty-five pounds per year in addition to housing, and the society would add an additional ten pounds to compensate the schoolmaster for being the catechist for the parish. To find an appropriate candidate, the society directed Honyman to consult with The Reverend Samuel Johnson at Stratford, Connecticut, and obtain from him a recommendation of an Anglican graduate of Yale College who upon ordination would be qualified to take up the position. Upon selection, the S.P.G. would pay for the candidate to go to England, where he would be ordained under the sponsorship of the society, eventually returning to Newport to take up the position as arranged.[76] By this time, James Honyman had been rector for forty-four years and was about seventy-three years old. He clearly needed assistance in managing the parish as well as in running the school, although he was active enough to report that he had baptized forty-seven people the previous year. Sixteen of them had been blacks, two Indians, and eleven adults that he had instructed. On the first Sunday in February 1748, Rhode Island was gripped by a deep cold spell, but Honyman carried on with his schedule to celebrate the Eucharist. Suddenly, in the midst of his sermon, he was, as he later described it, "seized and senses stupefied...so that my people carried me out of my pulpit home to bed."[77] Partially paralyzed, Honyman never fully recovered, and it was obvious that he needed assistance. The Reverend James MacSparran visited him at this time and presided over the vestry meeting that month, trying to find a schoolmaster and an assistant. They first turned to Joseph Cleverly of Braintree, Massachusetts, but eventually settled on the man Samuel Johnson had recommended: Jeremiah Leaming.

Born in 1719 at Middletown, Connecticut, Leaming had graduated from Yale in 1745. In April 1748, he left Newport for London, carrying with him a letter from Honyman that certified his qualification "both as to Morals and Learning" for holy orders. In June, he arrived in London and applied to the Society of the Propagation of the Gospel, which in turn recommended him to the bishop of London, who ordained him on 19 June 1748.[78] By the end of September, Leaming was back in Newport, carrying with him his orders as deacon and priest. He immediately took up the position of schoolmaster and assistant. He quickly found hard work at hand, "by reason of Mr. Honyman's great Age and Infirmities."[79] He soon found himself obliged to give two sermons a week as well as run the school, where by the end of the year he had seventy-two pupils, of which fifty-two were Trinity parishioners, with "nine dissenters, six Quakers, and five Baptists."[80]

Leaming had also brought back with him the S.P.G.'s encouragement for another one of Honyman's educational projects: a library. Long an advocate of the idea that learning and wide reading would confirm intelligent readers in the ways of Anglicanism, Honyman had strongly supported the plans that had developed out of the group that he, George Berkeley, and others had organized in 1730, "the Society for the promoting of Knowledge and Virtue," better known locally as "the Literary and Philosophical Society." In 1747, Abraham Redwood donated five hundred pounds to purchase books for the library. The new organization was chartered with Honyman on the first board of directors and Edward Scott the first librarian.[81] Encouraged by having several parishioners as key members of the library, Honyman had sought the assistance of both the S.P.G. and the S.P.C.K. for the new library, as an obvious complement to the work of the Kay School and to that of his parishioner Edward Scott's Latin School. Returning from his ordination, Leaming brought back a report that the S.P.G. would gladly assist the library with appropriate books.

In reply, Honyman happily wrote about the new Redwood Library in 1748: "It is an uncommon projection and I hope that it will be of general use to this part of the world and certainly deserves the attention of generous lovers of mankind."[82] In a postscript, Honyman added, "I am glad you approve of the preliminaries of our catalogue. I drew them as carefully as I could to prevent any

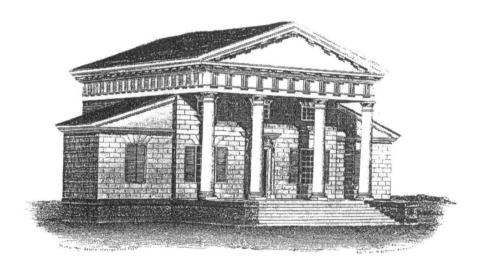

The Rev. James Honyman's certificate that he had carried out King George II's order in council to say the proper form of the prayers for the royal family in the appropriate places in the liturgy at Trinity Church. Dated 5 July 1741, the certificate was witnessed by church wardens John Bannister and Peleg Brown.

Parish Records. Collection of the Newport Historical Society.

Redwood Library, 1750. Print from George Champlin Mason, Extra Illustrated, Reminiscences, *vol. 4, 260-B.* Collection of the Newport Historical Society.

mischief that may be suggested by the Great Enemy to frustrate so excellent a Design." Interestingly, in December 1750, when the Library Company voted an equal assessment on all its members to raise the £1,200 necessary to complete its building, Ezra Stiles related the members to their churches. Of the ninety-three members, forty-four were Anglicans, eighteen were Quakers, sixteen Presbyterians (i.e., Congregationalists), thirteen Baptists, and two Jews.[83]

Although severely hindered by his paralytic disorder, Honyman still managed to carry on and write his annual reports to the S.P.G.. In October 1749 he described Trinity as the largest of any Anglican church in the area, "yet is so crowded that they must either enlarge it beyond the voice of a speaker or build another for the reception of such as cannot be accommodated in that church."[84]

Finally, on 2 July 1750, Honyman died, at seventy-five years of age. The congregation paid the funeral expenses, and he was laid to rest just outside the north door of the church he had built, next to his first wife, Elizabeth Carr Honyman, who had died in 1737.[85] For those who regularly pass by to attend services at Trinity Church today, the inscription on James Honyman's tomb still serves as a reminder of the achievements of a man who was "an excellent scholar, a sound divine, and an accomplished gentleman." The difficult moments in the first years of his tenure were long forgotten, and he had fully earned respect as a man "of venerable and ever worthy memory." Honyman had successfully served a parish "which by divine influence on his labors, had flourished and exceedingly increased."

Notes

1. Wm. King Covell, *The Organs of Trinity Church* (London: Musical Opinion, 1935), p. 13.
2. Mason, *Annals*, p. 25: Letter to Nicholson, 12 December 1710.
3. Lambeth Palace, S.P.G. 16, fo. 66: Letter from Honyman to the S.P.G., 12 July 1711. No description of the altarpiece is known to exist.
4. Rhodes House, Papers of the U.S.P.G. C/AM 9: Honyman to the S.P.G., 26 July 1717.
5. Quoted in Pennington, *Rhode Island*, p. 15.
6. Rhodes House, loc. cit., Honyman to the S.P.G., 20 June 1722.
7. Lambeth Palace, Fulham VIII, fo. 145: Letter from Honyman to Secretary, S.P.G., 19 November 1723.
8. Sydney V. James, *Colonial Rhode Island* (New York: Charles Scribner's Sons, 1975, p. 126 note.
9. Mason, *Annals*. Report of Vestry Meeting, 18 September 1719.
10. Carl Bridenbaugh, *Cities in the Wilderness: The First Century of Urban Life in America, 1625–1742* (New York: Alfred A. Knopf, 1964), p. 25.
11. Quoted in ibid., p. 263.
12. Rhodes House, Papers of the U.S.P.G., A13, letters 544 and 563: S.P.G. to Honyman, 18 April 1718 and 13 July 1719.
13. Ibid., pp. 123, 284–85, 445.
14. Newport Historical Society, Land Evidence Records 1711–1727, Book 7, pp. 181–83. As mentioned in reapportionment of shares 26 December 1726.
15. Quoted in Pennington, p. 11.
16. Rhodes House, Papers of the U.S.P.G., B1, letter 176: Memorial of James Honyman to Francis Nicholson, 7 May 1714; A12, letter 472: S.P.G. to Honyman, 15 April 1717.
17. On this general issue, see Arthur Lyon Cross, *The Anglican Episcopate and the American Colonies* (New York: Longman, Green, 1902) and Carl Bridenbaugh, *Mitre and Sceptre: Transatlantic Faiths, Ideas, Personalities, and Politics, 1689–1775* (New York, 1962).
18. Letter from Jahleel Brenton to the S.P.G., 15 November 1710, quoted in Pennington, *Rhode Island*, p. 10.
19. Pennington, *Rhode Island*, p. 12.
20. Lambeth Palace, Fulham VIII, fo. 229: Letter from Honyman to the bishop of London, 25 June 1725.
21. Mason, *Annals*, p. 26.
22. Ibid.
23. James, *Colonial Rhode Island*, p. 190.
24. Lambeth Palace, Fulham VIII, fo. 188: James Honyman's Answers to Printed Questionnaire, 23 April 1723.
25. Mason, *Annals*, footnote on pp. 56–58.
26. Lambeth Palace, Fulham VIII, fo. 188: James Honyman's Answers to Printed Questionnaire, 23 April 1723.
27. Isham, *Trinity Church*, pp. 31–58; Mason, *Annals*, 25, 34, 51, 51 note 44, 52, 58, 69, 107, 126.
28. Lambeth Palace, Fulham IV, fo. 161–62: Petition to the king, Newport, 21 July 1725; Lambeth Palace, Fulham VIII, fo. 93: Rhode Island Clergy to the S.P.G., 21 July 1725.
29. Lambeth Palace, Fulham IV, fos. 174–75. Letter to bishop of London, 7 December 1725.
30. *Annals of King's Chapel*, vol. 1, p. 338.

31. Mason, *Annals*, p. 40.

32. Ibid., pp. 40–41.

33. Lambeth Palace, Fulham VIII, fo. 204: Letter from Honyman to bishop of London, 26 September 1726.

34. Rhodes House Library, U.S.P.G. A19, letter 267: S.P.G. to Honyman, 1 July 1725, and letter 466: Honyman to the S.P.G., 7 February 1727.

35. Rhodes House, Papers of the U.S.P.G., B1, letter 222: Honyman to the S.P.G., 7 September 1727.

36. Mason, *Annals*, footnote on pp. 43–45; The Rev. Daniel Goodwin, ed., *A Letter Book and Abstract of Out Services. Written during the Years 1743–1751 by the Rev. James MacSparran, Doctor in Divinity and sometime Rector of Saint Paul's Church, Narragansett, Rhode Island* (Boston: Merrymount Press, 1899), footnote p. 73.

37. Ibid.

38. Isham, *Trinity Church*, pp. 77, 81, 86.

39. Rhodes House, Honyman to S.P.G., 7 September 1727.

40. Ibid.

41. Rhodes House, Papers of the U.S.P.G., C/AM9, the New England Clergy to the S.P.G., Newport, 12 December 1727.

42. [James Honyman], *Faults on All Sides. The Case of Religion Consider'd: Shewing the Substance of True Godliness: wherein are also particulariz'd, Sundry Errors, Maxims and Corruptions of Men and Sects of this present Age, with Suitable Observations and Reflections thereon. With Some conclusive Reasons to perswade to Unity, Moderation and Charity. Presented to the Inhabitants (especially) of the Colony of Rhode Island; and all others who make Possession of the Gospel of our Lord Jesus Christ* (Newport: Printed for the author, and sold by E. Nearegreas and J. Franklin, 1728).

43. Luce and T. E. Jessop, eds., *The Works of George Berkeley, Bishop of Cloyne* (London: Thomas Nelson and Sons, 1955), vol. 7, pp. 369–71.

44. Quoted in H. P. Thompson, *Into All Lands: The History of the Society for the Propagation of the Gospel in Foreign Parts, 1701–1950* (London: S.P.C.K., 1951), p. 87.

45. Edwin S. Gaustad, *George Berkeley in America.* (New Haven, CT: Yale Univ. Press, 1979), pp. 8–13.

46. Mason, *Annals*, p. 46.

47. Berkeley's original notes for fourteen of these sermons are in the British Library, Addit. MSS. 39, 306, fos. 140–63; they have been published in A. A. Luce and T. E. Jessop, eds., *The Works of George Berkeley*, vol. 7, pp. 53–84.

48. Ibid., vol. 8, pp. 191–92: letter 137, Berkeley to Percival, 28 March 1729.

49. Ibid.

50. Ibid., vol. 8, p. 196: Berkeley to Thomas Prior, 24 April 1729.

51. Ibid., vol. 8, pp. 201–202: Berkeley to Percival, 30 August 1729.

52. Ibid., vol. 7, p. 121: S.P.G. Anniversary Sermon, 1732.

53. Lambeth Palace, Fulham V, fos. 4043; Letter from Thomas Harwood to bishop of London, Boston, 19 July 1731.

54. Rhode House, Papers of the U.S.P.G., C/AM 9: Letter from George Berkeley to S.P.G., 10 February 1733.

55. Holy Trinity Church, London, Archives of the Society for Promoting Christian Knowledge: CN3/ 4. Letter from Henry Newman to The Rev. Mr. Honyman, 19 October 1733. See also, letters from Newman to The Rev. Dr. Cutler, 28 July 1733 and 19 October 1733; Newman to The Rev. Dr. Berkeley, 7 November 1733.

56. Loc. cit., Letter from Henry Newman to Honyman, 24 October 1733.

57. Bridenbaugh, *Cities in the Wilderness*, pp. 455, 462, 464 note, 466.

58. Mason, *Annals*, pp. 57, 59, 63; Vestry Meeting February 25, 1733 /[34] and 8 July 1734. Alternatively, it has been argued that the mitres symbolize the archbishop of Canterbury and the bishop of London.

59. James Honyman, *A Sermon Preached at the King's Chapel* (Boston, 1733).

60. On Brenton, see, Ralph E. Carpenter, Jr., *The Arts and Crafts of Newport, Rhode Island 1640–1820* (Newport: Preservation Society of Newport County, 1954), pp. 156, 165, 183.

61. Delbert W. Tildesley, *St. Michael's Church in Bristol, Rhode Island*, 1718–1983 (Bristol, RI: St. Michael s Church, 1989), pp. 19–22. On the Kay Farm and Kay School in Bristol, see ibid., pp. 44–49.

62. Margaret Ballard, "Early Silver in Trinity Church, Newport, Rhode Island," *Antiques* (October 1981), pp. 922–25; on Russell, see Carpenter, *Arts and Crafts*, p. 157.

63. Mason, *Annals*, p. 67 footnote 68. Mason errs when he explains that the doors opened out onto Spring Street. The evidence of the original door at the east end of the south wall was found during the 1987 restoration, when a door for handicapped access was put in the same location.

64. Mason, *Annals*, pp. 70, 72.

65. John Woolverton, *Colonial Anglicanism in North America* (Detroit: Wayne State Univ. Press, 1986), pp. 189–96.

66. This and the following quotations in this paragraph are a summary of Honyman's letter of 18 September 1740 as reported in Lambeth Palace, S.P.G. IV, fo. V; 2: Minutes of the S.P.G., 16 January 1741.

67. Ibid.

68. Rhodes House, Papers of the U.S.P.G., Letterbook B11, letter 10, Honyman to S.P.G., 13 lune 1743.

69. "Memoir of Trinity Church, Newport, R.I., compiled by Henry Bull, Esq., at the request of the Rector, Rev. Francis Vinton. Recorded by John Sterne, Esq. In 1841–42." Undated and unidentified newspaper clipping, Newport Historical Society.

70. Newport Historical Society, Land Evidence Records 1711–1727, Book 7, pp. 181–83; Reapportionment of shares, 26 December 1726.

71. Rhodes House, Papers of the U.S.P.G., A24: letter 92, Berkeley to the S.P.G., 10 February 1733 and C/AM 9 of same date; letter 137: Honyman to the S.P.G., 20 September 1732.

72. Ibid., pp. 72–73.

73. Ibid., p. 75.

74. Mason, *Annals*, pp. 83–84, 87.

75. MacSparran, *A Letter Book and Abstract of Our Services*, p. 36.

76. Rhodes House, Papers of the U.S.P.G., B14, letter 9 and letter 14: Honyman to the S.P.G., 2 August 1746 and 15 October 1746; B15, letter 25: 17 September 1747; Lambeth Palace, S.P.G. V, fo. 111v: Minutes of the S.P.G., 21 November 1746.

77. Rhodes House, Papers of the U.S.P.G., B16, letter 8: Honyman to S.P.G., 20 April 1748.

78. Lambeth Palace, S.P.G. V, fo. 190: Minutes of the S.P.G., 17 June 1748; Rhodes House, Papers of the S.P.G., B16, letter 26: Honyman to the S.P.G., 19 October 1748; Mason, *Annals*, p. 89.

79. Lambeth Palace, S.P.G. V, fos. 171–172: Minutes of the S.P.G., 17 February 1749.

80. Rhodes House, Papers of the U.S.P.G., B16, letter 32: Leaming to S.P.G., 19 December 1748.

81. George Champlin Mason, *The Annals of the Redwood Library and Athenaeum, Newport, Rhode Island* (Newport, Redwood Library, 1891), pp. 10, 12, 18, 25, 31, 32, 34, 37, 44.

82. Loc. cit., letter 26: Honyman to S.P.G., 19 October 1748.

83. New Haven Colony Historical Society, Whitney Library, MSS 7: Ezra Stiles Papers, Box 1, Folder S: Meeting of the Company of the Redwood Library, 28 December 1750 [xerox copy at Redwood Library, Newport].

84. Lambeth Palace, MSS 11233, I (43): Minutes S.P.G., 20 April 1750.

85. His second wife, Elizabeth Cranston Honyman, survived him. She was the daughter of Governor Samuel Cranston. When she died she was buried next to her first husband, Capt. John Brown.

The first known image of Trinity Church is on the over mantle painted for the Phillips House, which once stood on Mill Street. The image can be dated to c. 1740, as it shows the Colony House, built in 1739, and the Cove, where the Marriott Hotel now stands, before Long Wharf was extended in 1741. In 1864, J. P. Newell made a lithograph of this painting and mistakenly dated it 1730.

Anonymous loan to the Newport Art Museum.

4
Growth and Affluence, 1750–64

In the mid-eighteenth century, Newport was at the height of its commercial prosperity in the colonial period. It was a city dominated by maritime commerce in molasses, rum, and slaves, dependent upon the sea and maritime industries for its prosperity. The people of Newport were largely loyal to the Crown, well aware that their own prosperity was directly hinged to the success of Britain's maritime empire. For a number of Newport's successful merchants, there was also a connection between their worldly success and their spiritual beliefs, which found expression in the Church of England.

Throughout the period, one of the main things that concerned Anglicans in America was the lack of a bishop in the colonies. The Great Awakening, which George Whitefield and others sparked, had reached its full force. Earlier the bishop of London had tried to extend his control by increasing the number of commissaries in the various colonies. By the end of the 1740s, there were commissaries in Virginia, Maryland, the Carolinas, Pennsylvania, Delaware, New York, and Massachusetts, but they had proved ineffective in dealing with some of the excesses that the Great Awakening involved. Many Americans felt that only a local, American bishop would have the direct influence and authority to control a figure such as Whitefield. There were other practical reasons as well, as the Trinity parish had seen when Jeremiah Leaming had had to travel all the way to London just for his ordination. In 1751, even Thomas Sherlock, the bishop of London himself, complained that "for a bishop to live at one end of the world and his church at another must make this office very uncomfortable to the Bishop and in a great measure useless to the people."[1] Sherlock felt that there was a great need for a bishop in order to regulate the practices of the clergy, who came from a variety of backgrounds. "A great part are of the Scotch and the Irish, who can get no employment at home and enter into the service more out of necessity than choice. Some others are willing to go abroad to retrieve either lost fortunes or lost character."[2] For these reasons, as soon as he had become bishop of London in 1748, Sherlock had recommended to the king that two or three bishops be appointed in America. In order to support his case, he refused to fill vacant positions among the commissaries, arguing that only an American bishop could do the work. He saw that a bishop would have no jurisdiction beyond the clergy and seeing that the pastoral offices were properly performed, and he rejected the thought that a bishop should not go to "New England, where the difficulties are so numerous it never was proposed to settle a Bishop in that Country."[3] Despite that, many critics of the Anglicans in New England continued to be suspicious that a bishop would be merely another tool for tighter imperial control from London.

While the broad concern remained, the immediate issue that faced Trinity Church parish in 1750 was to find a replacement for Honyman. James MacSparran from the Narragansett Church immediately asked to succeed him, but forty-two members of the parish expressed their preferences in a vote. Dr. Johnson of Stratford, the leading Anglican in the northern colonies, was preferred, with twenty votes; Robert Carter had thirteen votes, and Peter Bours, Jr., one vote. Johnson quickly declined the invitation, perhaps already having his eye on becoming the first president of King's College in New York City. In the interim period, Jeremiah Leaming carried on in charge of the parish, but the parish actively searched for other candidates. A committee of the vestry approached The Reverend John Beach, then the minister at Redding and Newtown, Connecticut; the parish had contributed to the fund to send him to London for his ordination in 1732. The S.P.G. approved of this appointment, but Beach declined on the grounds of ill health.[4]

About this time, an old Yale College acquaintance of Jeremiah Leaming's made his first visit to Newport: Ezra Stiles, a man whom many had already been recognized elsewhere as a potential minister. When the vestry learned of Stiles's arrival, they instructed Leaming to do everything in his power to persuade his old friend to take the position. Leaming took Stiles to the Kay schoolhouse, dismissed the students for the afternoon, and spent a long time discussing the merits and attractions of the parish with him. It was midnight by the time the two men retired to Leaming's house to sleep, but before doing so, Leaming had thoroughly explained the intellectual attractions of Newport and offered him an annual salary of two hundred pounds sterling. In the morning, Stiles thanked his old friend for his kindness but apologized that "all his Art and Address and fine offers were ineffectual."[5] While attracted by Newport, Stiles was uncertain of his religious convictions at that point, except for being convinced that if any form of Christianity was true, it was not the Anglican. In a few years' time Stiles would return to Newport, but he would come as pastor of the Second Congregational Church on Clarke Street, before returning to New Haven as president of Yale.

Isaac Stelle served as junior warden in 1759–60 and senior warden in 1769–61. In 1739, he married Penelope Goodson in Trinity Church and soon became a prominent figure in the parish and in the town. In 1758, he was a key figure in persuading the vestry to proceed with its 1746 decision to block off the north-south aisle at the back of the church and to build four new pews in that aisle to help relieve demand for the expanding congregation. For £200, he purchased the new pew on the north side of the south aisle, facing the south door. In 1761, he and his business partner, John Mawdsley, who also succeeded him as church warden, were among the leading local shipowners and merchants who established the United Company of Spermaceti Chandlers. This firm, known as the "Spermaceti Trust," was an attempt to control the colony's profitable whale-oil candle industry. Collection of the Newport Historical Society.

The parish next offered the position to The Reverend Marmaduke Browne, the son of The Reverend Arthur Browne, whom Dean Berkeley had encouraged to come from Ireland in 1730 to take charge of the parish in Providence. None of the parish's initiatives succeeded. Finally, in January 1734, the S.P.G. appointed Thomas Pollen as the new rector. Pollen had no prior American connections. He had graduated from Corpus Christi College, Oxford, in 1723 and had served at St. Antholin's Church, London, and as rector at Little Bookham, Surrey, before moving to Glasgow, Scotland, where he was at the time of his appointment to Newport. The vestry had declined to make several major decisions, pending the arrival of a permanent rector, deciding not to change the hour of the Sunday afternoon service or to engage an organist immediately. In 1752, the vestry did decide that the "pews be handsomely numbered with paint on each door."[6] At about the same time, the wardens' pews and the vestry room under the south stairs at the back of the church were converted to private pews, while a new room was made for the vestry by partitioning off a section in the tower. Shortly after Honyman's death, the S.P.G. had reduced the rector's pay by twenty pounds. The vestry had decided to offer the new minister fifty pounds, but to make up the shortfall the pew owners agreed to assess a permanent annual tax on the pews from 1 January 1753 onward to bring the salary up to the total of one hundred pounds sterling.[7] In further preparation for a new minister, the vestry decided to purchase a rectory, taking possession of a home at the corner of present-day Touro and High Streets in 1753 and renting it out until the new minister could arrive.

By this time, the parish was employing a number of people. In addition to the rector and the schoolmaster, who was paid to serve also as catechist and assistant to the rector, there was, from time to time, a school-usher, whose pay was met by the schoolmaster but reimbursed by the parish; an organist, paid twenty-five pounds a year; the clerk of the church at sixty to a hundred pounds a year; the sexton, at forty pounds; and a person to wind the clock in the steeple weekly, at twenty-six pounds a year.[8] During this interim period, Jeremiah Leaming and the vestry had a variety of decisions to make in regard to these appointments. On receiving news that the S.P.G. had appointed a minister, the vestry immediately began to search for an organist, but no permanent appointment was made until John Ernest Knotchell took the post, holding it from 1757 to 1769. In the interim from 1750 to 1757, Captain Bardin filled the position, as he had earlier.

Just at this time, the Great Awakening was continuing to have a major effect on religion in America. At this phase, the Awakening affected Anglicans in two ways. One was the stress placed on sermons, and the other, on music. Because of this, Anglican buildings built in this period characteristically had large, dominating, central pulpits. While later generations might complain that this obscured the holy table from view, Trinity had this feature from the very beginning, reflecting the fundamental importance of preaching to Rhode Island's historical religious atmosphere. With its early organ, Trinity was also well ahead of its time. Before the Awakening, most Anglicans in America preferred to use traditional music and texts, such the Te Deum, which had a biblical or long traditional use. Up through the American Revolution, many Anglicans had been suspicious of hymn singing, which the Wesleys had popularized. In Virginia and Maryland there were cases of people prosecuted for singing unauthorized hymns. In this context, it is interesting to note a dispute that broke out at Trinity in August 1753. The vestry temporarily dismissed John Grelea as clerk of the church when he refused to lead the singing of a hymn service because the organist, Bardin, played a different tune than the one the clerk had selected. Compounding the situation, Grelea refused to go on with the psalm when The Reverend Leaming requested him to do so. The issue was finally resolved eighteen months later, when Grelea was restored to his position and the clerk made responsible for selecting the tunes for the organist to play.[9]

Pollen and his family arrived in Newport in early May 1754 and took up residence at the new rectory. Jeremiah Leaming continued in his role as assistant, catechist, and schoolmaster. Shortly after Pollen's arrival, Leaming took over the responsibilities of librarian of the Redwood Library for a year. In 1758, the parish at Norwalk, Connecticut, called Leaming to be its rector; he was to remain there for the next twenty-one years. On Leaming's departure, the vestry appointed a search committee to find a replacement, but none being found, Pollen continued to carry out the responsibilities of both positions. During his years in Newport Pollen earned a reputation as a preacher, and a number of his sermons were published. One was on "Universal Love," preached in Trinity Church before the "Free and Accepted Masons" in 1756, while two of them had a patriotic tone and were related to the French and Indian War. The first of the latter was preached in May 1755, in connection with the embarkation of the four hundred Rhode Island men who had been raised to join other forces in an attack on Crown Point on Lake Ticonderoga. It was on a text from Psalm 118: "Save now, I beseech thee Lord. I beseech thee send now Prosperity."[10] (In the event, French forces did not wait to be attacked but met the encamped colonial troops on the shores of Lake George. The Rhode Islanders had just arrived

Peter Harrison was the self-taught architect who designed the Redwood Library, Touro Synagogue, and the Brick Market. Raised a Quaker in Yorkshire, the young sea captain became an Anglican on his marriage to the socially-prominent Elizabeth Pelham in Newport in 1746. Characterized as "First American Architect," Harrison is credited with a number of other important buildings elsewhere. Known to other Anglicans for his design skills, The Reverend Henry Caner of Boston commissioned him in 1749 to design the new King's Chapel, Boston. The historian Carl Bridenbaugh has also attributed St. Michael's Church, Charleston, South Carolina, to him. In January 1762, Harrison was one of the forty-eight Trinity parishioners who pledged the money to expand the church building to the eastward to accommodate two new bays of pews. Portrait by Louis Sands after Nathaniel Smibert's 1756 portrait. Collection of the Redwood Library and Athenaeum.

and were able to help prevent the complete loss of the British position, but the planned attack on Crown Point was canceled.) Pollen preached his second war sermon in March 1758, dedicating it to the British commander in chief, Lord Loudon, and titling it "The Principal Marks of True Patriotism."[11] Some of these troops later participated in the successful siege of Louisbourg.

In an another area of his ministry, Pollen was discouraged by his lack of success in converting and baptizing the racial minorities in Newport. This concern had become the main focus of a third Anglican Missionary Society that joined the S.P.C.K. and the S.P.G.. Established in 1730, it was named the "Associates of Dr. Bray," commemorating the man who had founded the two earlier organizations (and had died that same year). In 1755, the secretary of the Associates wrote to Pollen asking him about his progress in this area. In his reply, Pollen reported that there were very few Indians "in or about the town"; those who were there had mixed in with the rest of the population. "Almost all of them are (as the term is here) of some Christian Society or another."[12] On the other hand he was deeply concerned about the African-Americans, "who for the most part are unbaptized, and in the same state of heathen ignorance as the wild Indians." When he questioned the baptized blacks in the congregation as to why slave owners did not baptize their slaves, "they said they could not tell unless the Masters thought that their servants would by baptism come too near themselves."[13] Despite this, Pollen declared, "I do not despair of meeting with success in my attempts (thro' God's grace) of converting and baptizing some of them."[14] Proposing his own plan of action, Pollen decided to move by degrees, educating the slave owners in the congregation on the necessity of baptism and persuading them, at least, not to oppose his efforts with slaves.

In 1760, the Associates of Dr. Bray elected Benjamin Franklin as their president. Then in the midst of his stay in London as an agent of Pennsylvania, Franklin had served on their board of directors and earlier had played a key role in establishing a school for blacks in Philadelphia. As president of the Associates, Franklin wrote to Pollen in Newport, proposing that Trinity Church establish its own school for slave children. Upon receiving the letter in mid-July 1760, Pollen called a meeting of the vestry to consider the matter. It agreed that the slave children in the school would belong to some member of the congregation and that half would be boys and half girls. They agreed that the mistress of the school would be a churchman, whom they would pay twenty pounds sterling per year, and that each slave master who had slave children in the school was to supply wood to keep the school warm in the winter.[15]

Just as Pollen was beginning the search for appropriate children for this new school, the parish at Kingston, Jamaica, called him to be its new rector. Pollen immediately accepted the new position. Privately, Pollen had not been entirely happy in Newport, and the trouble seems to have centered on his pay. In telling the Associates of Dr. Bray about the plans for continuing the school for slave children after his own departure, Pollen wrote that members of the congregation want to continue them. However, he did not recommend that they be allowed to do so on their own, "for they are on many accounts unfit to be trusted with the management of it."[16] Shortly after arriving in Jamaica, Pollen would write to one of his former Newport parishioners pointing out the differences between the two parishes in a way that said much about the attitudes of the Newport congregation:

> Our church [at Kingston] is in mourning [on the death of King
> George II], which I believe, is more than you can say of yours.
> This, if it be true, proves we make a grater show of loyalty than
> you, tho' not of religion; for I cannot find there came to the
> Church when it was open one person extraordinary, either to
> see the decoration, or to hear me, the new preacher. The former
> [in Kingston] take care to pay the parson, but do not care to
> hear him preach; the latter [in Newport] take care to hear the
> parson preach, but do not care to pay him.[17]

Immediately upon Pollen's resignation, "an incident quite unexpected to us," the vestry wrote to the S.P.G. and requested that it appoint The Reverend Marmaduke Browne in Pollen's place; at the same time, Browne himself applied for the position.[18] His father, The Reverend Arthur Browne, had served as rector of the parish in Providence for nearly six years and then moved on to New Hampshire, where he had been rector of the parish at Portsmouth. Like him, his son had graduated from Trinity College, Dublin, and had returned to New Hampshire, where he was then an itinerant minister. In recommending him, The Reverend Henry Caner of Boston told the society that young Browne's conduct in his itinerant work had been "unexceptionally prudent, and his abilities qualified him to be useful among a people of higher improvements than those with him he now resides."[19]

In the meantime, the Anglican clergy of New England met in Boston and jointly signed a petition congratulating George III on his accession to the throne and, once again, renewing their request that a bishop be sent to America.[20]

While both Browne and the parish repeatedly requested the appointment, the S.P.G. took its time. In November 1761, Marmaduke Browne wrote to

THE
BOOK
OF
COMMON PRAYER,
And Administration of the
SACRAMENTS,
AND OTHER
Rites and Ceremonies
OF THE
CHURCH,

According to the Use of the

Church of England:

Together with the

PSALTER or PSALMS
OF
DAVID,

Pointed as they are to be Sung or Said in CHURCHES.

OXFORD:

Printed by *THOMAS BASKETT*, Printer to the
UNIVERSITY. M DCC XLV.

This 1745 edition from the parish's book collection shows the full title of the
Book of Common Prayer as it was used in England from 1662 to 1800 and
during the entire colonial period at Trinity Church.

the society that he had done his best to meet the needs of the Newport congregation while also meeting his responsibilities as an itinerant minister in New Hampshire. During 1761, he made the 140-mile trip to visit Newport eight times. Pleading with the society not to censure him for taking this initiative without authority, he asked it to consider the serious circumstances of Newport, "composed chiefly of proselytes from the numerous Sects, with which the Colony of Rhode Island abounds: who as they were not educated in any fixed Principles of Religion, are extremely wavering and unsteady."[21]

Months later there was still no formal decision from London, but Browne continued his visits and had baptized thirty-three infants and seven adults, four whites and three blacks, and received eight more for communion, bringing the regular communicants up to 103. This figure, Brown wrote, was "scarcely one fourth the part of the constant attendants upon divine service, so prevalent is lukewarmness and inattention to our truest interest among us."[22] In January 1761, the vestry had decided to take matters in its own hands and elected Browne to the position, establishing his salary at one hundred pounds sterling. Only months later did Newporters learn that the society had immediately approved the appointment on receipt of the first letter but that the letter informing them of this had been lost due to the disruptions of communications across the Atlantic during the Seven Years' War.

In November 1762, Browne began to look for a schoolmistress for the parish's planned school for slave children. After making a thorough search for an appropriate candidate, Browne reluctantly reached the same conclusion that his predecessor already had and appointed Mrs. Mary Brett to the position, on the same terms that Pollen had previously suggested to her. Mrs. Brett was the widow of Dr. John Brett, who was said to have studied at the University at Leiden and was highly regarded as an eminent medical authority in Newport. "She is a sober, well-disposed woman, sufficiently qualified for the business she undertakes, and I hope will acquit herself in a manner answerable to the pious and charitable views of the worthy Associates," Browne wrote, but the fundamental problem the school faced was much larger. "The unaccountable prejudice entertained by many in the Plantations that learning and instruction has only a tendency to render Negroes greater Rogues than they would otherwise be is not without its adherents in this place."[23]

Soon Mrs. Brett was operating a school with thirty children, fifteen boys and fifteen girls, and a library of several hundred volumes. Browne explained to the S.P.G. that he had chosen a woman rather than a man for the

The Reverend Marmaduke Browne, minister of Trinity Church, 1760–71. During his years at Trinity, the parish expanded dramatically, attracting many wealthy and influential merchants, and the church building was expanded to accommodate the large congregation. In 1764, he became one of the founding fellows of the college that has since become Brown University. John Smyth carved this bas-relief portrait in marble in Dublin in 1795, probably from a portrait owned by his son, Dr. Arthur Browne of Trinity College, Dublin, who donated this monument in memory of his parents. The monument directly overlooks the spot at the front of the church where Browne's body was buried under the floorboards in 1771.

position "as by that means the girls may be instructed in knitting and sewing as well as in reading and the principles of Christianity."[24] Browne regularly visited the school to inspect it and gave instruction to the mistress and the scholars from time to time. When the children reached proficiency, Browne made a point of having them show their knowledge publicly at church so "that the unreasonable prejudices which too much influence numbers against the instruction of the Negroes, may by their good behavior in time be brought to abate."[25]

In the period 8–13 July 1763, Benjamin Franklin returned to Newport to visit family members. During his visit he visited Trinity Church and, as a representative of the Associates of Dr. Bray, called on Marmaduke Browne to discuss the parish's progress with the school for slave children.[26]

In the mid-eighteenth century, the Anglican Church throughout the American colonies benefited from a rapid rise in immigration from England. This can be seen in the census figures of the time, which show that in the twenty-year period from 1753 to 1774, the population of Newport grew from 6,753 to 9,209. In 1755, 18.27 percent of the population was black. In 1755, the total number of blacks in Newport was 1,234. Twenty years later that total had increased only by twelve, while the number of whites had increased by 2,456.[27] The increased numbers of English immigrants put heavy pressure on Trinity Church. In the autumn of 1763, Browne estimated that some nine hundred people were Church of England and that about 120 were regular communicants.[28]

Some of the wealthy merchants who arrived in Newport at this point found that there were no pews available for purchase. At their instigation, the vestry examined ways to enlarge the church. Up to that point there had been no possibility of enlarging the building, since it filled its lot. In the forty years between 1726 and 1762 Spring Street had settled in its present position, leaving a narrow, irregularly shaped strip, twenty-six to thirty feet wide, between the east end of the church building and that street.[29] In 1762, the vestry acquired this land to enlarge the church.

The new addition was twenty-six feet in length, increasing the size of the building by a third and adding thirty-six new pews, at an estimated cost of six hundred pounds sterling.[30] The burden of the cost fell entirely on the merchants who wanted to purchase the new pews, a group that included such names as John Bannister, Christopher Champlin, Francis Malbone, and Peter Harrison.[31] As Browne reported, in terms of its cost it was "an exertion the more

Benjamin Franklin had close family connections with Newport. While serving as the London agent for the colony of Pennsylvania in 1760, The Associates of Dr. Bray, an Anglican organization devoted to promoting religious education for Indians and Afro-American slave children, had elected Franklin as their president. Well acquainted with Newport, Franklin knew that Trinity had been considering such a school and immediately wrote the minister to encourage the school, which was established later that same year. In July 1763, Franklin visited Trinity to inspect the school's progress under the direction of Mrs. Brett. This school may possibly have been located in the Peter Bours House at 47 Division Street. Portrait of Benjamin Franklin by Charles Bird King.

Collection of the Redwood Library and Athenaeum.

extraordinary at this juncture as the persons concerned had been very great sufferers during the course of the war which has been remarkably unfavorable to the trade of this colony."[32] The building was cut in two sections, and the eastern wall, with the two easternmost bays, was moved twenty-six feet. The intervening space was filled in to create two new bays, and a new brass chandelier was added to match those that had been placed in the church in 1728. This enlargement made Trinity Church "one of the largest houses for public worship in New England," giving the main body of the building an overall dimension of ninety-six feet in length and forty-six in width.[33] Even then it was not too large; as Browne reported, "not withstanding the addition, there is still room wanting to accommodate all who would willingly attend, and the further growth of the congregation is in some measure prevented."[34]

In other places this pressure might have led to the establishment an additional parish to meet the demand, but Newport presented a difficult situation. In terms of their religious beliefs, Browne's only complaint was the reticence of his parishioners to take communion, "which does not proceed so much from their leading unblemished lives, as from the wrong notions they have imbibed and persist in adhering to of that sacrament, not withstanding the reiterated evidence that have been made to remove it."[35]

Browne reported that many Newport Anglicans believed, as did others in Newport and Rhode Island generally, that "religion should not bring any expense upon them. They are fond of the Church, they like religion, but they like it cheap."[36] This was all the more noticeable as Newport increasingly became the home for prosperous merchants and as many successful Quaker and Baptist businessmen began to join the Anglican Church.

By 1760, the Pastor of the Congregational church on Clarke Street, The Reverend Ezra Stiles, was reckoning that the two Congregationalist meetings in Newport made up the largest single denomination in town, with 228 of the 772 families in Newport, and that the Baptists followed with 190 in four congregations. The 169 Anglican families (plus eighteen widows and thirty-one bachelors) made up the third denomination, but the largest single congregation of any in Newport. In numerical order, the 105 Quaker families followed them. Over the next decade, Trinity kept pace with the growth of Newport, maintaining its relative position as the third largest among the different groups, with two hundred of the 980 families in town, while the Baptists took the lead over the Congregationalists.[37] In this period, however, members of Trinity Church held a disproportionate percentage of the town's wealth, with twenty-seven of the top fifty taxpayers; a number were among the 222 families that owned at least one slave, while others invested in the slave trade.

In analyzing the social fabric of Newport in this period, historians have found that there were connections between wealth, occupation, and religion in Newport, as shown in the following tables.[38]

Occupations of Anglicans in Newport

OCCUPATIONS	NUMBER	PERCENTAGE OF TOTAL NUMBER IN NEWPORT
Merchants	74	49
Retailers	4	16
Artisans	7	6
Mariners	23	49
Farmers	1	8
Misc.	1	9
Unknown	25	24
Total, all occupations	135	29

Family Size of Anglicans in Newport, 1760

FAMILY SIZE (TAX GROUP CATEGORY)	NUMBER	PERCENTAGE OF TOTAL OF CATEGORY IN NEWPORT
1–2	1	3
3–4	4	7
5–6	24	28
7–8	28	30
9–10	61	45
Unknown	17	31
Total	135	29

Newport artisans tended to be Congregationalists and Baptists, regardless of how wealthy they were. In all wealth groups, more merchants tended to be Anglicans than non-Anglicans. Within merchants as a group, the wealthier the merchant, the more likely he was to belong to Trinity Church. There was also a connection between wealth and the size of household, which included servants and slaves as well as members of the family. Here again, Anglican households tended to be larger than the average, as they were wealthier than the average. By the middle of the eighteenth century, Trinity Church had clearly grown into an affluent parish of leading merchants, but its days in that role were numbered.

Notes

1. Lambeth Palace, Fulham Papers XIII, fol. 41–44: Letter from The Bishop of London to The Reverend Dr. Dodridge, 11 May 1751.
2. Ibid.
3. Ibid.
4. Lambeth Palace, S.P.G. V, fo. 298: Minutes of the S.P.G., 19 October 1750.
5. Quoted in Edmund S. Morgan, *The Gentle Puritan: A Life of Ezra Stiles, 1727–1795* (New York: W. W. Norton, 1962), pp. 109–10.
6. Mason, *Annals,* p. 102.
7. Ibid., pp. 105–106.
8. Ibid., pp. 92, 94–95, 111, 112, 114–16.
9. Ibid., pp. 109, 114.
10. Thomas Pollen, *A Sermon Preached in Trinity Church, Newport, Rhode Island, on Thursday, May 29, 1755. Upon occasion of the Embarkation of some of the Colony's Troops, in Order to go against the Enemy.* Published at the Desire of the Council of War, at Newport (Newport: 1757).
11. Thomas Pollen, *The Principal Marks of True Patriotism. A Sermon Preached in Trinity Church, at Newport, in Rhode Island, on the 5th day of March 1758 By Thomas Pollen, M.A., and humbly dedicated to His Excellency, John Earl of Loudon* (Newport: 1758).
12. Rhodes House, MS Bray Associates/N. America/1, fo. 5: Letter from Thomas Pollen, 6 July 1755.
13. Ibid.
14. Ibid.
15. Leonard W. Labaree, ed., *The Papers of Benjamin Franklin* (New Haven, CT: Yale Univ. Press, 1966), vol. 9, p. 201: Minutes of the Associates of Dr. Bray; Rhodes House, MS Bray Associates/N. America/ 1 f 5: Letter from Thomas Pollen, 12 August 1760.
16. Ibid. Letter from Pollen.
17. Mason, *Annals,* p. 112 footnote 117: Letter from Thomas Pollen to Dr. John Brett, 12 March 1761.
18. Rhodes House, Papers of the U.S.P.G., C/AM9: Newport Congregation to the S.P.G., 13 September 1760; Marmaduke Browne, to S.P.G., 17 October 1760.

19. Loc. cit., Letter book B22, letter 100: Letter from Henry Caner to the S.P.G., 6 October 1760.

20. Lambeth Palace, MS 1123 111 (218) (219): Petition of the New England Clergy, 26 January 1761.

21. Rhodes House, Papers of the U.S.P.G., C/AM 9: Marmaduke Browne to S.P.G., Portsmouth NH, 5 November 1761.

22. Loc. cit., Letter from Browne to the S.P.G., 11 June 1762.

23. Rhodes House, Ms. Bray Associates/N. America/1 f 5: Letter from Browne to John Waring, 29 November 1762.

24. Rhodes House, Papers of the U.S.P.G., C/AM9: Letter from Browne to S.P.G., 9 January 1763.

25. Ibid.

26. Papers of Benjamin Franklin, vol. 10, pp. 278, 299–300.

27. Elaine Forman Crane, *A Dependent People: Newport, Rhode Island in the Revolutionary Era* (New York: Fordham Univ. Press, 1985), p. 76.

28. Rhodes House, Papers of the U.S.P.G., C/AM 9: Browne to the S.P.G., 29 August 1763.

29. Norman Morrison Isham, *Trinity Church in Newport, Rhode Island: A History of the Fabric* (Boston: Printed for the Subscribers, 1836), p. 26.

30. Rhodes House: Papers of the U.S.P.G., C/AM 9: Letters from Browne, 9 January and 29 August 1763.

31. A full list is in Mason, *Annals,* pp. 124–25.

32. Ibid.

33. Ibid.

34. Loc. cit., Letter from Browne, 29 February 1764.

35. Ibid.

36. Ibid.

37. Crane, ibid., p. 131.

38. The following are extracts from the tables in Lynn Withey, *Urban Growth in Colonial Rhode Island: Newport and Providence in the Eighteenth Century (Albany: State Univ. of New York Press, 1984), pp. 128–29, compiled from Franklin B. Dexter, ed., Extracts from the Itineraries and Miscellanies of Ezra Stiles* (New Haven, CT: Yale Univ. Press, 1916), pp. 12–17, and other sources.

Joseph Wanton served as governor of the colony from 1769 to 1775. He had served as junior warden in 1739–40 and senior warden in 1740–41 and, later, served regularly as a member of the vestry. On two occasions, he helped to raise funds for an organist's salary, and in 1750 he promised to pay the balance that his fellow parishioners were unable to raise. Portrait by an unknown artist.
Collection of the Redwood Library and Athenaeum.

5

A Loyalist Church in the Era of Revolution, 1764–81

The political issues that arose in the American colonies during the 1760s and '70s over taxation and over the regulation of commerce slowly created divisions among people who were basically loyal to England. The tensions created a civil war in the American colonies in which the Anglican Church played a role; they were clearly reflected in the Newport parish.[1]

The situation for Anglicans varied from region to region, often depending on whether or not the governments of a particular colony had established and supported the Anglican Church. In New England, where the colonial government did not support the church, the Anglican clergy was largely dependent upon support and guidance from London. Because of this, New England clergy were often leaders of the movement that saw a moral obligation to support the British government's policy, as the economic and political basis of their own and their parishioners' lives. At their ordination, all clergymen had promised before God and the Church to obey the king. In addition, the Book of Common Prayer also contained a collect, in all the offices and Sunday services, that asked the Lord to "strengthen our most gracious Sovereign Lord, King George . . . that he may vanquish and overcome all his enemies."[2] Thus, throughout these years both the clergy and the laity at Trinity Church were, by and large, loyal supporters of the Crown. By the 1760s, the religious tensions that had been so obvious at the beginning of the century in Newport had gradually withered, and an uneasy coexistence had taken its place.[3] Not all Loyalists in Newport were Anglicans, however. As others around them came to support the Patriot cause, Anglicans in Newport and elsewhere found themselves in a particularly difficult position, both torn in their loyalties and on the losing side. These fluctuations in opinion and status played a determining role in the development of the parish in the years between 1764 and 1783.

During the 1760s, the government in London was continuing to try to deal with the difficult task of administering the American colonies, facing the rising costs of both closer supervision and better defense. To meet these needs, customs officials as well as the Royal Navy became more vigilant, and Parliament began to pass a series of new taxes. By and large, the Trinity congregation supported closer ties with Britain, both politically and through the church. At this time, at least three pew owners at Trinity played a key role. Dr. Thomas Moffat, a physician from Edinburgh; Martin Howard Jr., a lawyer; and George Rome, a local agent for the London firm of Hayley and Hopkins, took their own initiative, though probably with widespread support from other Anglican churchmen. Critical of the colonial government and its management of affairs, although not otherwise involved in local politics, Moffat, Howard, and Rome firmly believed in the benefits to be found in parliamentary supremacy and tight control from London. With this in mind, in the autumn of 1764 they sent a petition to the king requesting that the Crown revoke the colony's 1663 charter and establish Rhode Island as a royal colony, with a Crown-appointed governor.

When this became public knowledge, it sparked a political controversy that soon developed into a pamphlet war. The issues quickly merged with other aspects of local politics, as well as with the controversy surrounding the 1764 Sugar Act. This act of Parliament had touched on Newport's economic well-being in its most sensitive spot, by placing a tax on its most important trading commodity: molasses. Newport merchants imported it from the West Indies in order to manufacture rum, a portion of which was used as a commodity in the slave trade.[4] In the mid-1760s, this intersection of local and imperial issues was the basis of a movement toward revolution in Rhode Island, a movement that branded the entire Trinity congregation as royalists. This was not entirely true, as some prominent Patriots, such as John Collins and Robert Elliott, were Anglicans, but by and large, a list of Tories in Newport reads like a list of the members of Trinity Church, including the descendants of several of the colony's first settlers.[5]

The following year, Parliament passed the Stamp Act, requiring a tax on many public documents as a means to raise money for the defense of the American colonies. It was widely opposed on the grounds that it violated the rights of the colonists as Englishmen by levying a tax on them without representation in Parliament. Ezra Stiles reported, "In Newport was the greatest Body of Advocates of the Stamp Act of any Town in America. The Custom House Officers, officers of the three men of war, and about one hundred gentlemen Episcopalians openly called the opposition [to the Act] Rebellion."[6] Before Parliament repealed the Stamp Act in 1766, riots occurred in several cities, and those in Newport were among the most violent. Opponents to the act rioted in front of the Wanton-Lyman-Hazard house on Broadway, the home of Trinity Church member Martin Howard, Jr., and at the home of Stamp Master Augustus Johnson at the corner of present-day Division and Mary Streets. The crowd burned effigies of Howard, Johnson, and Dr. Thomas Moffat, forcing them to seek shelter on board HMS *Cygnet* in the harbor.[7] Marmaduke Browne reported to London,

> It is with no small degree of pleasure that I can declare that whilst this country in general was activated by an intemperate zeal, to say no more, in opposition to an Act of the British Parliament, nothing of this spirit appeared in our congregation; many members of it on the contrary, openly protested against such notions & illegal proceedings & that at a time when such opposition was attended with no inconsiderable designs to their persons & interests.[8]

While the church and the congregation were continually involved in the most important political issue of the day, there were other matters of concern for the rector and the vestry. In June of 1765 Browne had complained to the S.P.G., "I have now a large and heavy cure, much resembling that of a city cure in England, which requires diligence and industry to discharge the duties of it faithfully."[9] Much of the burden arose in connection with the two Trinity Church schools. Marmaduke Browne had served as both rector and as schoolmaster of the school operated on the funds from the Nathaniel Kay bequest, while Mrs. Brett continued to operate the school for slave children.

In Browne's opinion, the school for slave children was not going as well. "This neglect, I conceive to be in some measure owing to the contempt incident to the colour & slavery of the Blacks, which renders their masters for the most part extremely negligent of their future interest, they consider them as living purely for the service & if their instruction interferes in the least with this servitude it must be entirely neglected."[10] At the same time, the schoolmistress was "too much disposed to earn her money without exertion."[11] In order to stir the vestry into action, Browne arranged for the secretary of the Associates of Dr. Bray in London to write a letter to the parish, complaining that the school was not meeting expectations.

In November 1765, the letter of complaint arrived and produced the effect that Browne wanted. The vestry appointed a committee of three to oversee the school. They moved to increase enrollment, bringing it up to twenty-six boys and girls, and the schoolmistress responded with greater diligence in teaching. The entire situation weighed heavily in Browne's thoughts. "Could people be brought to consider their slaves as of the same species with themselves they would pay more regard to their temporal & eternal welfare than the planters in America general do." Too many treated slaves as cattle, Browne lamented. "I shudder when I reflect on the load of guilt....I could wish they would either leave them in a state of liberty or at least make them some sort of amends for the loss of it by teaching them with humanity & instructing them in the truth of Christianity."[12] Some of the issues surrounding educating slaves involved more general local attitudes toward education generally.

Browne noted that the people in general "depend so much on the spirit as to make choice of gifted mechanics for their teachers to the utter neglect of grammar schools or other nurture of instruction."[13] Moreover, "their method of teaching here is bad, & they are in general poor grammarians."[14] Browne felt that Trinity's schools should try to counteract these trends with Christian education that provided both broad, liberal learning and sound instruction in reading and writing. In Browne's view, "the untutored, undisciplined youth of this licentious Colony, who for want of such instruction, are perhaps, in general, the worst formed as to their manner & principles of any youth in the British Dominions."[15]

For many Quakers and Baptists in Rhode Island, higher education was snobbish and tied to Anglicanism. In the early years many had disdained higher education, except for the specialized training that a physician required. By the 1760s local Baptist attitudes were slowly changing, and there were those who saw the value of having their own college to train ministers who could rival the graduates of the Anglican-dominated colleges at Williamsburg, Philadelphia, New York, and New Haven.[16] In 1761, Ezra Stiles at the Second Congregational Church in Newport began to develop a project to join with other Christians to affirm their common faith in free inquiry, hoping to establish a college that would unite all of Rhode Island's various denominations. He was dissuaded from going forward with his plan immediately, but in 1763 there arrived in Newport a delegation of Baptists, headed by The Reverend James Manning, a Baptist who had graduated from the College of New Jersey at Princeton. Aware of Stiles's interest in establishing a college, the Newport Baptists asked him to draft a charter for the proposed institution. He came up with a formula by which a college would be established in Newport and governed by an alliance between

The parish's school for poor boys produced some notable products. The future portrait painter Gilbert Stuart (top) was enrolled at the age of six. He spent nearly ten years at the school, under the instruction of the school-master, The Reverend George Bissett, and the organist, John Knotchell, before going on to study art and classics in Britain. His friend and classmate Benjamin Waterhouse (bottom) later went on to become a leading physician, who introduced the practice of vaccinations in America, and a professor at the Harvard Medical School. Self-portrait and portrait of Dr. Benjamin Waterhouse, both by Gilbert Stuart.

Collection of the Redwood Library and Athenaeum

Congregationalists and Baptists. Many people agreed with Stiles that Newport, as the colony's center of culture, was the most appropriate place for a college. As an example of local interest in Newport, twenty-one of the sixty-two people who signed the initial petition requesting that the General Assembly grant a charter for a college were stockholders of the Redwood Library.

In his draft charter, Stiles proposed a Corporation for the College that would have two branches: the Trustees, who would always have a majority of Baptists, and the Fellows, who would always have a majority of Congregationalists. Approved by both groups, the proposed Charter was submitted to the General Assembly. That body, however, dominated by Baptist members, was unwilling to give so much power to the Congregationalists, and it altered the formula.

In 1764, the General Assembly formally created the College of Rhode Island (renamed Brown University in 1804). The college's charter specified that there would be thirty-six trustees, of whom twenty-two would be Baptists, five Quakers, five Episcopalians, and four Congregationalists. The charter also established twelve Fellows, eight of whom were to be Baptists, with "the rest indifferently of any or all denominations." These were the most learned men in the colony, and they became the college's first faculty. Named in the charter as a Founding Fellow of the college was Trinity's rector, The Reverend Marmaduke Browne.[17] The permanent location for the college remained a matter of much controversy up until 1770. Although residents of Newport County donated a larger sum of money for construction of the college's first building than those of Providence, The Reverend James Manning and the other Baptist leaders of the college preferred to locate it in Providence, where the Baptists were more numerous. When the vote went against them, Ezra Stiles and a number of others in Newport petitioned the Assembly to establish a rival college there "on the plan of equal liberty to Congregationalists, Baptists, Episcopalians, Quaker." The plan passed in the lower house of the General Assembly but failed in the upper.[18]

On the parish level, Browne had found that it was too difficult to be both a rector and a schoolmaster. Because of the general weakness of education in the local area, however, he could find no local person qualified to send to England to be ordained for this position. As a schoolmaster, Browne wrote, "no person will be so agreeable to us as an Englishman."[19] Also, and as in so many other things, money was a key issue in bringing plans to fruition. Unlike several of the other colonies, Browne reminded the authorities in London, Rhode Island had a law that explicitly protected any person from being obliged to support a

A
SERMON
PREACHED IN

TRINITY-CHURCH,

NEWPORT, RHODE-ISLAND,

On MONDAY, JUNE 3, 1771;

At the FUNERAL

OF

Mrs. ABIGAIL WANTON,

LATE CONSORT OF

The Hon. JOSEPH WANTON, jun. Esq;

Who departed this Life on Friday, May 31, 1771, in
the 36th Year of her Age.

By GEORGE BISSET, M. A.

Published at the request of the relatives of the deceased.

NEWPORT: Printed by S. SOUTHWICK, in QUEEN-STREET,
MDCCLXXI.

Col. Joseph Wanton, Jr., son of Governor Wanton, served as junior warden in 1756–57 and senior warden in 1757–58. In 1756, Colonel Wanton married and purchased a new home for his wife, Abigail. Active in politics, maritime trade, privateering, and the slave trade, he purchased the 1748 building on present-day Washington Street known today as "Hunter House." Immediately enlarging the structure, he and his wife gave the building its present appearance, adding a second chimney and the entire south portion of the house.

church or ministry. "They may pay or refuse to pay as they see fit, that is support or starve their minister, unless wholly subservient to their humours."[20] Lands donated for this purpose were then yielding forty-three pounds, twelve shillings, six-pence in rents, and a house eight pounds more.

Responding in March 1767, the S.P.G. recommended The Reverend George Bisset as "Master of Mr. Kay's Grammar School" and assistant minister of Newport's large parish.[21] Born in Old Deer, Aberdeenshire, Bisset had gone from Scotland to London several years previously. He seemed particularly suited to the appointment. One observer noted that "his skill in languages, both ancient and modern, is uncommon and the whole cultivation of his mind seem equal to the singular purity of his manners."[22] In November 1767 Bisset arrived in Newport and took up his duties.

Remaining in Newport for a dozen years, Bisset quickly earned a reputation as a fine teacher. In this period, Trinity's Kay School produced some distinguished graduates, taught both by Bisset and the church organist, Johann Knotchell. Notable among the students was the future artist Gilbert Stuart, who later remembered Knotchell's strict discipline and Bisset's kindness. From Knotchell, Stuart learned his lifelong appreciation for music; he was grateful for the many occasions in which he was allowed to sit next to Knotchell when he played the organ during services. Other classmates included a future pioneer in the use of vaccination, Dr. Benjamin Waterhouse, and the rector's son, Arthur Browne, who would eventually become a well-known writer and academic in Ireland.[23]

A few weeks after Bisset's arrival, Browne wrote to the S.P.G. asking for a six-to-eight-month leave of absence to go to Ireland. There Browne wanted to settle the legacy that his wife Ann had left to their son Arthur on her death in 1767. At the same time, he wanted to arrange for the boy's eventual admission to Trinity College, Dublin, where both Marmaduke and the boy's grandfather, The Reverend Arthur Browne, had graduated. The society granted the leave request, but Browne and his son delayed their departure until 1769.

In the meantime, carpenters reported that the church tower, built with the main structure in 1724–26, was in serious condition, having been damaged in 1761. In April 1768, the vestry voted to tear down the old tower and to build an entirely new one, eighteen feet square and sixty feet high. Financing this new construction project proved difficult; it required both a loan and a special assessment on pew owners.[24]

While the new tower and its steeple were under construction, the vestry also initiated a petition to the government of the colony that the church be granted a charter of incorporation. The General Assembly granted the request, the first to any church in Rhode Island, and Trinity was incorporated as the "Minister, Church Wardens, Vestry and Congregation of Trinity Church, in Newport."[25]

With repairs and incorporation completed by June 1769, Browne and his young son Arthur finally set out for Ireland to make arrangements for the boy's education and inheritance. In addition, Browne was to go on to London, to procure a new stop for the organ. On Browne's departure, the vestry placed The Reverend Bisset temporarily in charge of the parish. Browne continued to receive his salary as rector during his absence. Bisset soon encountered difficulties and threatened to leave the parish unless his salary was raised and the schoolmaster's house was either put in order for him to occupy or let so that he could receive a portion of the rent. The vestry denied the request and took steps to look for a replacement for Bisset, but the issue soon disappeared. Up until that time, the organist, Johann Knotchell, and his wife Johanna had occupied the house on the Kay School property rent free. On Knotchell's death in October 1769, Capt. Charles Bardin once again took over as the organist; Johanna Knotchell was allowed to remain in the house until the following Easter. On her departure, the vestry repaired the house and allowed Bisset, a bachelor, either to occupy it, as was his right in his capacity as the schoolmaster, or to receive the eight-pound annual rental from it.[26]

In August 1770, after visits to Dublin, London, and Antwerp and an eleven-week voyage across the Atlantic, Browne and his fifteen-year-old son returned to Newport. Shortly after his return, Godfrey Malbone brought to fruition efforts that his father, Col. Francis Malbone, had begun in founding an Anglican church at Pomfret, Connecticut. A number of Newport's Anglicans had contributed three or four hundred pounds to the construction of the building, which took its architectural inspiration from Trinity. By the spring of 1770 the building was nearing completion, and Trinity planned to mark the final phase with a ball. At the last moment the church suddenly postponed these plans, as Browne grew gravely ill.[27] He suffered for months with a "slow and lingering fever,"[28] though he continued some of his parish duties.[28] Suddenly seized by convulsions in mid-March 1771, he died four days later on 16 March at the age of about forty.[29] The following day was a Sunday; Ezra Stiles, the Congregational minister, ever critical of Anglicans, noted in his diary, "The Episc° or Trinity Chh shut up & no Service performed in it all day, on Account of Mr. Browne's Death; tho' Mr. Bisset the Assistant Minister is in Town.

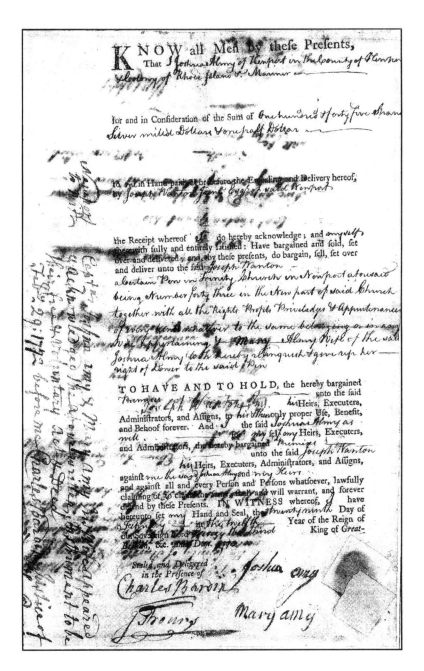

Pew deed, 1772.
Sale of Pew 43 "in the New part of said Church" for 145 and a half "Spanish
silver milled dollars" by Joseph Wanton, Jr., to Joshua and Mary Almy. The
document was witnessed by Charles Bardin and John Bours. Document from
George Champlin Mason, Extra Illustrated Reminiscences, *vol. 5, 309-A.*
Collection of the Newport Historical Society.

Superstitious!"[30] The vestry met the next day at the rectory and unanimously voted to bury Browne "in a decent manner, at the expense of the Church, and every mark of respect in their power shewed to his memory."[31]

Browne's funeral took place on 21 March, and it was the most elaborate one recorded in Trinity up to that date, honoring a very successful minister and scholar. As a tribute to him, the pall-bearers included Newport's two Congregational ministers, Ezra Stiles and Samuel Hopkins, along with several Anglican clergymen: The Reverend John Usher of Bristol, The Reverend John Graves of Providence, The Reverend Samuel Fayerweather of Narragansett, and The Reverend Luke Babcock of Phillipsburg, New York. Three Newport churches tolled their bells at one o'clock in the afternoon. At two, the pallbearers began the procession from the rectory, at the corner of High and Touro Streets, to the church. There a crowd of some one thousand to 1,200 gathered to hear Bisset preach his sermon, on the text from Psalm 110:12, "so teach us to number our days." At the end of the service, Browne was buried under the church, his body lowered through the floor "just before the chancel & on the North side of the Pulpit."[32]

Immediately following Browne's death, the vestry formally requested that Bisset officiate as rector. He could use the rectory and receive the fifty-pound salary that the parish had provided Browne, supplementing the fifty pounds received from the S.P.G., pending the society's confirmation of that arrangement. In its request to the society to continue this stipend, the vestry argued that it still needed a schoolmaster, had paid a considerable amount for the rectory, and had rebuilt the steeple; despite donations, it was four hundred pounds in debt.[33] Hearing of Trinity's request, The Reverend Henry Caner of Boston objected. Writing to inform the society of Browne's death and the subsequent appointment of Bisset, "a person of very respectable character[,] to succeed him," Caner remarked, "I think it my duty to say that the Church of Newport is esteemed as well able to give a Minister an honorable support as any church in New England, especially since by a late law of the Colony they are become a Corporation."[34] Others in the region felt the same way. An anonymous letter writer from Taunton, Massachusetts, suggested to the S.P.G. that Browne's salary supplement be transferred to Taunton from Newport, "the continuation of which has long been a robbing of other churches." In October, the vestry members were stunned to receive notification that the S.P.G. had terminated entirely its financial support of the rector. However, the vestry responded swiftly, confirming that it would pay Bisset the same salary that

Browne had received, giving him the proceeds of the Kay donation as part of his salary and raising pew taxes in order to so.[35]

Bisset's ministry was a successful one. As early as 1770 he began to earn a reputation as having his own mind. On 30 January of that year he declined to give the customary sermon on the anniversary of the execution of King Charles I in 1649, the first time that it had been omitted in Newport since the parish's establishment.[36] Bisset soon became noted also for his sermons. His first published sermon was given at the funeral of Mrs. Abigail Wanton, the thirty-six-year-old wife of Deputy Governor Joseph Wanton, Jr.[37] Bisset leveled another very effective sermon against the Universalist preaching of The Reverend John Murray, who had visited Newport in 1773. Entitled "The Trial of a False Apostle," it was printed and widely circulated.[38] In April 1773, Bisset married Penelope Honyman, the granddaughter of The Reverend James Honyman and daughter of the colony's onetime attorney general, James Honyman, Esq.

Shortly after Browne's death in 1771, his son Arthur wrote a formal letter to senior warden John Bours requesting the church wardens' assistance in continuing his education. He explained that his grandfather, The Reverend Arthur Browne, had declined to write to the S.P.G., suggesting that it would be best for Trinity's wardens to write explaining that he had been left "wholly unprovided for" and that there was a "great chance of losing a liberal education" in Ireland.[39] In response, the wardens wrote to the S.P.G. on behalf of the sixteen-year-old boy, explaining that Marmaduke Browne had made plans for his son to attend Trinity College, Dublin, but that Arthur now had only a little household furniture, a small library worth perhaps fifty pounds, and a small legacy from his mother's family of forty pounds per year. Bours wrote that in this child he had very early "discovered marks of a lively genius, and was from thence prompted to use his endeavours to give him an education suitable to his capacity."[40] With additional support from both the S.P.G. and the parish, Arthur Browne soon was able to make the journey to Ireland, where he matriculated at Trinity College in March 1772.

Trinity's two schools both continued in operation. Bisset himself taught the Kay School, while Mrs. Brett continued as headmistress of the school for slave children, receiving an annual salary of twenty pounds. Making a formal visit to her school for the first time in November 1771, Bisset found the school was well attended, with thirty black children, as shown in the following report:[41]

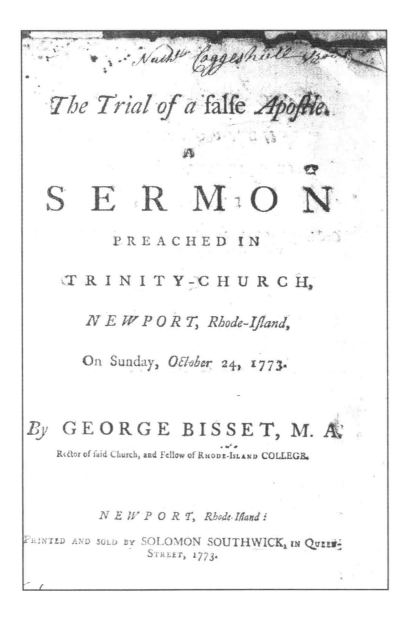

Nath.ᵗˡ Coggeshill

The Trial of a false Apostle.

A

SERMON

PREACHED IN

TRINITY-CHURCH,

NEWPORT, Rhode-Island,

On Sunday, *October* 24, 1773.

By GEORGE BISSET, M. A.

Rector of said Church, and Fellow of RHODE-ISLAND COLLEGE.

NEWPORT, Rhode-Island:

PRINTED AND SOLD BY SOLOMON SOUTHWICK, IN QUEEN-STREET, 1773.

The Reverend Bisset's sermon, The Trial of a False Apostle, *was a very effective and widely circulated criticism of the Universalist preaching of The Reverend John Murray. Bisset was a widely admired preacher; the Newport Herald of 24 April 1788 said in Bisset's obituary, "The style of his composition was remarkably elegant, and his reasoning seldom failed to force conviction on the minds of his hearers. As a divine he was liberally distinguished for the sanctity of his manners and the liberality of his sentiments. As a scholar he was free from pedantry, and as a gentleman he possesses the social virtues in an eminent degree, and never once lost sight of his sacred functions."*
Collection of the Redwood Library and Athenaeum.

List of the Negro Children, 23 November 1771

Mr. Ayrault sends 1	Mr. Whitehorne sends 1	Mrs. Chaloner sends 1
Mr. Dickinson sends 1	Captain Wilkinson sends 1	Mrs. Honyman sends 1
Mr. Honyman sends 2	Captain Duncan sends 3	Mrs. Cahoon sends 1
Mr. Thurston sends 2	Captain Cooke sends 1	Mrs. Scott sends 2
Mr. Johnston sends 2	Captain Sherman sends 3	Mrs. Thurston sends 3
Mr. Hunter sends 1	Captain Freebody sends 1	Free Negros 3

Total 30

The following April, Bisset visited again and found Mrs. Brett had maintained the school in similar condition, but in October 1772 he reported, "I found everything out of order. The woman had been sick and there were not more than two or three Negroes who regularly attended."[42] Bisset visited the school every day for a while, and upon Mrs. Brett's recovery the numbers rose to seventeen consistently attending. From that period onward, Bisset found that Mrs. Brett, given close supervision, managed her school more diligently. In general, its pupils found it much more difficult to attend in the wintertime than in the summer, since many slave owners preferred to keep them at home rather than to send the additional firewood necessary to keep the school. Apparently Bisset was tempted from time to time to replace Mrs. Brett with someone more diligent, but, Bisset admitted, "as the teaching of blacks is not here reputed very creditable, I believe I should find it difficult to get a better."[43] Somewhat disappointed, Bisset told the Associates of Dr. Bray, "Your charitable benefaction here has not all the good effects I could wish, yet I am far from thinking that it is misapplied."[44] Nevertheless, by the spring of 1774 there were thirty-eight black pupils attending, which "is as many as one person can instruct," Bisset commented.[45]

The vestry was able to ease George Bisset's heavy burden of parish duties in October 1771, when it chose The Reverend Willard Wheeler to take up the dual position of schoolmaster at the Kay School and assistant minister. Wheeler formally accepted the appointment in April 1772.[46] A 1755 graduate of Harvard, Wheeler had been ordained in England in 1767 and had served a parish in Georgetown, Maine, from 1768 until he came to Newport in 1772. Shortly thereafter, William Selby arrived from England to take up the position of organist.

In the political crisis that gathered momentum following the Boston Tea Party in December 1773, Parliament passed the Coercive Acts. When in June 1774 the Royal Navy blockaded Boston and began to interfere in Newport's commerce, Bisset earned a reputation for his pro-British views, while other ministers in Newport lauded the Patriot point of view. In one sermon, according to Ezra Stiles, Bisset "took as his Text—Fast not as the Hypocrites—and preached a high Tory sermon inveighing (by allusions) against Boston and N. England as a turbulent ungovernable people."[47] In April 1773, violence broke out when militia forces clashed with British soldiers at Lexington and Concord. By May, Connecticut, Rhode Island, and Massachusetts had voted to send troops to support the colonial cause. Shortly thereafter, Congress appointed George Washington to command the forces besieging the British at Boston, assigning four major generals under him. Soon the Continental Association agreed on an economic policy of nonintercourse with Britain.

Simultaneously, Capt. James Wallace in HMS *Rose* began to assert the power of the Royal Navy in Narragansett Bay, systematically closing off Newport to shipping. The customs office closed, and there were widespread rumors that Wallace intended to bombard and burn Newport. Trinity was already associated with this ship, as Lt. James Conway, Royal Marines, had been buried in the churchyard in May.[48] The growing fears of Wallace and the *Rose* were well justified; Wallace fired several shots at Newport in July 1775 and also bombarded Portsmouth and Bristol. Landing parties from ships of the Royal Navy came ashore to find food, and several of their members were accused of looting. Stopping all wood-carrying boats and ferries to Aquidneck Island, Wallace demanded that the island be cleared of the colony's troops and that his sailors be allowed ashore to provision his ships. To stave off disaster, seventy-four of Newport's leading citizens, representing the leaders of both the Loyalist and the Patriot factions, signed a declaration of allegiance to the Crown, supporting the established civil authority until the issues could be reconciled between Britain and her colonies.

Dependent upon maritime trade for its economic survival, Newport was caught between two forces. On the one side, the Royal Navy demanded that the town abide by British trade restrictions; if they did so, Newporters would become the enemies of their fellow colonists. On the other hand, if they flaunted British regulations and followed the other colonies in withholding trade with the British, they would destroy the town's own economic well-being. Heavily criticized, Newporters fought hard to maintain their reputation and their livelihoods.

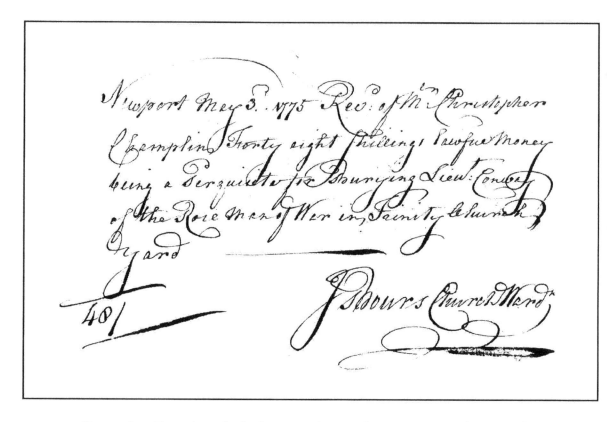

Christopher Champlin, who had previously served as a junior warden, was also the local victualling agent for the Royal Navy in Newport. Champlin paid the forty-eight shillings for Conway's burial in the churchyard, as this receipt from senior warden John Bours attests. Manuscript from George Champlin Mason, Extra Illustrated Reminiscences, *vol. 5, 327-A.*

Collection of the Newport Historical Society.

Unable to help them, Washington advised Rhode Island to meet Wallace's demands. Very few people in Newport now openly defended British policy, but many saw that moderation and accommodation with the British were the only ways to save their livelihoods.

After much wrangling, Newport obtained the consent of the General Assembly to negotiate with Wallace on supplying his ships, arguing that the destruction of Newport could not possibly serve the common cause. While this was going on, Newport merchants tried valiantly to carry on their trade at sea, but their cargoes were often seized. Wallace's stranglehold over shipping at Newport and in Narragansett Bay led Rhode Island's delegation in the Continental Congress to advocate the establishment of an armed force to oppose the British at sea. Congress agreed to this in October 1775, establishing the Continental Navy, headed by Ezek Hopkins of Providence.

In December 1775, the *Newport Mercury* whipped up patriot support with reports that Wallace intended to celebrate Christmas by burning the town. While this was going on, Patriot propaganda also created widespread fear of Tories. As the threats continued and fear spread, many townspeople began to leave the city. The Rhode Island authorities passed an act that demanded a declaration of fidelity to the American cause, on pain of execution. At one point, nearly a hundred suspected Loyalists were rounded up in Newport.[49] In December 1775, one of Washington's major generals, Charles Lee, appeared in Rhode Island. In Newport on Christmas Day, he summoned eight local Tories to appear before him that evening and asked each to renounce Tory views, assert their faithfulness to the Patriot cause, and declare their willingness to bear arms when called upon to do so by Congress.[50] Among them were Bisset, Dr. William Hunter, Col. Joseph Wanton (the former deputy governor of the colony), John Bours, and customs collectors Nicholas Lechmere, Richard Beale, John Nichol, and his son—all of whom were Trinity parishioners. Of these, Lee exempted Bisset, as a clergyman, and Hunter, as a physician, from the oaths, but Wanton, Beale, and Lechmere, who refused to sign, were taken into custody and removed to Gloucester, in the northern part of Rhode Island.[51]

During an unusually cold winter, many Newporters had found it impossible to obtain supplies and firewood. Faced with additional threats from British forces, many left. In January 1776, the General Assembly reported to the Continental Congress that the town was "reduced to so deplorable a state" that many of the wealthy inhabitants have not only left the town but the colony."[52]

Ezra Stiles recorded in his diary, "So great is the Evacuation of the Town, I judge more than three Qu^{rs} of the Inhabitants are removed. If so of 9,200 souls in the Town last year are not above 2,500 left."[53] By spring, Newport's once-flourishing commerce was at a standstill. The colonists' self-imposed policies of nonimportation and nonexportation had ruined many Newport merchants, while Wallace's seizures of ships brave enough to try to evade the blockade had finished the remainder. Newport's wharves and harbor, the pulse of the town, lay quiet. With many of its members leaving town, the parish had to struggle to carry out its work. On 15 April 1776, a vestry committee called upon The Reverend Willard Wheeler, informing him "that the Vestry and Congregation are greatly disappointed and dissatisfied with regard to his school, and that as many difficulties arise from the unhappy state of public affairs, in collecting the rents and taxes of the Church, to support the officers, they would have no objection to Mr. Wheeler's being removed to another more advantageous living.[54] At this point, Wheeler's name disappears from Trinity's records; after the war he became rector of St. Andrew's Church in Scituate.

During the early months of 1776, the Second Continental Congress, meeting in Philadelphia, slowly moved toward independence for the colonies. The Rhode Island General Assembly, however, began to lose patience with the slow pace of politics in the middle colonies. Reasserting its right to admiralty jurisdiction that it had abandoned at the beginning of the century, Rhode Island created its own admiralty court and quickly commissioned privateers to take British ships. The local elections in 1776 did little to change the sentiments of the General Assembly, although some of the well-known British sympathizers lost their seats; despite the desperate situation in Newport, no Tory majority arose to moderate the General Assembly's policies. Encouraged by the election results, the Assembly took a radical step on 4 May 1776 and became the first of the American colonies to repudiate allegiance to King George III. The Assembly declared that the king, "forgetting his dignity, regardless of the compact most solemnly entered into, ratified and confirmed to the inhabitants of this colony by his illustrious ancestors," had sent fleets and armies to America "to confiscate our property and spread fire, sword, and desolation throughout our country, in order to compel us to submit to the most debasing and detestable tyranny."[55] In doing this the Assembly was, while withdrawing its allegiance from the king, maintaining the form of government of the charter of 1663. The principal change was to forbid the use of the king's name in public commissions, oaths, or ceremonies. This action struck directly at the Anglican liturgy, with its prayers for the king and the royal family.

Little immediate public notice was taken of the General Assembly's action, although the service book in use at Trinity Church seems to have been altered at this time to conform with the assembly's action. Two months later, on 4 July 1776, the Continental Congress went much farther and declared "That these United Colonies are, and of Right ought to be Free and Independent States; that they are absolved from all Allegiance to the British Crown, and that all political connection between them and the State of Great Britain, is and ought to be totally dissolved." The first news of independence reached Newport from Philadelphia on 8 July; the full text of the Declaration of Independence was published on Saturday, 20 July.

Immediately upon receiving the full text of the declaration on 18 July, the Rhode Island General Assembly voted its approval, its members declaring their support for it "with their lives and fortunes."[56] Immediately thereafter, they changed the name of the government to "The State of Rhode Island and Providence Plantations." The Assembly next took direct aim at Anglicans, with their collect for the king and other rubrics in the 1662 Book of Common Prayer, specifying in "An Act to Punish Persons who shall acknowledge the King of Great Britain to be their Sovereign":

> That, if any Person within this State, shall under Pretence of Preaching or praying, or in any Way or manner whatever acknowledge or declare the said King to be our rightful Lord and Sovereign, or shall pray for the success of his Arms, or that he may vanquish or overcome all his enemies, shall be deemed guilty of a high misdemeanor, & shall be presented by the Grand Jury of the County where the Offence shall be committed, to the Superior Court of the same County; and upon Conviction thereof shall forfeit and pay, as a fine to and for the Use of this State the sum of One hundred pounds legal money and pay all costs of prosecution; and shall stand committed to Gaol until the same be satisfied.[17]

Ezra Stiles recorded in his diary that this occurred on a Saturday and that "instantly thereon the People of the Chh. Of England in Newport cried out of persecution, went and removed all their Prayer Books &c shut up the Church; and had no Service in it last Lordsday, tho' Mr. Bisset their parson was well & walking the streets."[58]

State officials confronted about ninety suspected Tories in Newport and demanded that they make the "Test Declaration," but most, at first, refused. In the face of this recalcitrance, the General Assembly began to consider forcible removal of the Tories into the interior of the state. When a bill to this effect passed the lower house of the Assembly and was taken up for consideration in the upper chamber, all but eleven of the suspected Tories changed their minds and agreed to subscribe to the declaration. After officials sent these eleven off, Godfrey Malbone and several other prominent merchants spoke in their favor, arguing that they were peaceable people. Ezra Stiles noted, "This was Tories vouching for Tories—the House, instead of receiving it, said this gave reason to suspect the Petitioners, & ordered them before them, & tendered the Test, [to] which they subscribed."[59] Another case was that of Anglican layman George Rome, who directly provided HMS *Rose* and other British vessels with supplies; Rhode Island officials seized his tannery as well as his home on Newport's Parade.[60]

Anglicans were not the only ones who were subjected to this. The authorities also called two Baptist ministers and the Moravian minister; two of them declared they were conscientious objectors. Isaac Touro at the synagogue was exempted as a foreigner. The question was raised whether or not to force George Bisset to make the declaration, but "it was considered he had been sufficiently handled by General Lee last winter."[61]

During this period, no public Anglican services were held in Trinity Church. In late August 1776, Stiles observed, "The Chh of England in America is exceedingly & really affected with the present Revolution."

> The Clergy especially seem to be generally at Difficulty about
> reconciling an Omission of prayers for the King in the Liturgy
> with their oath of Canonical Obedience & the Oath of Alle-
> giance: and I believe they have generally shut up their Chhs.
> thro' the United States. . . . They are all shut up by themselves
> in Rhode Isld. & Connecticutt States.[62]

Stiles's view was an accurate description of the situation he saw around him in Newport, but it was not correct for all of America. Two-thirds of the signers of the Declaration of Independence had been Anglican laymen, but they were from the southern and middle colonies. The situation in New York and New England was quite different; Anglican laypeople there widely supported the British, and in these areas one found widespread persecution of Anglicans.[63] In general from 1776 to 1778, the Anglican clergy in areas under control of American forces ceased using the liturgy and refrained from public preaching, occasionally meeting only to say the Lord's Prayer or reading a printed sermon. There were a few notable exceptions, particularly the churches in Newton and Huntington, Connecticut, which continued to use the liturgy and to pray for the king, but this was not the case in Rhode Island. At the end of 1778, the bishop of London authorized the Anglican clergy in America to reopen their churches and to resume using the Anglican liturgy, omitting the prayers for the king and the royal family.[64]

Newport's particular situation temporarily changed when on 8 December 1776 a squadron of Royal Navy ships escorted into Narragansett Bay a large fleet of army transports carrying Gen. Sir Henry Clinton and British troops. The local troops retired from Newport without offering effective resistance. Several months before, George Washington had written the governor of Rhode Island, "I feel myself much concerned on account of your appreciation for the town of Newport and the Island of Rhode Island. Circumstanced as I am, it is not possible for me to grant any assistance."[65]

On 9 December, about three thousand British troops entered Newport, where they "published the King's proclamation, and formally took possession of the Town and erected the King's Government & Laws."[66] In these circumstances, Trinity Church could freely open its doors and resume using the Anglican liturgy with the prayers for the king; other church buildings in town were gradually converted into hospitals and barracks. George Bisset remained at Trinity Church throughout this period, and British soldiers joined the remaining members of the Congregation at services.

Apparently, army units could attend "church parade" at Trinity on rotation. One young officer, Lt. John Peebbles of the Royal Highland Regiment, the Black Watch, left his impressions of the 1776 Christmas Day service: "Went to Church and heard a very good sermon inculcating peace among men—a very neat Church wt, a handsome organ the Gift of Dr. George Berkley Bishop of Cloyne, a good many inhabitants in church some decent looking People & the women tolerably well dress'd for Yanky's."[67] On the following Sunday, he reported his battalion went to church "in form" and apparently having forsaken its kilts: "Our company dress'd in britches for the first time. . . . A Chaplain preach'd, the Church full, some pretty looking Girls."[68]

British forces remained in Newport until October 1779. At least one British officer was buried in the churchyard during this period; Lt. Lowther

Mathews of the 62d Regiment of Foot died in January 1779 and was buried close to the north door.[69] In the autumn of 1779, General Clinton ordered the consolidation of British forces in the area at New York, in order to facilitate further British military operations in the southern colonies. The soldiers quickly and unexpectedly evacuated Newport on Monday, 25 October. The Reverend George Bisset had already prepared his sermon for the day before the departure, but British army authorities kept the townspeople off the streets as they hurried the troops on board the transports that Sunday. Bisset, along with about thirty other Tory sympathizers in town, accompanied the troops to New York. Having experienced the persecution of 1776, they had no desire to repeat the experience. A year later, still in New York City, Bisset had an opportunity to give the sermon he had intended for the Newport congregation that last Sunday. It was entitled, "Honesty the Best Policy in the Worst of Times," and in it Bisset consoled fellow loyalists in their tribulations:

> The true Christian will reflect that he is only called to tread
> in the steps of the great captain of his salvation, who was made
> perfect through suffering; who went surrounded by a sea of
> troubles, yet did not let go the cause that he had in hand, but
> set his face forward like flint, and did not fail, neither was dis-
> couraged, until he had brought forth judgement into victory.[70]

Following the departure of the British army and of the loyalists that accompanied it, Rhode Island militia forces, along with Continental soldiers under Gen. Horatio Gates, reclaimed Aquidneck Island. Within several days, two American soldiers entered the church and tore down part of the altarpiece on the east wall over the altar. The most accessible symbols of the British crown, the altarpiece included the king's arms, the lion and the unicorn. Other symbols of British power, including the bishop's mitre (which many thought to be a crown) on the top of the weather vane, as well as the crown and mitres on the organ case, were out of reach. Reportedly, about forty of the loyalists who remained in Newport were imprisoned. General Gates gave Trinity Church to The Reverend Gardiner Thurston for the use of the Second Baptist Church (also known as the Sixth Principle Baptist Church) while its meeting house was being repaired.[71]

gracious Sovereign Lord King *GEORGE*; and so replenish him with the grace of thy Holy Spirit, that he may alway incline to thy will, and walk in thy way: Endue him plenteously with heavenly gifts; grant him in health and wealth long to live; strengthen him that he may vanquish and overcome all his enemies; and finally, after this life, he may attain everlasting joy and felicity, through Jesus Christ our Lord. *Amen.*

¶ *A Prayer for the Royal Family.*

Almighty God, the fountain of all goodness, we humbly beseech thee to bless

The Governor and Council of this State, endue them with thy holy Spirit, en ~~with~~

Here endeth the Order of Morning Prayer

Advocate Christ.

¶ *A Pray*

Almi giv with one common and dost or three in thy N; their requ Lord, the of thy ser expedient us in this thy truth, come life

2

THE Jesu of God, a the Holy evermore.

A Prayer for the royal family altered in May 1776, two months before the Declaration of Independence, when Rhode Island became the first colony to revoke its allegiance to King George III. ". . . bless the Governor and Council of this state, endue them with thy holy spirit, enrich them with thy heavenly grace: . . ."

Under the terms of the corporation, the church buildings, the school-house, rectory, and other properties remained in the hands of the congregation and wardens. The latter since 1771 had been senior warden John Bours and junior warden Isaac Lawton. On 27 April 1780, the remaining members of the congregation met and decided to rent out the church's properties for the best price they could obtain, making necessary repairs to the rectory, the church building, and the fencing around the yard. Within a few days they had found paying tenants for the properties. After Bisset's departure in October 1779, no Anglican clergyman had permanently resided in Newport. It is possible that lay members of the parish continued to hold Anglican services, but there is no mention of this until 1782. However, Johann Knotchell did remain as organist, until his death in 1783. From time to time, visiting Anglican clergyman visited Newport and conducted weddings; also, several burials in the churchyard are recorded.

With Newport and its harbor being open and undefended, a French naval squadron under the command of Adm. Charles d'Arsac de Ternay entered on 11 July 1780. There were seven ships of the line, two frigates, and two smaller warships escorting transports carrying 5,500 soldiers of the French army under the command of the comte de Rochambeau. Shortly thereafter, a squadron of British ships under Admirals Marion Arbuthnot and Sir George Rodney blockaded Newport in an effort to trap the French forces there. The thirty-two-gun French frigate *Hermione* engaged a British vessel. Her commanding officer, Captain La Touche-Tréville, was gravely wounded in the action, as was first lieutenant, de Valernais. When the ship returned to Newport, the wounded officers were brought ashore. De Valernais died and was buried with naval honors in Trinity's churchyard on 22 July.[72]

The French forces remained in Newport for nearly a year. During that period, on 15 December 1780, Admiral de Ternay died of "putrid fever" (typhus) at his headquarters, now known as the Hunter House, on present-day Washington Street. One of the French army officers, Jean-Baptiste-Antoine de Verger, briefly noted in his diary for that date, "The Chevalier de Ternay died. The whole army was paraded for his funeral."[73] The Anglican presence must have seemed minimal to the Frenchmen as at this point that Verger added, "He was buried in the Baptist cemetery"—when in fact the admiral was buried in the Trinity churchyard.[74] None of Newport's churches had impressed this officer, who had earlier written, "All the buildings consecrated to religious worship, except the Jewish synagogue, are but of wood and not especially notable."[75]

George Washington at Trinity.
No documentary evidence has yet been found to support the long, oral tradition in the parish that George Washington worshiped in Trinity Church. Washington visited Rhode Island on four occasions: in 1756, 1776, 1781, and 1790. He visited Newport on every occasion, except in 1776. Most accounts attribute his visit to Trinity to the 1781 visit, when he stayed at the Vernon House on Clarke Street as a guest of General Rochambeau. There are no surviving records of regular services during that period. The parish had no clergyman, as The Reverend Bisset had departed with the British troops, and the church building had been rented to the Sixth Principle Baptist Church. However, John Bours apparently acted as lay reader for the few remaining Anglicans in Newport, and he was certainly the key figure behind the rebirth of the parish after the Revolution. Only one piece of circumstantial evidence supports the tradition. There is a receipt that shows that on 5 March 1781, the day before Washington arrived in Newport, Bours purchased two pairs of black silk gloves. When holding services in this period, clergymen typically wore such gloves.

The death, funeral procession, and burial of Admiral de Ternay at Trinity Church became a major event in Newport. The admiral had died at 5:30 in the morning. From sunrise to sunset throughout that day, his flagship, the seventy-four-gun ship of the line *Duc de Bourgogne*, flags at half mast, fired a cannon every half-hour. The burial took place on the following day, a Saturday. Later in the day, the funeral cortege made an impressive sight as it wound its way through the streets of the city from Hunter House. Nine Catholic chaplains from the fleet and the army led the cortege. Following them, sailors from the flagship carried the casket, with the senior officers of the fleet as a guard of honor. French troops and seamen marched behind, making a long, colorful, and impressive display. As the casket came in sight of the *Duc de Bourgogne*, lying at anchor in the harbor, the flagship fired a fifteen-gun salute. From Washington Street the funeral cortege continued up Long Wharf, turned south along Thames Street, and then up Church Street to the churchyard. Newport residents lined the streets to watch as French military bands played the dirge. The sailors carried the casket into the churchyard, where the nine chaplains chanted the Catholic burial service. As the sailors slowly lowered the coffin into the grave, each regiment represented fired three salvos with muskets, and the French warships in the harbor repeated the final salute. As the last shovel of earth filled de Ternay's grave, the flagship broke Captain Destouches's command flag and raised the white flag of France to the masthead.[76]

Some time soon thereafter, French forces erected a temporary memorial, on which was inscribed in French:[77]

Here lies Charles Louis D'Arzac de Ternai.
Knight of the Order of Saint John of Jerusalem
former governor of the isles of France and of Bourbon
Admiral of His Most Christian Majesty's Navy
Commander of the French Squadron sent in 1780 to assist
the United States of America
Died 15 December 1780, age 57

The vestry continued to function during the period of the French occupation of Newport, managing the church property. Several burials took place. Among them was that of another soldier, this time an American volunteer from Connecticut, Heathcote Muirson, who had been mortally wounded while assisting the French in an action against a British position on Long Island.[78]

Buried in an unmarked grave, the young American patriot joined casualties from both sides of the conflict in Trinity Churchyard. About this time, the Kay schoolhouse, which had not been used as a school since 1779, was torn down.[79]

When the French forces left Newport in the summer of 1781 to join in operations in Virginia, Newport was in extremely bad condition. The foundation of trade and of economic livelihood was largely destroyed, and many of the most prominent residents were gone. Numerous buildings had been destroyed. Only a handful of Trinity's congregation remained. The Anglican Church faced serious difficulties throughout America, and little attempt could be made to repair them in the period following the Franco-American victory over the British army at Yorktown in September 1781 and the formal cessation of hostilities on 4 February 1784. The situation in Rhode Island was typical of that faced by loyalists throughout the new country. Nine states exiled loyalists, and nearly every state expelled them, barred them from the professions, seized their property, and nullified their rights. A total of one hundred thousand loyalists left the former British colonies and went to Canada. Many from Newport, like The Reverend George Bisset, eventually settled in New Brunswick, where he founded Trinity Church at St. John's in 1786. Others went to Nova Scotia and Upper Canada. Some found partial compensation for their losses through the British government's Loyalist Claims Commission, which functioned from 1783 to 1790. In states where the Anglican Church had been formally established and supported by tax revenues, it was disestablished. Some of the southern colonies did not allow their former Anglican parishes to reorganize themselves as independent, self-supporting churches until after 1783.

Due to the affluence of its congregation, Trinity Church had lost its financial backing from the S.P.G. even before the Revolution, but now Trinity no longer had a parish of wealthy merchants to support it. As a self-governing corporation, it did remain in control of its buildings and lands, although as the state seized the private property of individual loyalists, this remained for the moment a matter of question. The war of 1776–83 had brought British, American, and French troops to Newport. Unlike in other places, many of the city's wooden buildings had survived, but its former thriving economic and social life had not. The war had destroyed the political, social, and economic contexts in which Trinity Church had been founded. Still, the war had not entirely scattered its congregation. As there had been eighty-some years before, a small group of devoted people were prepared to begin again as Newport slowly began to reweave the fabric of its institutional life.

Notes

1. Crane, *A Dependent People,* pp. 3–6.

2. 1662 Prayer Book, quoted in Robert Pritchard, *A History of the Episcopal Church* (Harrisburg, PA: Morehouse, 1991), p. 75.

3. Elaine F. Crane, "Uneasy Coexistence: Religious Tensions in Eighteenth Century Newport," *Newport History,* vol. 53. no. 3 (Summer 1980), pp. 101–11.

4. David S. Lovejoy, *Rhode Island Politics and the American Revolution, 1760–1776* (Providence, RI: Brown Univ. Press, 1969), pp. 31–51.

5. Crane, *A Dependent People*, p. 129.

6. Quoted in Bridenbaugh, *Mitre and Sceptre,* p. 255.

7. Crane, *A Dependent People,* pp. 111–114; Neil R. Stout, *The Royal Navy in America, 1760–1775: A Study of the Enforcement of British Colonial Policy in the Era of the American Revolution* (Annapolis, MD: Naval Institute Press, 1973), pp. 92–96; Edmund and Helen Morgan, *The Stamp Act Crisis: Prelude to Revolution* (Chapel Hill: Univ. of North Carolina Press, 1953), pp. 47–52, 144–51, 191–94.

8. Rhodes House, Papers of the U.S.P.G. C/AM 9: Letter from Marmaduke Browne, no date.

9. Loc. cit.; Letter from Browne to The Reverend Dr. Daniel Burton, 1 June 1765.

10. Loc. cit., MS Bray/N. America/ lf5: Letter from Browne to John Waring, 6 November 1764.

11. Ibid.

12. Loc. cit.; Letter from Browne, 10 June 1768.

13. Loc. cit.; Letter from Browne to Burton, 1 June 1765.

14. Loc. cit.; Papers of the U.S.P.G., C/AM 9: Letter from Browne to Burton, 19 September 1764.

15. Loc. cit.: Letter from Browne to Burton, 1 June 1765.

16. James, *Colonial Rhode Island,* pp. 215–16, 221.

17. John Russell Bartlett, ed., *Records of the Colony of Rhode Island and Providence Plantations, in New England.,* vol. 6 (Providence, RI: Knowles and Anthony, State Publishers, 1861), p. 387. See also, Morgan, *The Gentle Puritan,* pp. 204–206, and Walter C. Bronson, *The History of Brown University, 1764–1914* (Providence, RI: Brown University, 1914), pp. 1–50, 493–507.

18. Bronson, *Brown University*, p. 50.

19. Rhodes House, U.S.P.G., Browne to Burton, 19 September 1764.

20. Ibid.

21. Lambeth, Fulham Papers XXIII, fo. 230. S.P.G. to Bishop of London, 21 March 1767.

22. Rhodes House, Papers of the U.S.P.G. C/AM 9: Letter from James Elphinstone, Kensington, 18 February 1767.

23. George Champlin Mason, *The Life and Works of Gilbert Stuart* (New York: Charles Scribners, 1894), p. 4; "Waterhouse, Benjamin (1754–1846)," *Dictionary of American Biography*, vol. 19, pp. 529–32; "Browne, Arthur (1756–1805)," *Dictionary of National Biography*, vol. 7, p. 41; Richard McLanthan, *Gilbert Stuart: Father of American Portraiture* (New York: Harry N. Abrams in association with the National Museum of Art, Smithsonian Institution, 1986), pp. 17–18, 21.

24. Mason, *Annals*, pp. 121, 136–38.

25. Bartlett, ed., *Records*, vol. 6, p. 573.

26. Mason, *Annals*, pp. 140–43.

27. Franklin Bowditch Dexter, ed., *The Literary Diary of Ezra Stiles, D.D., L.L.D.* (New York: Scribner's, 1901), vol. 1, pp. 30–31, 93–94, 219.

28. Rhodes House, MS Bray/N. America/ lf.5: Letter from Browne to Waring, 14 December 1770.

29. Loc. cit., Papers of the U.S.P.G., C/AM 9: Letter from The Reverend John Graves to S.P.G., 25 March 1771.

30. *Diary of Ezra Stiles*, vol. 1, p. 96.

31. Mason, *Annals*, p. 144.

32. *Diary of Ezra Stiles*, vol. 1, p. 96. This would seem to be in front of the altar, just to the south of where his monument was later placed.

33. Rhodes House, Papers of the U.S.P.G., C/AM 9: Trinity Church to the S.P.G., 17 April 1771.

34. Loc. cit., Papers of the U.S.P.G., B22, letter 125A: The Reverend Dr. Henry Caner to S.P.G., 9 April 1771.

35. Mason, *Annals*, pp. 150–52; *Diary of Ezra Stiles*, vol. 1, pp. 179–80.

36. *Diary of Ezra Stiles*, vol. 1, p. 35.

37. Mason, *Annals*, footnote on pp. 145–46: Letter from Arthur Browne to John Bours.

38. Rhodes House, Papers of the U.S.P.G., C/AM 9: Warden of Trinity Church to Burton, 24 May 1771.

39. Loc. cit., MS Bray, N. America /I f.5. List enclosed in letter from George Bisset to Waring, 23 November 1771. There is a similar list in the same series of documents for 30 April 1772, listing thirty-one black children: Mr. Hunter one, Captain Duncan three, Mr. Honyman three, Mrs. Cahoon one, Captain Buckmaster one, Captain Sherman three, Captain Freebody one, Mrs. Thurston two, Mr. Thurston three, Mrs. Honyman one, Mrs. Lyndon one, Captain Sneel one, Mr. Johnston two, Mrs. Mumford one, free negroes three, Captain Wickham one, Captain Dupee two, Captain Wanton one.

40. Loc. cit., Letter from Bisset to Waring, 17 October 1772.

41. Loc. cit., Letter from Bisset to Waring, 13 November 1773.

42. Ibid.

43. Loc. cit., Letter from Bisset to Waring, 21 May 1774.

44. Mason, *Annals*, pp. 151, 155.

45. George Bisset, *A Sermon Preached in Trinity Church, Newport, Rhode-Island on Monday 3 June 1771; At the Funeral of Mrs. Abigail Wanton, late consort of the Hon. Joseph Wanton, Esq., who died on the 31st of May in the thirty–sixth year of her Age* (Newport: Solomon Southwick, 1771).

46. George Bisset, *The Trial of a False Apostle. A Sermon Preached in Trinity Church, Newport, Rhode Island, on Sunday, October 24, 1773* (Newport, RI: Solomon Southwick, 1773).

47. *Diary of Ezra Stiles*, vol. 1, pp. 148–49.

48. See grave 108 in *Semper Eadem*, vol. II-B.

49. James, *Colonial Rhode Island*, pp. 347–49; Crane, *A Dependent People*, pp. 120–23.

50. "Declaration or Test," in Bartlett, ed., *Records of the Colony of Rhode Island,* vol. 7, p. 567.

51. *Diary of Ezra Stiles*, vol. 1, pp. 646–47.

52. Quoted in Crane, *A Dependent People*, p. 123.

53. *Diary of Ezra Stiles*, vol. 1, p. 649.

54. Mason, *Annals*, p. 158.

55. Bartlett, ed., *Records of the Colony of Rhode Island*, vol. 7, pp. 522–23.

56. Ibid., p. 581; also Diary of Ezra Stiles, vol. 2, footnote on pp. 27–28.

57. Ibid., transcribed from the Newport Mercury, 22 July 1776; also printed in full in Bartlett, ed., *Records of the Colony of Rhode Island*, vol. 7, pp. 585–86.

58. *Diary of Ezra Stiles*, pp. 27–28.

59. Ibid.

60. Bartlett, ed., *Records of the Colony of Rhode Island*, vol. 7, pp. 549–50.

61. *Diary of Ezra Stiles*, p. 29.

62. Ibid., p. 45.

63. Robert Pritchard, *A History of the Episcopal Church*, pp. 75–79.

64. *Diary of Ezra Stiles*, vol. 2, pp. 314–15.

65. Letter from George Washington to the governor of Rhode Island, 17 September 1776.

66. *Diary of Ezra Stiles*, vol. 2, pp. 95, 97.

67. Ira D. Gruber, ed., *John Pebbles' American War: The Diary of a Scottish Grenadier, 1776–1782*, Army Records Society, vol. 13 (Phoenix Mill: Sutton Publishing for the Army Records Society, 1998), p. 74.

68. Ibid., p. 75.

69. See grave 81 in *Semper Eadem*, vol. II-B.

70. *George Bisset, Honesty the best Policy in the Worst of Times, Illustrated and proved from the Exemplary Conduct of Joseph of Arimathea, and its consequent Rewards with an application to the case of suffering Loyalists. A Sermon intended to have been preached at Newport, Rhode Island, on the Sunday, preceding the evacuation of that Garrison by his Majesty's Troops, and afterwards preached at St. Paul's and St. George's Chapels, New York, on Sunday, October 8, 1780* (London: W. Richardson, 1784).

71. *Diary of Ezra Stiles*, vol. 2, p. 386.

72. Mason, *Annals*, p. 162. The grave is unmarked, and its location not known. For the naval action, see Maurice Linÿer de la Barbée, *Le Chevalier de Ternay: Vie de Charles Henry Louis d'Arsac de Ternay. Chef d'escadre des armées navales (1723–1780)* (Grenoble: Editions des 4 Seigneurs, 1972), tome 2, p. 591.

73. Howard C. Rice, Jr., and Anne S. K. Brown, eds., *The American Campaigns of Rochambeau's Army, 1780, 1781, 1782, 1783* (Providence, RI: Brown Univ. Press; and Princeton, NJ: Princeton Univ. Press, 1972), vol. 1, p. 125.

74. Ibid.

75. Ibid, p. 124.

76. Allan Forbes and Paul F. Cadman, *France and New England*. 3 vols. (Boston: State Street Trust Company, 1925–29). vol. 2, pp. 49–50. Maurice Linÿer de la Barbée, *le Chevalier de Ternay*, vol. 2, pp. 639–42.

77. As recorded in the journal of Francisco de Miranda, 5 September 1784: "cit-git, Charles Louis D'Arzac de Ternai. Chevalier de l'ordre de Saint Jean de Jerusalem, ancien gouverneur des isles de France, et du Bourbon, Chef d'Escadre des Armées navales de S.M.T.C. Commandant l'Escadre Française envoyé en 1780. au Sucours des Etats-Unis de l'Amerique. Mort le 15. Decembre 1780, agé de 57. ans." John S. Ezell, ed., *The New Democracy in America: Travels of Francisco de Miranda in the United States, 1783–84*, trans. by Judson P. Wood (Norman: Univ. of Oklahoma Press, 1963), p. 139.

78. See information on Muirson and his monument in *Semper Eadem*, vol. II-A.

79. "Memoir of Trinity Church, Newport, R.I., compiled by Henry Bull, Esq., at the request of the Rector, The Reverend Francis Vinton. Recorded by John Sterne, Esq. In 1841–42." Undated and unidentified newspaper clipping, Newport Historical Society.

John Bours, c. 1770. In this portrait, Bours appears in private contemplation while reading a book. On several occasions, fellow Trinity parishioners urged him to take holy orders. One of Newport's leading merchants, Bours owned a shop at the sign of the Golden Eagle, as well as slaving vessels and two slaves. He served as junior warden in 1765–66, senior warden in 1766–67 and 1771 to 1786, clerk of the vestry 1786–89, 1796–99, and a member of the vestry from 1800 until 1811. Bours was the key person who maintained the parish's property after the departure of the Reverend Bisset in 1779. From 1779 to 1786, he served as the lay leader for the remaining Anglicans in Newport and led the revival of the parish in the 1780s. In addition to his career as a merchant and his work at Trinity, he also served as treasurer and president of the Redwood Library. Portrait by John Singleton Copley. Collection of the Worcester Art Museum.

6

Beginning Again, 1781–1810

In the period between 1781 and May 1790, when Rhode Island became the last state to ratify the Constitution, the people living along the shores of Narragansett Bay were well known for being "otherwise-minded." Still displaying some of the attitudes toward self-government that had characterized Rhode Island in the colonial period, the new state resisted the trend toward a polity of united states and experimented with being completely independent from others, charting its own course in a bid to create a separate economy. With the references to the Crown removed, King Charles II's charter remained the state's constitution for another half-century, even after Rhode Island finally joined the federal republic.

While this was going on, Anglicans in other parts of America began to think about ways to reorganize and rebuild in the context of the new country. The first sustained movement took place in Maryland, where The Reverend Dr. William Smith, the former provost of the College of Philadelphia, began to convene meetings to discuss the future of the church. By 1783 he and the clergy in that area had taken a number of lasting steps. Most importantly, they adopted "Protestant Episcopal Church" to replace "Church of England. " In doing this, they wished to differentiate themselves from Roman Catholics, while at the same time reaffirming the importance of bishops, by adopting the word "episcopal"—from the name of a mid-seventeenth-century church party in England that had favored retention of bishops. In addition, they explicitly separated themselves from Great Britain and agreed to organize a state convention of churches that would be the authority for the church, governing through state-granted charters a synod of laity and clergy. They also identified their own candidates for the clergy and elected a candidate for their bishop.[1] One of Smith's former students, The Reverend William White, rector of the united Philadelphia parishes of Christ Church and St. Paul's and formerly the chaplain to the Continental Congress, carried Smith's work forward in a 1782 pamphlet, *The Case of the Episcopal Churches In the United States Consider'd*. He suggested that other states should take similar action and made suggestions for a national organization.

As this was going on, the Newport parish was struggling just to breathe life back into Trinity. Vestry records for the annual meeting on Easter Monday 1782 (a tradition going back at least fifty years before) give the first hint since 1779 that regular Episcopal services had been taking place. In that meeting, the congregation decided that an allowance for the sexton and the clerk would be made from the collections taken on the first Sunday in each month, beginning in May 1782. A year later, in July 1783, immediately following the death of Johann Knotchell, the vestry employed John Meunscher as the organist, paying him one dollar a Sunday. From that point forward, activity around the church increased. In August, for example, The Reverend Daniel Fogg of Christ Church, Pomfret, Connecticut, came to Newport to marry Peggy Malbone, the daughter of Francis and Margaret Malbone, to Capt. Edwyn Stanhope, RN. (In 1807, as a vice admiral, Stanhope would be created a baronet, recognizing his service as second in command to Admiral Ford James Gambier at Copenhagen.)

On the national level, William White was continuing to serve as a catalyst in reviving the Anglican Church. However, certain Episcopalians in the three New England states of Connecticut, Massachusetts, and Rhode Island objected to White's ideas about a voluntary association of clergy and laity. They pointed out that the historic episcopate was the essential characteristic of the church and the essential agent through which the Holy Spirit was conveyed. Pursuing their own course, Connecticut clergy had secretly elected two candidates as bishop in 1783. One was a former schoolmaster and minister of Trinity church, Jeremiah Leaming; the other was Samuel Seabury. The sixty-six-year-old Leaming declined the appointment, but Seabury accepted and, in June 1783, set sail for Britain, hoping to be consecrated.

Seabury had been born in 1729 at North Groton (now Ledyard), Connecticut, the son of The Reverend Samuel Seabury, Sr., and his second wife, Elizabeth Powel of Newport. Her father, Adam Powel, had served as a vestryman at Trinity from 1719 and successively as junior warden and senior warden in 1721–23. His wife, Elizabeth's mother, was the daughter of Gabriel Bernon, one of the original founders of the Newport parish. The young Seabury had gone to Scotland in 1752, where he studied physics and anatomy at the University of Edinburgh, before being ordained by the bishop of London the following year. Returning to America, he had served in New Jersey and Long Island before returning to Connecticut. Like many other Anglican clergymen, he had been a loyalist. In 1774, he authored a series of pamphlets against the Continental Congress and the activist group Sons of Liberty, using the pen name "A. W. Farmer." Later, during the war, he had served as chaplain of the King's American Regiment.

The Right Reverend Samuel Seabury. Bishop Seabury was the first American to be consecrated a bishop in the Church of England. Immediately after his consecration, on his way back from Britain to take up his position as bishop of Connecticut, he stopped in Newport and performed his first marriage as a bishop and delivered his first sermon in America as a bishop, on 25 June 1785. He declined a call to also become rector of Trinity, but was formally elected to serve additionally as the first bishop of Rhode Island from 1790 until his death in 1796.
Collection of Trinity Church.

Arriving in London in 1783, he, like several candidates from Maryland awaiting ordination, found that the most difficult hurdle was the English law requiring candidates to take an oath of allegiance to the Crown. Since the ordinands from Maryland had been approved by the Maryland state convention, chartered by the state legislature, Parliament allowed their ordination in England in August 1784. Seabury, had been recommended only by a secret meeting of the Connecticut clergy, where the Congregational Church was established by law. Although cordial, the English bishops and the archbishop of Canterbury were sensitive about creating further ill will between Americans and Britons. They felt that they could not proceed with Seabury's consecration without the consent of American governmental authorities, without the approval of the laity, and without a formally established diocese. With the way momentarily blocked, Seabury went to Scotland, where through Trinity's former rector, The Reverend George Bisset, he made contact with three nonjuring bishops (who had declined to swear allegiance to the Crown): the bishop and coadjutor bishop of Aberdeen and the bishop of Ross and Caithness. These three consecrated him in Aberdeen on 14 November 1784. Immediately thereafter, he signed an agreement with the Episcopal Church in Scotland that recognized its legitimacy and agreed to promote the use in America of the prayer of consecration for communion use in Scotland. On this theological point, the Scots church differed significantly from the English. The Scots prayer came from the 1549 Prayer Book, while the English form came from the revised 1552 Prayer Book.

Bishop Seabury's mitre.
Bishop Seabury personally designed and wore this mitre as bishop of Connecticut and Rhode Island.
Collection of the Diocese of Connecticut.

During Seabury's absence in Britain, the clergy in Connecticut, Massachusetts, and Rhode Island had attended a meeting of clergy and lay delegates in New York City. There, delegates from nine other states joined to make plans for the first General Convention, to be held in Philadelphia in 1785. During this meeting, they also decided to proceed with plans to organize the church around state meetings, with a bishop for each state. Unhappy with what they were hearing, the New England clergy returned home to await Seabury's return.

In early 1784, the Rhode Island General Assembly recognized the Newport parish's right to dispose of property in North Kingston that Nathaniel Norton had donated to it in 1781. At the annual meeting on Easter Monday 1784, the parish voted to invest the proceeds from that sale and to make plans to settle a minister and arrange the means to pay him. The parish unanimously agreed to encourage John Bours, who had been a member of the vestry since 1765, clerk of the vestry, and the dynamic force behind the revival of the parish in 1781. With this thought in mind, the church's sixty-one pew owners formally signed a statement agreeing to the proposal to settle a minister.[2]

Three weeks later, a committee reported its plan to raise funds by a pew tax of twenty-eight shillings per year for each pew on the main floor and twelve shillings each in the gallery, in order to provide the minister an annual salary of £93.6.8. In addition, the minister was to receive whatever additional income he could from reviving what was now known as the Kay School and making use of the Kay donation, teaching ten poor boys and charging tuition for others. In the meantime, in order to encourage Bours to accept, the committee offered him a salary of thirty pounds a year and the use of the minister's house. After a long period of consideration, Bours eventually declined the invitation but agreed to stay on until a permanent minister was found and to "continue to keep the congregation together in the way we are."[3] The vestry simultaneously authorized him to invite The Reverend Moses Badger, a clergyman who was temporarily in Newport, to officiate occasionally.

As the vestry was taking these decisions, a visitor from South America, Francisco de Miranda, happened to visit Newport toward the end of his travels through the United States. In his diary for Sunday, 5 September 1784, he wrote: "At the Anglican Church I remained for the entire service, celebrated with great dignity. The organ accompanying the singing of psalms and the general good taste of the building and elegance of the gathering (certainly not large) giving a majestic air to the religious ritual."[5] Completing his description, he added parenthetically, "This is the only place in all this continent where a decent foreigner arriving at Church is not offered a seat by others."[5]

The situation at Trinity continued to develop along these lines until 25 June 1785, when an important figure unexpectedly appeared. A ship arrived from Halifax, Nova Scotia, carrying The Right Reverend Samuel Seabury, on his way home to Connecticut after consecration in Scotland. On the following day, he performed the marriage service in Trinity Church for Thomas Grosvenor of Connecticut and Ann Mumford, a family relation. Shortly thereafter, he preached a sermon from Trinity's pulpit before taking passage on a ship to New Haven on the following day. These were the first clerical acts that Seabury performed in America after being raised to the episcopate and the first by any bishop of the Episcopal Church in America.[6]

In July, a few weeks after Seabury's visit, a French warship arrived in the harbor and on the orders of King Louis XVI erected a low marble mausoleum over the grave of Admiral de Ternay.[7] The elaborate engraved memorial has since become a distinctive feature of the church. Even more importantly, at about the same time, Seabury's unexpected visit to Newport had created for the struggling little parish a key connection upon which it built its future.

A little more than a month after leaving Newport, Seabury called a convocation of the clergy at Middletown, Connecticut. This was the first of several meetings (like some that were being held in the middle states) in which no lay members but only the clergy participated. At this meeting, the clergy agreed to accept Seabury as their bishop and to "render him that respect, duty and submission which as they understand, were given by the Presbyters to their Bishops in the primitive Church when unconnected with, and uncontrolled by, secular power."[8] Immediately thereafter, the Trinity wardens were faced with a decision as to whether to follow the lead of William Smith and William White in the middle colonies or join Seabury and the Connecticut clergy.

Meanwhile, in Boston, a committee of Massachusetts and Rhode Island clergy had gathered to consider what changes might be proposed to the Book of Common Prayer and what steps should be taken to promote uniformity of worship. To this end, it proposed a convention in Boston for 7 September 1785 to decide whether or not to receive Seabury as bishop or to send delegates to the General Convention proposed by the middle states to be held later in September at Philadelphia. In a meeting of the Trinity congregation held on 22 August, the parish authorized John Bours to travel to Boston at the church's expense, with full power to join in and agree with any plan that might be adopted to promote the Episcopal Church. At the same time, they reserved to the congregation the right of approving or disapproving any proposed alterations in the forms of prayer.[9]

When the meeting took place in Boston, with both clergy and lay representatives from Rhode Island, Massachusetts, and New Hampshire, John Bours agreed to Trinity's participation. Following the meeting, he presented to the parish a number of proposed changes to the liturgy. The congregation approved these changes and appointed Bours once again to represent the parish at a second convention to be held in Boston, in which further plans were made to coordinate Episcopal worship in Massachusetts, Rhode Island, and New Hampshire. At this time, the New England churches were moving in a direction that was distinct from that of the churches in the middle states. New England, Bishop Seabury in particular, was attempting to develop a theology that clearly distinguished the Episcopalian Church from the Congregational churches that were prevalent in the region; Episcopalians in the middle states were taking a different course, tending to remove the aspects of the church that were different. In particular, Seabury and the New Englanders stressed the importance of the connection between baptism and confirmation, with an essential role for the episcopacy as the agent through which the Holy Spirit was conveyed. In this, Seabury was establishing the basis for an Episcopalian response to the Great Awakening. Building on the catechism that Thomas Bray had written for use in the colonies in the 1690s, in which he linked the covenant to the apostolic succession, Seabury now linked the episcopacy to the Holy Spirit.[10]

At this point, the views of Trinity's parishioners were very close to those of Seabury. In March 1786, Seabury was back in Newport. He had already ordained several priests, but on this occasion occurred the first ordination in Trinity Church. On 12 March Seabury ordained John Bisset a deacon and, three days later, a priest. A few weeks later, at the annual meeting of the parish on Easter Monday, the congregation agreed that it was time to move forward and obtain a clergyman.[11] On 21 April, Bours wrote directly to Bishop Seabury on behalf of the parish and invited him personally to accept a call as Trinity's minister, since in this early period a bishop also had responsibility for a parish as well as a diocese. Seabury replied in July declining the invitation, noting that "however agreeable such an event might be to me, the state of Connecticut does not seem to permit it."[12] Connecticut had just lost five clergymen and seemed to be on the verge of losing another; he felt that if he accepted the call to Trinity he would be less able to assist with those vacancies, and as a result, "my necessary absence from you, would leave your church unsupplied more frequently than it ought to be."[13]

However, Seabury told the Trinity search committee, "In the present scarcity of clergymen, no great choice can be had; but there is one in this state who is not under any engagement." On a recent visit to New Haven he had met The Reverend James Sayre, who was then living in Fairfield, Connecticut, and had discussed with him the opportunity of filling the position at Newport. "He has a good understanding, and appears to be well acquainted with and fully grounded in our holy religion. . . . He reads prayers much to my satisfaction. His voice is strong and, I believe, equal to your church."[14]

On this recommendation, the parish invited Sayre to preach at Trinity, and soon thereafter invited him to accept the position at a hundred pounds sterling per year. He accepted. John Bours continued to officiate until Sayre and his family arrived in Newport on 1 October 1786 to take up residence in the minister's house at the corner of High and Touro Streets. The vestry formally thanked Bours for the five years that he had led the parish, and Sayre immediately went into action: pew holders were required to pay their taxes immediately; the four pews that had been installed at the west end of the church in 1747, blocking the aisle between the north and south doors, were removed and the owners accommodated with pews elsewhere. Although the parish had received Sayre warmly, a conflict soon developed, and Sayre attended no vestry meetings after 4 September 1787, just a year after his appointment. Sayre remained nominally in charge, but a great difference of opinion between him and the congregation soon became public knowledge.

At first, the dispute was mainly between John Bours, who had retained his office as clerk of the vestry, and the minister. Soon there was much personal friction between Sayre and various other members of the congregation as well. When Sayre tried, unsuccessfully, to remove the very popular John Bours from the vestry, matters became even more heated. Some members of the congregation charged that while Sayre, refusing to give communion to long-standing church members who were sick at home, had "received to the altar and administered communion to a vagrant Portuguese, who was an entire stranger to him until he saw him approaching with antic postures and gesticulations, beating his breast and crossing himself."[15] In another case, he refused to put to a vote an issue that the vestry believed should be resolved in one way or the other, changes to the Book of Common Prayer. In opposition to much of the congregation and other Episcopal churches in the region, Sayre, not wanting to make any break with the Church of England, would agree to no changes beyond omitting prayers for the king.

Pointing to the indissoluble nature of the conflict and the divisions it had created in the parish, the vestry appealed to Sayre and asked him to set a

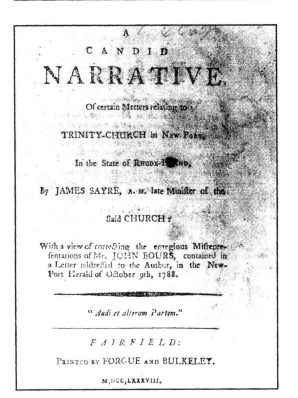

AN
APPEAL to the PUBLIC:
IN WHICH THE MISREPRESENTATIONS AND CALUMNIES, CONTAINED IN A PAMPHLET, ENTITLED,

A NARRATIVE
OF CERTAIN MATTERS RELATIVE TO
TRINITY CHURCH,
IN
NEWPORT,
IN THE
STATE OF RHODE-ISLAND,
BY A VERY *EXTRAORDINARY* MAN,
THE REV. JAMES SAYRE, A. M.
LATE MINISTER OF SAID CHURCH, ARE POINTED OUT, AND HIS VERY *STRANGE* CONDUCT, DURING THE TIME OF HIS MINISTRATION AT NEWPORT, FAITHFULLY RELATED.

BY JOHN BOURS,
MERCHANT, AND ONE OF THE VESTRY OF SAID CHURCH.

" Honor and fhame from no condition rife ;
Act well your part, there all the honor lies."

" Worth makes the man, and want of it the fellow,
The reft is all, but leather or prunella."   POPE.

NEWPORT (RHODE-ISLAND)
PRINTED BY PETER EDES, MDCCLXXXIX.

A
CANDID
NARRATIVE.
Of certain Matters relating to

TRINITY-CHURCH in New Port,

In the State of RHODE-ISLAND,

By JAMES SAYRE, A. M. late Minifter of the

Said CHURCH ;

With a view of correcting the egregious Mifreprefentations of Mr. JOHN BOURS, contained in a Letter addreffed to the Author, in the NewPort Herald of October 9th, 1788.

" *Audi et alteram Partem.*"

FAIRFIELD:
PRINTED BY FORGUE AND BULKELEY.
M,DCC,LXXXVIII.

The Reverend James Sayre, Minister of Trinity Church, 1786–88. The first Episcopal clergyman to settle in Newport after the Revolution, Sayre's tenure at Trinity was marked by controversy. His ministry created deep divisions within the congregation that soon became public through letters to the editors of the local newspapers and pamphlets. Several years later, Sayre's extraordinary actions in Connecticut led Bishop Seabury to excommunicate him.

Collection of the Redwood Library and Athenaeum

convenient date to terminate his ministry at Trinity. When that effort failed, the vestry appealed to Bishop Seabury "to prevail on Mr. Sayre to leave us, without coming to an open rupture."[16] Eventually the bishop was successful and arranged for Sayre to take a position at Stratford, Connecticut. Thereafter, the argument was carried on publicly and at a distance. Bitter charges and countercharges appeared in print, both in the *Newport Herald* and in pamphlets.[17] Soon after, Sayre became involved in similar squabbles in Connecticut; he died insane ten years later. Sayre's conduct had become so extreme that Bishop Seabury excommunicated him on 25 September 1793 for "depraving the liturgy, contravening the government and despising the discipline of the Protestant Episcopal Church in America."[18]

The deep divisions that had been created in the Newport parish as a result of Sayre's ministry were very slow to heal. Apparently the two opposing sides had about equal numbers of people, so votes at meetings of the vestry and of the congregation were inconsistent. For instance, at its 1789 annual meeting the congregation voted to reverse its 1786 decision to adopt changes to the liturgy and decided to revert to what had been used before that date. At the same time, the vestrymen entered into discussions with The Reverend William Smith, who had performed all marriages at Trinity since September 1787.

William Smith had been born in Banff, Scotland, in 1754 and studied at King's College, Aberdeen, where he had earned a master of arts degree. Ordained in Scotland, he was closely associated with the high church views of Scots Episcopalians. In 1784, he had immigrated to America, where he came under the influence of another, older, Reverend William Smith. After a brief career in Pennsylvania and Maryland, the younger Smith settled in Rhode Island in July 1787 at St. Paul's Church, Narragansett. Bishop Seabury thought highly of him, and Smith soon became his favorite clergyman. Seabury once wrote of him, "He would be very useful to me in bringing our people to a better knowledge of the real principles of their religion and to more submission to ecclesiastical discipline."[19] In May 1789, the Trinity Church vestry formally invited Smith to take services every other week in Newport, and also wrote to the vestry of St. Paul's, Narragansett, to ask its agreement to this proposal; both letters were favorably received.

In September 1789, the Boston clergy notified the Newport congregation of a forthcoming convention of the church to be held in Philadelphia. William Smith, serving part time in Newport, was not formally the rector. In a move reflecting its divisions, the parish chose The Reverend Samuel Parker of Boston

Articles for the Constitution of the Protestant Episcopal Church in the State of Rhode Island — Vizt.

Article 1. The Protestant Episcopal Church in the State of Rhode Island hath and aught to have in common with all other denominations of Christians full, and unalienable powers to regulate the concerns of their own Communion. —

Art. 2. Under the protection & agreeable to the Institution of our Lord and Savior Jesus Christ this Church shall always hold the three Orders of Bishop, Priest, and Deacon as essentially & indispensibly necessary to the right & due administration of the Word & Sacraments.

Art. 3. This Church shall continue in connection with the Church in the State of Connecticut as one Diocese untill it may be deemed by the then existing Convention expedient or necessary to have a Bishop to reside within this State. —

Art. 4. An annual Convention consisting of the Clergy, and one or more lay deligates from each Congregation shall be holden on the second Wednesday in July, or on any other day, appointed by the Bishop & Standing Committee of the State in each Parish by rotation and to be allways opened with prayers & a Sermon. —

Articles for the Constitution of the Protestant Episcopal Church in the State of Rhode Island, 1790. The first Convention of the Diocese of Rhode Island was held at Trinity on 18 November 1790 and adopted these articles for its governance. Article 3 stated, "This Church shall continue in connection with the Church in the State of Connecticut as one Diocese until it may be deemed by the then existing convention expedient or necessary to have a Bishop to reside within the State." Document in George Champlin Mason, Extra Illustrated Reminiscences, *vol. 5, p. 314-A.* Collection of the Newport Historical Society to represent it at the Philadelphia convention, not Smith. Aware of problems of the national church, the Trinity parish voted on 13 September 1789 that it would abide by and maintain the doctrine and discipline that they expected the forthcoming Philadelphia convention to establish.

At this point, Episcopalians were divided on the national level as deeply as they were in Newport. In effect, the church in America had split into three fragments; a group that eventually split off completely to become the Methodist Episcopal Church; a group associated with the middle and southern states; and the parishes of New England.

The three factions had become outwardly hostile to one another, but the convention that met in Philadelphia in the summer of 1789 was able to heal the breach between two of them. This convention recognized Seabury's consecration and created a House of Bishops and House of Deputies, with optional attendance by lay representatives. Most significantly for local parishes, the convention adopted the 1789 Book of Common Prayer. This eliminated some of the most contentious changes made to the Prayer Book in 1785–86, but it maintained such alterations as the omission of prayers for the king and royal family, a shortened psalter, and, interestingly, a slightly altered form of the Scottish prayer of consecration.[20] Reverend Smith of Rhode Island, who had connections to the leading figures on both sides—the elder Reverend William Smith and Bishop Seabury—was a key figure in building the consensus and, particularly, in introducing the Scottish prayer of consecration.

By this time, the Trinity congregation was determined to obtain a full-time clergyman. Meeting on 28 December 1789, it voted to offer the position formally to William Smith, who was very much interested in education and had become intrigued by the possibilities that Newport's Kay School offered for Christian education. With Smith's acceptance, the term "rector" was first used officially at Trinity, the parish having previously used the term "minister" in formal documents. Soon after Smith took charge, the parish reopened the Kay School. By autumn it was beginning to think further about the organization and unity of the church, which resolved to host the first convention of Rhode Island Episcopal churches, which met in Trinity Church on 18 November 1790. Trinity was represented by its new rector and two lay delegates, Robert N. Auchmuty and Maj. John Handy—the Newport patriot who had publicly read aloud the Declaration of Independence from the steps of the Court House in 1776.

Major John Handy, Rhode Island patriot. John Handy is most famous for having publicly read the Declaration of Independence, on its first arrival in Rhode Island, to the residents of Newport from the steps of the Colony House in July 1776; fifty years later in 1826 he again read it from the same steps. Elected senior warden in 1789, he served in that capacity until 1797. He was a lay delegate from Trinity to the first Rhode Island diocesan convention. His brother, William Handy, laid out many of the house lots on William, Thomas, and John Streets. John Street was probably named after John Handy. Miniature on ivory. 76.1.1.

Newport Historical Society.

At this meeting, William Smith was the catalyst in establishing the diocese of Rhode Island at Trinity Church. He delivered the sermon, opening what soon became Rhode Island's first church convention.[21] Shortly thereafter, the assembled clergy and lay delegates, representing the three Episcopal churches at Newport, Bristol, and Providence, voted. They formally accepted the canons established at Philadelphia, accepted the revisions in the Book of Common Prayer (1789), and declared The Right Reverend Samuel Seabury the first bishop of the Episcopal Church in Rhode Island. At its formation, the diocese consisted of only the three parishes, but the arrangement provided for other Rhode Island churches "as may in future accede to and become part of the established Episcopacy of the United States," as Seabury noted in accepting his additional responsibilities as bishop of Rhode Island. Acknowledging the long road ahead, Seabury replied to the invitation, "Next to doing as well as we wish is to do as well as we can."[22]

Smith readily joined in other Newport activities. In 1790, the Redwood Library was in deplorable condition, not yet having recovered from the ravages

A

DISCOURSE,

AT THE OPENING OF THE

CONVENTION

OF CLERICAL AND LAY-DELEGATES OF THE

CHURCH,

IN THE

STATE OF *RHODE-ISLAND.*

DELIVERED IN

TRINITY-CHURCH, NEWPORT,

Thursday, the 18th of *November,* 1790.

Pſal. cxxii. 7—9. *Peace be within thy Walls,
and Plenteouſneſs within thy Palaces. For my
Brethren and Companions Sake, I will ſeek to do
thee Good.*

By *WILLIAM SMITH,* A.M.

RECTOR OF TRINITY-CHURCH, NEWPORT.

PROVIDENCE: Printed by J. CARTER.

*The Reverend William Smith's
sermon at the opening of the first
Rhode Island diocesan convention,
18 November 1790. Smith was the
first clergyman at Trinity to use the
title rector rather than minister.*

Collection of the Redwood Library and Athenaeum.

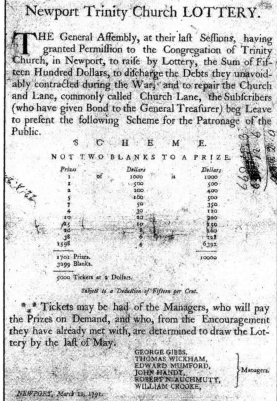

*Trinity's 1791 lottery was
designed to raise $1,500
to pay debts and to repair
the church. Document in
George Champlin Mason,*
Extra Illustrated Reminiscences, *vol. 5, p. 325-A.*

Collection of the Newport Historical
Society.

of the war. Its board of directors, which still included many Trinity parishioners, including John Bours, took steps to reestablish it, obtaining an act of the General Assembly toward this end. The Library Board elected William Smith as one of the seven Newport clergymen it made honorary members in1791. In addition, it elected Smith as the librarian for the year and voted that "the care and use of the Library Yard be annexed to the Librarian for the time being, that he be permitted to put a cow and a horse therein, but that no hogs be permitted or suffered to go therein."[23]

Under Smith's strong direction, the parish began to resume its former lively activity. Smith experimented with the use of the organ and chant during services, and he placed the Kay School on an active footing. By early 1791, Smith saw an urgent need to raise money to repay debts and repair the fabric of the church building and the lane along the north side of the property. With state approval, a parish committee was formed to run a lottery. It offered five thousand tickets at two dollars apiece, with 1,701 prizes, ranging from a grand prize of one thousand dollars down to 1,598 prizes of four dollars each. Each prize was subject to a deduction of 15 percent that went to the benefit of the church, a total of $1,500. As the years passed, Smith was involved in other programs to bring funds to the church. In 1796, the vestry accepted an offer from Richard Harrison for a 999-year lease on the seven-acre property that Nathaniel Kay had donated to the church (for an annual rent of three hundred silver dollars, or the silver bullion equivalent, which was to be put toward Kay's goal of schooling poor boys).[24] At the same time, the parish finally determined to dispose of the North Kingston land that Nathaniel Norton had donated in 1781, the sale of which the state had authorized in 1784 but which had not yet been sold. The vestry now agreed to sell it for whatever could be obtained and to use the proceeds to purchase lands that had formerly belonged to James Honyman, Jr., adjoining the church cemetery in Westerly, Rhode Island. As the cemetery expanded, the rector of Trinity was to augment his income with a fee for every burial.[25]

Having succeeded with the lottery and other fund-raising efforts, Smith arranged for Bishop Seabury to return to Newport for a week, during which time he held the first confirmation class in Newport.[26] He quickly earned a reputation for his sermons and his writings. In June 1791, he played a role in the establishment of Rhode Island's first Grand Lodge of Free and Accepted Masons, delivering the sermon on St. John's Day, which was later published."[27] A leading lay member of the parish, Christopher Champlin, was the first Grand

Master; others were parishioners George Gibbs, Benjamin Bourne, and Robert N. Auchmuty. During Passion Week that same year, Smith published a remarkable pamphlet of prayers and readings for the condemned.[28] Reminiscent of Honyman's ministry to the condemned pirates in the 1720s, this little volume was specifically designed to reach two men who were then in Newport's jail awaiting their execution, James Williams and Thomas Mount.

Smith's association with Trinity Church may also be associated with what has become a distinguishing feature of the church building: the placement of memorial plaques on the inside walls. When Smith first held services at Trinity, in November 1788, the first plaque was installed. It was given in memory of Sarah Atherton, one of Jahleel Brenton's daughters, who had twice been married in the church. In January 1775, she had married Joseph Wanton, Jr., the loyalist, and had begun her married life with him in Hunter House. They left with the evacuation of the British army in 1779, but she returned to Rhode Island after Wanton's death in New York City. In 1784, she had married a Jamaica planter, William Atherton, who donated the London-carved memorial after her death in 1787 at the age of thirty-five.

In 1794, when Smith was firmly in charge, the French frigate *Méduse* called at Newport. The ship's officers visited Admiral de Ternay's grave and found that the mausoleum that had been placed over it nine years earlier had been seriously broken and vandalized. They ordered seamen to reassemble the remaining pieces as a wall monument. They placed this monument outside, against the north side of the church building, where it remained until it was restored and brought inside in 1872–73.[29]

Clearly interested in the church's monuments, Smith approved plans to erect a monument to the memory of one of his predecessors, The Reverend Marmaduke Browne, and his wife, Ann. Donated by Browne's only son, Arthur, it was carved in Dublin. When the completed monument arrived in Newport in 1796, John Bours arranged for its installation. Still serving as clerk (as he would until his resignation in 1811), Bours had first joined the vestry during Browne's ministry and had played a role in obtaining the funds to send his son Arthur to Trinity College, Dublin. With the educational opportunity that the Kay School and Trinity parishioners had given him, Arthur Browne had gone on to a very successful academic career. He became a Fellow of Trinity College, Dublin, in 1777, Professor of Laws in 1785, Regius Professor of Greek in 1797–99 and 1801–1806 and was being repeatedly elected as member of the Irish Parliament for the college in 1783, 1790, and 1797. One of his works, *Miscellaneous*

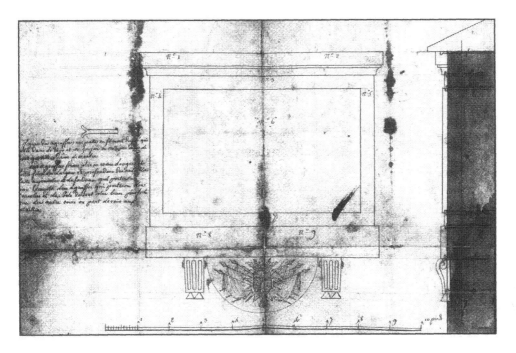

The memorial to Admiral de Ternay.
The officers and men of the French frigate Méduse *probably used this plan in 1794 when they converted de Ternay's vandalized mausoleum into a wall monument, placing it along the outside, north wall of the church. Detail from the manuscript in George Champlin Mason,* Extra Illustrated Reminiscences, *vol. 5, p. 326-A.* Collection of the Newport Historical Society.

Sketches, was widely read in its day and contained a brief essay on his youth in Newport.[30]

Despite Smith's activist role in building up the parish, deep divisions remained, typical of the "other-mindedness" that Rhode Islanders reflected. Smith certainly represented the larger trend in the Episcopal Church, through which the churches in New England and those of the middle and southern states were beginning to come together in a larger national church. Yet we know that an undercurrent of dissatisfaction continued within the Newport parish. Interestingly, this paralleled the rise of the Methodist Episcopal Church, which could trace its origins to the work of John Wesley and, locally, to the evangelism of George Whitefield a half-century before. In June 1790, Jesse Lee, a Methodist pastor and the founder of New England Methodism, preached in Newport, marking the first known Methodist service in Newport, although there was more such activity in Portsmouth. Little is known of those in Newport who became interested, except that a number were formerly members of other denominations. Given the origins of the Methodist movement, it would not be surprising to find that a number were from Trinity. Fifteen years later, some of the first incorporators of St. Paul's Methodist Church bore family names that were also found at Trinity, such as Gardiner, Mumford, Shaw, and Sherman.[31]

In April 1797, not long after Bishop Seabury's death, Smith resigned his position at Trinity to take up a new appointment at Norwalk, Connecticut. He eventually moved directly into the teaching work that had originally attracted him to Newport, going to the Episcopal Academy at Cheshire, Connecticut; in 1804 he was to be one of the founders of the *Churchman's Magazine.*

Immediately upon his departure, the vestry began the search for a replacement. Very quickly it settled on The Reverend John S. J. Gardiner, the assistant rector at Trinity Church in Boston, offering him a salary of five hundred dollars per year. During a ten-week visit to Newport, Gardiner was on the verge of accepting the offer but declined, noting, "On the one hand I reflected that I might prove the instrument in the hands of Providence of organizing a scattered church, and of reuniting a divided people; on the other hand, I was deterred from the undertaking from a sense of its extreme difficulty and by the fear that my best exertions would prove abortive."[32] While Gardiner examined his doubts about the Newport parish, the Boston church had raised his salary to eight hundred dollars, making the offer in Newport impractical to accept. In his place, Gardiner suggested that the parish consider Theodore Dehon, a young man then living in Cambridge, Massachusetts, who had graduated with honors from Harvard in 1795 and was about to enter holy orders after studying theology with The Reverend Dr. Samuel Parker, the rector of Trinity Church, Boston. After receiving a further recommendation from Parker, the vestry invited Dehon to Newport. After some negotiations over his salary, Dehon agreed to accept the appointment at a salary of seven hundred dollars per year, along with the use of the rectory.

The Right Reverend Edward Bass, rector of St. Paul's Church, Newburyport, had recently been consecrated as the first bishop of Massachusetts, in May 1797. Bass ordained Dehon at Newburyport on Christmas Eve, 1797, and Dehon entered on his new duties at Newport in early January 1798. Immediately upon Dehon's arrival, the vestry seemed to unite and display the activity of a beehive. Among other things, it created a standing committee to deal with the business of the church, and it built an addition on the north side of

Receipt for three month's tax on pews 44 and 45, paid on 30 June 1803. Interestingly, pounds and shillings were still in use in Newport. Document from George Champlin Mason, Extra Illustrated Reminiscences, *vol. 5, p. 319-A.*

Collection of the Newport Historical Society.

This type of cup, sometimes called a caudal cup, was used for Holy Communion in the seventeenth and eighteenth centuries. This piece bears no maker's mark or date, but the engraved crest of a unicorn above a crown with the motto "Praesto ut Praaestem" is said to be that of the Preston family. There is no definite record of when the parish acquired it, but it is probably the piece mentioned in the vestry minutes for 3 March 1806: "The Revd Mr Dehon has informed the Vestry, that at the last Christmas festival he received from Mrs. Catherine Malbone a valuable silver cup for use of the altar of Trinity Church."

the east end of the church for a vestry meeting room. New taxes were levied on pew owners, ranging from twenty dollars for a double pew to four dollars in the gallery. Within a year, other building projects were under way. In early 1799 construction began for a new building for Kay School at the corner of Mary and School Streets, using the accumulating funds from Richard Harrison's lease on the Kay lands. The new building went on the site of the dilapidated earlier school, forty feet by twenty feet, with an eight-foot-square bell tower rising eight feet above the roof.

In July 1798, the parish was host to a church convention. Abraham Jarvis had been consecrated bishop of Connecticut in 1797, but this was the first opportunity for the Rhode Island diocese to consider who would be its new bishop. Instead of following the state's earlier ties to Connecticut, the convention used Dehon's connections with Massachusetts and with Bass to elect the latter bishop of Rhode Island, a position that he held until his death in 1803.[33]

Among the memorable events that now took place in the church was a memorial service for George Washington. News of Washington's death at Mount Vernon on 14 December 1799 reached Newport eight days later. On the following day, 23 December, the Fraternity of Masons assembled at the Old Colony House and marched with muffled drums to Trinity Church, where Dehon delivered a sermon.[34] The commemoration of Washington's death continued on 6 January 1800, with a full-scale military funeral service that halted all other activity in town. Guns were fired every half-hour throughout the day from Fort Adams and Fort Wolcott. Townspeople brought a bier to the Parade and then carried it in a procession led by the Newport Guards and Newport Artillery, along with soldiers from Fort Adams, officers from the army, the navy, and the customs house, as well as members of the Society of Cincinnati. Following the bier and the pallbearers were representatives of the Masonic Society, the Marine Society, the Town Council, the Mechanics Association, and a number of Newport citizens. The procession passed along Spring Street to Trinity Church, where Reverend Dehon read a prayer and the participants heard a funeral anthem and an oration. Following the service, the procession continued on to the burial ground, where it buried the empty bier with a gun salute.[35]

When the schoolhouse was completed in 1800, The Reverend Abraham Bronson took charge as schoolmaster and assistant to the rector, but he remained for only a year. The Reverend Clement Merriam succeeded him and was in that position in December 1802, when Reverend Dehon became ill and

A

DISCOURSE,

DELIVERED IN

NEWPORT, RHODE-ISLAND;

BEFORE THE

CONGREGATION OF TRINITY CHURCH,

THE

MASONIC SOCIETY,

AND THE

NEWPORT GUARDS;

THE SUNDAY FOLLOWING

THE INTELLIGENCE OF THE DEATH

OF

GENERAL GEORGE WASHINGTON.

By THEODORE DEHON, A.M.

RECTOR OF TRINITY CHURCH IN NEWPORT.

NEWPORT: Printed by HENRY BARBER,

M,DCCC.

George Washington's death.

News reached Newport on Sunday, 22 December 1799, that Washington had died at Mount Vernon. A week later, the pulpit was draped in black, and the rector, The Reverend Theodore Dehon, delivered this sermon. On 6 January 1800, a full-fledged funeral service was conducted in Trinity, and a bier was carried from the church in procession to the Burying Ground.

Collection of the Redwood Library and Athenaeum.

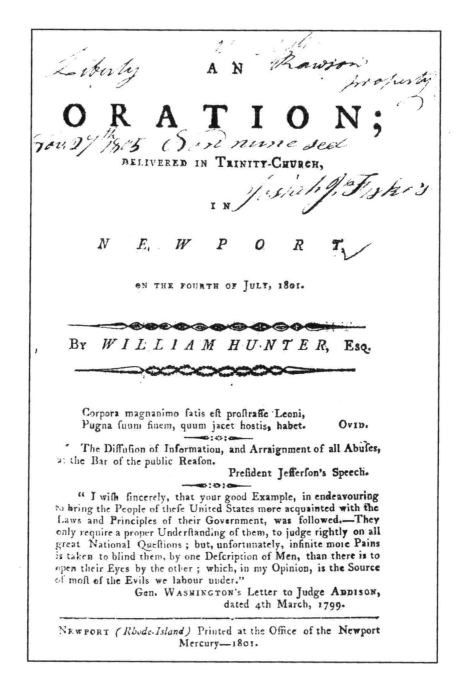

AN ORATION;

DELIVERED IN TRINITY-CHURCH,

IN

NEWPORT

ON THE FOURTH OF JULY, 1801.

By *WILLIAM HUNTER*, Esq.

Corpora magnanimo fatis eft proftraffe Leoni,
Pugna fuum fiuem, quum jacet hostis, habet.   Ovid.

The Diffufion of Information, and Arraignment of all Abufes,
at the Bar of the public Reafon.
President Jefferfon's Speech.

" I wifh fincerely, that your good Example, in endeavouring
to bring the People of thefe United States more acquainted with the
Laws and Principles of their Government, was followed.—They
only require a proper Underftanding of them, to judge rightly on all
great National Queftions ; but, unfortunately, infinite more Pains
is taken to blind them, by one Defcription of Men, than there is to
open their Eyes by the other ; which, in my Opinion, is the Source
of moft of the Evils we labour under."
Gen. WASHINGTON's Letter to Judge ADDISON,
dated 4th March, 1799.

NEWPORT *(Rhode-Island)* Printed at the Office of the Newport
Mercury—1801.

*The Fourth of July 1801. Rhode Island state representative William Hunter
delivered this oration to a special meeting of the Society of Cincinnati held in
Trinity Church on Independence Day. In 1811, Hunter became U.S. senator
from Rhode Island, and in 1834 he became minister to Brazil. He and his wife,
Mary Robinson Hunter, are both buried in the churchyard.*

Collection of the Redwood Library and Athenaeum.

had to take a leave of absence to recover his health in Charleston, South Carolina, until the following summer. During his absence Merriam took charge of the church, and Jabez Whitaker was hired to fill in temporarily as schoolmaster. In the following year, Dehon took another leave of absence for health reasons in Charleston, but by then Merriam had resigned, and there was no clergyman available. The vestry hired John Ward of Harrington, Connecticut, to take responsibility for the school and encouraged him to take holy orders. He eventually did this in 1805 and became the assistant minister.

In 1804, the thousand-pound bell that the church had acquired in 1741 cracked. The repair work was performed by the firm of Fenner & Crocker in Hartford, involving the recasting of the bell and use of additional metal, bringing it up to 1,200 pounds. When it was reinstalled in September 1804, the vestry directed that the sexton "ring her as usual, at sunrise, one of the clock, P.M., and at nine in the evening."[36] The new bell lasted less than two months. The parish immediately commissioned an entirely new bell, weighing 1,735 pounds, from the firm of Fenton & Cochran in New Haven. This bell remained in use until it too cracked in 1842.[37]

After the death of Bishop Bass, the Rhode Island Convention unanimously elected Benjamin Moore as its bishop and commissioned Dehon to go to New York to seek his acceptance. In the end, Moore declined to accept the responsibility, and for a time Rhode Island was without a bishop. Nevertheless, under Dehon's leadership the Newport parish consolidated its finances, its property management, and its quiet but active growth.

The vestry began to pay attention to details that had been long overlooked. Parishioners used braziers of hot coals to keep themselves warm in their pews during cold winter services. During the winter of 1806–1807, the vestry voted to install the first heating in the church, a stove placed in the middle aisle and using sea coal for fuel.[38] By 1810 the vestry had also been able to establish for the first time a permanent fund to support the rector, an issue that had been discussed at vestry meetings for a decade. By December of that year the vestry had raised the sum of $6,500 to be invested in bank stock until dividends brought the principal up to ten thousand dollars. When the fund reached this amount, the annual dividends were to be used to pay part of the rector's salary. Shortly after it was established, a bequest from Samuel Brown of Boston raised the fund to eleven thousand dollars.

Dehon's repeated visits to Charleston had established many friends for him there and brought him repeated invitations to stay permanently in South

Carolina. He refused them all until December 1810, when St. Michael's Church in Charleston (whose building was probably designed by Trinity's former parishioner Peter Harrison) asked him to become its rector.[39] Leaving Newport and accepting this post, Dehon soon became the second bishop of South Carolina, serving from 1812 until his premature death from yellow fever in 1817. By the time of his departure from Newport, Dehon had fully reestablished the parish, completing the work that John Bours had begun in 1781. As Henry Bull recalled in 1842, "Mr. Dehon proved very acceptable to the society, which again united in the bonds of harmony and Christian fellowship, flourished and increased to an overflowing congregation. The pews were again all occupied to a degree almost equal to what they had been in the days of Mr. Honyman."[40]

It had taken a full thirty years for Trinity Church parish to adapt and to recover from its devastating losses from the ravages of the Revolution.

Notes

1. Robert Prichard, *A History of the Episcopal Church* (Harrisburg, PA: Morehouse, 1991), pp. 82–83.
2. Mason, *Annals*, pp. 166–67, listing the individual names of the pew owners.
3. Ibid. p. 169: Letter from Bours to the Wardens, Vestry, and Congregation, 26 July 1784.
4. John S. Ezell, ed., *The New Democracy in America: Travels of Francisco de Miranda in the United States, 1783–84.* trans. by Judson P. Wood (Norman: Univ. of Oklahoma Press, 1963), p. 139.
5. Ibid.
6. F. Edward Beardslee, *Life and Correspondence of the Rt. Rev. Samuel Seabury, D.D.* (Boston: Houghton Mifflin, 1881), p. 206.
7. See details on de Ternay's grave and monument in *Semper Eadem*, vol. II-A and B.
8. Mason, *Annals*, pp. 173–74: Letter from Samuel Parker to Messrs. Bours and Malbone, 15 August 1785.
9. Ibid., p. 175.
10. Pritchard, *History of the Episcopal Church*, p. 90.
11. Kenneth Walter Cameron, *The Younger Doctor William Smith 1754–1821: The Role of Seabury's Brilliant Scottish Presbyter in the Formative Period of the Diocese of Connecticut: A Divinity Story* (Hartford, CT: Transcendental Books, 1980), p. 12.
12. Ibid., pp. 179–80: Letter from Seabury to committee of the congregation of Trinity Church, 17 July 1786.
13. Ibid.
14. Ibid.
15. "Memoir of Trinity Church, Newport, R.I., compiled by Henry Bull, Esq., at the request of the Rector, Rev. Francis Vinton. Recorded by John Sterne, Esq. In 1841–42."
16. Mason, *Annals*, p. 186 footnote: undated draft letter to Seabury.
17. [James Sayre] *A Candid Narrative of certain Matters relating to Trinity-Church in New Port, in the State of Rhode Island, by James Sayre, A.M, late Minister of said Church: With a view of correcting the Egregious Misrepresentations of Mr. John Bours, contained in a Letter addressed to the Author in the Newport Herald of October 9th 1788* (Fairfield: Forgue & Bulkeley, 1788). [John Bours] *An Appeal to the Public; in which the Misrepresentations*

and Calumnies contained in a pamphlet entitled 'A Narrative of Certain Matters relative to Trinity Church, in Newport, in the State of Rhode Island,' by a very extraordinary man, the Rev. James Sayre, A.M., late Minister of said Church, are pointed out and his very strange conduct during the time of his ministration at Newport, faithfully related. By John Bours, Merchant, and one of the Vestry of said Church (Newport: Peter Eades at the office of the *Newport Herald*, 1789).

18. Cameron, *The Younger Doctor William Smith 1754–1821,* p. 40; See also, Archives of the Diocese of Rhode Island, Special Collections, University of Rhode Island, Kingston: Series "Other Churches," Box 51.

19. Quoted in Bruce Steiner, *Samuel Seabury, 1729–1796: A Study in the High Church Tradition* (Athens: Ohio Univ. Press, 1971), p. 336.

20. Pritchard, *History of the Episcopal Church*, p. 96.

21. [William Smith] *A Discourse at the Opening of the Convention of Clerical and Lay Delegates of the Church, in the State of Rhode Island, delivered in Trinity Church, Newport, Thursday, the 18 of November 1790. Psalm cxxii, 7–9. By William Smith, A.M., Rector* (Newport, Rhode Island, 1790).

22. Mason, *Annals,* pp. 198–99: Letter from Seabury to Rhode Island Clergy, 1 December 1790.

23. Mason, *Annals of the Redwood Library*, p. 76.

24. Ibid., pp. 208–209.

25. Ibid., pp. 162, 164, 165, 210.

26. Cameron, *The Younger Doctor William Smith 1754–1821*, p. 36.

27. William Smith, *A Discourse delivered Before the Grand Lodge of the Most Ancient and honorable Fraternity of Free and Accepted Masons of the State of Rhode Island and Providence Plantations in Trinity Church, Newport, on the 27th day of June 1791, celebrating the Festival of St. John the Baptist* (Providence, RI: Bennett Wheeler, 1794).

28. William Smith, *The Convict's Visitor: or, Penitential offices (in the antient way of liturgy) consisting of prayers, lessons and meditations, with suitable devotions before, and at the time of execution* (Newport, RI: Peter Edes, 1791).

29. Allan Forbes and Paul F. Cadman, *France and New England*, 3 vols. (Boston: State Street Trust Company, 1925–29), vol. 2, pp. 51–52.

30. Arthur Browne, Esq. "America," in *Miscellaneous Sketches: or, Hints for Essays* (London: G. C. & J. Robinson, J. Johnson, and R. Faulder, 1798) vol. 2, pp. 193–211.

31. Rev. Charles Stenhouse, *Historical Sketch and Directory of the First Methodist Episcopal Church, Marlboro Street, Newport* (Newport, RI: Milne Printery, 1903).

32. Mason, *Annals*, pp. 212–13: Letter from Rev. John S. J. Gardiner to Churchwardens and Vestry, Trinity Church, Newport, 11 September 1797.

33. Rhodes House, Papers of the U.S.PG., C/AM 9: Convention of the Protestant Episcopal Church of Rhode Island, meeting in Trinity Church, 11 July 1798.

34. [Theodore Dehon], *A Discourse delivered in Newport, Rhode Island, before the Congregation of Trinity Church, the Masonic Society, and the Newport Guards, the Sunday Following the Intelligence of the Death of General George Washington. By Theodore Dehon, A.M., Rector of Trinity Church* (Newport, RI: Henry Barber, 1800).

35. Mason, *Annals*, pp. 222–23.

36. Ibid., p. 243.

37. Arthur Howard Nichols, "The Bells of Trinity Church, Newport, R.I." (April 1916), pp. 147–49.

38. Mason, *Annals*, p. 263 and note.

39. Carl Bridenbaugh, *Peter Harrison: First American Architect.* (Chapel Hill: Univ. of North Carolina Press for the Institute of Early American History and Culture at Williamsburg, Virginia, 1949), pp. 63–67.

40. "Memoir of Trinity Church, Newport, R.I."

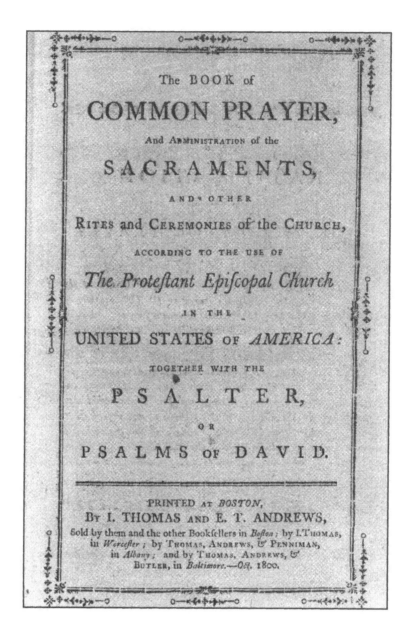

The BOOK of

COMMON PRAYER,

And Administration of the

SACRAMENTS,

AND OTHER

Rites and Ceremonies of the Church,

ACCORDING TO THE USE OF

The Proteftant Epifcopal Church

IN THE

UNITED STATES OF *AMERICA*:

TOGETHER WITH THE

PSALTER,

OR

PSALMS OF DAVID.

PRINTED AT *BOSTON*,
By I. THOMAS AND E. T. ANDREWS,
Sold by them and the other Bookfellers in *Bofton*; by I. Thomas,
in *Worcefter*; by Thomas, Andrews, & Penniman,
in *Albany*; and by Thomas, Andrews, &
Butler, in *Baltimore.—Oct.* 1800.

An 1800 edition of the American Book of Common Prayer. In 1789, the General Convention of the Episcopal Church adopted its first prayer book. For the major services, it was similar to the 1662 Book of Common Prayer that had been used throughout the colonial period. The 1789 version remained in use for more than a century from 1790 until 1892, but unlike later versions, it was subject to minor changes at each General Convention. These changes were reflected in succeeding standard editions, which appeared in 1793, 1822, 1832, 1838, 1845, and 1871. The 1892 Book of Common Prayer was replaced in 1928 and it, in turn, was replaced in 1979.

7

A Poor Parish in an
Impoverished Town, 1810–40

In the first half of the nineteenth century, Newport was a sleepy town. Its earlier preeminence as one of North America's leading commercial ports had vanished, leaving it in what would eventually become picturesque decay, but beset with serious social and economic problems. An English traveler, Adam Hodgson, noted in 1821 that "one of the churches in Newport is now more than an hundred years old; quite a piece of antiquity in this New World and there is a windmill 'tower' or something like it, which carries back the imagination of the natives to very distant times as their antiquaries have not yet discovered either its date or its object."[1] Additionally, he remarked that he had rarely seen "a more desolate place,"

> or one which exhibited more evident symptoms of decay. The wooden houses had either never been painted, or had lost their paint, and were going to ruin. A decent house, here and there, seemed to indicate, that some residents of respectability lingered behind; but the close habitations, with their small windows, and the narrow, dirty, and irregular streets, exhibited no trace of the attractions which once rendered this a summer resort for the planters from the South. . . . [A] few young men dropped in, in the course of the evening, but I soon found that, as usual in declining seaports, they were at a premium.[2]

Newport's island location no longer was an attraction to economic development as it had been in the mid-eighteenth century, when the island's wealth and economy had been based on maritime exchange. Established interests in Providence and elsewhere now blocked Newport's access to the new avenues of trade, which led inland first on roads and turnpikes, and then via the railroads. Most importantly, the Revolution had scattered the resourceful and determined merchants who had taken the risks necessary to build Newport into a successful entrepôt for the maritime trades. As another visitor noted in 1821, "Newport resembles an old and battered shield. Its scars & Bruises are deep & indelible. Commerce & all the Jews are fled. . . . The people are now so poor, that there are scarcely more than 10, or a dozen, who would have the courage to invite a stranger to his table."[3]

Following the Reverend Dehon's resignation in 1810, the parish schoolmaster, The Reverend John Ward, filled Trinity's pulpit for a short period, until a new rector could be appointed. During this period, in May 1810, the representatives of the twenty-two Episcopal churches in Massachusetts, Vermont, New Hampshire, Maine, and Rhode Island met in a convention at Boston to elect the first bishop of the newly created Eastern Diocese. The choice fell for the first time to a Rhode Island clergyman, The Reverend Alexander Viets Griswold, who had been rector of St. Michael's Church, Bristol, since 1804. Bishops William White of Pennsylvania, John Henry Hobart of New York, and Abraham Jarvis of Connecticut consecrated him at Trinity Church, New York City, a year later, in May 1811.

Meanwhile, in the summer of 1810, the clerk of the vestry, John Bours, had been in New Haven, where he met the rector of New Haven's Trinity Church, The Reverend Bela Hubbard. Hubbard suggested that Trinity might be interested in a young graduate of Yale, The Reverend Salmon Wheaton, as a candidate to succeed Dehon. Bours met Wheaton in New Haven and sent him to Newport with a letter of introduction to the churchwardens. For the previous two years, Wheaton had been assisting Hubbard at the New Haven church and had earned the recommendation of Bishop Jarvis of Connecticut. While negotiations were in progress with Wheaton, The Reverend John Ward left Newport, leaving Trinity without a clergyman. Arrangements were agreed upon, and Wheaton took up his duties in Newport on 1 November 1810. Reverend Dehon returned to Newport from Charleston for the occasion and delivered his last sermon in Trinity Church on 29 October 1810.[4]

Wheaton settled easily into the work of his new parish. Under Wheaton's guidance, a Quaker, John Rodman, became the schoolmaster of the Kay School. About the same time, John Springer became the sexton of the church, remaining in that position for thirty years, until 1840. The position of organist proved difficult to fill in these years, but Miss Mary Towle eventually took up the position, serving until she moved away in 1817. In other areas, Wheaton moved forward with the vestry on the plan that had earlier been established to raise funds for a permanent fund for the parish. By November 1811, the congregation had $6,050 in hand and invested.

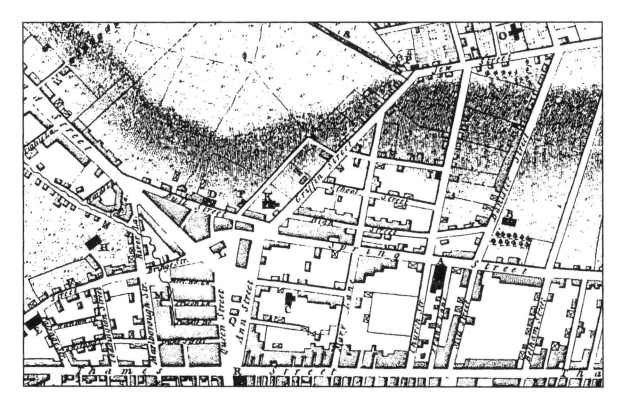

Newport in c. 1775.

"A" indicates Trinity Church on Spring Street.

*"B" indicates the First Congregational Meeting House on "Bannister" now
Mill, Street.*

"O" indicates The Redwood Library.

*"P" indicates "An Estate, the Donation of Nathanl Kay, late collector of his
Majesty's Customs, for the Support of an Assistant Minister in Trinity
Church & Schooling Ten poor Boys. "This is the land that was leased
for 999 years in 1833.*

*The minister's house, in use from 1753 to 1839, is shown on the map at the
corner of Griffen [Touro] Street and modern-day High Street.*

*"8" indicates a rope walk, the final portion of which was destroyed during the
Dorr Rebellion in 1844 and the space later turned into modern-day
Kay Street.*

*The building housing the parish's school for poor boys may be seen at the
corner of Division and Mary Streets.*

Enlarged detail from the map drawn by Charles Blaskowitz about 1774–75.

*William Faden published it in London in 1777. Print from George Champlin
Mason,* Extra Illustrated Reminiscences, *vol. 1.*

Collection of the Newport Historical Society.

Less than a year later, in September 1812, Wheaton married Dehon's sister, Ann, at Trinity Church, Boston. Within six months, as he had anticipated when he took the position in 1810, he found that his salary was insufficient to raise a family. The nation was then in the midst of the War of 1812, and Newport, like all of New England, was suffering from the Royal Navy's blockade of commerce. "It is with pain that I behold the gloomy state of our political affairs and calamities with which this town is visited," Wheaton wrote to the wardens in April 1813, "Under all these circumstances, it is not without much reluctance that I feel myself obligated to make further demands upon your goodness, in order that according to divine appointment, I may *live of the gospel*."[5] However justified Wheaton's request, the congregation felt that it could not afford to provide him additional income that year by raising pew taxes, due to "the distress of the times."[6] The rector and the vestry renewed their efforts to increase the fund to the point where it could directly benefit the church budget.

In the summer of 1814, the situation of the town was not good, and British forces threatened the region. As a precaution, Major General Sheldon asked and received permission from the parish to have the church bell rung and a signal lantern shown in the tower in case of an alarm. At the same time, sentries were placed in the church tower to guard against accidental fire in the steeple.[7] In August, the British burned Washington and began a major military effort in the area around Lake Champlain, but there were no major events in the Newport area aside from the tight coastal blockade.

To relieve the rector's financial situation, the vestry agreed to pass the collection plate immediately after the sermon every Sunday, increasing it from the monthly passing. Also, it advanced the rector fifty dollars on his salary and gave him a gift of ten cords of wood to heat the rectory. Even when the war ended and with it the immediate threat of invasion, the people of the parish remained in severe economic distress. The vestry conscientiously looked at every possible means of increasing the parish's income and reducing its debts. As part of this effort, the vestry realized that it could no longer effectively manage the church's property or operate on the basis of the 1769 charter of incorporation.

In May 1816, a committee began to draft new and revised articles, completing its work in October. The vestry submitted the revised charter to the Rhode Island General Assembly for its approval. With the approved document in hand in early November, the vestry immediately had the charter inscribed on vellum parchment and had the Rhode Island secretary of state authenticate the

Seal of Trinity Church.
In November 1816, the vestry first
authorized an engraved brass seal
for the Corporations use on official
documents.

document. Immediately moving to acquire the paraphernalia of a corporation, the vestry commissioned a brass circular seal for use with its official documents. It had a raised cross in the center, the head of which was surrounded by the words "God Send Grace," and the entire circle was surrounded with a band bearing the legend, "Trinity Church, Newport, R.I. Incorporated 1769."

In early January 1817, the corporation met in a special meeting to accept formally the charter as approved by the General Assembly. Putting its most crucial provision into effect, the vestry elected Samuel Fowler Gardner as the parish's first treasurer. He served until the next regularly scheduled annual meeting on Easter Monday. Moving quickly, the vestry also voted to liquidate three shares of its stock in the Rhode Island Bank, in order to meet outstanding debts. At the same time, the parish began legal action against Richard Harrison, who had variously damaged and destroyed the house, stable, fences, and out-buildings on the Kay estate, which he had taken on a 999-year lease from the church in 1796.

As a result of its reorganization, under Wheaton's direction the parish took a large number of actions in 1817. The seating arrangement within the church was altered so that the first four pews at the west end of the center aisle were reserved and labeled "For Strangers," mending the problem that Francisco de Miranda had experienced thirty years before. The financial circumstances of parishioners did not improve dramatically, and the practice of passing the plate every Sunday, even for a penny, was reduced to a quarterly event. In 1818, the spire was painted, and the wind vane and balls were gilded. In other changes, the vestry authorized painting the outside of the pews a "stone color" (they had earlier been a faux rosewood pattern), and it authorized whitewashing the outside of the church building. The vestry authorized that the Creed, Lord's Prayer,

Commodore Oliver Hazard Perry.
Baptized at Trinity on 13 January 1795, Perry and his wife occupied pew 14 in
the north aisle. In 1818, he served on a vestry committee to raise funds to repair
the church. Portrait by Samuel Mason. Collection of Redwood Library and Athenaeum.

and Commandments be lettered and gilded; it also passed a regulation that reflected the growing racial prejudice in the country—banned blacks from sitting in the lower pews.[8] At that time, the African-American members of the congregation were limited to the raised pews at the back of the north and south galleries.

To finance these changes, the vestry appointed a fund-raising committee consisting of four parishioners that included Commodore Oliver Hazard Perry and a future governor of the state, William C. Gibbs. As part of the resolution of its financial affairs, the parish reached an accommodation over the Kay estate in 1820 with Richard Harrison, receiving an income more proportionate to the higher current value of the property than that provided in the original 1796 agreement. Issues surrounding Harrison's lease of the Kay estate remained until 1830, when the family settled the matter by paying $1,200 and returning the property to the church.

Slowly, members of the congregation came to the conclusion that the parish needed to protect the permanent fund as an endowment and not allow the use of the principal for operating expenses. A committee was formed in 1823 to examine the issue, and in 1827 the parish petitioned the Rhode Island General Assembly for an act that established the fund "permanently and untransferable," except by a vote of three-quarters of the male members of the corporation, and "unimpaired and undiminished" by any act of the corporation.[9] In order to clarify procedural matters, the General Assembly further modified the charter in June 1828.[10]

Though the parish had wisely established and protected its small endowment fund, the financial condition of the parish, like that of Newport in general, was so poor that there was not enough money to carry out all the projects that many may have wished for. During his early years, Wheaton had repeatedly asked for an increase in his salary to support more fully his own activities; while the vestry acknowledged the merits of his case, they could not responsibly approve further expenditures from their severely limited resources. The members of the parish were in such difficult financial straits that pew taxes were reduced to five dollars a year; even at this level, many parishioners could not afford the expense, leaving a number of pews to revert to the church. The vestry offered to sell pews in the gallery at ten dollars apiece, with an annual tax of one dollar, but could find no takers. Several attempts were made to reintroduce weekly collections at services, but these moves were repeatedly stymied by parishioners' lack of cash to make even the smallest donation on a weekly basis. To make ends meet, the parish treasurer regularly had to resort to small loans.

John Gilpin's watercolor sketches of Trinity Church, 1830. Collection of Redwood Library and Athenaeum.

The financial issues became even more acute after the spring of 1833, when a number of parishioners became so dissatisfied that they decided to form a parish of their own, one with greater evangelical spirit and activity. This reflected the continuing debate among Episcopalians between the "High Church" advocates, who stressed the apostolic succession and baptismal regeneration, and the "Evangelicals," who stressed adult renewal of faith.[11] The dissenters included a number of prominent and long-time members of the Trinity parish. Among the leaders of the new parish were T. C. Dunn, Alexander P. Moore, Charles H. Mumford, James Mumford, Henry Potter, Joshua Sayer, Jacob Smith, Stephan T. Northam, Silas Ward, and William Weeden. In February 1833 they named themselves Zion Episcopal Church, obtained the services of The Reverend John West as rector, and hired Russell Warren of Bristol to design a new building for them at the corner of Touro and Clarke Streets. Built by parishioner and master carpenter William Weeden, the new church was in the form of an Ionic prostyle temple, one of the very first Greek Revival buildings in Newport.

While some members of the congregation felt that there was enough interest in town to warrant two Episcopal parishes (at least one person originally intended to maintain pews in both), it did create practical difficulties. The creation of the new parish seriously weakened Trinity, drawing away some thirty families. In this same period, another twenty families left the parish for other churches, although newcomers to Trinity balanced the losses and increased the size of the parish by some 30 percent over what it had been at the outset of Wheaton's tenure in 1810. At the same time, however, the new Zion parish was faced with the very heavy financial burden of paying for its new building and providing for its own clergy and staff, a burden it could not sustain.

The financial crisis that all this created for Trinity led the vestry to turn to its 1734 endowment in land from Nathaniel Kay, land that had reverted to the parish in 1830 after the settlement of Richard Harrison's 1796 lease on the original eight-acre Kay estate. In 1833, the vestry once again leased the land for 999 years. This time, Lieutenant Governor George Engs leased the land from Trinity Church, for 999 years, for $3,300. Shortly thereafter, Engs proceeded to subdivide the land for the construction of summer homes: this was paralleled by development along Catherine Street and South Touro Street (Bellevue Avenue). This lease and other similar leases of property brought immediate cash to the corporation. In fact the parish and all of Newport benefited indirectly. These land developments began to bring Newport out of its long-term economic depression.

Zion Episcopal Church.
In February 1833, a group of parishioners left Trinity to establish the second
Episcopal parish in Newport. Russell Warren designed their new church building,
one of the first Greek Revival buildings in the city, at the corner of Clarke and
Touro Streets. It remains standing today as the Jane Pickens Theater. P2711
Collection of the Newport Historical Society.

The Trinity vestry continued to maintain its building and to pay its salaries, but despite cash inputs, it repeatedly borrowed money to do so. In one case, the vestry even refused to pay the $17.50 assessment levied by the diocese for an assistant for Bishop Griswold, who had become presiding bishop in 1836. At the same time, the vestry formally denied the right of the diocese or of the state Convention to tax Trinity; it agreed however, to pay a $12.50 assessment to defray the cost of printing the proceedings of the Convention.[12] Ever in search of funds, as well as trying to expand the accommodation for the African-American members of the parish, in 1836 the vestry rebuilt and put up for sale the pews the black members of the parish occupied in the south gallery getting ten dollars apiece for the newly refurbished bench pews.

Finally, at the annual parish meeting on 1 April 1839, the parish took radical action to reform its financial situation. The meeting authorized the creation of a committee, composed of all forty-one male lay members of the Corporation, to examine the state of the finances and recommend a new course of action. Within a month, the committee had reached a solution, which was quickly approved by the parish on 29 April. The new plan discontinued the total financial dependence of the rector on the corporation and instituted in its place a plan of annual contributions, much like that used by other religious organizations in Rhode Island. Taking into account the disparity of financial means within the parish, the new plan was "to allow such as are possessed of much to contribute in some proportion to their worldly means, to that which is wanted by the whole association."[13] As part of the plan, the parish shifted to supporting the rector from private and voluntary annual contributions. From this point, the corporation ceased to provide directly for the rector, beyond the annual interest received from the Permanent Fund and the benefit received from the use of a two-acre lot of land at the top of the hill, bounded by present-day Greenough Place and Catherine and Beach Streets. To pay existing debts, the parish sold the house at the corner of Touro and High Streets, which had been used as the rector's residence since 1753. In addition, it sold the house occupied by the sexton next to the schoolhouse, and also a portion of the Kay School lot that was not needed for the use of the school. To increase members, the parish decreased taxes on the pews to six dollars; incidental expenses were to be paid by instituting a monthly collection.

Immediately upon the Corporation's approval of these actions, Wheaton resigned as rector, with effect from Easter Monday 1840. Looking back on his thirty-year tenure, Wheaton noted that the church building had been maintained effectively and that he had been the key instrument in establishing the permanent fund. Despite the substantial loss of parishioners with the establishment of Zion Church in 1833, the parish had actually increased in size by a third since 1810 and the church funds had doubled in the same period. In resigning, Wheaton remarked, "I am gratified in knowing that I shall leave your Church in excellent repair, and well endowed, with a congregation large and able to sustain it."[14]

The new financial plan went into effect immediately. In Wheaton's final year the interest from the Permanent Fund was not sufficient to pay his usual salary, but parishioners donated to special subscriptions, collecting $236 to make up the deficit. For his final year, Wheaton was allowed to use the rectory rent-free, although the parish sold the building and its entire lot at public auction for $1,900. The south side of the school lot, with the sexton's house, brought three hundred dollars at auction. When these sales had taken place, the vestry finance committee reported that the church's assets then comprised the church building and its land, the school house and its lot (now reduced in size to

CHARTER

OF

Trinity-Church,

IN

NEWPORT, (R. I.)

WITH THE

CONSTITUTION

OF THE

PROTESTANT

EPISCOPAL CHURCH,

IN THE

STATE OF RHODE-ISLAND.

NEWPORT, (R. I.)

PRINTED BY WM. & J. H. BARBER,

1823.

1816 charter.
In October 1816, the parish revised its 1769 charter to conform to the laws of
the United States and the state of Rhode Island. In 1823, the parish printed two
hundred copies of its charter along with the diocesan constitution.

Collection of the Newport Historical Society.

twenty-five by forty-eight feet), a two-acre vacant lot at the top of the hill, the Permanent Fund of $10,640, and the Church Fund of $3,046.61. Inside the church, a large number of pews had reverted to the Corporation. The parish owned all but eight of the pews in the gallery and thirty pews on the ground floor, four of which housed stoves to heat the building.

The thirty-year period from 1810 to 1840 coincided with the period of Wheaton's rectorship of Trinity. Both the parish and the town were clearly marked by financial strain. By the 1830s, the situation was slowly beginning to change for the better.

Notes

1. Adam Hodgson, *Letters from North America, Written during a Tour in the United States and Canada* (London, 1824), vol. 2, pp. 134–35.
2. Ibid., pp. 132–33.
3. Gertrude Selwyn Kimball, ed., *Pictures of Rhode Island in the Past 1642–1833 by Travelers and Observers.* (Providence, RI: Preston & Rounds Co., 1900), p. 170.
4. Mason, *Annals,* pp. 277–85: Correspondence with and about Wheaton, July–October 1810.
5. Ibid., p. 302: Letter from Wheaton to Wardens, Vestrymen and Congregation, 12 April 1813.
6. Ibid., pp. 302–303: Committee of the Congregation to the Rector, 23 April 1813.
7. Ibid., p. 306.
8. Winthrop D. Jordan, *White over Black: American Attitudes toward the Negro, 1550–1812* (Chapel Hill: Univ. of North Carolina Press, 1968), pp. 414–26.
9. Ibid., pp. 345–46; George Champlin Mason, *Annals,* pp. 22–3.
10. Ibid., First series, pp. 346–47.
11. Pritchard, *A History of the Episcopal Church,* pp. 118–23.
12. Ibid., Second series, pp. 53–54.
13. Ibid., Second series, p. 62: Report of the Committee on Finances, 29 April 1839.
14. Ibid., pp. 64–65: Letter from Reverend Wheaton to the Corporation, 29 April 1839.

View of Trinity Church by J. P. Newell, c.1860.
On 4 May 1846, Thomas Pratt placed the following advertisement in the
Newport Daily News:

House to Let

The subscriber has several chambers to let in his house directly opposite Trinity
Church Burying Ground. There is probably no more desirable spot in Newport
for those whose souls are not entirely steeped in sin. . . . The occupant may sit at
the window and view that last home of man in all its mysterious and solemn
grandeur and seriously reflect upon the great uncertainty of all things human.

8

Renewed Vitality, Renewed Conflict, 1840–66

The installation of a new rector in 1840 happened to coincide with the beginnings of economic development for the entire Newport community, some of which was indirectly stimulated by Trinity, through its 999-year lease of the Kay estate. Like other organizations in town, Trinity began to show signs of vitality that had not been seen in three-quarters of a century. As this economic revival was taking place, the parish search committee to find a successor to Wheaton began meeting in October 1839. It found its prime candidate within a week.

He was Francis Vinton, born in Providence in 1809 the grandson of a Jacobite refugee from Scotland who had immigrated to Massachusetts in 1717. Vinton had graduated from the U.S. Military Academy at West Point in 1830. As a second lieutenant, he had served in the Indian wars at Fort Snelling, Minnesota, and in Georgia and Alabama, earning the thanks of Congress and a grant of land in Indiana for his services. While assigned to Fort Independence at Boston, he used his spare time to study law at the Cambridge Law School and was admitted to the bar at Portsmouth, New Hampshire, in 1834. Resigning from the army in 1836, he studied for the priesthood at the General Theological Seminary. Bishop Griswold ordained him a deacon in 1838 and priest in 1839. As a missionary, Vinton first organized the Church of the Ascension in Wakefield and soon took over additional responsibility for the services being held in Kingston. Shortly afterwards, the nascent St. Stephen's Church in Providence called him as its rector. Soon after, Trinity entered into negotiations with the intention of obtaining his services upon Wheaton's departure to take up the rectorship of St. Michael's Church, Johnston, New York. In November 1839, Vinton initially agreed to accept the post, at a salary of $1,250 per year. Vinton's reluctance to leave St. Stephen's in 1840, while its new building was barely started, as well as the death of his wife that year, delayed his arrival in Newport until Easter 1841.

Vinton's tenure at Trinity was brief, but it was marked by the rapid strengthening of the parish. While at Trinity he began his career as a noted

The Reverend Francis Vinton, rector of Trinity Church, 1840–44. An 1830 graduate of West Point, Vinton received the thanks of Congress for his service in the Indian Wars in Georgia and Alabama. Resigning from the army in 1836, he studied at the General Theological Seminary and was ordained a priest in 1839. While in Newport, he married Elizabeth Perry, the only daughter of Oliver Hazard Perry. He became a very well-known clergyman in New York City and professor of ecclesiastical law and polity at General Theological Seminary.

preacher, publishing his first sermons during this period, several of them combining his knowledge of military life and devotion to patriotic duty with his religious teaching.[1] While in Newport, Vinton married Elizabeth Mason Perry, a parishioner and the only daughter of the naval hero Oliver Hazard Perry. While her marriage to Vinton in 1841 deprived her of the fifty-dollar annuity for life that Congress had voted her on her father's death in 1819 (in an unprecedented provision for the care of a naval officer's dependents), she went on to a happy marriage that eventually produced twelve children.[2] During his tenure in Newport, Vinton inspired longtime vestryman Henry Bull to write the first memoir of the parish's history.[3] Vinton's four-year period in Newport coincided with the revival of Newport as a summer resort, the development of "the Top of the Hill" area, and Alfred Smith's opening of South Touro Street (later, Bellevue Avenue) for development.

A number of the southern summer residents were Episcopalians, and they began to attend services at Trinity. One of them, a member of one of Georgia's oldest leading families, was George Jones, whose ancestors had been among the staunch Anglicans who had been aides to Lord Oglethorpe in Virginia during the early eighteenth century. The Jones family plantation, "Wormsloe," south of Savannah, dated from that time. In 1839, George Jones purchased a

Jones offering plates.
Mrs. Sarah Jones presented these offering plates to the parish on Easter Day, 1843. Her son, George Noble Jones, built the house known as "Kingscote" in 1841. She died there in 1844 and is buried in the churchyard. The smaller plate is engraved on the bottom: "What shall I render unto the Lord for the benefits he hath done unto me? I will offer thee an oblation of Thanksgiving and call upon the name of the Lord. Trinity Church, Easter Day 1843, Presented by Mrs. Sarah Jones."

large lot in Newport on the corner of Bellevue Avenue and Bowery Street. There, in 1840-41, Jones commissioned the architect Richard Upjohn to build the first of Newport's elegant summer cottages (which under its second owners, the King family, came to be called "Kingscote" in 1880). Jones apparently intended the house as a year-round home for his widowed mother, Mrs. Noble Wimberly Jones II, and his younger sister.[4] In 1843, Mrs. Noble Jones donated a set of silver alms basins to the church, the first substantial gift of silver that the parish had received in nearly a century. On her death the following year, her son purchased a family burial lot at the northwestern edge of the churchyard along Church Street. He maintained a strong interest in the parish, serving on the vestry in 1845.

The Jones family was only one of several well-to-do summer Newport visitors who began to attend services at Trinity and to assist the parish in its work during the Vinton years. As a result, the parish was soon able to obtain the services of Henry Erben of New York, one of the most celebrated American organ makers of the day, to replace the working parts of the century-old instrument that George Berkeley had presented to the church. In mid-1844, Vinton resigned to take up the position of rector at Emmanuel Church in Brooklyn, New York. (The works of the old organ followed him, remaining in the antechapel there until that parish merged with Grace Church, Brooklyn. At that point the organ works returned to Rhode Island, remaining for nearly forty-five years at St. Mary's Church, Portsmouth, before they disappeared.)[5] Vinton went on to serve Trinity Church and All Saints Church, and to become a professor at the General Theological Seminary. In New York, he played a continuing role in the life of the Newport parish, encouraging many of his wealthy parishioners in New York to attend summer services at Newport. In addition, he played a key role in organizing the Sons of Rhode Island in that city, helping to strengthen the Episcopalian ties between New Yorkers and Rhode Islanders.

In October 1845, parishioner Henry Hunter, sitting in his family pew, wrote to his brother in the navy,

> Henry Davis, son of the cobbler down town preached in Trinity Church last Sunday. I thought I heard the indignant ghost of Godfrey Malbone thumping on the floor underneath. Our regular pastor, an eloquent, high-toned epicurean gentleman is sick from eating mushrooms.[6]

Going on, he commented, "I wish to present the church a transparent painting for the window over the altar, in place of the dirty white cotton curtain that hangs there to remind us of anything but the 'beauty of Holiness.' "[7]

In 1845, the parish selection committee considered a slate of six possible candidates to succeed Vinton as rector, finally selecting The Reverend Robert B. Hall of Plymouth, Massachusetts, for the position. In March 1846, the bishop of Rhode Island, The Right Reverend J. P. K. Henshaw, ordained and instituted Hall as rector of Trinity. At the outset of his rectorship, Hall moved to improve the methods of charity in the parish. One of his main concerns was to try to eradicate the public image of the Episcopal Church in general, as well as of Trinity parish, as a church of the rich rather than of the poor. Aware that donations would probably flow more readily if they were assigned to definite local projects rather than vaguely defined ones in other areas, Hall proposed several initiatives. First, he suggested that every donor to the church be informed of the object of his or her donation. Since 1816, for

The Reverend J. H. Black's annual report for 1865–66. The Reverend Black served as rector from 1863 to 1866; this is his annual report up to the time he resigned in April 1866. George Champlin Mason, Extra Illustrated Reminiscences, *vol. 5, p. 318-A.* Collection of the Newport Historical Society.

Receipt for one quarter's pew tax, 1 April 1840.
Junior warden Christopher Grant Perry signed this receipt for the three-dollar tax that the senior warden, George Champlin Mason, paid.

instance, the parish had annually distributed funds to the poor at Christmas, but this had always been done as an anonymous gift from the church. Secondly, in order to solve the long-standing issue of providing worship space for visitors and for the poor, he proposed that a portion of the offertory be used to rent the pews in the south gallery for the use of visitors and others who did not own pews. In this way, nearly a hundred seats became available, while the financial obligations to the corporation were also met. Finally, Hall proposed that the parish initiate its own local missionary work in Newport, by establishing a chapel for "a larger class of our community who will need to be reached by the blessed influence of the Gospel and the Church," as Hall wrote. "I refer, especially, to residents of the 'Point,' so called, where I am credibly informed, and am assured by observation likewise, that large numbers of families live without the means of grace."[8] Hall envisioned that this new ministry would require about half the annual plate collection. The remainder would still provide fifty dollars for the bishop's salary and seventy-five dollars for the support of music at Trinity and the Sunday School, support a donation to a mission in the West, and maintain the annual donation to the poor of Newport.

The corporation immediately approved Hall's plan and directed him to proceed with carrying it out. One of the first things that he did was to discontinue the use of the Kay School as a day school and to convert the building for use as a Sunday school. In connection with this change, the parish donated the schoolhouse bell to the newly-established parish of Holy Cross in Middletown. Hall was able to implement only part of his plan, as he soon became seriously ill. Less than six months later, he resigned to accept the rectorship of St. James Church at Roxbury, Massachusetts, due to the state of his health, "which had been so disastrously affected during his residence" in Newport.[9] Instead of proceeding further with Hall's financial plan, the vestry decided to place the donations and weekly offerings in an investment fund, until it reached the amount of five thousand dollars, for the sole purpose of repairing the church.

On 5 November 1846, the parish elected The Reverend Darius Richmond Brewer of Concord, New Hampshire, to succeed Hall, with effect from the first Sunday in December. When he took up his duties, one of the aspects of the parish that deeply concerned Brewer was its narrow definition of membership in the church. In June 1847, the vestry had requested and received the approval of the General Assembly to alter its charter, widening membership in the corporation from "each white male owner of a pew" to "each owner of a pew," either male or female, and allowing them to vote by proxy. A year later, Brewer went farther and asked that the vestry abolish pew ownership entirely. There were many people who wanted to do away with the ownership of pews, as it tended to bring inappropriate distinctions into the church and made it difficult for visitors and those who could not afford or obtain a pew to worship. "The practice was entirely unknown for the first fifteen hundred years of the Christian Church, and has not been common more than two hundred years." Brewer warned, "Unless Trinity is made free, an effort will be made to build another Church, upon that principle."[10] Despite the rector's strong feelings on the issue, the vestry postponed indefinitely any further consideration of the matter.

By 1848, Brewer found that due to the pew arrangement, Trinity could not accommodate the large number of people who wanted to attend church during the summer months. At the same time, there was a demand for visiting clergymen to preach at Trinity. Faced with this dilemma, Brewer came up with the idea of building a chapel, which could both relieve the situation at Trinity and provide a pulpit for visiting clergy. The Reverend Brewer privately arranged for purchase of land and for the construction of a free chapel on Church Street. Richard Upjohn designed the building, and it was built in 1850. In support of this work, Phoebe Bull, the daughter of longtime Trinity vestryman Henry Bull, was the largest contributor, donating $2,500.[11]

During the annual meeting of the corporation in April 1849, the parish appointed a committee to examine the physical condition of the church building and ascertain whether there were any funds belonging to the church that could be used for building repair. Within a week the committee made a full report to the parish, finding that the steeple needed extensive repairs and the building needed to be painted. The committee obtained estimates on the work to be done and found that the cost would be approximately $1,300. At the same time, it reported that there were no funds readily available for building repairs.

In this context, the committee brought attention to what it considered the parish's recent misuse of the 1734 Kay endowment and its neglect of the donor's intentions in making the bequest. In a detailed report, the committee traced the history of the Kay donation, showing that for many years the parish had fulfilled Nathaniel Kay's intention to use the rents and income from his lands to support the education of ten poor scholars in the principles of the Episcopal Church. Due to the difficulty in obtaining regular payment of the rents and the further problem of obtaining an episcopally ordained schoolmaster, as

All Saints Chapel.
Trinity's rector The Reverend Darius Brewer built this private, free chapel on
Church Street in 1850 to protest against the owned-pew system. In 1858, it was
moved to the corner of Cottage Street and Old Beach Road, where it soon
became the center of a major controversy within the parish. P2709. Collection of the
Newport Historical Society.

required in Kay's will, members of the vestry had gradually forgotten the original purpose for which this income was intended as it dealt with other financial problems. The committee lamented that if it had been maintained as intended, in 115 years it "would have constituted a magnificent endowment for a high school—a school, which would have contributed to the prosperity of the Town, as well as the prosperity of the Church." The committee went on to point out, "This fund, like all charitable funds, belonged to the poor. It was an estate placed under the guardianship of the rich, to be devoted to the education of the poor. Whatever amount has been heretofore taken from this fund, has been so much taken from the poor."[12] The surviving remnant of the Kay bequest consti-tuted the Church Fund. This fund could not be used for building repairs, but must be reserved for charitable purposes. The committee pointed out that while changed circumstances might justify deviations from the literal application of a bequest, they did not justify the complete nullification of a donor's wishes. Since the Kay bequest was "a sacred trust in their hands to be devoted to a special purpose," it could not be used for the proposed maintenance of the building, which would have to be dealt with by donations for that purpose or from weekly collections.[13] As a result of this report, the corporation voted to reconstitute the Kay Fund, restoring it to the original purposes.

By the 1840s, Newport had developed some industry. Several cotton mills had been built on the southern shore of Newport Harbor, and the workers employed in them began to build homes in that area, expanding the city to the southward in what would much later become known as "the Fifth Ward." As this part of the city expanded, several people began to be concerned about the religious welfare of the workers. In October 1850, Brewer became interested in establishing an Episcopal mission there, establishing it on the same free system that he had unsuccessfully proposed for Trinity two years earlier but was using at All Saints Chapel. Three Trinity parishioners became the key figures in promoting this work. Once again, Phoebe Bull was a leading figure; she was joined by Elizabeth Wormeley, the daughter of Rear-Admiral Ralph Randolph Wormeley, Royal Navy, who had retired to live in Newport, and by Miss Char-lotte Tew. The mission work began in a building that had formerly been used by the Free Will Baptists and soon became known as Emmanuel Church. In Sep-tember 1851, the three ladies arranged for a collection to be taken at Trinity for the benefit of this mission. Brewer officiated at the services there, in addition to his work with the regular Trinity parish.

As an experiment in 1851, Brewer arranged for The Reverend John L. Gray to hold services at Emmanuel for three months. They were so successful that in the following year, Brewer engaged The Reverend Kensey Stewart to fill that position for three years, on a salary of five hundred dollars, raised by subscription. When Stewart resigned to accept a call from a parish in Virginia, Brewer took up the duties at Emmanuel again. Between 1 June and 1 October 1854, Brewer and the vestry arranged for the weekly collections at Trinity to be designated for constrcting a new church building at the corner of Spring and Dearborn Streets. Trinity vestrymen Samuel Powel, Marshall Slocum, and Edward King served as the building committee for the project and collected the funds for the parish.

By April 1855, Brewer had still not been able to find an assistant to take on the work at Emmanuel. He was having difficulty coping with the work of both parishes, and he found in particular that the demands that Trinity placed on him had become too onerous. "I do not feel myself equal to it, either in body or mind," Brewer wrote.

> The amount of pastoral duty is so great, the necessity of hard
> study in preparation for the pulpit is so constant, the congrega-
> tion, especially during the summer is so large, and is made up
> of such a variety of character and taste, that my strength is often
> exhausted without meeting their wishes.[14]

Feeling that he could more effectively handle the work at Emmanuel, in April 1855 Brewer resigned as rector at Trinity after eight years of service to take up his part-time job on a full-time basis. Brewer oversaw the completion of the new building, which was inaugurated in June 1856 when the bishop of Rhode Island celebrated the marriage of Brewer and Charlotte Tew, principal donors of the new church and chief activists in promoting its work.[15] Regular Sunday services began two days later. After three further years at Emmanuel, Brewer succeeded, with the continuing financial support of Trinity parishioners, in putting Emmanuel on a self-supporting basis.

In April 1857, Brewer formally wrote to the senior warden at Trinity thanking the parish for the "long continuance of its nursing care and protection" for Emmanuel. Brewer reported that Emmanuel could now care for its own needs through the contributions of its own parishioners and no longer needed to be a drain on Trinity's resources.[16]

In the meantime, Trinity selected The Reverend Alexander G. Mercer as the new rector, to succeed Brewer. Coinciding with this change in clergy, many new ideas, approaches, and complaints were circulated within Trinity. Among the first changes in 1855 were two new memorials added to the church walls, remembering Georgina Clarke Pell and Commodore Oliver Hazard Perry. At the same time, other parishioners began to object to the fumes from the stove used for heating in the winter. Fourteen prominent ladies of the parish petitioned the vestry in November 1855, refusing to attend services in the winter unless better ventilation could be introduced. Investigations were made into feasibility of digging out a cellar to a depth that would accommodate a furnace. Others petitioned to keep carriages from passing along Spring Street in the vicinity of the church during services. Examinations were made to alter the old pew arrangement and to create "slips" in their place. To mark his own rectorship, Mercer presented to the parish a pair of silver goblets to be used for Communion; they were first used on Easter Sunday 1857. In another change, gas lighting replaced candlelight in 1858.

The church building, then 130 years old, must have seemed antique and out of fashion to Mercer. From the time of his arrival at Trinity, he had been uncomfortable preaching from the high pulpit, with its sounding board suspended overhead. First, he had the sounding board raised, but when this did nothing to relieve its "depressing effect" on him he had it removed, to the consternation of many parishioners in the years between 1855 and 1859. The parish stored the sounding board, but in order to get it out of the building, it had to be sawed in two. The congregation continued to protest, and Mercer reluctantly restored the sounding board to its rightful place in 1859. Today, the underside of the sounding board has a smooth surface, betraying no sign of the tumult of the 1850s. One can speculate that perhaps the underside of the sounding board once had the "Union Jack" pattern of paneling that seems to characterize Richard Munday's work (as it can still be seen under the balcony at the Colony House, under the sounding board at the Seventh Day Baptist Meeting House, and on the ceiling of the two pews at the back of Trinity); if so, it was probably lost during its replacement in 1859.

The sounding board was not the only controversy that Mercer encountered. Two more major issues arose nearly simultaneously, one surrounding All Saints Chapel and the other around the question of whether or not to construct a new building. Both were tied to Trinity's growing size, particularly during the summer months.

The Reverend Alexander G. Mercer, rector of Trinity Church, 1855–60.

The Mercer chalices. The Reverend Alexander Mercer ordered this pair of communion chalices from New York, and they were first used at Easter, 1857. A century later, Trinity's clergy felt they were too tall for use and unsuccessfully fitted one of them with a weight to convert it to a vase.

In order to deal with the increasing size of the parish, the idea of either enlarging the present church or building a new one came before the vestry. The committee circulated a questionnaire to parishioners and pointed out,

> The enlargement of the present building would be attended by almost insurmountable obstacles; and if it could be effected, would involve an expense disproportionate to the advantage accruing from it. The erection of a new building, therefore, forces itself upon us as a matter of necessity. There are obvious reasons why the Church should be built of stone, and after the model of the old English parochial churches, as best adapted to Episcopal worship.[17]

The committee pointed out that the 1724-26 building could be torn down and a new one built on the old site but that this would be very difficult to do without injuring and disturbing the old graves. From the committee's point of view, the only practical option was a new building on a new site. Supporting this view, Mercer wrote to the vestry that he opposed demolishing the old church: "It is a venerable relic, which it is a sort of virtue to preserve; and to destroy it would do violence to many hearts."[18] When the matter was put before parishioners in May 1858, they overwhelmingly opposed either expanding the church or building a new church on a new site. The proposition quickly died, in the face of the strongest possible opposition.

Several months after this crisis receded, seventy ladies of the parish presented a petition to the vestry in response to a rumor that Mercer was about to resign and to accept a call to "a Church of much greater influence and importance than our own."[19] As a result of this petition, the vestry appointed senior warden George Champlin Mason to call on the rector to discuss the situation and find out if there was anything that was objectionable at Trinity that the vestry could remedy. While Mercer made no public reply to the petition, the vestry immediately granted him his request to preach at the chapel during the summer months and at any other time that he found convenient.

The chapel soon became the next crisis. The origin of the issue went back a few years. In the spring of 1857, shortly after Brewer had announced that Emmanuel Church was able to proceed on its own finances, Brewer had decided to sell his financial interests in this private chapel to Mercer for four thousand dollars, to finance Emmanuel's new spire. Trinity parishioners raised the required sum by subscription, the sale took place, and Mercer operated the chapel,

Emmanuel Church as it appeared c. 1880–1900.
Three ladies from Trinity Church, Miss Phoebe Bull, Miss Charlotte Tew, and
Miss Elizabeth Wormeley, worked to create an Episcopal Mission among the
factory workers in the southern end of Newport in 1850. Attracted by their
work, Trinity's rector, The Reverend D. Richmond Brewer, resigned in 1855
and married Charlotte Tew to carry on the ministry at Emmanuel.
Photo Courtesy of Emmanuel Church.

at first along the lines of a free chapel for summer visitors that Brewer had initially envisaged. Soon, however, Mercer began to reverse Brewer's earlier practice and to send the visiting clergy to Trinity, while he habitually took the summer services at the chapel. While the parish was not entirely happy with this, the vestry continued to approve his preference to preach in the chapel rather than at Trinity. Beginning in the spring of 1858, as the controversy over a new building for Trinity was in progress, parishioners began to question Mercer's motives, but the matter did not break out into a full-fledged controversy until Mercer decided to move the chapel from its Church Street location to a new lot at the corner of Beach and Cottage Streets, enlarge it by adding transepts, and finance the move and the alterations through pew rentals to wealthy summer visitors. When Mercer's decisions in regard to the chapel became more widely known throughout the parish, fundamentally changing the basis upon which the chapel had been established, many parishioners began to oppose Mercer.

TRINITY CHURCH.

Woodcut of Trinity Church.
This woodcut by Whitney Jonelyn-Annin, Jr., was originally made for George Champlin Mason's 1854 book Newport and Its Early History *and used subsequently in many publications. George Champlin Mason,* Extra Illustrated Reminiscences. Collection of the Newport Historical Society.

The matter simmered until the spring of 1860. In March, Mercer proposed a plan "to produce harmony unaffected and cordial" with the parish. To achieve this, Mercer suggested that the rector be given two additional months of vacation, that the vestry appoint an assistant who could preach in the absence of the rector, and that the bishop of Rhode Island alternate with the rector during the summer months in preaching at the chapel and the church. Consideration of the matter was put off until the annual meeting on Easter Monday.

At the annual meeting, Mercer's plan failed to bring harmony or agreement. During a series of highly charged meetings, the corporation passed several closely divided resolutions, but it agreed unanimously that the parish recognized no other building for public worship except "the Church edifice" and the school on Church Street, clearly excluding the chapel as part of the parish. The course of the proceedings was interrupted when both the secretary and president of the corporation resigned. Nevertheless, vestryman Charles Hunter introduced a formal protest against the rector's plan, pointing out that the rector's intentions involved a marked deviation from the parish's accustomed mode of procedure. The plan created a rivalry between a new, private chapel and an old established church, separating rich from poor. The plan placed Trinity at a disadvantage, diminishing its strength, while the rector benefited from the exclusive control of finances in a privately pewed and rented chapel. Furthermore, the critics pointed out, the rector had proceeded in developing the chapel into a full-fledged parish without consulting the bishop, allowing it to also diminish the strength of the other existing Episcopal churches serving the community, Zion and Emmanuel.[20]

Following the introduction of this protest, a letter from the rector was read, withdrawing his plan. Charles Hunter then introduced a motion requesting the rector's resignation, noting that "the connection of The Reverend A. G. Mercer with Trinity Church has led to unhappy differences, and we fear, incurable disturbances" within the parish.[21] The motion failed to pass by a vote of thirty-four to thirty, whereupon the senior and junior wardens, the secretary, the treasurer, and six vestrymen resigned. Two days later, on 21 April 1860, Mercer formally resigned as rector.

Mercer's resignation from Trinity did not end the conflict over All Saints Chapel. Two weeks before, the vestry of Zion Church had submitted a formal protest to the bishop of Rhode Island noting that Mercer's operation of the private chapel had adversely affected Zion Church, reducing attendance and collections by 20 percent in comparison to previous years. After Mercer reported to the bishop that he intended to open his chapel as usual in the coming season, the bishop called for a meeting between Mercer and the rectors of Zion and Emmanuel Churches. Shortly thereafter, 120 members of Trinity Church presented a petition to the bishop requesting a full investigation of the matter.

A week after Mercer's resignation from Trinity, Bishop Thomas March Clark held the investigation, convening in a room at the Aquidneck House a hearing that was attended by vestrymen and parishioners from all three of Newport's Episcopal parishes. After prolonged discussion and debate, Bishop Clark ruled that under the canons of the Episcopal Church he could not allow All Saints Chapel to open without the consent of both Trinity Church and Zion Church, since the chapel and those two churches were all in Newport's Third Ward. Zion had already lodged its disapproval, and following the meeting at Aquidneck House, Trinity's vestry met and passed a resolution that reiterated the protest that had been registered and approved at the Trinity's 19 April annual meeting.

In reaction to this decision, the supporters of All Saints Chapel petitioned the Newport City Council, at its regular monthly meeting on 1 May 1860, to alter the boundary between the Third and the Fourth Wards. Under Bishop Clark's ruling, the boundary of the ward was the key issue. Altering the boundary placed the chapel in a ward that contained no other Episcopal church, and therefore there would be no objection under the canon law that the bishop had applied. Aware of this reasoning, the City Council agreed and altered the boundary so that the chapel, located at the southeast corner of Cottage and Beach Streets, was in the Fourth Ward.

Following the City Council's action, a group of former Trinity Church parishioners reported to Bishop Clark that they had been "driven to leave Trinity Church by a series of unparalleled outrages, such as no Christian Man can submit to." In order to find "peace and growth in Christianity," they petitioned the bishop and the Standing Committee of the diocese to establish a fourth parish in Newport at All Saints Chapel. On consideration of this request, the bishop and the Standing Committee, acting in council on 12 May 1860, requested that all the parties to the dispute withdraw their petitions, as the first step in resolving the conflict. By this, the diocese requested All Saints to withdraw its petition to form a new parish, while Zion and Trinity were both requested to withdraw their objections.

All parties to the dispute were dissatisfied with the diocesan Standing Committee's approach. The "Chapelites," as they had now become known, proceeded to name their parish "Christ Church, Newport," but in deference to the bishop they agreed to suspend their request for three days to see if Trinity and Zion complied. In the meantime, the Trinity vestry carefully considered the situation and decided to reject the request, "compelled by a sense of duty to continue their protest."[22] Although Zion Church did not make a formal response to the bishop's request immediately, the diocese proceeded to develop a new plan to solve the problem. In their decision, the bishop and the Standing Committee announced that a new parish was not necessary in Newport and withheld their consent to the petition to establish Christ Church, asking that the petitioners withdraw their request. The bishop and the Standing Committee then proceeded to propose informally that the diocese purchase the building and property at the corner of Cottage and Beach Streets by autumn. With this suggestion, they intended to remove the objections to a private chapel, placing its use under the joint control of the rector and wardens of Trinity, Zion, and Emmanuel Churches, and allowing Mercer to continue using it during the summer of 1860. Under the bishop's plan, the chapel would revert to being a free chapel, without rented or owned pews, sharing the collections among the three parishes.

The objections continued, and in June 1860, the diocese expressed reluctance to close the chapel entirely, while at the same time it declined to redefine the parochial limits of the Newport Episcopal churches in a manner that would make the chapel a fully independent parish. Reversing its previous suggestion, the diocese allowed Mercer's services, "so long as the Chapel is held as private property, the revenues to be applied at the sole discretion of the owner, liable to be occupied by a clergyman subject to no control, as far as the management of the chapel is concerned . . . ; it not being requisite that he should even be connected with the diocese."[23] Following this, the corporation of Trinity Church met and agreed to authorize the vestry to withdraw its protest in regard to All Saints Chapel. At the same time, the corporation passed a resolution that approved the vestry's previous actions in making its protest, on the grounds that it had been based upon statements of fact regarding the interests and rights of the parish.

With the situation temporarily relieved, in the summer of 1860 the parish proceeded with its search for a new rector. The bad effects of the dispute over All Saints Chapel lingered on, casting a pall over all the Episcopal churches

Pew 37
This late-nineteenth-century photograph shows the paneling in this pew and also one of the gaslight fixtures installed in 1858.

Trinity Church Choir, 1861.

in Newport. Zion Church took no action to remove its protest, and in the midst of their own debate over this issue, Zion's rector resigned to accept another call. Unable to find a clergyman who would accept a call to Newport in this situation, the Trinity vestry elected the bishop of Rhode Island as its rector and voted "that he be urged to accept the call, as indispensable to the peace and harmony of the churches of this city."[24]

Clark declined to accept the rectorship of Trinity, being then also the rector of Grace Church in Providence as well as bishop of Rhode Island. Upon receiving his letter in early April declining the invitation, the annual meeting of the corporation immediately elected The Reverend Oliver H. Prescott as rector for one year. Prescott waited four months to reply formally, and when he wrote to the wardens and vestry to accept the rectorship, he carefully noted that he was "reserving to myself the right of resignation thereof whenever it may seem to me expedient."[25] During the eleven months between Mercer's resignation and the date when Prescott took up his duties as rector, thirty-three different clergymen officiated at Trinity's services.

In the meantime, on 11 June 1861, Bishop Clark and the Standing Committee of the diocese had consented to the establishment of All Saints Parish in Newport, completely reversing the position they had taken in the previous year and without consulting the other parishes in Newport. While disappointed in this action and puzzled by the reversal in policy, the Trinity vestry decided quietly to cease contention in the matter. Five weeks later, however, Bishop Clark issued a pastoral letter, which was apparently read aloud only to the Trinity congregation. The bishop devoted the entire letter to the controversy surrounding All Saints Chapel, appealing to all to cease from further contention and noting that

> in the case before us we have exhausted every possible device
> to settle the controversy by counsel and fraternal appeal, and,
> failing in all these efforts, we have reluctantly consented to the
> organization of a new Church, as the only way to secure perma-
> nent peace, and to provide for the opening of the Chapel during
> the summer months, which we have always considered to be
> very desirable.[26]

Surprised by the bishop's unexpected public letter, the Trinity congregation took great offense at it. Two weeks later, the vestry replied in a firmly worded letter declaring that while disagreeing with the bishop, "as 'loyal Churchmen we have submitted to your decision without cavil or opposition.' We therefore consider your Pastoral Letter as uncalled for, and its reprimands and admonitions not deserved by the congregation." Noting the fact that the country was in the midst of a civil war, the vestry remarked, "In the present unhappy state of our country, we seek comfort and consolation in the religious services of our Church, and, at least, we hope to find peace and tranquility within the bounds of our Sanctuary."[27]

Further exchanges between the bishop and the parish fully defined the motivations behind the actions that each had taken and revealed some basic misunderstandings on both sides. The vestry was not aware that some members of the parish had privately communicated with the bishop, falsely accusing him of collusion with Mercer and gaining financial benefit from the chapel. At the same time, the vestry had not understood that the bishop fundamentally opposed Mercer's plan for the chapel and had unsuccessfully implored him to abandon it. By the end of August 1861, mutual confidence and good will was restored between the parish and the diocese, but further turmoil continued in the parish. By the autumn of 1861, two new issues had arisen: music and the selection of a permanent rector.

In December 1861, the parish's committee on music reported that a boys' choir could furnish all the music needed by the parish. The current organist, Mr. Tourgee, had been unable to devote time to training a boys' choir. In his place, the vestry appointed Henry S. Cutler, the director of music at Trinity Church, New York, to the adjunct position of director of music at Newport. To do this, the vestry granted Cutler the authority to hire a deputy, but payment and all responsibility for the parish's music remained with Cutler. At the same time, the committee recommended that a thousand dollars be spent in making permanent repairs to the organ. A piano was purchased and placed in the schoolhouse for the use of the organist in "drilling" the choir. By January 1863, however, this arrangement had proved to be a failure. At that point, in addition to the outlay for organ repairs and purchase of a piano, the parish was spending seven hundred dollars a year for the choir, a greater cost than any other Protestant church in Newport, and getting a product that brought only criticism from all quarters. "Music is a most important element in the worship of the Episcopal Church," the committee reported, "but the Style of music now in use in Trinity Church is wanting in devotional influences, too monotonous in its character, insufficient

Pew deed.
On 27 June 1857, Jesse Chase sold pew 79 to Daniel B. Fearing for $475.
B2-F19. Collection of the Newport Historical Society.

and defective in its execution, and is in no wise calculated to promote the high and holy purpose for which it was designed." In its place, the vestry approved the committee's recommendation of "The Psalms and Hymns and Chants of the Prayer Book, in the order of its arrangement, sung to the most approved and popular tunes, long in use and familiar to all."[28] The arrangement with Cutler in New York was soon terminated, and control returned to the vestry.

Meanwhile, a dispute was growing over the rector. In April 1861, the vestry had appointed Prescott for one year. Early the following year, the corporation met to consider his permanent appointment. On 7 February 1862, a meeting was held in which sixteen corporation members were present, holding a total of thirty-one proxies. This meeting voted to elect Prescott permanently as the rector, but many parishioners considered it a "packed vote." The meeting had been hastily organized at an unusual time, when several key members of the parish were out of town. A few weeks later, at the annual meeting on Easter Monday, the corporation considered a motion to rescind the proceedings of the February meeting as illegal, since no quorum had been present. When brought to a vote, the motion failed to pass, but only by the slimmest margin. The parish was clearly divided in its opinion of Prescott.

In early April 1862, Prescott refused, in these circumstances, to give a decisive answer to the invitation; he accepted it only with the qualification that he could resign at any time and that he would not be formally instituted as rector. A month later, the issue was still a matter of concern; a motion was tabled indefinitely, calling for a minister who would command an almost unanimous vote of the corporation.

In the months that followed there were a number of clashes between the rector and the vestry. During the summer of 1862, Reverend Prescott informed the vestry that the Sanitary Commission's Portsmouth Grove Hospital for the war wounded, located at present-day Melville and under Lady Superintendent Kate Prescott Wormeley of Newport, had offered him an appointment as its chaplain. Prescott had requested an extended three-month summer vacation to fulfill the post, if he should decide to accept it. The vestry, however, declined to consider his request until he made up his mind whether or not he would accept that position.

Then, in January 1863, the vestry began to question the rector's distribution of some of the Christmas offering to the poor, something that the vestry had done itself for the past forty years. After several requests, Prescott declined to give a detailed accounting, only asserting that he had made the distribution in accordance with the canons of the church. Several meetings and exchanges took place, but the rector refused to join with the vestry in distributing the portion of the Poor Fund that remained in its hands and declined to identify the recipients of his own distribution. Finally, the vestry proceeded to distribute the funds without knowing whether or not there was any duplication, but this was followed by continued debate over the proper manner in which to distribute alms. As a result of the dispute, Prescott announced in mid-January his intention to resign at Easter 1863. Upon receiving permission from the bishop, Prescott informed the corporation that he would resign ten days after being informed that his successor had been selected.

At the annual meeting at which this occurred, the corporation elected George Champlin Mason as senior warden. He had previously held this post in 1855–59, but with this election he began the longest term of any senior warden up to that time, remaining in office for twenty-six years, from 1863 to 1889. Under his stewardship, many key decisions were made. He was strongly seconded by the junior warden, Samuel Engs, who served from 1863 until his death in 1886. Their first task in bringing calm to the parish was to form a search committee to select a new rector.

By June 1863, the search committee had called a Reverend Eccleston of Newark, New Jersey, as the new rector. However, Eccleston did not reply to the call. The vestry then discharged the committee and formed a new search committee. While the search for a new rector was going on, Clement C. Moore, one of Trinity's prominent parishioners, died at the age of eighty-three on 10 July 1863. Moore, the son of a bishop of New York, The Right Reverend Benjamin Moore (1748–1816), had spent a distinguished academic career as professor of Greek and Hebrew literature at the General Theological Seminary in New York City. He had compiled a dictionary and written several academic books, but even in his day he was most famous for having written the classic American Christmas poem for children "The Night before Christmas." Moore had retired from General Theological Seminary in 1850 and purchased a home in Newport the following year, located at the corner of Greenough Place and Catherine Street, part of the old Kay lands that Trinity had leased to others for 999 years. Becoming a regular parishioner at Trinity, Moore purchased pew 59 from Mrs. Elizabeth C. Perry and remained in Newport until his death. On the Sunday following Moore's funeral in Trinity, Prescott preached and later published a memorial sermon for Moore, in what was Prescott's last major contribution to the parish.[29]

Just a week later, the new search committee unanimously selected The Reverend John H. Black of Sing Sing, New York, as Trinity's new rector. After meeting with a member of the committee, Black immediately accepted the offer and reported that he would take up his duties in August 1863. Immediately upon the corporation's approval of the selection, the vestry appointed a committee to inform Prescott that a successor had been chosen and arranged the date of 30 July for Prescott to pass on the official parish records that he had in his possession.

Trinity School,
Christmas Term.

Kay Scholars average on
examina &Term. Year.

Thomas Blackler - 95 - 9.66 - - -
George H. Carr - - - 67 - 8.06 - 8.28.
Benj. W. Hammond - 53 - 7.17 - 7.25.
Robert H. Preece - - 65 - 7.40 - 7.52.

I would respectfully recommend
to the committee that Blackler, Carr,
and Preece be continued in their
scholarships, and that (if possible)
a substitute be found for Hammond,
who ranks very low in deportment
and scholarship. On the next page
will be found the averages for the
whole school.

John Anketell.

Newport, Dec. 14, 1866.

Trinity School, 1866.
In 1866, The Reverend John Anketell ran a Classical School in Newport for a
year with forty-eight pupils. The vestry voted him the proceeds of the Kay Fund
for that year, amounting to $180, on the understanding that four boys from the
parish would have scholarships. This document is his report to the vestry on the
Kay scholarship Students. B2-F10. Collection of the Newport Historical Society.

The vestry representatives called on Prescott at the appointed time and received an old Bible, a volume of old parish records, and the new parish record, wrapped in a sealed package and addressed to the new rector, The Reverend J. H. Black. Later, the vestry committee opened the package and was surprised to find in the section of the volume reserved for recording marriages, baptisms confirmations, and other services, "an ex-parti recital of the difficulties between the late rector and the Vestry, with copies of his own letters to the wardens, vestry and corporation, but in no instance a copy of the communications addressed to him on the subject in dispute—the whole statement being calculated to give his successors, and to all who under whose observation the Parish record may come in future years, the most unjust and unfair impression."[30]

On receiving this report, the vestry voted to bring the matter to the attention of the bishop. With his permission, the vestry suggested expunging the inappropriate material from the record before it was transferred to the new rector, replacing it with factual entries that recorded the dates of Mercer's resignation, Prescott's appointments, resignation, and termination of his connection with the parish on 30 July 1863. The bishop was unable to advise the parish on the legality of making such a change and advised it to seek legal counsel. However, the vestry did not wish to take the matter beyond the church and in the end passed on the records unaltered to Black.

Black took up his duties, and shortly thereafter the vestry began to consider an alteration to the charter, eliminating the use of proxy votes. The practice of voting by proxy had been at the source of much of the conflict in the previous twenty years, allowing nonresident pew owners to control the corporation, to the detriment of the regular members and attendees. In January 1865, the Rhode Island General Assembly granted a change in the charter, repealing the 1847 amendment that had allowed proxy voting by pew owners, although the Assembly declined to go further, as many in the parish wished, to widen the right to vote beyond pew owners.[31]

In April 1866, after only three years as rector, Black announced his resignation, due largely to the small salary of two thousand dollars per year that he had received. Accepting his resignation, the vestry voted him an additional one thousand dollars in appreciation for his work. During his short time at Trinity, the parish had begun to recover from the split that had rent it for so long. The Christmas alms were once again distributed without disputes. A new monument had been installed to the south of the altar, commemorating The Reverend Salmon Wheaton. Once again thoughts had turned to Nathaniel Kay's 1734

Trinity Church decorated for Christmas, 1866.
View from the south gallery. Note the flues from the four heating stoves located in the north and south aisles converging over the central aisle, and the monument to Georgina Clarke Pell, the daughter of Duncan Pell, in its original location in the chancel to the south of the altar. The Pell monument remained in that location from its installation in 1855 until early 1867.

Collection of the Newport Historical Society.

bequest for maintaining a school and educating ten poor boys. The restored Kay Fund had grown to three thousand dollars and now produced nearly two hundred dollars per year in income. In April 1866, the vestry voted to award this income to The Reverend James Anketell, who opened a classical school in Newport for the academic year 1867 with forty-eight pupils and was willing to educate four poor boys and be an assistant to the rector.

Despite these encouraging signs, the parish divided once again over the choice of a new rector. In August 1866, the selection committee divided into two camps, submitting a majority report and a minority report. The majority favored calling The Reverend James H. Rylance, the rector of St. Paul's Church, Cleveland, Ohio, while the minority favored The Reverend Canon, Isaac P. White, D.D., of Montreal, Canada. Upon receiving the reports, the vestry first called Rylance, offering him a salary of $2,500 with an additional five hundred dollars for housing. Rylance declined the call, and the vestry unanimously proceeded to call White. In making the parish's agreement with White, the church wardens, George Champlin Mason and Samuel Engs, wrote: "We are truly sheep without a shepherd. The services of the Church have been duly administered, but the pastoral tie is missing, and we long to cement the bonds that are to make us one."[32] While awaiting White's arrival, The Reverend Henry D. Sherman acted as interim rector, until White took up his new position. The parish remained deeply divided by the conflicts of the preceding decades.

Notes

1. Francis Vinton, *The Destinies of Our Country: A Sermon Preached on the National Fast Day, March 15, 1841 and by request, on the Fifth Sunday after Trinity, in Trinity Church, Newport, R.I.* (Boston: J. B. Dow, 1841).

    Francis Vinton, "The Reception of the Newport Artillery by their townsmen, Thursday, May 19, 1842, 3 o'clock, p.m.," *Herald of the Times. Extra* (Newport, RI: James Atkinson, 1842).

    Francis Vinton, *Loyalty and Piety: or the Christian's civil obligations defined; a discourse preached in Trinity Church, Newport, R.I., on Thursday, July 21, 1842, the day of public thanksgiving* (Providence, RI: Burnett & King, 1842).

    Francis Vinton, *The Church, her Lord's almoner to the world, a sermon preached in Grace Church, Providence, before the missionary convocation of the church in Rhode Island. . . . Jan. 10, 1844* (Providence, RI: n.p,, 1844.

    Francis Vinton, *A Remembrance of the Former Days: Being the farewell discourse to Trinity Church, Newport, R.I., preached on the fifth Sunday after Trinity, July 7th, 1844* (Providence, RI: Samuel C. Blodget, 1844).

2. John K. Mahon, "Oliver Hazard Perry: Savior of the Northwest," in James C. Bradford, ed., *Command under Sail: Makers of the American Naval Tradition 1775–1850* (Annapolis, MD: Naval Institute Press, 1985), p. 140.

3. "Memoir of Trinity Church, Newport, R.I., compiled by Henry Bull, Esq., at the request of the Rector, Rev. Francis Vinton. Recorded by John Sterne, Esq. In 1841–42," reprinted in Wilkins Updike, *A History of the Episcopal Church in Narragansett, Rhode Island,* second edition edited enlarged and annotated by The Reverend David Goodwin (Boston: Merrymount Press, 1907), vol. 2, pp. 150–77.

4. J. Walton Ferguson, *Kingscote; Newport Cottage Orné* (Newport, RI: Preservation Society of Newport County, 1973), pp. 6–10.

5. Wm. King Covell, *The Organs of Trinity Church Newport, R.I.* (London: "Musical Opinion, 1935); article reprinted as a pamphlet from *The Organ,* vol. XIV, no. 56 (April 1935), p. 8.

6. Mason, *Annals,* Second Series, pp. 117–21: Letter from Rev. Hall to the Corporation of Trinity Church, Easter Monday 1846.

7. Ibid., pp. 122–23: Letter from Hall to the Corporation of Trinity Church, October 29, 1846.

8. Ibid., p. 133: Letter from Rev. D. Richmond Brewer to the Corporation of Trinity Church, 10 June 1848.

9. Richard M. Bayles, ed. *History of Newport County, Rhode Island, From the Year 1638 to the Year 1887* (New York: L. E. Preston & Co., 1888), p. 457. Mason, *Annals*, Second Series, p. 181.

10. Ibid., pp. pp. 137–42: Report of the Committee of 8 April 1849. Quotations from p. 140.

11. Ibid., p. 142.

12. Ibid., pp. 158–59: Letter from Rev. D. R. Brewer to the corporation, 9 April 1855.

13. Bayles, ed. *History of Newport County*, p. 456.

14. Mason, *Annals*. Second Series, p. 168: Letter from Rev. D. R. Brewer to George C. Mason, Senior Warden, 12 April 1857.

15. Ibid., p. 169.

16. Ibid., p. 170, note 37: Letter from Reverend Mercer to the vestry, 4 May 1858.

17. Ibid., pp. 171–72: Petition from the Ladies of Trinity Church, 30 July 1858.

18. Ibid., pp. 189–90: Protest of 19 April 1860.

19. Ibid., p. 192: Charles Hunter's resolution, 19 April 1860.

20. Ibid., p. 213: Letter from the vestry of Trinity Church to Bishop Thomas Clark, 16 May 1860.

21. Ibid., p. 217: Resolution of the Standing Committee, Diocese of Rhode Island, 15 June 1860.

22. Ibid., p. 224: Minutes of the Vestry, 21 March 1861.

23. Ibid., p. 226: Letter from Rev. O. H. Prescott to the Vestry, 5 August 1861.

24. Ibid., pp. 227–30: Pastoral letter from the Bishop of Rhode Island, 20 July 1861.

25. Ibid., pp. 230–33: Letter from the vestry of Trinity Church to the Bishop of Rhode Island, 9 August 1861.

26. Ibid., p. 245: Report of the Committee on Music, 2 January 1862 [1863].

27. O[liver] S[herman] Prescott, *The Power of the Resurrection: A Sermon Preached in Trinity Church, Newport, R.I. on the Seventh Sunday after Trinity, 1863, being the Sunday following the Funeral of Clement Clark Moore, L.L.D.* (Newport, RI: Charles E. Hammett, Jr., 1863). The funeral was held in 15 July 1863, and Moore's remains were taken for burial in St. Luke's Churchyard, New York.

28. Ibid., p. 266: Report of the Committee to receive the Parish Record, 20 July 1863.

29. Ibid., First series, p. 347; Second Series, pp. 270–72.

30. Ibid., pp. 282–83, footnote 41, Churchwardens to Reverend Canon White, 29 October 1866.

31. Ibid., First series, p. 347; Second Series, pp 270–72.

32. Ibid., pp. 282–83, footnote 41, Churchwardens to Rev. Canon White, 29 October 1866.

The Reverend Isaac R White, rector of Trinity Church, 1866–75.
White's appointment as rector marked a new period of tranquility and growth in
Trinity's history. On 27 April 1867, the Newport Mercury *reported on the Easter*
service and noted the unmistakable growth and prosperity of the parish: "Never
since we can remember have this congregation been more united or bound in bonds
of deepest affection closer to their pastor than they are now to their present
esteemed rector." Collection of the Newport Historical Society.

9

Peace, Stability, and Growth, 1867–1907

With The Reverend Dr. Isaac White's arrival from Canada to begin his ministry in Newport during January 1867, the parish immediately began to show new signs of growth and stability. White brought with him an entirely new outlook for Newport. Born in Sunderland, England, in 1818, he had graduated from the University of Cambridge and had had a parish on the Isle of Jersey before immigrating to Canada. For fifteen years, he had been rector of a parish in Chambly, Quebec, fourteen miles from Montreal, and then had become a canon of the Anglican cathedral in Montreal for four and a half years, before coming to Newport.

In one of the first moves to revitalize the church after White's arrival, the corporation voted at the annual meeting in April 1867 to authorize plastering over the two bull's-eye windows in the chancel and the casement windows on both the east and west walls of the church building. This was the first major step toward creating an entirely new and more contemporary atmosphere for worship inside the church. At the same time, 140 years after its construction, the first stained glass window was installed. A window of simple design, on opaque glass with a colored border and a large cross, now dominated the window over the altar. With the competing light from the bull's-eyes and the other windows removed, a somber and shadowed light, more in tune with current Victorian taste, set a very different tone and marked a new era in the parish's history.

In describing the changes, the *Rhode Island Mercury* noted that the window at the east end was "chaste in design, yet beautiful in expression."[1] Going on, the journalist wrote of the "new, rich and appropriate altar cloth of crimson embroidered with gold also above the chancel a superb blue and gold corona or chandelier with lights formed in the shape of a crown affording a most brilliant appearance in the evening and lighting that portion of the church with fine effect."[2] During the Easter service in 1867, the church was crowded and "with its profuse floral decorations on the altar, around the chancel and on the reading desk . . . presented an appearance rarely if ever before witnessed within its venerable walls."[3]

In connection with White's appointment, one of the vestry's first concerns was to find adequate housing for the new rector. Even before his arrival, White had expressed concern about this matter, as he had obtained private information about the cost of living in Newport that did not seem to match the parish's five-hundred-dollars-a-year housing allowance. Since the parish sold the house at the corner of High and Touro Streets in 1839, it had not owned a rectory. During Black's tenure as rector in 1865, the vestry had voted to begin to raise subscriptions for a new rectory and to search for a suitable house or piece of land upon which to build a home. Little had been achieved in raising any new funds by the end of 1866, when White's appointment and imminent arrival made it an urgent issue. After White's arrival, in January 1867, a new vestry committee reported on the various alternatives.

The vestry determined that it had the authority to invest up to ten thousand dollars of the parish's capital funds in land, providing it did so for the benefit of the parish. Investigation showed that most rental properties ranged at seven hundred to a thousand dollars, with only one house available at five hundred a year. Consulting the real estate agents, the vestry found that suitable houses for sale in Newport would cost ten to fifteen thousand dollars, while a new, modern building could be built for $11,500, plus the cost of the land. Calculating that the rector's five-hundred-dollar allowance was equivalent to the interest on principal of seven thousand dollars, the committee suggested discontinuing the allowance and investing seven thousand dollars in the new rectory, while raising the remainder of the cost from subscription. An architect, presumably the senior warden himself, George Champlin Mason, or a member of his architectural firm, provided building plans and offered to superintend construction free of charge. In the meantime, the vestry allowed White six hundred dollars a year to rent property until the funds could be raised.[4]

The plans for building a new rectory were quickly overtaken by an even more urgent need: expanded facilities for the parish Sunday school. At the April 1867 annual meeting, the matter was raised of the overcrowded and inadequate conditions for the Sunday school in the old Kay schoolhouse. At that time the corporation delegated power to the vestry to take what action it thought necessary to remedy the situation. After considering the situation, the vestry decided to purchase the land and building that the Moravian church had used on the northwest corner of Church and High Streets. The Moravian, or United Brethren,

Kay Chapel. In 1867, Trinity purchased the building and land previously used by the Moravian Church at the northwestern corner of Church and High Streets, moved the Moravian graves to the Island Cemetery, and constructed this chapel for use of the Trinity Sunday School. Building funds came from the sale of the School Street schoolhouse. Dedicated to the educational purposes that the Kay legacy was designed to serve, it was first used for Lenten services in 1869.

Collection of the Newport Historical Society.

church had been active in Newport from the mid-eighteenth century but at this point had declined in numbers and was no longer using this property. In the summer of 1867, Trinity purchased the property for two thousand dollars and planned to remove the known graves that were on the site to a designated area in the Island Cemetery and to sell both the wooden building that the Moravians had used as well as the old Kay School and its lot. With the proceeds of these sales and additional funds from the Kay Fund, the vestry planned, at first, to build a stone schoolhouse on the new site, which was to be named the Kay School House. On further examination, however, the cost to construct a stone building proved to be too high. At first it seemed as though the new building would have to be constructed of wood, but enough donations had been received so that the vestry was soon persuaded to compromise and to build it of brick.[5]

In early December 1867, neighboring Zion Episcopal Church, located in the Greek Revival building at the corner of Clarke and Touro Streets, ceased to operate. This development brought the need to accommodate members of that parish. Rethinking the new building itself, along with Benjamin Finch's donation of an additional piece of land adjoining the north side of the new lot, the vestry had entirely new plans drawn for a larger building and chapel. By the end of 1868, the Shiloh Baptist Church had purchased and occupied the Old School House on School Street. At this point, several parishioners, headed by David King, objected to the use of the Kay legacy for purposes other than education, as Nathaniel Kay had specified in his will of 1734. They argued that the proceeds of the sale of the old Kay schoolhouse should be deposited with the Kay Fund as it had been reconstituted in 1849.[6] While the vestry did not agree to the proposal, it did order the installation of a plaque that stressed the purpose of the building. In part, the inscription read: "This building, designed for the use of the Sunday School, was erected by the Vestry A.D. 1869, in part with funds left by him to the 'Minister, Church Wardens and Vestry of the English Church in Newport' for educational purposes."[7]

Although not formally consecrated or named by the bishop of Rhode Island until 27 August 1875, when its debt had been fully paid off, the new Kay Chapel was used for Lenten services as early as the spring of 1869.[8] The total cost for land, building, and furnishings had amounted to $20,410. In the end, the parish had paid this amount from subscriptions and the sale of the old property, leaving the Kay Fund of three thousand dollars, as it had been reconstituted in 1849, relatively untouched. Believing that the parish had fully complied with the terms of the Kay bequest by building the new Sunday school building, the corporation allowed the vestry to apply the interest from the Kay Fund to a fund that would protect Kay's grave and those of others in the churchyard. As part of this effort, the Composite Iron Works completed installation of the iron fence and gates on the Spring and Church Streets sides of the property, at a total cost of $1,870, by the end of 1870.[9] This was not the only improvement that was made to the old church. The stoves that had stood in the main part of the church were removed. In order to heat the building in a more modern way, William Fludder began excavating for a cellar under the building in the autumn of 1869; he installed a cement floor with steps and a doorway leading into a new furnace room and built two chimneys, all for a total of $983.[10]

The construction of the iron fence to protect the stones in the old graveyard was only one aspect of a revived appreciation for the parish's past that arose following the building and subsequent naming of Kay Chapel. Not only did the vestry commission a detailed study of the records in regard to how the parish had handled the Kay bequest over the previous 135 years, but individual parishioners also became interested in preserving the remnants of the past.[11] In 1865, the vestry had appointed Duncan Pell and George Mason as a committee

Levi P. Morton.

In 1870, the New York banker Levi Morton purchased both pew 78 in Trinity and his Newport summer home, "Fairlawn," on Bellevue Avenue. Subsequently, he served as a congressman from New York in 1879–81. He declined to run as vice president on the Republican ticket with James Garfield in 1881, but served as minister to France in 1881-85. While serving as vice president of the United States under Benjamin Harrison in 1889–1893, he exchanged Newport for a summer residence at Rhinebeck on Hudson. He sold "Fairlawn" in 1890 and William K. Vanderbilt, then building "Marble House, "purchased pew 78 from him in 1891. In 1997, Salve Regina University purchased "Fairlawn" to house its Pell Center for International Relations and Public Policy. From *Harpers Weekly*, vol. 32, no. 1645 (1888), p. 472. Collection of the Redwood Library and Athenaeum.

View of Trinity from Spring and Church Streets.

This late-nineteenth-century view clearly shows the fence that Composite Iron Works made for the churchyard in 1870 and the two chimneys installed in the same year, when the heating stoves were removed from the main part of the church. PI543. Collection of the Newport Historical Society.

to put the graveyard in order and to renew the stones over the graves of The Reverend James Honyman and his family, as well as of Nathaniel Kay. To further this work, in 1874 Martha Littlefield left a legacy of two thousand dollars, directing its investment as the first permanent fund for maintaining the churchyard and preserving its monuments. In her will, she asked that particular attention be paid to the Brinley, Malbone, Littlefield, Sands, and Kay monuments, with their inscriptions.[12] At about the same time, the marquis de Noailles, then ambassador of France in Washington, requested that he be allowed to preserve the grave of Admiral de Ternay. He asked to place a new stone over the original gravesite and to move the remnants of the original marble mausoleum on the outside north wall of the church to some location inside, for their preservation.[13]

In the summer of 1870, the *Boston Journal* wrote, "Old Trinity is the most fashionable place of worship and it is crowded to its utmost capacity every Sunday morning."[14] Describing the scene, Mrs. Jennie Pitman wrote, "the miserable sinners' dress as if for the opera—riding to church with their best turnouts, which block the streets all about for some distance. Of the twenty million dollars worth of taxable property in Newport—thirteen million is represented by this congregation."[15]

To finish off the transformation of the church building that had begun in 1867, the vestry voted in December 1873 to allow the senior warden, George Champlin Mason, to paint the ceiling of the church "according to his judgment."[16] The work was completed by the end of March 1874, in time for Easter; the vestry formally voted its unanimous thanks to Mason for "the thorough and tasteful manner in which he decorated the Church."[17] Completely changing the simple colonial lines of the interior, Mason had added decorative borders to enhance the subtle vaulted ribs of the ceiling plasterwork, along with an ornate border around the chancel apse and a tiled effect in its lower area.

As early as 1846, Trinity's rector, The Reverend Robert B. Hall, had noted the need for a mission in "the Point" area of Newport, but this initiative had fallen by the wayside. In 1874 the issue reemerged in connection with The Reverend Isaac White's initiative to interest young men in the work of the parish. In order to do so, White established a guild, first called the Guild of Trinity Parish, later St. Stephen's Guild.[18] At first, there was no clear objective for the group, other than establishing a Christian fellowship for young men within the parish. As president of the guild, White organized monthly meetings where the participants read papers on various topics and discussed issues of mutual interest. At one of these early meetings, the issue came up that the guild

Interior of the church as it looked between 1874 and 1897.
This view shows George Champlain Mason's decoration of the church interior.
The first stained-glass window is in place over the altar. The east windows and the
bull's-eye windows in the chancel have been plastered over. Mason's decorative
borders highlight the vaulting in the ceiling, along with his decorative painting of
the lower part of the chancel. Note the pew boxes under the Browne and Wharton
monuments, the Victorian altar and chairs in the chancel, and the stone font that
stands in front of the clerk's desk, and the three-armed gaslight fixtures.
Collection of the Newport Historical Society.

might engage in missionary activity. At the same time, someone noted that there was no church of any kind in the Point area and that few people from that part of town attended any church in other parts of the city. At first, the group let the subject drop and took no action.

However, about a year later, in the summer of 1875, the subject arose again, and the guild decided to undertake active missionary work. At that time, it rented a room in a house at 27 (then numbered 15) Third Street, at the corner of Third and Poplar Streets. This was the home and workshop of Peter Quire, an

African-American shoemaker. His wife, Harriet, was the principal owner of the property, having purchased it before she married Peter in 1865. Both, however, were active parishioners of Trinity Church and very interested in bringing the church to the Point. Mrs. Quire personally prepared for the guild's use what was probably a vacant apartment or unused room on one of the upper floors of the house.[19] There, Dr. White conducted the first formal service of the new mission on Sunday evening, 11 July 1875. White preached a sermon, and the Trinity Church choir sang. Among those present at the first service was a close friend of White's (and Newport summer resident), The Reverend Dr. Henry A. Coit, the rector of St. Paul's School, Concord, New Hampshire. During that summer, Coit played an active leadership role in the new mission and made a number of donations to outfit the new room.[20]

These services on the Point proved to be popular, and soon the little room at Third and Poplar could no longer hold the number of people who wanted to attend. After considering their options, the guild decided to solicit donations to build a small chapel for services, with room for a Sunday school. By the end of November 1875, there was enough money available to purchase land and begin building. The Reverend Dr. White and the two wardens, George Mason and Samuel Engs, agreed to be the trustees of the mission chapel and its funds, but at the same time, it was agreed that the vestry of Trinity Church was not to be responsible for the support, maintenance, or management of the mission.[21] A lot was purchased on Poplar Street, and George Champlin Mason personally furnished the architectural plans for a building to accommodate 150 people. It soon became apparent this was going to be too small, and Mason altered the design so that it would be big enough for an additional hundred people to attend services. Mason's original concept of the building did not include a bell tower, but the city of Newport proposed that if a tower were added, the city would provide a bell as well as contribute to the cost of the tower, on condition that the bell also be used as a fire alarm for the Point area.[22]

Just as all these plans were being brought to fruition, The Reverend Dr. White suddenly died—on 26 December 1875, at the age of fifty-seven. As he had been the moving force behind the new mission, his death brought everything to a momentary standstill on the Point. The bell had just been installed in the new tower, and even before it rang for the first service in the new building, it tolled the death of the building's founder. White's funeral was held on 30 December at Trinity; Bishop Clark delivered the eulogy. The bishop noted the abundant Christmas greens that decorated the church, pointing out that "over

St. Johns Chapel.
Designed in 1875 by Trinity's senior warden, George Champlin Mason, this
building first served as Trinity's Mission Chapel in Newport's Point section.
The city of Newport contributed to the cost of its bell tower, on condition that
its bell also serve as a fire alarm in the Point section.
Collection of the Newport Historical Society

these Christmas greens which adorn these walls there hangs the sable drapery of mourning." He went on to comment on White's significant accomplishments during the nine years of his ministry in Newport:

> His work here will abide long after his earthly form has crumbled to ashes. Look at the substantial and beautiful [Kay] Chapel, free from all pecuniary encumbrance, which has replaced the small and uncomfortable building in which the Sunday School was once gathered; look at the condition of this ancient church, and the sacred enclosure that surrounds it; the complete repair, the new furnishings, the beautiful embellishments which adorn the walls, all effected with no disturbance of the connections which hallow the antique and peculiar style of the sanctuary; and all in a degree the result of his indomitable energy and irrepressible assiduity. [23]

At the family's request, White was buried in the Trinity churchyard to the west of the tower, and a monument donated by the vestry and designed by George Champlin Mason was placed over the grave.[24] In the spring of 1876, his wife, Catherine White, donated to the church a three-foot-high brass cross, engraved "To the Glory of God and in memory of Rev. I. P. White," which stood on the altar for more than seventy-five years.

To fill the pulpit until a new rector could be chosen, the vestry unanimously voted to invite The Reverend Dr. Alexander Mercer, who had served as rector during the tumultuous years between 1855 and 1860. In accepting, Mercer took care to point out "that I do not assume full care of all the work and interests of the parish, but only such care as is necessary."[25] The vestry went to work immediately in search of a successor and within a fortnight of White's death had produced a list of thirteen candidates. Immediately proceeding to an informal vote, seventeen corporators met in a special meeting of the corporation and chose, by a vote of fifteen to one, Newport summer resident The Reverend Henry Coit, who had played such an important role in Trinity's mission on the Point. After carefully considering the offer, Coit decided that he could not leave his work at St. Paul's School, where he had been for twenty years.

The Point mission, disappointed that one of its principal supporters was not able to accept the rectorship at Trinity, continued with the assistance from The Reverend R. B. Peet, rector of Emmanuel Church, who held regular services

Interior of Trinity Church, c. 1875.
This view may well show the church as it was decorated for Christmas at the time of Isaac White's death on 26 December 1875.
Collections of the Newport Historical Society.

in the room at Poplar and Third Streets until the new building was ready. In February, the mission formally took up the name that White had suggested for it, the Free Chapel of St. John the Evangelist, and a number of Trinity parishioners made contributions to the new chapel. The Trinity Church Sunday School presented handsomely bound prayer books, altar service books, hymnals, and a Bible. On the evening of Sunday, 13 February 1876, a large congregation gathered to open the new St. John's Chapel at its first service—so large, in fact, that not all could get inside the building. A number of clergymen were present, including The Reverend Dr. Mercer, who delivered the first sermon in the building on this occasion. During the following year, the Trinity Church choir sang regularly, until the chapel congregation organized its own choir in the following year.

In March 1876, the corporation considered three additional names for the rectorship. After consideration, it chose The Reverend Dr. George J. Magill, rector of St. Paul's Church, Wickford, as the new rector of Trinity. The vestry requested that Dr. Mercer continue his work with the parish until Magill could take up his new position after Easter. Shortly after his arrival, Magill presided at his first meeting of the vestry on 19 May. Consistent with White's active restoration of the parish to a normal routine, Magill's tenure was remarkable for its quiet activity.

The first major issue that greeted Magill was a report from the committee on repairing the bell. In the following months, arrangements were made to recast and enlarge the large, 1,876-pound bell. Meneely & Company of West Troy (now Watervliet), New York, carried out the work, amalgamating the metal from the previous bell to produce a new one weighing 3,500 pounds. At the committee's direction, two inscriptions were cast on the bell. On one side the inscription read, "Vivos Voci. Mortuos Plango. When I do ring God's praises sing, when I do toule pray heart and soule." On the other side, a very misleading inscription was placed: "The Gift of Queen Anne to Trinity Church, Newport, R.I., 1709. Recast in 1843. Recast and doubled in weight, 1876." In fact, the 1876 bell included only metal from the 1843 bell and not the earlier ones. The parish's second bell, an eight-hundred-pound one made in 1709, had cracked and had been shipped to England in 1740 to be exchanged for a new thousand-pound bell. That bell had lasted until 1804, when two more bells, each cast anew successively, replaced it.[26]

In 1880, the parish proceeded to install a new organ, which remained in place until 1902. Hook and Hastings & Co. replaced the works that Henry Erben of New York had installed in 1844, partially using the original 1733 case built by Richard Bridge and partly the tower behind it. As early as 1862 the Music Committee had reported that repairs to the Erben organ, which contained two stops from the original Bridges organ, would do little toward its permanent improvement. However, when the change was made in 1880, Hook and Hastings fitted the Erben organ into a new case and installed it in Kay Chapel. The new organ in Trinity was a great improvement over the old, having a manual compass of fifty-eight notes and a pedal register of twenty-seven notes. In the new installation, the largest pipes of the organ, sixteen-foot open wood, were placed on either side of the old case.[27]

On taking over his duties at Trinity in 1876, Reverend Magill took an active interest in the affairs of the parish's mission on the Point. Through his efforts, the remaining debt was paid off, a cause to which the vestry of Trinity donated six hundred dollars, in addition to its regular annual donation to the Free Chapel as part of its missionary work. In August 1877, Trinity's rector obtained the services of his brother, The Reverend W. I. Magill, at St. John's. From his first service in early August 1877, W. I. Magill began weekly celebrations of Holy Communion, St. John's thus becoming the first church in the diocese

The Reverend George J. Magill, D.D., rector of Trinity Church, 1876–98.

Magill's years at Trinity were marked by a wide number of initiatives and new missions. On his death, Mrs. J. P. Swan donated ten thousand dollars to the parish in his memory. For many years it was the largest single endowment the parish maintained. Its income was restricted first for use to the support of Magill's widow and, then, to support their invalid daughter, Gertrude, who died in 1958. At that point, it reverted to the Trinity Endowment Fund.
Collection of the Newport Historical Society.

The 1876 bell.
This bell included metal from the 1843 bell, doubling it in size. When this bell was made, it was thought that the 1843 bell was a recasting of the 1709 bell, and the inscription on it carries this incorrect information.

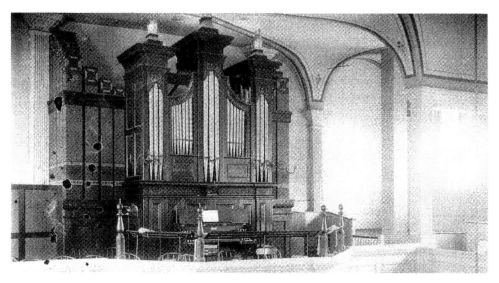

The Hook and Hastings Organ, c. 1880-1902.
This damaged image shows the church's third organ, installed in 1880, with gas-
light fixtures at the corners of the original organ case and the sixteen-foot open
wood pipes behind the organ. Details from Mason's 1874 ceiling decoration can be
seen here. Note that the western windows have been plastered over.
Collection of the Newport Historical Society.

Engraving of Trinity Church
from Frank Street, c. 1888.
This view shows the stone cross in
the churchyard, designed by George
Champlin Mason, over the grave of
The Reverend Isaac White.
From Bayles History of Newport
County *(1888). P273.*
Collection of the Newport Historical Society.

to initiate this practice, which continued without a break during Magill's three years there. During this period, Mrs. John J. Astor donated funds to build and furnish the St. John's Reading Room.

In the summer of 1881, W. I. Magill resigned to take up another appointment, and The Reverend Samuel P. Watters succeeded him. Newly graduated from General Theological Seminary, Watters was ordained to the priesthood at Trinity a week after his arrival at St. John's. He remained for about fifteen months; The Reverend S. Wilson Moran of Wisconsin took over in February 1882.

Upon his appointment, Moran began to work energetically to enlarge the St. John's congregation. Within a few months, his congregation had grown to nearly a hundred, including eighty members of Trinity. With this growth of interest in the Point area under Moran's leadership, the communicants at St. John's decided that it was time for them to establish themselves as a fully independent parish, which occurred on 22 September 1882. Five weeks later, with the approval of the diocese and Trinity, Moran took responsibility as the first rector of the newly established parish, on All Saints Day 1882.[28] The rector and wardens of Trinity Church continued in their original capacities as trustees of St. John's Chapel until 7 April 1890.[29]

As early as March 1883, Magill had reported that up to that time, he had been so engrossed in the parish's missionary work that he had not yet had time to bring an important question to the vestry's attention. He reported that he had long felt that the parish, then the third largest in Rhode Island, should have a permanent home for its rector. He had found the need to house-hunt and move, in Newport's fluctuating real estate market, an embarrassment for one of his position.[30] The vestry appointed a committee, headed by the rector, to undertake the necessary fund-raising and planning, but the work proceeded slowly. Finally, in April 1889, six years later, the committee reported that it had fully completed its work. For the total cost of $15,051.99, the committee had purchased a lot facing Cottage Street at the corner of Old Beach Road and had erected a new gambrel-roofed house "complete in all its appointments" as the new rectory, and presented it to the parish free of all debt and liens.

Magill's years at Trinity were marked by a wide variety of initiatives and missions. In May 1886, he inspired the St. Stephen's Guild to begin publishing the parish's first newspaper, *The Trinity Messenger*, which recorded many of the activities of that time. In association with summer resident Mrs. John J. Astor, Magill and Trinity became involved with a project to raise funds to bring sick and poor children for periods in the summer from New York City to Newport. As Magill explained, "Living in the cool and health-giving breezes of Newport, we are liable to forget the misery of those to whose poverty and wretched surroundings is added the intense heat of a crowded city."[31]

In another initiative, Magill picked up on an issue that had arisen within the national church and within the larger Anglican communion. As early as 1862, the General Convention of the Episcopal Church in the United States had established a committee to examine possible relationships with branches of the Lutheran Church that had preserved their historical episcopate. One particular focus was the Church of Sweden. In 1888, bishops from the worldwide Anglican communion met at Lambeth Palace in London. This, the Third Lambeth Conference, agreed to a proposal similar to that of a "quadrilateral" that William Reed Huntington had successfully proposed for the General Convention in 1886. This established the four basic elements that Episcopalians should expect in any national church: Holy Scripture, the Nicene Creed, the sacraments of Baptism and Eucharist, and a local adaptation of the historical episcopate.[32] Along with this endorsement, which opened the way to closer connections with

Trinity Church rectory.
Built by the parish in 1889, the newly built building cost $15,051.99, including land, construction, and furnishings. This rectory stood facing Cottage Street at the corner of Old Beach Road. It was used as the rectory from 1889 to 1905.
Collection of the Newport Historical Society.

other denominations, the Lambeth Conference specifically encouraged a close connection with the established Lutheran Church of Sweden. This move had a local impact for the Trinity parish. About this same time, a substantial number of Swedish immigrants were coming to Rhode Island. Some worked in industries in the Providence and Pawtucket areas and in Newport; a number of summer residents started to employ them in household staff positions.

At Grace Church, Providence, a thirty-eight-year-old Swedish emigrant, John Gottfried Hammarsköld, had been ordained a deacon in 1888 and a priest in the following year. In what would become the origin of St. Ansgarius Church in Providence, the bishop of Rhode Island appointed him superintendent of the Episcopal diocese's Swedish mission. Hammarsköld began to encourage services in Swedish in Providence, Pawtucket, and Newport. His first service in Newport was held in Kay Chapel in February 1889, although most of the service was in English, with psalms sung in Swedish. At Trinity, the rector noticed that in Newport "Swedes attended the service of Methodists and put their children into Methodist Sunday Schools not because they like Methodist Doctrine, but because they love their mother tongue."[33] Within a year, The Reverend Axel Z. Fryxell had succeeded Hammarsköld in caring for the groups in Providence and Pawtucket, but in Newport, Trinity decided to carry on the work as a parish mission. Very early on, the parish established St. Ansgarius' Guild. In 1890, the parish obtained the services of The Reverend John Hedman. Beginning his ministry on Advent Sunday, he soon gathered a group of 130 people interested in Swedish services. In Lent of the following year, he held Swedish services on Ash Wednesday and every Friday at 8 P.M. for a growing congregation.[34]

Not all Swedes who had immigrated to America were interested in maintaining doctrines similar to those of the Swedish state church. Indeed, a number had immigrated just to get away from these pervasive religious doctrines. Many of them had a desire for a more evangelical outlook than either the Swedish Lutheran Church or the Episcopal Church provided. This group within the Kay Chapel Swedish congregation began to look elsewhere and soon split to form a new group, but a number of the original Swedish group stayed with Trinity. Among those who stayed were families with such names as Anthony, Lawson, Lindroth, Selander, and Johnson. Those who split away soon established their own church, the Svenska Evangeliska Zion Luterska Församling (the Swedish Evangelical Zion Lutheran Church). In 1895, they built their own wooden church building on nearby Corné Street in Newport, laying the foundation for

Swedish baptismal certificate, 1892.
This document, in Swedish, records the baptism of Albert Hector Johnson on 22
June 1892 by the pastor of the Scandinavian Mission of Trinity Church, The
Reverend John Hedman. Trinity Church Records, Newport Historical Society.

today's St. Peter's Evangelical Lutheran Church.[35] Meanwhile, Trinity maintained its Swedish services as a formal parochial mission; they were discontinued within a few years, and the remaining congregation joined the larger services at Trinity and Kay Chapel.

At the annual meeting of the Trinity corporation in 1889, George Champlin Mason tendered his resignation as senior warden after a total of forty-one years as a member of the vestry; LeRoy King was elected in his place. Having been the steadying hand within the parish for so long, Mason had one remaining major contribution to make. Long interested in historical matters, he had been one of the original founders of the Newport Historical Society in 1853, as well as being a prominent local architect and editor of the *Newport Daily News*. He had published in 1884 his *Reminiscences of Newport*, which had included several chapters relating to Trinity Church. Now in retirement, he turned to publishing transcriptions of historical documents about Newport. As senior warden, he had clearly learned that many issues in the management of the parish could not be understood without ready access to the historical record. In August 1888, the vestry had learned that Mason had been diligently copying the parish's old vestry records, searching for supplementary documents and annotating them. The vestry appointed a committee to invite Mason to publish this material. By December 1889, donors had provided a sum that was sufficient for publication, and in the following year the Evans Printing Company of Philadelphia printed 350 copies for Mason (whose name appeared on the title page as the publisher) of the *Annals of Trinity Church, Newport, Rhode Island, 1698–1821*.[36] It is not easy to explain Mason's choice of the ending date of 1821. It did not mark a change in rectors or any other major epoch in the parish's history, but the division may have been one of editorial convenience, marking the annual meeting in which the senior and junior wardens changed. Perhaps, more significantly, it included the date, unmentioned in the volume, of the author-editor's birth in 1820.

The following year, Mason published his *Annals of the Redwood Library and Athenaeum*, which contained many documents relevant to the early history of Trinity, with several of its rectors, schoolmasters, and other parishioners among its founders.[37] Meanwhile, Mason continued to gather and transcribe documents on the history of Trinity in his own lifetime. In December 1892, a member of the vestry, Dr. V. Mott Francis, undertook to raise a further subscription to raise enough money to publish the remainder of Mason's work, taking the published record down to 1892. The national financial crisis of 1892

George Champlin Mason.
Mason served as senior warden of Trinity Church for twenty-six years, from 1863
to 1889, having first become a vestryman in 1848. A man of varied talents, he was
deeply interested in the history of Newport, and of Trinity. He transcribed and
published the known early records of the parish in his two-volume Annals of
Trinity Church *as well as wrote the* Annals of the Redwood Library, Newport and
Its Cottages, *and a volume of* Reminiscences of Newport. *In addition, he was a*
founder of the Newport Historical Society, the editor of the Newport Daily News,
as well as the decorator of the church interior in 1874, designer of the Isaac
White's gravestone in the churchyard, and architect of many structures in Newport,
including "Chepstow," maintained by the Preservation Society of Newport County.
Collection of the Newport Historical Society.

made fund-raising a difficult task, and with less than half of the needed two thousand dollars on hand, Dr. Mott proceeded on his own to publish the book. Mason died in February 1894, and, not wanting to abandon the project, Mott persevered. When the new volume appeared, entitled *Annals of Trinity Church, 1821–1892, Second Series*, it contained Mason's dedication to The Reverend Salmon Wheaton, who had baptized him and of whom he retained to the end of his life "a vivid impression of his kindly presence and life of holiness."[38] In addition, the volume contained The Reverend George J. Magill's sermon in memory of Mason.[39] The period of years chosen for this volume (1821–92) almost exactly coincided with those of Mason's own life (1820–94), but in the case of the second volume, it ended with the Rhode Island General Assembly's revision to Trinity's charter.

Originally issued in 1769, Trinity's corporate charter had been amended to conform to state laws in 1816, and with further minor amendments in 1819, 1828, 1847, and 1865.[40] By 1889, it was clear that several further amendments were needed to bring the charter up to date, the most obvious one being, in the light of a need to raise the value of the endowment fund to meet current costs, raising the limitation set by earlier documents on the total value of property that the corporation could hold.[41] The vestry appointed a committee to undertake an evaluation of the charter and to make recommendations, including raising the limit on the value of church property from $40,000 to $100,000. At the annual meeting in June 1890, the corporation approved the committee's report that recommended alterations to allow the increase in value. In addition, in order to accommodate some summer residents, such as Cornelius Vanderbilt who had just been newly elected to the vestry at the same meeting, the date of the annual meeting was changed from Easter Monday to the last Monday in June. A further change allowed pew owners to be "those who attend public worship in said Church," instead of the earlier restriction to those "who profess to worship in the Protestant Episcopal Church."[42] Following this, the committee sought legal counsel to advise on the proper procedures to obtain the needed legislation. For the sum of ten dollars, attorney Patrick J. Galvin reviewed the matter and recommended a number of changes that required further action at the next annual meeting, in June 1891. To complicate matters further, when the issue arose before the next annual meeting, no official minutes of the 5 June 1890 meeting could be found, raising a range of procedural and substantive issues. A new committee for revising the charter took charge and proceeded to submit its report at the annual meeting of April 1892. These issues were finally resolved

Detail from the Newport City atlas. This map shows Kay Chapel at the corner of Church and High Streets, with the outline of the Guild Hall constructed by William Gosling in 1892 adjoining the chapel along High Street. Adjoining the property to the West is the J. P. Swan property that Mrs. Jane Swan donated to the parish in 1901, on the condition that it be redeveloped with a new building for the parish's educational purposes. Unused by the parish, it reverted back to Mrs. Swan after five years by the terms of the donation. In this case, the vestry's dilatoriness preserved an important eighteenth century house, the Finch-Green Collins House at 40 School Street, which was eventually purchased three-quarters of a century

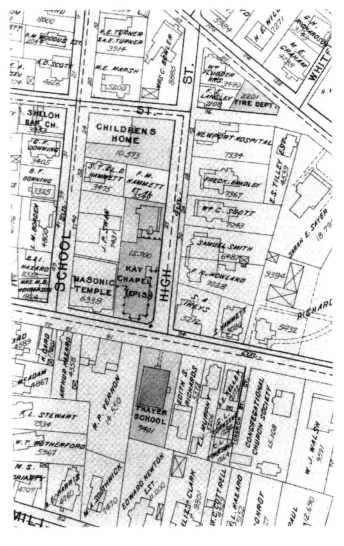

later and restored by the Newport Restoration Foundation. Atlas of the City of Newport (Springfield, MA: I. J. Richards, 1907), plate 3. Collection of the Newport Historical Society.

with a new version, which passed the General Assembly on 3 May 1892, raising the property limits to $250,000.

In October 1892, the vestry began to solicit donations to build a guild house for the parish. After rejecting the initial bids for its construction, the vestry obtained new plans for a smaller brick hall to adjoin Kay Chapel on High Street, and it commissioned William Gosling to construct it, on plans drawn by Wilbur, at the cost of eight thousand dollars.[43] The building was completed in the spring of 1895.

In January 1897, repairs to the church were made, and the interior and exterior were repainted. It was discovered that the north side of the church was gradually sinking and that the building had become unsafe. Some of the timbers and sills had rotted away. Rather than abandon the old church, the vestry hired Dudley Newton to reinforce it. A larger cellar was dug and constructed with a substantial stone foundation, reinforced with brick and iron piers. The north side of the building was reshingled, for a total cost of ten thousand dollars.[44] In connection with this renovation, Mrs. Lewis McCagg donated brass gas brackets to the church, in keeping with the eighteenth-century chandeliers hanging over the center aisle. At the same time, the vestry agreed to move the stained-glass window over the altar to the south gallery and to install in its place a window in memory of LeRoy King, as well as the stained-glass window to the memory of Mrs. John H. Davis. This was followed by similar requests from Sara Rives, Jane Whiting, and Oliver Hazard Perry Belmont.[45] As a result of this, the vestry began to establish rules concerning memorials on the church walls.[46] The vestry decided that the Davis and Whiting windows would establish the standard color scheme for all subsequent windows. At the same time, the vestry commissioned a third chandelier to replace the one that had been removed when the flue for the heating stoves had been installed. It was designed to match the original one dated 1728 in the center aisle.[47]

In the spring of 1898, the parish began to plan for a two-hundredth-anniversary celebration of the founding of the parish, but these plans were marred when in April 1898, The Reverend Dr. George Magill asked for a two-month leave of absence to undergo surgery. Soon after, he died in New York City. Although the vestry offered to arrange for the funeral and burial in the Trinity churchyard, Magill had expressed a wish to be buried alongside his twin sons at Richmond, Quebec. Upon receiving the family's wishes, the vestry renewed its offer to have the funeral at Trinity and was profoundly disappointed that it was too late to change the arrangements.[48] Nevertheless, the church was draped in mourning, and the vestry, in accordance with the family's wishes, placed a memorial tablet on the east wall of the church. Also in his memory, Mrs. Jane P. Swan of "Daleswell," Gibbs Avenue, Newport, donated ten thousand dollars to be held in trust by the parish, the income of which was to be paid semiannually to Magill's widow and his invalid daughter, Gertrude, during their lifetimes, and then to revert to the Trinity endowment fund. At that point, the Magill Fund became the largest single fund held by the parish, nearly equal the combined total of the three others—the Littlefield, the endowment, and the Poor Fund.

Shortly after Magill's death, The Reverend Frederick Irving Collins took up responsibilities as minister in charge of Trinity. In November 1898, the vestry unanimously chose The Reverend Edward Rousmaniere of Grace Church, New Bedford, as the rector, with a salary of four thousand dollars per year plus the use of the rectory. At a meeting of the corporation, the senior warden, George Gordon King, placed in nomination Rousmaniere's name, but a member of the corporation nominated The Reverend Henry Morgan Stone, of the Berkeley Memorial Chapel in Middletown. Rousmaniere won in a vote of twenty-one to four, but when notified of his election, he declined the call to leave his New Bedford parish.[49] In February 1899, the vestry unanimously recommended that Stone be the new rector, with a salary of $2,500 per year with the use of the rectory. At a special meeting of the corporation, Rousmaniere repeated, by a telegram that was read out to the group, his decision to decline the call to Trinity, and Stone was unanimously elected rector. He assumed his duties in April 1899.

On 23 April 1899, the parish's first Tiffany stained-glass window was unveiled in the church, the gift of Mr. Lispenard Stewart, in memory of his mother.[50] Another, in memory of Cornelius Vanderbilt, soon followed. A pew owner and former vestryman of Trinity, Vanderbilt had been incapacitated by a stroke several years before, and his death brought forth a particularly profound sense of loss within the parish community. In a long minute, the vestry noted that he had

> walked quietly with us in humbleness and gentleness and simple hearted devotion. . . . For though God had charged him with the stewardship of vast wealth he administered it with a consecration that is seldom found among men of smaller means and less distracting temptations. . . . Mr. Vanderbilt saved many a man's belief in human nature and in God. High and low respected him alike. Rich and poor believed in him and reverenced his faith.[51]

There was a limit to the physical improvements desired in the church; when in late 1899 it was proposed that a toilet be added, the vestry declined to make an addition to the building for that purpose. At the same time, however, a member of the vestry reported that he had petitioned the City Council to lay a sidewalk on the west side of High Street for use of Kay Chapel and the Guild Hall. In January 1900, the vestry also petitioned the General Assembly for permission to sell the rectory at the corner of Cottage and Beach Streets and to

The Reverend Henry Morgan Stone, rector of Trinity Church, 1899–1904.

Illness forced the thirty-four-year old Stone to resign from Trinity. Unable to recover his health, he died four years later and was buried in Trinity's churchyard, alongside The Reverend Isaac White.

Collection of the Newport Historical Society.

Cornelius Vanderbilt II.

Cornelius Vanderbilt was the grandson of Commodore Cornelius Vanderbilt, the founder of the Vanderbilt fortune, and eldest son of William Henry Vanderbilt. On his father's death in 1885, he became the richest man in America as head of the family and its business interests. That same year, he purchased the Pierre Lorillard Estate, "The Breakers," in Newport and bought two pews in Trinity Church, which he combined to accommodate his family. Deeply interested in the Episcopal Church and the YMCA, he was elected a vestryman at Trinity in 1890. The date of the annual corporation meeting was temporarily changed to accommodate him and other summer residents. Active in parish activities, his death in 1899 brought a deep sense of loss within the parish community. A Tiffany window was installed in the church in his memory and, in his will, he left funds to build Newport's Mary Street YMCA, which nearly a century later was converted to a hotel, named Vanderbilt Hall. From Harper's Weekly, *vol. 30, no. 1515 (1886), p. 20.* Collection of the Redwood Library and Athenaeum.

reinvest the proceeds in other real estate. Upon the advice of real estate agents, the vestry set a minimum price of nine thousand dollars on the property, but no bids were received higher than $7,250. As a result, the vestry did not sell the property.[52]

In 1901, a number of parishioners requested permission to install memorial tablets and stained-glass windows in the church.[53] Like several other requests, these were granted, but for one reason or another, the donors failed to carry out their intentions. This situation created a major problem for vestry members, who did not know whether they should consider a particular location permanently reserved, or whether or there was enough space available for the new monuments that were being proposed.[54] In order to deal with the situation, the vestry ruled that permissions for such installations would expire one year after they had been approved, and it requested that all future designs for proposed memorials be submitted in advance to the vestry.

In May 1901, Mrs. Jane Swan donated the Finch estate on School Street, abutting the west side of the lots occupied by Kay Chapel, specifying that this property should be redeveloped with a new building for parochial purposes within five years.[55] While accepting this gift, the vestry did not act immediately on its requirements to build a building. Moving in other areas, however, in early 1902 the vestry contracted with Hook and Hastings & Co. to construct a new organ for $6,500.

On 22 April 1903, The Reverend Henry Morgan Stone resigned as rector, reporting that he had not been well for some time. He had considered asking for a leave of absence, but he felt it would be wiser to resign, as his physicians had advised that the only way he could recover his health was "to move to another climate and mode of life."[56] In expressing his regret, Stone wrote, "No man could be happier in a parish than I have been in this and nothing but coercion of this imperative sort could induce me to leave. As it is I do not know what else to do."[57] The vestry, however, refused to accept his resignation and offered him instead a year's vacation. In his absence, the assistant, The Reverend Ernest J. Dennen, as well as The Reverend Henry S. Nash, officiated. By November 1904, Stone, writing from Colorado Springs, formally resigned as rector, having found that his health made it impossible for him to continue.[58] In reluctantly accepting his resignation, the vestry noted, "The Gospel of Jesus Christ has been devotedly taught and all our parochial bonds, branching in all directions, have been knit together with golden threads of love and sympathy."[59]

On receiving news that the archbishop of Canterbury would visit the United States, the vestry immediately requested that the archbishop hold a

The Oak Leaf Communion set. One of the most interesting of the nineteenth-century silver pieces in the parish's collection is this flagon, paten, and chalice made by E W Cooper, Amity Street, New York. No record of its donor has yet been found, but it first appears in the parish's 1890 census of silver. Each piece is inscribed. The flagon bears the words "Glory be to God on High," the chalice, "Drink ye all of this," and the paten, "Lord for evermore give us this bread."

The Engs and LeRoy Chalices. The Chalice and Paten on the left are both engraved "In Memory of Samuel Engs, Junior Warden. Trinity Church, November 14, 1886." Samuel Engs first became a vestryman in 1841 and continued to be junior warden from 1863 up to the day of his death, recorded on the pieces.

The Chalice on the right is engraved "Trinity Church, August 19, 1885." It was donated in memory of Daniel LeRoy. The patten and both jeweled, gold-lined, chalices are stamped "J. & R. Lamb, New York, Eng. Sterling." All three pieces were in regular daily use at the end of the twentieth century and the beginning of the twenty-first century.

service in Trinity to "permit the congregation to express their gratitude for what this parish owes to the Great Society [for the Propagation of the Gospel], to do honour to the Mother Church and to her Primate."[60]

In March 1905, the vestry and the corporation elected The Reverend Walter Lowrie as rector, at the rate of three thousand dollars a year plus the use of the rectory. On acceptance, to take effect in May, Lowrie, the assistant at Emmanuel Church, chose not to occupy the rectory, as he wished to remain at his residence at 11 Kay Street.

During the previous year, the endowment fund had more than doubled with the bequest of five thousand dollars from Mary LeRoy King, along with ten thousand dollars in the Magill Fund and nearly fourteen thousand dollars in the General Investment Fund, $2,600 in the Littlefield Fund, $2,700 in the Poor Fund, and $5,217 in a fund for a new parish house.[61] An envelope system was introduced in 1906. The vestry ordered that the hangings on the pulpit were to remain permanently and not to be removed for any purpose. Since the parish had not improved the Finch estate land on School Street donated by Mrs. Jane Swan in 1901, it reverted back to Mrs. Swan, as specified by the terms of the donation.[62] In early January 1907, the American Church in Rome selected Lowrie as its rector. With the approval of the bishop in charge of foreign churches, Bishop Potter of New York, Lowrie accepted the appointment, serving in it until his retirement in 1930. Having been at Trinity for just two years, Lowrie told the vestry that he had long had an interest in the Church of "St Paul within the Walls" at Rome and that it was the only possible appointment that could lure him away from Newport.[63] Upon the corporation's acceptance of his resignation, Lowrie left to take up his new duties in Italy. (Already showing signs of his future scholarship, he would eventually write thirty-eight scholarly volumes during his career, including works of biblical criticism and studies of Kierkegaard and Karl Barth.) In regretfully accepting his resignation, the corporation noted that the parish had lost "the valuable services of one so eminently qualified to fulfill the arduous duties of rector, . . . a clergyman of high scholarship and purity of life."[64] Upon request of the vestry, pending the formal selection of a new rector, the responsibilities of the parish devolved upon the assistant minister, The Reverend Stanley C. Hughes, who had been with the parish for less than a year.

In the forty years since Isaac White had come to Newport in 1867, Trinity parish had grown remarkably. White and George Magill, during their long years of pastoral care, had eradicated the serious conflicts that had divided the parish in the mid-nineteenth century. By the turn of the century, Trinity had returned to being a stable parish. It had recovered its membership and its resources. In many ways, the quality of its clergy, the membership in the parish, and the nature of its outreach to the community echoed that of a century earlier.

As it had in the 1760s and early 1770s, Trinity during the last three decades of the nineteenth century counted among its members many prominent community and business leaders. Newport continued to grow as a summer resort with the arrival of many new summer residents, who were also some of the nation's leading business and social leaders. Trinity benefited from their interest in and generosity to the two-hundred-year-old parish. The work of the parish among the poor and the African-American communities in Newport continued and was expanded under this influence. In addition, with their broader knowledge of the business world and the world beyond Newport, a number of key summer residents provided leadership and guidance, making both formal and informal suggestions that helped gradually to place Trinity's practical affairs, as a corporation, under sound management and on an increasingly firm financial footing. In addition, the interest of the summer residents in their wintertime parishes led them to bring leading clergymen from New York and other places, establishing further ties for the parish with the national church and its missions.

The Reverend Walter Lowrie, rector of Trinity Church, 1905–1907.

After spending only two years in Newport, the American Church of "St. Paul within the Walls" in Rome called Lowrie as its rector. He remained in Rome until he retired in 1930, becoming a leading scholar and interpreter of the works of Kierkegaard and Karl Barth. In retirement, he became a Newport summer resident and returned to Trinity's pulpit on occasion.

Notes

1. Mason, *Annals,* Second Series, pp. 273, 281–86.
2. Ibid., pp. 290, 293–95.
3. Ibid., pp. 330–31; Minority Report by David King.
4. Ibid., p. 304, fn 46.
5. Ibid., pp. 303 fn 45; 348–49, fn 50.
6. Ibid., pp. 334–35.
7. Ibid., pp. 304–305.
8. Ibid., pp. 308–32.
9. Ibid., pp. 272, 344–45: Will of Martha Littlefield.
10. Henry B. Anthony, "The Chevalier de Ternay," in *Memorial addresses on several occasions delivered in the Senate of the United States by Henry B. Anthony, a senator from Rhode Island* (Providence, RI: Sidney S. Rider, 1875).
11. Mason, *Annals,* Second Series, 8 December 1873, p. 341.
12. Ibid., p. 343.
13. NHS, Parish Records: Records of St. Stephen's Guild, 1874–1888.
14. Ron Potvin, "The Christmas Explosion of 1934," unpublished manuscript; Henry G. Turnbull, ed., *A Century on the Point: Notes from the History of the Zabriskie Memorial Church of St. John the Evangelist* (Newport, RI: St. John's Church, 1975); Lorraine Le H. Dexter, "Steps from Trinity Church to the Point."
15. Loraine Le H. Dexter, "The Zabriskie Memorial Church of St John," *Newport History,* 49, pt. 4 (Fall 1975); "History of the Free Chapel of St. John the Evangelist, Newport, R.I., 1875–83" (Newport, 1935), pp. 1–8.
16. Mason, *Annals,* Second Series, 30 December 1875, p. 350.
17. *History of the Free Chapel,* pp. 8–9
18. *A* Mason, *nnals,* Second Series, Extracts from Bishop Clark's eulogy of Rev. Dr. White, 354–57, fn 53.
19. Ibid., pp. 352 fn 51, 363, 366.
20. Ibid., p. 353: Rev. A. G. Mercer to the Vestry, 7 January 1876.
21. Arthur Howard Nicholas, "The Bells of Trinity Church, Newport, R.I.," 70 (April 1916), pp. 148–49.
22. Wm King Covell, *The Organs of Trinity Church* (London, 1935), pp. 9–10.
23. *History of the Free Chapel,* pp. 17–19.
24. Mason, *Annals,* Second Series, p. 410.
25. Vestry Minutes, pp. 378–79: Magill to the corporation, 26 March 1883; pp. 401–405: Report of the Committee on the Rectory, 22 April 1889.
26. "New York Fresh Air Fund," *The Trinity Messenger,* vol. Ill, no. 3 (July 1888), p. 11.
27. Robert W. Pritchard, *A History of the Episcopal Church* (Harrisburg, PA: Morehouse, 1991), pp. 151, 188–91.
28. *Trinity Messenger,* vol. IV, no. 3 (July 1889), p. 10.
29. "Our Scandinavian Mission," *Trinity Messenger,* vol. V, no. 8 (December 1890), p. 30; vol. V, no. 10, (February 1891), p. 39: University of Rhode Island, MS Coll. 41: Records of the Episcopal Diocese of Rhode Island, Box 12, Folder 124, Anna Brophy, "The Swedish Episcopal Church in Rhode Island, 1888–1903."
30. Edith Sestrom Pedersen, *St. Peter's Evangelical Lutheran Church, Newport, Rhode Island: A Century of Witnessing and Grace, 1892–1992* (Baltimore: Gateway Press, 1993), pp. 10–13.
31. George Champlin Mason, *Annals of Trinity Church, Newport, Rhode Island, 1698–1821* (Newport, RI: George C. Mason, 1890).

32. George Champlin Mason, *Annals of the Redwood Library and Athenaeum.* (Newport, RI: Redwood Library, 1891).

33. "Dedication," George Champlin Mason, *Annals of Trinity Church, Newport, Rhode Island, 1821–1892* (Newport, RI: V. Mott Francis, M.D., 1894), [p. 1],

34. Ibid., pp. 447–54: "A Sermon in Memory of George C. Mason, Esq., preached in Trinity Church, Sunday, February 18, 1894, by Rev. George J. Magill, D.D., Rector."

35. These are summarized in *Annals*, First Series, pp. 341–47.

36. Mason, *Annals*, Second Series pp. 407.

37. Ibid., pp. 417–18.

38. NHS, Parish Records, Vestry Minutes, 3 September, 4 December 1894.

39. Ibid., Vestry Minutes 8 June: Letter from the Rector, Warden and Vestry to the Congregation, 18 June 1897.

40. Ibid., 18 January 1897.

41. Ibid., 10 February, 7 July 1897.

42. Ibid., 7 July 1897, 9 July 1901, 13 August 1901.

43. Ibid., 11 April, 26 May 1898, 18 December 1899.

44. Ibid., Letter of Rev Edward Rousmaniere to the Wardens and Vestry of Trinity, 4 December 1898.

45. Ibid., Vestry Minutes, 15 May 1899 with letter from Lispenard Stewart to Rector, Wardens and Vestry, 23 April 1899.

46. Ibid., 18 September 1899.

47. Ibid., 9 April; 10 May, 20 July, 19 September 1900.

48. Ibid., 10 June, 13 August, 23 August, 8 October, 12 November, 12 December 1901, 1 September 1903, 4 October 1904.

49. Ibid., 10 June 1901.

50. Ibid., 13 May, 23 May 1901.

51. Ibid., 23 April 1903: Letters of Rev. Stone to the Vestry, to the Junior Warden, 22 April 1903.

52. Ibid.

53. Ibid., 19 November, letter of Rev. Stone, 15 November 1904.

54. Ibid., Resolution, 27 November 1904.

55. Ibid., Resolution of 26 June 1904.

56. Ibid., Report of the Annual Meeting, 24 April 1905.

57. Ibid., Vestry Record 1906–1926, p. 17, 26 July 1906.

58. Ibid., p. 24, 17 January 1907.

59. Ibid., p. 25.

60. Ibid., Resolution of 26 June 1904.

61. Ibid., Report of the Annual Meeting, 24 April 1905.

62. Ibid., Vestry Record 1906–1926, p. 17: 26 July 1906.

63. Ibid., p. 24: 17 January 1907.

64. Ibid., p. 25.

The chancel as it appeared about 1900.
A new stained-glass window was installed in 1898 in memory of senior warden
LeRoy King. Note the bull's-eye windows are still closed and the brass cross still
standing on the altar in memory of The Reverend Isaac White. The Victorian altar
was still in place until 1915 and the lower part of the chancel was painted a dark
shade until 1911. Collection of the Newport Historical Society.

10

Wars, Restoration, and Anniversaries, 1907–49

In the four decades between 1907 and 1949, the world was twice engulfed in war. Although far distant from Newport, the effects of these wars were keenly felt at Trinity. The presence of the U.S. Navy in Newport gave those events a vivid immediacy, as did the service of many parishioners in uniform. At Trinity, one figure dominated those decades. When The Reverend Stanley Hughes had first come to Newport in February 1906 to take up duties as assistant minister at Trinity, he began an association that lasted for thirty-eight years, including service as both rector and rector emeritus. Only James Honyman served longer at Trinity.

Hughes was a Princeton graduate who at forty years of age in 1907 had been a Presbyterian minister before becoming an Episcopalian only two years before. When The Reverend Lowrie left Trinity in January 1907, the members of the vestry began an intensive search for a new rector. They considered a number of names and received a large number of letters, but after a full discussion they settled on Hughes, Lowrie's assistant. The vestry's nomination was unanimously approved by vote of the corporation in April 1907. He was offered a stipend of three thousand dollars per year and a monthly rental of fifty dollars for housing until the vestry could furnish the rectory for him.[1] Shortly afterwards, the vestry began negotiations with Mr. W. D. Sayer to rent the house at 135 Touro Street, with an option to purchase the property as the rectory, which was eventually done, in August 1908, for twelve thousand dollars.

As always, the church building required maintenance, and business matters needed attention. Interest in historical preservation and the city's colonial past was just reawakening in Newport during these years, and a number of people sought to remove some of the accretions that had grown in the Victorian era.[2] To that end, Mrs. G. L. Rives donated funds to repaint the church in June 1911, "beautifully done to the great and lasting satisfaction of all who see it."[3] In the process, much of the remaining neo-Renaissance decoration inside the church was painted over.

In April 1912, the corporation voted to widen participation in parish affairs by changing the charter to allow not only pew owners but anyone who rented a pew for one full year or more to vote at corporation meetings and hold parish office.[4] To evaluate the parish's financial condition, the vestry appointed a committee, composed of Herbert Bliss, J. I. Greene, and Clarence A. Carr, to examine income and expenditures over the previous five years.

The Financial Committee reported that the parish's annual income from taxes on pews, rental of parish-owned property, and investment income averaged $8,587.57 per year, whereas the yearly expense averaged $10,613.92, leaving a typical annual deficit of two thousand dollars to be covered by donations or, more commonly, by loans. Annual donations varied so much from year to year that the committee recommended that pew taxes be increased to cover the immediate shortfall in income and that for the long term the endowment fund, which then stood at $16,525, be increased to $100,000.[5]

This view of the chancel, taken a few years later, shows remnants of the earlier decoration with the Victorian altar still in use, but the bull's-eye windows opened. The box pews on either side of the chancel are clearly shown.

Collection of the Newport Historical Society.

View looking to the east up Frank Street, c. 1907. Clarence Stanhope took this photograph standing in Frank Street in front of the P. J. Murphy property, as shown on the detail from the 1907 city atlas.

Photo P2721; Atlas of the City of Newport (*Springfield, Mass.: I .J. Richards, 1907), plate 3.* Collection of the Newport Historical Society.

In considering the shortfall in income that the report had identified, the senior warden, George Gordon King, suggested that individual contributions needed to be both more regular and larger. A new way to approach this, he told the vestry, was to adopt the idea of the "duplex" envelope system, which had been highly successful in other parishes. The vestry approved his suggestion, and to start it they inaugurated Trinity's first every-member canvass in December 1912. Through it the parish issued 128 weekly pledge cards and eight additional cards for annual, semiannual, or quarterly pledge payments. Based on the information that the canvass produced, the rector appointed a committee to prepare the parish's first balanced budget, based on a firm estimate of income for the coming year.[6] This was duly done for 1913–14, at $15,521.

To stabilize further the parish's financial situation, the vestry agreed to a resolution presented by the senior warden for the establishment of an "Advisory Committee of Three." Composed of corporation members who were not on the vestry but were knowledgeable about matters of money, it was to be consulted in all matters relating to the financial welfare of the parish. All matters of great expense, including new construction and large building repairs, as well

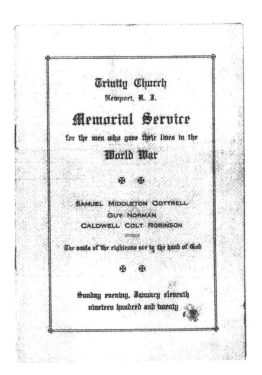

Memorial service for the Men who died in World War I.

Parish records. Collection of the Newport Historical Society.

as the allocation of any budget surplus, required its approval. To undertake these duties, the corporation elected a series of well-known individuals, many of them summer colonists. The first three were Gen. William Ennis, Gov. (later Senator) George Peabody Wetmore, and Lispenard Stewart. In later years, such prominent summer residents as Arthur Curtiss James, John Thompson Spencer, William Fitzhugh Whitehouse, and Willing Spencer served on the committee.[7]

In April 1915, William G. Schwartz, a German immigrant who had been sexton of the parish since 1888, was forced to retire due to ill health. Both summer and year-round residents loved him for the care and punctuality with which he had long carried out his duties, at both Trinity and Kay Chapel. In recognition of his twenty-eight years of service to the parish, the annual meeting of the corporation voted him a wage—specifically not a pension—of six hundred dollars a year for the remainder of his life.[8]

The international situation was growing increasingly grim, but the United States maintained its neutrality for another year. The increasing strain took its toll on America's armaments industry. One of the most prominent figures affected was Newport summer resident Col. Charles L. F. Robinson, a former colonel of the Newport Artillery and the current head of the Colt Manufacturing Company.

On his death from the strain of war-related work, his wife donated two silk American and Rhode Island flags for display in the church.[9] The following year, 1 April 1917, with American entry into the war, the vestry authorized the purchase of two more American flags and poles, one to be erected outside over the church and the other on the High Street guild house.[10]

Although the Naval War College suspended its operations for the duration of the war and many of its officer-students and staff were posted to sea duty, Newport quickly began to look like an armed camp. Some seventy-five thousand naval recruits passed through indoctrination at the Naval Training Station on Coaster's Harbor Island. The rapid increase of naval activity brought with it a temporary housing shortage as well as an influx of many young men and also of a new type of sailor, women "yeomanettes." Newport businesses welcomed, and many Newport citizens opened their homes to, the young sailors and naval officers. A number of organizations ran "Home Hospitality" programs, and churches throughout Newport welcomed the young servicemen and women. As part of its welcome effort, Trinity Church kept its parish house open every night of the week for social activities.[11] Just outside the Naval Training Station gate near the corner of Training Station Road and Third Street, the grounds of the Episcopal Church-related Cloyne School (which its headmaster

Processional cross.

In 1920, John D. H. Luce presented this brass processional cross to Trinity Church in memory of his father, Rear Admiral Stephen B. Luce, U.S. Navy, the founder of the Naval Training Station and the Naval War College in Newport. A longtime member of the parish, Admiral Luce's naval funeral had taken place in the church in 1917. The cross has been in regular use since 1920.

The fourth organ, 1920–30.

Hook & Hastings Company exchanged the organ it had installed in 1880 for another much larger instrument in 1920, with the detached console shown in this photograph. Electric lighting had been installed in 1918 and the old gaslight was removed at that time, as shown on the fixtures on the organ. Note that new round pipes replaced the square ones of 1880 behind the original organ case. Hanging from the gallery rail is one of the flags that Mrs. Charles Robinson had donated in memory of her husband in 1917. Hook and Hastings refurbished the 1880 instrument and sold it to St. Augustine's Church, Andover, Massachusetts.

and Trinity parishioner, Dr. Oliver Huntington, had named for Bishop George Berkeley's diocese in Ireland) were leased as a naval barracks, to help ease the housing strain. In other war-related issues, the vestry authorized the Rhode Island Trust Company to transfer the ten-thousand-dollar Magill Fund from its account and invest it in Liberty Loans. This was soon followed by similar investments of portions of other parish trust funds.[12]

The furnishings used in the chancel and in connection with services gradually began to change in this period. In 1915, Mrs. Sara J. Pattison inherited from her cousin, William Gilpin, the parish's original altar table, which had been used in the original 1700 church but had been removed from the present church in 1861. She donated it back for use in its original location.[13] A few years later, the stone font that had been placed in the church at the same time was donated to Holy Trinity Church, Tiverton.[14] In 1918, electric lighting replaced the gaslights in the church and, the following year, in the rectory.[15] In

1920, John D. Henley Luce presented to the parish a brass processional cross in memory of his father, Rear Admiral Stephen B. Luce (1827–1917), a longtime member of the parish since his days with the Naval Academy in 1861–65, and the founder of the Naval Training Station in 1883 and of the Naval War College in 1884.[16] This cross was still in regular use in the year 2001.

In the same years, services at Kay Chapel included worshippers from other churches. In order to assist the Greek Orthodox congregation in Newport, which was just begun to form in 1914, the vestry invited it to use Kay Chapel temporarily for services. It continued to make use of the chapel for this purpose until 1923, when it built its own St. Spyridon Church on Thames Street.[17]

More space for expanding activities remained an urgent problem for Trinity. In 1922, Hughes revived the plan that Stone and his assistant minister, Dennen, had put forth twenty years before to replace the parish house on High Street. As in 1902, there was only one building to use as a hall, and a small dwelling house for parish activities. As Hughes wrote in 1922,

> Things are worse now that they were twenty years ago, you see;
> far worse. Nobody knows the fearful handicap the Clergy are
> working under till he comes down to the parish house and
> works with them. Clubs and Societies clamor for the same room
> and there is constant friction. The shower-rooms and locker-
> rooms are not fit to be seen.[18]

A committee was formed and donations collected for this work, estimated to cost $100,000. Most of the needed money was donated by Arthur Curtiss James. After consulting several architects, the parish chose Frederick R. King to provide architectural drawings for the new building. The Grand Lodge of Free and Accepted Masons was invited to participate in laying the cornerstone on 23 September 1923. The building was fully completed in January 1925, and the committee ended its responsibilities with a report that the new structure had cost $123,231.08.[19]

In 1919, the Rhode Island General Assembly approved the corporation's latest amendment to the charter, changing the annual meeting to the second Monday in January; at the same time it established the vestry as having seven members. The two wardens were additional, ex-officio members.[20] In January 1925, in order to improve further the financial management of the parish, the Corporation formally constituted the vestry as a trust committee to supervise the

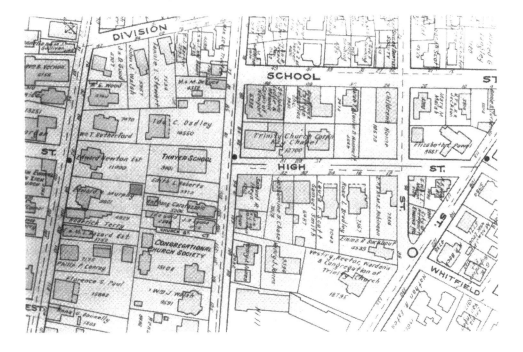

Detail from city atlas.
This detail shows the location of the church rectory at 135 Touro Street. Owned by
the parish from 1907 to 1929, it was conveniently located a short distance from
Kay Chapel. The building was later destroyed to make way for the Viking Hotel.
The outline of the Kay Chapel complex shows the buildings available for parish
activities. Atlas of the City of Newport (Springfield, Mass.: I. J. Richards, 1907), plate 3. Collection of
the Newport Historical Society.

parish's funds, now amounting to more than sixty-seven thousand dollars, and
authorized the Newport Trust Company to act as custodian for the trust funds.
At the same time, it authorized the treasurer to sell the twenty-seven thousand
dollars in Liberty Bonds that it had purchased during World War I and to reinvest the money in other securities.[21]

In terms of maintenance on the church building itself, there had been
concern for a number of years about the deteriorating condition of the wooden
shingled roof on the church and about the fire hazard it created. Newport had
suffered a number of serious fires. Rogers High School had been gutted by fire
in 1920, and the entire third floor and cupola of City Hall had been destroyed in
March 1925, during a fire in which the city had lost its first fireman in the line
of duty.[22] At first, the vestry made plans to replace the dry wood shingles with

asbestos, as a new city ordinance encouraged.[23] However, Leroy King had proposed that the parish hire a competent architect to survey the building and prepare plans showing the exact location of monuments and its layout, in case a disastrous fire required replacement of the building. Along with these precautions, electrical service to the church was placed underground, and a new and safer furnace was installed in the cellar; however, it would be 1931 before the first sprinkler system was installed.[24]

In conjunction with this work, plans were also begun to celebrate in 1926 the two-hundredth anniversary of the building as a place of worship.[25] In order to carry out the restoration work on the church building, the vestry had been in contact with the Society for the Preservation of New England Antiquities (S.P.N.E.A.). The vestry laid out four objectives for restoring the church:

1. Restoration—only if a certainty exists as to the original form of construction in all detail.
2. Elimination—whenever and so far as possible, if incongruous jarring decoration, ornamentation or furnishing.
3. The integrity and prolonged life of the original structure to be the prime object.
4. A definite containing policy along the above lines so that Posterity may receive from us and our successors of the Parish, as near as possible in its pristine beauty and well considered dignified proportions, this Gem of Colonial American Churches.[26]

Subsequently, the vestry obtained the services of the restoration architect Norman Isham of Providence as consulting architect in the renovation of the church.[27] Already acquainted with Newport, Isham had done the 1915 restoration of the Redwood Library and had given a series of lectures on colonial architecture that had helped to open many people's eyes to the importance of Newport's colonial architecture.[28] His first task at Trinity was to dissuade the vestry from putting asbestos shingles on the roof in its attempt to conform to the city's fire code. "The church, of course, is really a national monument. It ought not to be injured in any way and I know the vestry is far from meaning to injure it, but this green asbestos would be a distinct and almost irreparable wrong to the ancient fabric," Isham advised the rector.[29] Despite his professional authority, not everyone on the vestry was persuaded that Isham was right. In the

Norman Isham's 1927 concept for restoring the chancel.

The restoration architect Norman Isham painted this signed watercolor drawing as his concept for the work he undertook to restore Trinity to its original colonial appearance, with the royal arms over the altar. Isham Papers. Collection of the Newport Historical Society.

absence of Mrs. Harold Brown from Newport, a member of S.P.N.E.A.'s council, vestryman Henry Barton Jacobs took it upon himself to appeal directly to S.P.N.E.A. to arbitrate the dispute. Only when S.P.N.E.A. secretary William Sumner Appleton replied that "he would not have the temerity to venture to differ with Mr. Isham" did the vestry vote to install a more appropriate gray slate roof.[30]

With this recommendation of his authority, the vestry soon afterward agreed to Isham's longer-term proposals to restore the church. These included returning the chancel to a Christopher Wren style, restoring the royal arms to the altarpiece, installing a new chancel rail, hanging a red curtain at the east window, removing the ugly iron bars that propped up the wine-glass pulpit and restoring it to its original condition, using electric candles in the fixtures in the nave and in the galleries, adding cabinetry to the original organ case to conceal the pipes that had been installed in 1920, removing the chandelier in the chancel, and painting the building inside and out.[31] With the decision to restore the church to its colonial look, the vestry also went on record to oppose the erection in the future of any metal memorial tablet that was inconsistent with the colonial style.[32]

With the restoration of the building being planned, the parish formally celebrated its two-hundredth anniversary with a communion service on 1 August 1926. The church was full beyond capacity, with chairs in the aisles and many worshipers standing. The order of worship was printed in a special folder, illustrated on the cover with an etching of the church by Anne B. Henshaw. The bishop of Rhode Island, The Right Reverend James DeWolf Perry, gave the sermon.

One of the events that had been planned for the event was to publish a history of the parish, but Norman Isham would not have his study completed and off the press for another ten years. Referring to this, the bishop declared, "The magic touch of the historian is not needed now to surround us with the vanished scenes of yesterday. The subject of our celebration stands before our eyes. . . . Let it tell the story." Recounting the history of the parish briefly, Bishop Perry noted that the Anglican Church had played a key role in the history of the English-speaking peoples and that Trinity, the "Westminster Abbey of New England," was "among her fairest children . . . , calling the future to heed the message of past years."[33] In his sermon, Perry remarked that over the past two centuries, eleven men had entered the priesthood from Trinity Church, an average of one every twenty years.

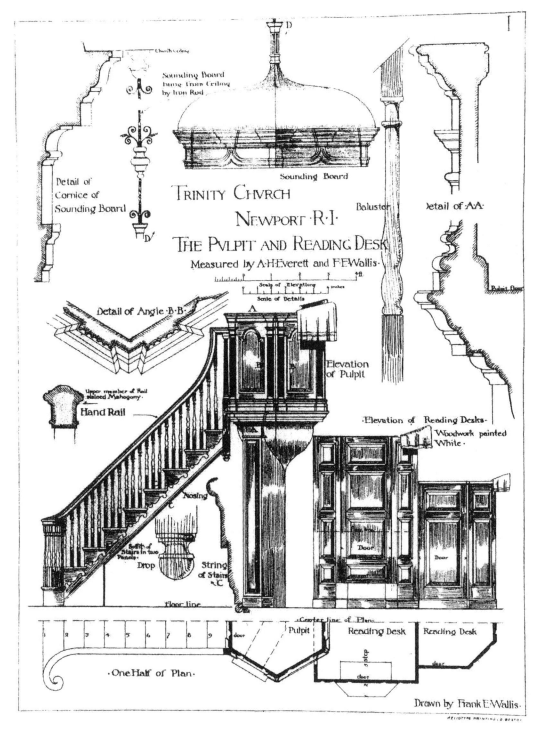

Architectural drawings of the "Pulpit and Reading Desk" and "Beadle's Pew." H. Everett and F. E. Wallis measured the church for these heliotyped drawings in the late 1920s. P2707, P2708 Collection of the Newport Historical Society.

TRINITY·CHVRCH·NEWPORT·R·I· ·BEADLE'S·PEW·
Measured and drawn by Frank E. Wallis.

II

scale of Elevation
6 inches
scale of details

ceiling line

gilt top

Beadle's
Wand

Two Panels
on End of
Pew

Pew Door
swings out

cushion

floor of Pew

Two steps up
from main floor
to floor of Pew

B B

floor line

Main Entrance to Church   Front Elevation.

Section thro Pew

center line

One half of Ceiling

Moulding of all Panels

Detail of B·B

There are two of these Pews,
one on each side of Entrance,
all Woodwork,
Painted White.

Dado Cap

Detail of Cornice

Section

Pew hinge

Guilloche from Organ

Rail from Gallery Stairs · Drop from Gallery Stairs

The service in the church was only one of a series of events in the first week of August in 1926 that celebrated the building's two-hundredth anniversary.[34] On Monday evening, the entire parish was invited to a reception held at the parish house, from 5 to 7 P.M., with dancing until 10 P.M. In another notable event that closed the week of celebration, the Art Association presented a pageant of ten tableaux, performed on an outdoor stage on the grounds of the Griswold House. More than a thousand people attended the pageant, chaired by Miss Helena Sturtevant and directed by Francis Carpenter. Prominent members of the Newport summer colony as well as Trinity parishioners had purchased seating space for group parties. Among them were Mrs. Hugh D. Auchincloss, Mrs. Miguel de Braganza, Miss Martha Codman, Mrs. Arthur Curtiss James, and Mrs. J. T. Spencer.

Each of the tableaux marked an important incident in Rhode Island history. Most were performed before a backdrop of the exterior of Trinity, painted with assistance from local artist William Cotton. Many prominent Newport residents played roles in the production. For example, John Howard Benson played Conanicus, and Erich Taylor played Wanumetonomy, in the tableau illustrating the Indian sale of the island in 1637. Mrs. Sidney Wright organized

The Reverend Stanley Hughes, standing at the altar at Easter, c. 1920.
Rector of Trinity Church, 1907—41, and rector emeritus, 1941—44.

the scene recreating Smibert's famous "Bermuda Group" portrait of Dean Berkeley with his family and friends. Mrs. William V. Pratt, wife of the president of the Naval War College, organized the scene showing George Washington attending Trinity Church, while Gen. James Parker, U.S. Army, played Washington, and Capt. Rufus Zogbaum of the War College faculty played Washington's aide. Other tableaux included the baptism of Stephen Decatur in June 1752, the arrival of Bishop Seabury in 1788, and the marriage at Trinity on 13 October 1811 of Mary Gibbs, the daughter of prominent merchant George Gibbs, to Thomas William Moore, the British vice consul at Philadelphia.[35]

The main feature and finale of the tableaux depicted the First World War. Based on a scenario written by Mrs. Virginia Potter and staged by Frank W. Shea of New York, it had five scenes showing Peace, Defiance, War, Surrender, and Benediction. In the first scenes, Miss Ruth Yarnell played "Peace," while Michael Urban of the Naval Training Station played "War." As "War" menaced "Peace," "France," played by Anne Burr Auchincloss, walked on stage, followed by the "Allies," each appearing in costume with appropriate national music: Mrs. Gustave J. S. White was "Belgium," Mrs Hugh Auchincloss, Jr., was "Russia," and Countess Alexandrine Beroldingon was "Italy," with others representing Japan, China, Greece, Czechoslovakia, and America. At a dramatic point in the performance, Mrs. Robert Potter, the author of the scenario, appeared on stage as "Germany." Walking defiantly past "Peace," she saluted "War" and strutted back to center stage. Various soldiers symbolized the progress of the war, until Mrs. Morris de Peyster appeared on stage as "The Greatest Mother of the World" and brought the "Allies" together. In the last scene, "Germany" laid down her sword and shield, and "Good," played by Trinity's rector The Reverend Stanley Hughes, pleaded for Germany to be taken back among the world's nations. All the nations then knelt on stage alongside "Good" as the Trinity Church choir sang "The Battle Hymn of the Republic." For the final verse of Julia Ward Howe's hymn, a company of apprentice seamen from the Naval Training Station joined the Trinity choir. Upon its completion, Hughes said the benediction. As he spoke, the figure of "Germany" moved on stage and again joined the family of nations. At the conclusion of the performance, the American flag was hoisted, and Conrad's Orchestra, joined by the Naval Training Station and Fort Adams orchestras, played "The Stars and Stripes."[36]

Following the celebration, the parish got down to the work of restoration. By 1928 Robert A. Smith of Newport, the general contractor, had completed the main work of Isham's restoration. In addition to the carpentry and painting

The fifth organ, 1930
Along with Isham's restora-
tion of the church interior,
the parish contracted with
the Skinner Organ Company
to replace the Hook &
Hastings Organ of 1920,
which had not been
satisfactory. At that time,
Isham designed the
enlarged organ case
that echoed the original
1733 case.

involved in restoring the chancel to its colonial appearance, Isham also installed the altar rail and hung twenty-six yards of Italian red Georgian damask at the east window. Following information that Isham had researched and provided, the parish commissioned the Irving & Casson - A. H. Davenport Co. of Boston to carve and paint a replica of the royal arms, as used by Queen Anne in 1702–1707, to be placed above the altar, where both research and local information suggested it had hung in the parish's first church and in the present church from 1726 until 1779.

Through Miss Edith and Miss Maud Wetmore, the parish obtained two matching "William and Mary"-style chairs to be placed in the chancel. "They belong to a friend of English descent," she wrote Isham, "and were brought over from England more than 125 years ago."[37] In the process of this work, Isham created a full set of architectural drawings and measurements of the building, in case it ever had to be reconstructed.[38]

In the spring of 1929, the parish sold the rectory at 135 Touro Street; Hughes had not used it since the death of his wife. The proceeds of the sale were deposited in a newly created Rectory Fund, the annual interest from which was to be paid to the rector in lieu of a rectory.[39] At about the same time, the vestry entered into a contract with the Skinner Organ Company to build a new organ for the church, at the cost of $15,375. The vestry subsequently sold the old instrument to William W. Laws, who rebuilt it as several smaller instruments.[40]

Among the issues that had long occupied Norman Isham in his plans for restoring the church were details regarding the royal arms to be placed over the altar. After correction of some errors in the first attempts, then repairs of damage incurred in shipping the arms back and forth between the church and the shop, the arms were finally ready for installation in 1930. In December 1930, Hamilton Fish Webster donated funds to install the arms over the altar, where Isham had planned. In February 1931, however, this final touch to the restoration project had created a major uproar at the annual corporation meeting. Mrs. Daniel B. Fearing moved that the corporation reject the placement of the arms. Clarence Cass seconded the motion, and numerous other members raised objections to it. In light of the patriotic and heated discussion that followed, Miss Elizabeth Smith, a member of the committee on fabrication, rose and asked permission to change her earlier vote, which had favored the royal arms. When brought to a vote, the motion against replacing the royal arms over the altar was unanimously carried.[41] At that point the arms were removed, and they disappeared from view.

One further pair of restoration-related improvements was made the following year, when two small bells were added to the chimes in order to complete the scale of notes, and an electric system was installed to ring them.

Meanwhile, many in Newport and in the country at large had been ruined in the stock market crash of 1929 and in the early years of depression that followed. Newport had an unemployment rate of about 20 percent in 1930. The city's summer social activities declined notably by 1932, and the absence of the Atlantic Fleet from Narragansett Bay was felt in the years between 1927 and 1934. Despite this downturn in the economy at all levels, Trinity's membership can be estimated at seven to eight hundred. There were three Sunday services in the chapel and one in the church, plus several weekday services. While pew owners dominated the church, the chapel had free pews, open to everyone. The neighboring parish house on High Street was the scene of numerous theatrical

The church after the Isham restoration.
This photograph shows the drapery and hangings on the pulpit as Isham designed
them. What appears to be a cross in the window over the altar is actually a shadow
created by the closed shutters.

presentations and of parish and community activities. There was economic chaos in the county and in Newport, but Trinity's investments largely escaped the disaster. At the annual meeting in January 1932, the treasurer reported that the parish's trust funds had actually grown substantially and now amounted to $224,644.79.[42] A year later, at the very bottom of the Depression, the Newport Trust Company reported that the market value of the proportion held in bonds and stocks was $168,302. At the same time, the Statistical Department of the Trust Company reported,

> Considering the present condition of the industry, we have no hesitation in classifying this list as an extremely good one. Based on market value, 50% of the holdings are yielding less than 5%, while 70% yield less than 6%. The remaining 30% is of lower grade in varying degrees but only one issue is actually in default. Some of the companies whose bonds yield more than 6% will not survive the depression. But on the other hand some of them will, and their issues will appreciate in price. . . . Our only advice can be, therefore, to retain present holdings for the time being.[43]

During the following year, Hughes suggested that the parish might produce a yearbook as a means to promote parish work. Mindful of financial considerations, he suggested using advertisements to pay fully for its production. The novel idea of advertising proved to be a contentious one; some thought it improper for a church. The secretary of the vestry recorded in the minutes that the vestrymen did "not take kindly to this procedure & discussion on the folly of present day advertisement was carried on."[44] Nine years later, in 1941, the vestry still opposed the use of advertising; in that case, the issue was solicitation for a sound-movie projector for use by the parish.[45]

As the tercentenary of Rhode Island approached in 1936, the vestry gave permission to exhibit some of the parish's colonial silver, including the Queen Anne chalice and paten, on the condition that they were exhibited in a fully-protected glass case. This request gave rise to additional thoughts about the danger of theft. It was then that the vestry purchased a safe for the silver.[46]

In September 1936, Norman Isham published his history: *Trinity Church in Newport, Rhode Island*. Daniel Berkeley Updike printed the book for the parish at his Merrymount Press, with all rights remaining with Trinity.

The Lafayette observance, 20 May 1934.
Samuel Kerschner took this photograph of the churchyard ceremony at the grave
of Admiral de Ternay, marking the centenary of Lafayette's death. P2725.
Collection of the Newport Historical Society.

A Trinity church team at the High Street parish house, c. 1925.
Back row, left to right: Billy Codgas, The Reverend Harold Dunn, John Hatch
Front row, left to right: John Rodda, Bill Adair, Bill Burke, Billy Good,
Harry Andrews.

Berkeley chocolate pot. This silver chocolate pot was made by the London silversmith Paul Crespen in 1725 and brought to Rhode Island by Dean George Berkeley in 1729. In 1731, as Dean Berkeley was leaving Newport, he gave it as a farewell gift to Daniel Updike, a Trinity vestrymen and the attorney general of the colony. Members of the Updike family passed it down from one generation to another until 1936. At that point, Daniel Berkeley Updike, a distinguished book designer, printed Norman Isham's architectural history of Trinity Church in Newport at  *his famous Merrymount Press and presented his family heirloom to Trinity, following publication of Isham's book.*

With its publication, Isham and Updike created a distinguished piece of printing as well as a major contribution to the historical understanding of the parish. The edition was limited to a thousand copies, which were sold to subscribers for five dollars apiece. Not surprisingly, Isham's work concentrated on the architectural history of the building and the knowledge of the fabric that the author had gained as the parish's consulting restoration architect since 1923. The book's publication raised one old issue, which Hamilton Fish Webster of "Pen Craig" brought to the attention of the vestry. In 1925, when the history was originally planned, several donors had agreed to replace the antiquated heating system in the church, which by that time had become a fire hazard. They had been promised that in recognition of their donations to the fabric of the church, the vestry would include their names in the appendix of that book, among the donors to the Restoration Fund of 1925. In the event, that was not done; Webster requested that his letter be made a part of the official parish record to rectify that omission.[47]

Trinity weather vane.

Samuel Kerschner took this photograph of Trinity's original weather vane while it was on the ground for repairs after the 1938 hurricane. P2728. Collection of the Newport Historical Society.

On 21 September 1938, one of the most devastating hurricanes in Newport's history struck the Rhode Island coast and Narragansett Bay at high tide, with no advance warning. The storm killed six people in the city of Newport and caused an estimated five million dollars in damages. Among Newport's churches, the First Baptist Church lost its spire, but Trinity's was spared. Damage to the church was less than for others, but the glass in two windows had to be reset, and the large window under the clock had to be repaired, along with other repairs to the roof and steeple amounting to more than three thousand dollars.[48]

As war loomed once again, Newport became the base of operations for numerous destroyers protecting transatlantic convoys. The number of sailors in town would eventually increase to levels far above what the city had experienced in 1917; the base expanded from Coaster's Harbor Island to the Coddington Cove area and across Narragansett Bay. At this early stage, half a year before the United States had formally entered the war in late 1941, the vestry unanimously approved Hughes's suggestion that the parish invite the "boys of the fleet and of the forts" to services at Kay Chapel and entertain them at the Parish House on Sunday evenings as the parish had during the last war.[49]

On 24 July 1941, Hughes announced his resignation due to ill health, but he noted that "the Parish is in sound condition and with God's blessing and guidance we may confidently expect that it will go forward to new and greater usefulness."[50] On Hughes's recommendation, the assistant minister, The Reverend W. Eugene Snoxell, became minister in charge of the parish. In accepting Hughes's resignation with deep regret, the corporation elected him "Rector

Emeritus for the rest of his natural life" and unanimously approved a minute, drafted by vestryman Dr. Stephen B. Luce, describing Hughes's many contributions to the parish. Among the rectors of the parish, only Honyman had served longer, and Hughes earned accolades equal to those given Honyman for his devotion to the parish:

> No minister of the Gospel in Newport of any denomination
> has been so beloved and respected as Dr. Hughes. At his
> thirtieth jubilee [in 1937], the reception in his honor was
> attended by Roman Catholic Priests, Jewish rabbis, and
> ministers of all other creeds in the city. In the communion
> of the Episcopal Church, both high and low churchmen have
> turned to him for advice and guidance. His influence in civic
> affairs is attested by his activity in Masonic affairs, his chap-
> laincy of the Sons of the American Revolution, his past
> chaplaincy of the Newport Artillery Company, his appoint-
> ment to the Directorate of the Redwood Library, and his
> election as First Vice President of the Newport Historical
> Society.[51]

Choirboy Roger Gilman, c. 1934.
This formal portrait was taken to mark Gilman's record for sixty-six months of perfect attendance in Trinity's choir. His brother-in-law, Ralph Whitman, subsequently surpassed this record with seventy months. A life-long Trinity parishioner, Gilman (1918–99), was one of the 262 Trinity parishioners who served in World War II. Graduating from the Massachusetts Merchant Marine Academy in 1938, he became the country's youngest licensed cargo ship-master in 1943 at the age of twenty-five. Among many wartime voyages, he served on the Murmansk run, later becoming master of salvage ships and a coastal pilot.

Parish Records. Collection of the Newport Historical Society.

Luce, a distinguished archeologist as well as grandson and namesake of the Naval War College's founder, went on to describe Hughes's many contributions to the diocese and the parish, noting that he was "essentially a scholar—brought up in the old disciplines of Latin, Greek and Hebrew—a lover of books with a profound understanding and appreciation of research. To this, he adds those qualities of a pure loving heart which are the principal characteristics of a true teacher and pastor."[52] He noted that the parish was made up of "hetero-geneous elements[:] . . . the summer visitors, the officers of the Army and Navy stationed here, as well as those who reside here permanently."

> There is not an element in the Parish to whom Dr. Hughes has
> not affectionately ministered, and there are none of them, rich
> or poor, white or colored, who do not appreciate the devotion
> he has so unselfishly bestowed and who are [not] praying for
> him at this time of his illness.[53]

Kay Chapel in the 1930s.
This interior view of Kay Chapel shows the paintings that W. F. Whitehouse
donated to the parish. In 1944, they were given to St. George's Church, Newport.

The Reverend Lauriston Livingston Scaife, rector of Trinity Church, 1942–45.

In early January 1942, the daughter of Cornelius Vanderbilt II, Countess László Széchenyi, endowed the Vanderbilt Family pew for ten thousand dollars, accompanying her letter with the first half of the donation.[54] In appreciation for her continuing interest in the parish, the corporation elected her a member of the Committee of Advice, succeeding Arthur Curtiss James. At this time, pew rents continued to form a substantial portion of the parish income. At the annual meeting, the treasurer reported that pew rents had contributed $7,964, based upon an annual rent of 25 percent of the value of each pew. Looking ahead at the coming year, the treasurer used recent experience to project a balanced budget at $18,077, with income of two thousand dollars from plate collections, three thousand dollars from the envelope system, $7,500 from pew rents, and five thousand dollars from endowments. Among expenditures, salaries to the clergy and parish officers ($9,900) was the largest single category, followed by three thousand dollars each for music and for general operating expenses.[55]

On 21 December, the committee to select a new rector reported that about thirty men had been recommended and that it had received several direct applications for the position. After considering the candidates, the committee recommended The Reverend Lauriston Livingston Scaife of St. Thomas's Church, New York, as the new rector. Scaife arrived in Newport to take up his new duties on 1 May 1942, along with a new assistant minister, The Reverend Kenneth W. Cary. Among Scaife's first initiatives, he combined the "Parish Purse" and the "Parish Poor Fund" into a single fund, which was named the "Rector's Discretionary Fund." At the same time, on his recommendation, the vestry set in motion plans to purchase a rectory, one that was dignified and in keeping with Dr. and Mrs. Scaife's needs. In July 1942, the vestry approved the purchase from Mrs. C. J. Guthrie Nicholson of the property at 287 Gibbs Avenue, for ten thousand dollars.[56] In another initiative, in September, Scaife introduced a new official parish publication, *The Trinity Tower.*

The 1944 parish budget reflected for the first time a general and continuing plan to raise funds to donate to activities outside the parish. Setting aside a thousand dollars, the vestry planned donations that included varying amounts to the General Theological Seminary, the American Red Cross, St. Andrew's School, and the Army and Navy Commission. The parish's invested funds had reached a value of $298,000, to fund annual expenses of $29,000. During the year, seven thousand dollars were budgeted for renovations to Kay Chapel.

In connection with the Kay Chapel renovation, in 1944 Mrs. Prescott Lawrence donated funds in memory of her daughter to construct a small chapel within the Kay Chapel building, to be named Calvary Chapel. In addition, the newly renovated Kay Chapel featured a completely renovated chancel, newly redone floors and pews, and interior walls painted a light buff color. On 17 September 1944, the bishop of Rhode Island, The Right Reverend James DeWolf Perry, consecrated Calvary Chapel and rededicated Kay Chapel, paying special tribute to the memory of the rector emeritus, The Reverend Stanley C. Hughes. The Reverend Nelsin W. Bryant, rector of St. George's Church, delivered the dedicatory sermon before an overflow congregation. As part of the renovations, the paintings in the chapel, which had been donated by Mr. W. F. Whitehouse, were, with his approval, passed to St. George's Church. In his dedication the bishop also blessed a new pulpit, given in memory of Carl Gustave Richardson by his family; a prie-dieu and a sedilla given by Miss Mae Rounds in memory of her parents, Mr. and Mrs. George Rounds; a new Bible in memory of Rear Adm. Livingston Hunt, given by his wife; a pair of candlesticks for the altar, in memory of Theodore Johnston Bigalke, USNR, who had lost his life in the war; and eight ecclesiastical lanterns, given by Miss Helen Powers in memory of Thomas Powers.[57]

Bishop Perry granted Scaife leave of absence from 1 November 1944 to volunteer for service as a navy chaplain. Commissioned a lieutenant (j.g.), Scaife reported for training at the College of William and Mary in Williamsburg. Noting that "clergymen who have served in Newport churches have heard the call to join the armed forces," one newspaper commented,

> If he had chosen, Chaplain Scaife could have remained with his family in Newport. Since the death of his father-in-law, Commander Carnochan, in an airplane crash last year, those who know the Trinity rector best believe he has set his heart on becoming a naval chaplain. He started steps toward this end some

weeks ago. His being in uniform now means that he is doing what he believes is more important for his country.[58]

In order to administer the affairs of the parish more efficiently, by having one single head, the vestry, with the advice of the bishop, appointed The Reverend William Murray Bradner to serve as priest in charge, authorizing him to use the rectory during this period. Six months later, in June 1945, while still on leave of absence, serving first on Okinawa and then on board the transport USS *Montauk*, Scaife resigned as rector in order to accept a call from Calvary Church in Pittsburgh, where the Scaife family had lived for several generations, and where Arthur B. Kinsolving, brother of Mrs. John Nicholas Brown of Providence and Newport, had been rector.[59] In a special meeting of the corporation following Scaife's resignation, the vestry moved the immediate promotion of The Reverend Bradner to become rector.[60]

William Murray Bradner was the son of The Reverend Lester Bradner, who had been rector of St. John's Church, Providence, and later the educational director for the diocese of Rhode Island. The young Bradner had been born in New York City and graduated from Yale in 1922, and from the Episcopal Theological Seminary in Cambridge in 1925. Ordained in Oregon, he had served as a deacon at Ascension Cove between 1926 and 1928. In 1928–31, he had been secretary of the department of religious education in the diocese of New York; then rector of Grace Church, Medford, in 1931–38; and canon precentor at the Washington National Cathedral in 1938–41. For many years, he and his family had retained their Rhode Island connections, spending their summers in North Kingston.[61]

The Reverend William Murray Bradner rector of Trinity Church, 1945–49.

In an early initiative, Bradner made immediate arrangements to deposit with the Newport Historical Society, on indefinite loan, the original S.P.C.K. library of the parish. The surviving books, which had arrived in Newport in the earliest days of the parish and constituted the first library in the colony, were stacked in the basement of the church and were in need of care.[62] Not long afterward a book collector found one of the original volumes, still bearing its original label as "Belonging to ye Library of Road Island' printed in gold on the cover, in an auction catalogue, and he donated it to the collection.[63] Among other changes, Bradner was the first to ban the use of cameras in the church building during services.

During the war years, the number of communicants in the parish rose from two hundred in 1942 to about one thousand in 1946, with many servicemen and women among them. The parish Role of Honor at Easter 1945 listed 253 names and, typically for the period, the weekly *Tower* included news and extracts of letters from servicemen abroad. Typical for the period were 1944 parish statistics showing that a total of 44,855 individuals had attended 225 Sunday services and 204 weekday services during the year.

In September 1945, the sexton, John Ernest Medlock, retired after twenty years of devoted service to the parish. Born in 1873 at Tempsford, Bedfordshire, in England, he had come to America as a boy of eighteen in 1892. He had been employed by a number of Newport families, including Daniel B. Fearing, for two decades before he became sexton of Trinity Church in 1925. With those families, he had made many trips to Europe, crossing the Atlantic twenty-eight times; he had lived in Rome for seven years as well as in France, becoming fluent in both Italian and French. His upbringing in the Church of England, along with his faithful and intelligent service, gave him an unusual dignity in and love for his duties. As the vestry noted on his death, "His respect for, and faithful observance of, all the traditions of the Episcopal Church was something never to be forgotten."[64]

In February 1946, Bradner submitted a plan for organizing the vestry into standing committees, each chaired by the rector, to deal with specific matters: finance, property, music, canvass, and ushering. This arrangement replaced the organization that Hughes had introduced in 1912; among other things, it replaced the Advisory Committee on Financial Affairs, on which several very prominent summer residents had served over the years.

In March 1946, on the recommendation of the president of the Naval War College, Vice Adm. William S. Pye, the privilege of using a pew on the

The rectory, 1946–74, 81 Rhode Island Avenue.

main aisle in Trinity, which had been extended to him during his presidency of the college from 1942 to 1946, was also extended to his successor, Adm. Raymond Spruance.[65] Spruance's daughter Margaret was married to Gerard S. Bogart in the church in 1948, toward the end of Spruance's presidency of the college.[66]

Upon his appointment, Bradner had advised the vestry that the rectory was much too large for him to maintain; he recommended that the vestry obtain a smaller house for the rectory. It took some time to find a buyer for the property, but in March 1946 the parish sold the property at 287 Gibbs Avenue for twelve thousand dollars to Vice Admiral and Mrs. Pye. In its place, the vestry was able to purchase 81 Rhode Island Avenue from Mrs. Christine Andrews, for fifteen thousand dollars, as the new rectory.[67]

In 1947, the charter of the corporation was revised for the first time in more than fifty years. With the advice of the law firm of Edwards & Angell of Providence, the changes allowed the parish to increase the value of its property holdings from $250,000 to the value of $1,500,000, and they thoroughly modernized the language of the charter. The vestry was altered from a nine-member board to a board elected for a three-year term with nine vestrymen, a senior warden, junior warden, secretary, and treasurer. At the same time, the corporation adopted a detailed set of by-laws that specified the procedures for the annual meetings and the duties of the rector, churchwardens, and vestry as well as the secretary, treasurer, and the standing committees. Modifying Bradner's earlier plan, the by-laws established five committees (membership, nominating, finance, pews, and auditing) and provided that no amendment to the charter could be made without the approval of two-thirds of the members at two consecutive meetings of the corporation.[68] After their introduction by Rep. James H. Kiernan (D-Providence) and the entire Newport delegation, the Rhode Island General Assembly approved these changes to the charter, and Gov. John O. Pastore signed them into law on 9 January 1948.

Section three of the new charter provided that "each and every adult communicant in regular standing in the Protestant Episcopal church who is a regular member of, worshipper in, and contributor to, said Trinity Church in Newport shall be a member of said corporation." In order to determine exactly who was a member, the vestry decided that all who contributed to the envelope system, or who made contributions through the office where they were registered by name, would in the future be considered "regular contributors."[69]

In April 1948, the parish began to make plans for celebration of its 250th anniversary. The Anniversary Committee, chaired by Dr. Stephen B. Luce, with Cdr. Robert S. Carr, USNR (Ret.), as vice chairman, arranged several special services and a full week of observances. The celebration opened on Sunday, 4 July 1948, with a service of morning prayer and a sermon by the Venerable Anthony R. Parshley, archdeacon of the diocese of Rhode Island, who spoke on "The Church and the Union." Outlining the history of the Anglican and Episcopal Church in America, Parshley concluded, "Ours is a compelling heritage." At this anniversary, he said, "we meet not to take cognizance of the brightest flowers and fruits of the years, but to see that the deep roots of prayer still draw the primal elements to sustain and nourish."[70]

Special services followed throughout the month. The main celebrations were concentrated in the week of 11 July. The Reverend George Handisyde, rector of a parish in Sussex, England, launched them with a sermon linking the Newport parish with its Anglican roots.[71] On Wednesday evening, 14 July, The Right Reverend William L. Essex, bishop of Quincy, Illinois (assistant rector under The Reverend Stanley Hughes at Trinity in 1910-13), returned to the pulpit. At the same service, the Trinity choir, joined by the Swanhurst Choral Society, sang the Magnificat, in a setting by Trinity's first organist, Carl Theodore Pachelbel. The Reverend Albert C. Thomas of the First Baptist Church in Providence, a Rhode Island congregation with similar spirit and historic interest, preached on "The Church and the Community" at the 18 August service, while on 22 August, former Trinity rector and now bishop of Western New York, The Right Reverend Lauriston Scaife, preached on "Christian Behavior."

Before beginning his sermon, Scaife remarked, "I shall be eternally thankful to the members of this congregation . . . for the splendid and generous response to my short ministry in this parish—a response which gave me confidence [and] . . . which has stood me in good stead these recent years."[72] In connection with the anniversary, a display of historical treasures, including old linen, silver, and prayer books, was set up in the parish house. The Reverend Charles Russell Peck, rector of Christ Church, the "Old North Church" in Boston, gave an illustrated lecture on his church, so similar in design to Newport's; Dr. Stephen Luce spoke on Trinity and its long line of community leaders who had served as wardens and on the vestry.

In 1946 or 1947, Ward Printing, owned by vestryman Henry Wilkinson, published the very first, limited run of an illustrated pamphlet on the parish's history: *An Historical Sketch of Trinity Church.*[73] Reflecting public interest in colonial buildings, the recently established Preservation Society of Newport County suggested in April 1949 that the parish open the church building to visitors during the summer months and outlined a proposed agreement between the two organizations to do this. The vestry so authorized the rector.[74] The years from 1945 to 1949, as a curate, The Reverend A. Royston Cochran, would recall, "included the closing years of World War Two and the excitement of V-J Day. Trinity Church was a booming parish throughout the period with one of the largest Church Schools in the Diocese."[75] With effect from 1 July 1949, Bradner resigned as rector. During the autumn, The Reverend Archie H. Burdick provided much of the pastoral care and assisted in directing the Church School.

In October, the parish called The Reverend James R. MacColl III, who was able to officiate at his first service on 11 December. Born in Evansville, Indiana, the thirty-one-year-old MacColl had graduated from St. Paul's School in Concord, New Hampshire, and from Princeton University in 1941, where he had majored in English literature. Going on to graduate from the Episcopal Divinity School in 1943, he had served briefly at Trinity Church, Toledo, Ohio. Commissioned as a naval chaplain, he had first ministered to fighter pilots at Vero Beach, Florida. Later, he had served at the naval hospital in Dublin, Georgia, until his discharge. He had become assistant rector at Christ Church in Winnetka, Illinois, before coming to Newport.[76]

The parish that MacColl came to at the end of 1949 was an active and strong one, reflecting the growth and stability that had emerged through Stanley Hughes's long service beginning in 1907, and which had been sustained through the continuing work of Dr. Scaife and Bradner. The financial condition of the parish remained solid, with income and expenses at $35,114.02 in 1949, despite a deficit of $1,632. By this time, investments had come to provide the largest source of income, amounting to nearly nine thousand dollars, followed by pew rents at $6,860, and plate collections, including weekly pledges, at only $3,088. Reflecting the vitality and strength of the parish during nearly half a year without a rector or an assigned priest in charge, all parish activities continued in 1949, as they had for many years. The parish officers and each member of the vestry performed all the tasks necessary to maintain the parish's many activities, in addition to the daily work of parish secretary, Gustava Stenholm. Among these activities there were women's organizations, such as the Altar Society under Mae Rounds, and the Guild of the Christ Child, under Mrs. Carl Gustafson. Margaret Parker managed the Church School, and the choirs were under her husband, the organist, Raymond Parker. The Young People's Fellowship was under Mr. and Mrs. J. Crocker Titus; girls' basketball was played under Mrs. George A. Thurston and Mrs. John B. Lawton; the Scouts met under Raymond F. King and Capt. Robert S. Simpson. Men and women of the navy and Marine Corps stationed in Newport, although often in Newport for relatively short periods of duty, remained a vital element of the congregation. Not only attending services, many servicemen and women played key roles, teaching in the Sunday school, leading in the Men's Club program, and generally being active in the parish.[77]

While much had changed for Newporters in the forty years between 1907 and 1949, some things remained the same and were a continuing inspiration. The daily weekday ringing of Trinity's chimes at five o'clock for fifteen minutes remained a special moment for the entire city. "Drivers of cars inching their way along the narrow confines of Spring Street find that for a little while they do not mind the slow going traffic as cars string out behind stop lights. Harried pedestrians forget their cares and worries and listen," a journalist wrote. "For the classic perfection of Trinity's spire, it may be that the chimes within have at least as much significance to those who listen as has the pure beauty of line that greets the eye. And the playing of hymns from the steeple would seem to supplement its function of 'pointing the soul to God.' "[78]

Notes

1. Newport Historical Society, Vestry Minutes 1906–1926, pp. 37–39: 25 April, 9 May 1906.

2. Eileen Warburton, *In Living Memory: A Chronicle of Newport, Rhode Island, 1888–1988* (Newport, RI: Newport Savings and Loan, 1988), p. 53.

3. Ibid., p. 157: letter from Rector to Mrs. Rives, 12 July 1911.

4. Ibid., pp. 151, 167, 178, 179, 180: 17 April 1911, 13 March, 24 March, 2 May, 10 May 1912.

5. Ibid., typed sheet laid in at pp. 166–67: Report of the Committee, 4 March 1912.

6. Ibid., p. 190: 16 January 1913.

7. Ibid., p. 204: minutes of the annual meeting, 24 March 1913; p. 320: 1 April 1918; p. 455: January 1925.

8. Ibid., p. 248: 3 January 1915; Obituary, *Newport Mercury,* 22 May 1915.

9. Ibid., p. 296: 9 Nov 1916; Obituary, *Newport Mercury,* 8 July 1916.

10. Ibid., p. 299: 1 April 1917.

11. Warburton, *In Living Memory,* p. 58.

12. Ibid., pp. 331, 333: 28 April 1918, 10 October 1918.

13. Ibid., p. 271: 7 October 1915; letter laid in from Mrs. Sara J (Mrs. E. J.) Pattison to Rev. Hughes, Boston, 1 October 1915.

14. Ibid., p. 310: 8 June 1917.

15. Ibid., pp. 316, 317, 330, 336.

16. Ibid., p. 367.

17. Ibid., p. 250: 3 February 1915.

18. *Parish Notes,* anniversary number, Trinity Church, June 1922, p. 1.

19. Vestry Minutes, pp. 450, 453: 8 January 1925; Construction Account 1924.

20. Ibid., p. 346.

21. Vestry Minutes, p. 456: Resolution passed during the annual meeting, 12 January 1925; laid in back of volume: Agreement between Trinity Church and Newport Trust Company, 19 January 1925.

22. Warburton, *In Living Memory,* p. 64.

23. Ibid., p. 462: 13 September 1925.

24. Ibid., p. 83: 10 May 1931.

25. Ibid., p. 461: 2 July 1925.

26. Society for the Preservation of New England Antiquities (SPNEA). Correspondence File Newport, RI-Trinity Church: Letter from H.W. Hare Powel, secretary Restoration Committee, to William Sumner Appleton, secretary, SPNEA, 18 August 1923.

27. Newport Historical Society, Isham Collection, Box A-11 Folder 114: Correspondence 1923–1928, Isham to H. W. Hare Powel, 22 August 1923.

28. Warburton, *In Living Memory,* p. 53.

29. Newport Historical Society, Isham Collection, Letter from Isham to Rev. Stanley Hughes, 18 August 1925.

30. SPNEA Correspondence, Henry Barton Jacobs to William Sumner Appleton, 14 September 1925.

31. Vestry Minutes, 1926–1950, p. 21: Special Meeting, 11 July 1927; Norman Isham, *Trinity Church in Newport, Rhode Island.* (Boston: 1936), pp. 110–11. Isham Correspondence 1923–28, Box A-11, file 114: Rev. Hughes to Isham, 8 July 1927, 12 July 1927.

32. Ibid., p. 22: 17 July 1927.

33. "Bishop Perry Gives Historical Sermon: Trinity Church Opens Observance of Bi-Centennial Anniversary," *Newport Daily News,* 2 August 1926, p. 1.

34. "Trinity Church to Observe Two Hundredth Anniversary Next Week," *Newport Daily News,* 31 July 1926, pp. 2–3.

35. "Recollections of Old Newport Recalled,*" Newport Daily News,* 5 August 1926, pp. 1, 9.

36. Ibid.

37. Newport Historical Society, Isham Papers, Box A-11, file 114, Correspondence 1923–28: Tessitura Italiana, New York, to Isham, 27 February 1928; LeRoy King to Isham, 21 May 1928; Edith Wetmore to Isham, 8 August 1928; Irving & Casson-A. H. Davenport Co. to Isham, September 1928.

38. These drawings are now in ibid., Box A-12. In July 1943, The Boston Blueprint Com-pany made copies for the parish in 1942; these, too, have been deposited in the Newport Historical Society.

39. Newport Historical Society, Vestry Minutes., p. 46: 7 March 1929.

40. William King Covell, *The Organs of Trinity Church*, pp. 11–13.

41. Newport Historical Society, Vestry Minutes, pp. 73, 77: 20 December 1930; Minutes of the continued annual meeting, 2 February 1931.

42. Ibid., p. 91: annual meeting, 11 January 1932.

43. Ibid., p. 111: Industrial Trust Company, "Analysis of Securities of Trinity Church, New-port," December 6, 1933.

44. Ibid., p. 107: undated [August 1932],

45. Ibid., p. 216: [July 1941],

46. Ibid., pp. 136–37: 12 April; 10 May 1936.

47. Ibid., p. 143: Hamilton Fish Webster to Edward Ellis, 26 October 1936.

48. Ibid., pp. 175, 178, 181: undated [September] 1938, 13 November, 8 January 1939.

49. Ibid., p. 214: 11 May 1941.

50. Ibid., p. 271: Hughes to vestry, 24 July 1941.

51. Ibid., pp. 220–22: Minutes of A Special Corporation Meeting, 12 August 1941. Hughes died in Newport, 14 December 1944.

52. Ibid.

53. Ibid.

54. Ibid., p. 230: Vestry Minutes 11 January 1942.

55. Ibid., p. 232: Minutes of the annual meeting, 12 January 1942.

56. Ibid., p. 245: Special Meeting of the Vestry, 7 July 1942.

57. "Trinity Holds Rededication Service," *Newport Daily News,* 17 September 1944.

58. Trinity Church Scrapbook, 1944–1951. Clipping dated 6 November 1944.

59. Vestry Minutes, 1924–1950, pp. 336–37: letter from Scaife to Henry C. Wilkinson, secretary of the Vestry, 25 June 1945.

60. Ibid., p. 338: minutes of the Special Meeting of the Corporation, 11 July 1945.

61. "Trinity Vestry Names Associate Minister," *Newport Daily News*, 2 November 1944.

62. Ibid., p. 334: minutes; p. 342: letter Herbert Brigham to Rector.

63. "246-Year-Old Volume Returned to Trinity," *Newport Daily News*, 16 October. 1947.

64. Ibid., p. 331: minute 10 June 1945, "John Ernest Medlock"; Obituary, *Newport Daily News*, 23 April 1945.

65. Ibid., pp. 360, 362, 364, 365: minutes, 10, 20, 24, 27 March, 14 April 1946.

66. Trinity Scrapbook, 1944–51: "Margaret A. Spruance and Gerald S. Bogart to Wed in Trinity Church," *Newport Daily News,* 22 May 1948; Trinity Church Marriage Register, 22 May 1948; This corrects the statement in Thomas Buell, *The Quiet Warrior: A Biography of Raymond A. Spruance* (Boston: Little Brown, 1974), p. 395, that the marriage took place at the President's House, Naval War College; in fact, it was the wedding reception after the Trinity service, that occurred there.

67. Ibid., p. 362; Minutes 20 March 1946.

68. Ibid., p. 402: suggested Amended Charter; Suggested By-laws.

69. Ibid., p. 454: Minutes of the annual meeting, January 1948.

70. Trinity Church 250th Anniversary Committee Records; "Trinity Church Opens Anniversary Program," *Newport Daily News,* 6 July 1948.

71. "Trinity Church Told of Anglican Communion," *Newport Daily News,* 11 July 1948.

72. "Bishop Scaife Returns to Preach at Trinity," *Newport Daily News,* 22 August 1948.

73. Letter from Rev. A. Royston Cochran to Hattendorf, 21 February 1996.

74. Vestry Minutes, p. 461: minutes 10 April 1949; Pew Deeds 1926–54: letter from Clerk of the Vestry to Pye, 23 November 1942.

75. Letter from Cochran, 21 February 1996.

76. "Trinity Parish Extends Call to New Rector," *Newport Daily News*, 20 October 1949.

77. Ibid., p. 489: "Report of the Rector. Rev. James R. MacColl III to the Corporation of Trinity Church," January 9, 1950.

78. Trinity Scrapbook, 1944–1951, "Trinity Chimes Long Popular," undated clipping c. August 1950.

Trinity Church from the northeast, at the corner of Spring and Church Streets.
P674. Collection of the Newport Historical Society.

11

New Ventures in a Battle for Survival, 1950–73

In his first report to the corporation in January 1950, The Reverend MacColl noted, "It is both a humbling and inspiring experience to come to this parish as its rector. . . . To stand in the Church and to think of all that is symbolized in that beautiful and dignified building, to feel with one's heart the cumulative effect of the faith and consecration that have made it what it is shakes and stirs my soul." At the same time, while MacColl fully appreciated the historic and inspirational nature of the fabric of its historic church building, he detected a darker side to the picture. "There are a few, I regret to say, who feel that Trinity has seen its best days, who have intimated to me that Trinity may in future years be remembered more for its past than for its present, that it may be heavy on tradition and lean on dynamic Christian activity." Setting the tone for the next half-century of parish life, MacColl declared, "To believe even one morsel of this kind of thinking is to indict ourselves and the vitality of our faith."[1]

In April 1950, when it became clear that no curate would be available among the current graduating class of any seminary in the country, the vestry hired John Rupp, who had previously served for ten years as executive director of the Newport Armed Services YMCA, to serve as co-coordinator of parish activities from 1 July. The responsibilities of this new position included being administrative assistant to the rector; developing and coordinating parish activities, with special emphasis on the High School Group, organization of a Young Married Group and the Men's Club; promotion and public relations, including with armed services personnel; and planning and administration of the every-member canvass for 1950.[2] When The Reverend Peter Chase arrived in the following year to serve as curate, Rupp continued in this valuable service to the parish, remaining in the position until 1954.

In the summer of 1950, the country once again faced the prospect of war; this time, it was in Korea. In response to this new international situation, MacColl wrote to President Harry S. Truman, informing him that our first president had worshiped here. "Few parishes in our land have shared as much of our nation's history as this one," MacColl wrote "and we want you to know that our prayers are with you and your advisors in this crucial hour." On 28 July, Truman personally replied to MacColl.[3]

THE WHITE HOUSE
WASHINGTON

July 28, 1950

Dear Dr. MacColl:

      I certainly appreciate your kind let-
ter. It is a source of strength to know that
you and the congregation of Trinity Church are
including a remembrance of me in your prayers.
My sincere thanks to you, and please convey to
your parishioners an assurance of my deep gratitude to them also. Support of this kind really
means a lot to me.

      Very sincerely yours,

Harry Truman

Reverend James R. MacColl, III,
Trinity Church,
Newport,
Rhode Island.

Letter from President Harry S. Truman to The Reverend James MacColl.
On 25 June 1950, North Korea, prompted by the Soviet Union, attacked South Korea.
Two days later, President Truman ordered U.S. forces to aid South Korea as part of
a United Nations police action. As these events were taking place, the international
crisis was deeply felt in Newport, and Reverend MacColl wrote to the president,
sending the parish's prayers. Reproduced courtesy of The Reverend James MacColl, III

In February 1951, the rector called a special meeting of the vestry to consider the news that Hetty S. A. H. G. Wilks had made a bequest to Trinity Church of 1/140th of her estate, estimated to be worth a total of $100 million. The eighty-year-old widow of Matthew Astor Wilks, who died in 1928, had lived in almost complete seclusion since her husband's death but had managed her vast holdings personally up until a year before her death. "A tall slim woman who spent her time scanning the financial pages of newspapers, she learned the art of fortune gathering from her mother [Hetty Green of New Bedford], who brought her up in near austerity."[4] Her mother had begun her fortune from whaling, and her daughter had carried on building on the basis of the fortune she had inherited.

This largest single bequest that Trinity had ever received came as a complete surprise to the parish, which was named in her will, one of sixty-three beneficiaries, including Harvard, Yale, Columbia, and Vassar. She had attended All Saints Chapel in her youth and had been fascinated by Trinity but had no known recent connections. Her husband, a nephew of both John Jacob Astor, who had once lived at "Beaulieu" on Bellevue Avenue, and of William B. Astor, who had owned "Beechwood," was known to have visited only in the 1880s.

Not long afterwards, the parish received news that it was also the beneficiary of the estate of Hamilton Fish Webster, a prominent member of the community, who had died at his Harrison Avenue estate, "Pen Craig," in September 1939. Following the death of his wife in 1951, the Newport Trust Company distributed two shares of the estate, amounting to forty-five thousand dollars, to be held in trust to establish the Hamilton Fish Webster Fund, the income from which was to be divided into three funds to be used to restore, beautify, and refurnish the interior and exterior of the church, Kay Chapel, and the Parish House, respectively.[5] The first impact of these gifts was the immediate need for the General Assembly to revise the charter, increasing the tax-free limitation on the corporation's assets from one and a half to two and a half million dollars.[6] This was expeditiously done and signed by the governor in a month's time.[7]

For the longer term, these gifts could eventually be the means by which the parish could free itself from pew rents and taxes as the largest single sources of parish income. At the annual meeting in January 1952, MacColl told the parish, "It is my hope and that of several vestrymen and corporation members that the day will come when all pews in Trinity Church will be free pews." In making this plea, he echoed sentiments that had been heard for more than a century, but MacColl made a point of not criticizing pew owners, as they had been very helpful and considerate; however, the parish did need to make extra space for general use on Sundays. The pew system had been widespread in the country and "had been a source of financial security for countless parishes," MacColl said, but "throughout the Church today, it is generally felt that the Christian view on this matter is that all pews should be free and held in the name of the Church."[8] Not wishing to change the system arbitrarily, he asked that pew owners consider deeding their pews to the corporation, something that had actually been practiced for some time, as well as helping make extra space each Sunday for general use, "especially today when an ever increasing number of service men are attending Church."[9]

While these events were going on behind the scenes and in vestry meetings, the parish remained prominent in a variety of public activities. With the benefit of his experience as a reserve-duty naval chaplain, MacColl played a key role in welcoming the officers and men of the cruiser HMS *Superb* to Newport in August 1951. At the city's official welcoming luncheon in honor of Vice Admiral Sir Richard Symonds-Tayler, commanding the American and West Indies Station, held at the Viking Hotel, MacColl delivered the benediction.

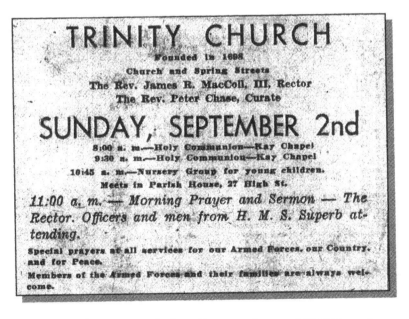

Morning prayer and sermon with the officers and men of HMS Superb, *2 September 1951.* Collection of the *Newport Daily News.*

ORDER OF SERVICE

IN MEMORY OF

HIS BRITANNIC MAJESTY

KING GEORGE VI

1895 - 1952

TRINITY CHURCH
NEWPORT, RHODE ISLAND
FRIDAY EVENING, FEBRUARY 15, 1952
AT 7:45 O'CLOCK

Joint memorial service in memory of King George VI by the Episcopal churches of the Newport Convocation, held on the day of the king's funeral in London.

During the ship's week-long stay in port, fifty officers and men came ashore from Superb at Government Landing to attend Sunday services, joining parishioners "in songs and prayers that crossed the Atlantic with other Britons nearly three centuries ago."[10] The ship's commanding officer, Capt. W. J. Bankes, RN, read the first lesson, and her chaplain, D. S. Bennett, assisted. After the service, the rector presented each of the British guests with a small commemorative tile made for the occasion, showing Trinity and its churchyard.

Less than a year later, on 15 February 1952, Trinity was the scene of a memorial service for King George VI, on the evening of his funeral in London. Out of respect for the late king, the American flag on City Hall was flown at half staff. MacColl conducted a candlelight service that included Arcangelo Corelli's *Trio Sonata for Strings and Organ*. The Reverend Dr. Robert Mercer, rector of St. George's Church, read the New Testament lesson and the Collect for the Dead, while The Reverend Hubert Buckingham of Holy Trinity Church, Tiverton, read the prayers. In the address, The Reverend Harold Forster, chaplain of St. George's School, noted that the nobility and strength of the king's character had stemmed from his Christian faith and had earned him widespread respect.[11]

Some weeks later, the archbishop of Canterbury, The Most Reverend Geoffrey Fisher, wrote to the Trinity clergy, "We have been deeply moved in this country by the great volume of sympathy and affection from United States citizens." The king had been a great man, he wrote, "a good, godly and dutiful man." In concluding his letter, the archbishop expressed his personal pleasure at the news that Capt. John H. Zimmerman, officer in charge of the Naval Chaplains School in Newport, had joined the Trinity parish, where he often preached and assisted at services. Zimmerman had recently returned from England, where he had served as a chaplain on the staff of the commander, U.S. Naval Forces Europe; he had been, Fisher wrote, "so deeply valued by us when he was in this country. [12]

As the church acquired its unexpected new funds, it found new opportunities to use them. One of the first initiatives was to hire the parish's first full-time

Aerial view of Trinity Church, showing Coddington School and the crowded properties between Frank and Mill Streets Collection of the Newport Historical Society.

director of education, Miss Elizabeth S. Elliott, to manage the Church School, with its thirty teachers and 350 children. In another initiative, in December 1951 the vestry Property Committee reported that the neighboring Coddington School, built in 1867 on the lot to the south of the church near Spring and Mill Streets, might be purchased and removed. Then in derelict condition, it was a fire hazard and hampered access to the church, should it be threatened with fire. The Property Committee proposed beautifying the property, providing additional parking near the church, and erecting a colonial-style building conforming with the style and dignity of the main church.[13] In purchasing the school property from the city for nine thousand dollars, Reverend MacColl wrote to the city clerk, "If permitted to purchase this property, the corporation of Trinity Church plans to demolish the School building and improve the property in the meticulous keeping of all that was characteristic of Eighteenth Century Newport."[14]

Upon the City Council's approval of the sale, the vestry immediately moved to engage a contactor to demolish the old school. As this was going on, the parish received its share, $615,000, of the distribution from the Wilks estate. The sum of $22,483.70 was immediately spent from the principal to pay outstanding notes on the Parish House, rectory, and the Coddington School property. All the parish's outstanding bills were paid, and all debts liquidated. The remainder, $411,347.96, was allocated to the Hetty S. A. H. G. Wilks Fund, $350,000 of which was invested.[15]

In planning the future use of the Coddington School site, MacColl and the parish, in cooperation with the Preservation Society of Newport County, projected an attractive park along the south side of the building. The initial idea called for moving the eighteenth-century building known as the Pitt's Head Tavern to the site from its location on Charles Street, but this plan never came to fruition.[16] A new group, the Friends of Trinity Church, was established to further the site improvement project. Among the leaders of the group were Mrs. Guy Fairfax Cary, Mrs. George Henry Warren, Jr., Mrs. Charles Howland Russell, and Cyril B. Judge, chairman of the vestry committee for the preservation of the fabric of Trinity Church.

Meanwhile, attention was devoted to repairing the damage from a boiler explosion at the High Street Parish House and making necessary repairs to the old church structure, which was carefully surveyed for the chairman of the Property Committee, Rear Adm. Henry E. Eccles. During 1952–53, the carpet, cushions, and upholstery were renewed in all pews that were not privately owned, burgundy then being used for corporation pews. Among the other improvements made at this time, the parish acquired a new dossal for the curtain behind the altar, and new pillows and hangings for the pulpit. Antique chairs were purchased and refurbished for use in several of the pews in the gallery, and the small room to the south of the altar was converted to a sacristy.

In August 1952, Mrs. Emily Coddington Williams of "Villa Ross" on Bellevue Avenue, the widow of W. Henry Williams of New York, died in Paris. The bond for her twenty-million-dollar estate was the highest in the history of Newport's probate court, and it contained a legacy of $300,000 for Trinity. In a two-and-a-half-year period, the parish had received four large legacies. "Humility and gratitude move us to the feeling that we should share a portion of this blessing with our Diocese in thankfulness," the vestry declared.[17] With its newfound financial strength, the corporation acted on the vestry's recommendation and voted to donate sixteen thousand dollars from the income of the endowment to the Episcopal Charities Fund of the diocese of Rhode Island to build a dormitory at the Episcopal Conference Center at Pascoag.[18]

Famous military and naval officers continued to visit Trinity, bringing with them echoes of the Cold War and international events that linked the parish with its past and the present. In October 1952, Vice Admiral Pierre Barjot, commanding French naval forces in the Indian Ocean, was in Newport to visit the Naval War College. Visiting Vernon House, Colony House, and the Newport Historical Society to see a display of mementoes relating to the French army in Newport in 1780–81, he placed a wreath on Admiral de Ternay's grave. Some months later, Field Marshal Viscount Montgomery of Alamein, then Deputy Supreme Commander Allied Forces in Europe, came to Newport for the same purpose and also visited Trinity. Just prior to Montgomery's arrival at the church, the 5 P.M. church bells peeled out "God Save the Queen" in addition to the usual afternoon hymns. When Montgomery arrived to view the church, Vice Admiral Richard Connolly, president of the Naval War College, introduced him to Newport police chief Samuel H. Durgin. "Chief, are there any Communists in Newport?" Montgomery demanded to know. "Not a one, Marshal!" Durgin replied. "Newport is one of the cleanest cities in the country."[19] The son of a clergyman and former secretary of the Society for the Propagation of the Gospel, Montgomery expressed special interest in Trinity's history. Completing his visit, he signed the church guestbook, which, MacColl told him, two other famous military men had also signed: Marshal Ferdinand Foch and General John J. Pershing.

The Reverend James R. MacColl III rector of Trinity Church, 1949–53.

Shortly after this visit, MacColl received a call to become rector of St. Thomas's Church in Whitemarsh, Pennsylvania, a suburb of Philadelphia. In submitting his resignation, effective September 1953, MacColl noted that the first set of objectives that he had undertaken in 1949 had been completed:

> The parish program of worship, work, and study has been set in motion, the parish staff has been built up to the limit, which is needed, and every member of the staff is loyal, hard-working, and competent. Buildings of the parish will have been put in excellent physical condition, and the finances, due to the good fortune of recent bequests and the ever-increasing generosity of our parishioners and friends, are sound and being efficiently managed.[20]

On MacColl's departure, the vestry appointed The Reverend Peter Chase as priest in charge of the parish. One of the very first events that occurred in this period was the opportunity to purchase the Schwamburger property at the corner of Frank and Spring Streets, adjoining the former Coddington School land.[21] Purchasing it for $16,100, the parish immediately demolished the building on the property, at the additional cost of $2,500, thereby adding to the open space on the south side of the church.

The parish had benefited from and expanded its activities through generous donations. At the end of 1953 it held investments totaling $955,721, which produced fifty-three percent of the income to fund a sixty-five-thousand-dollar operating budget.[22] Chase noted that the every-member canvass for 1953 had given a useful analysis of the parish. Old and lost parishioners had been found, and some inactive parishioners had renewed their interest. Still, the parish office was plagued by the fact that many parishioners changed their addresses without notification; the parish had much to learn about stewardship. "Perhaps the biggest disappointment from the point of view of contributions," Chase reported, "is the fact that the average weekly pledge is only 77¢ per week (the cost of three packs of cigarettes), and that only 9% of our contributors pledge more than that average sum."[23]

In December 1953 the vestry search committee nominated The Reverend Lockett Ford Ballard as the new rector; he arrived to take up his new duties on 1 February 1954. A graduate of Hamilton College and the General Theological Seminary, Ballard had served as curate at Christ the King Church in Greenwich, Connecticut, from 1940 to 1942, when had he enlisted in the army as a private. After basic training, he had gone to Officer Candidate School and had been posted to France as a forward observer in the 263rd Field Artillery Battalion of the Yankee (Twenty-sixth) Infantry Division. Wounded in combat, he had received the Bronze Star for action near Nancy, in October–November 1944. Upon his discharge from the army, he had become rector of St. Phillip's Church in the Highlands, Garrison, New York, before coming to Newport.

One of Ballard's first intentions was to establish firm long-range plans for the property across Frank Street and to the south of the church. To do this, Ballard appointed a planning committee, consisting of Leroy King and Henry Wilkinson, the senior and junior wardens, with Rear Admiral Eccles.[24] Meanwhile, the parish moved quickly to expand its holdings around the church. It purchased another lot for $11,500 and then purchased the strip of land to the west of the Coddington School property, running between Frank and Mill Streets.[25]

In the period 1955–57, the parish had two curates, The Reverend F. F. Rogers and The Reverend Alan Maynard, one of whom lived in the apartment in the High Street Parish House, while the other lived in an apartment the parish rented in town. Both of the curates were Anglo-Catholics, but as Maynard

The Right Reverend Evelyn Charles Hodges, D.D. (left), Anglican bishop of Limerick in Ireland, with Trinity's new rector, The Reverend Canon Lockett Ford Ballard, examines the Berkeley chocolate pot at the altar, 14 November 1954. Bishop Hodges was the first Irish Anglican bishop to visit Trinity since Bishop Berkeley.

recalled, "we found our rector to be theologically sound so that we were never uncomfortable. Because there were so many Navy personnel from a variety of backgrounds in Newport, the low-church rector, high-church curates, orthodox preaching and moderate liturgical practices seemed to attract a variety of persons."[26]

At the annual meeting in January 1955, the corporation approved construction of a new building on the newly acquired land. Designed by the firm of Wyeth & King of New York, which had designed the parish house on High Street in the 1920s, it was to be called "Honyman Hall." One of the architects, Frederic Rhinelander King, was the brother of the current senior warden, LeRoy King; their father, the elder LeRoy King, had also been senior warden. Well known for his architectural work, Frederic King had also designed the Seamen's Church Institute and several summer homes in Newport and on Long Island. The Church of the Epiphany and the National Women's Republican Club in New York City were his major works.

As part of the plan for Honyman Hall, the city of Newport granted an easement to allow the parish to install pipes across Frank Street so that the

Honyman Hall, built in 1955–56.
A modern building designed to fit in among Newport's colonial buildings, the doorway on the Mill Street side was an original, taken from a 1790 home in Bristol, Rhode Island.

church building could be further safeguarded from fire by being heated from a furnace located in Honyman Hall.[27] Ground was broken in May 1955 for the new building, but even before completion of the new building, its furnace was in use to heat the church. Meanwhile, to add to the property acquisitions in the area around the church, Dr. and Mrs. Alexander Hamilton Rice purchased and donated the house at 27 Church Street that Simeon Martin, a lieutenant governor of Rhode Island and one-time Trinity vestryman, had built in 1810. By a curious coincidence, the parish had sold the same piece of property to Martin in 1802.[28]

In other areas, Kay Chapel continued to be an active part of the parish, and as in the past, Trinity allowed its use by several nascent groups and congregations in need of a worship space. During 1955–58, for example, the Newport Church of the Nazarene used the building while it planned a building of its own.[29]

The year 1955 was one in which a number of Newport organizations, including the Preservation Society, the Newport Historical Society, the Redwood

Library, and Trinity Church, decided to publicize the city's colonial heritage. Trinity played a key role in the 175th Washington-Rochambeau anniversary celebration, a well-publicized event designed to draw attention to restoration work in Newport. Many colonial buildings, both public and private, opened to the public during the week of 4–14 July. The *New York Times* announced in a headline, "Newport to Memorialize Its Colonial Era."[30] The *Washington Post* featured a photograph of Trinity's spire, suggesting a motor tour from the nation's capital to "Little Rhody," while another newspaper announced, "Newport, a Living History Book, Dusted, Shined for Rochambeau Fete."[31] Among the many activities, Trinity held a service on Sunday, 10 July 1955, in which French ambassador Couve de Murville delivered an address from Trinity's pulpit; Hon. S. Walter Washington read the lessons and occupied the Washington pew. Afterward, the French ambassador and Secretary of the Navy Charles S. Thomas jointly placed a wreath on the grave of Admiral de Ternay.

Immediately following these events and in preparation for the dedication of the new building, Ballard wrote and published in the autumn of 1955 an expanded, new, illustrated brochure on the history of the church, designed for tourists and the general public visiting Newport: *Trinity Church in Newport*. In making other preparations for the dedication of Honyman Hall on 22 July 1956, Canon Ballard searched for something appropriate to welcome the invited guest of honor, The Right Reverend Robert W. Stopford, bishop of Peterborough, England. Bishop Stopford would represent the bishop of London and the Society for the Propagation of the Gospel at the ceremony and give the main address. Ballard discussed his plans with the rector of the Berkeley Memorial Chapel in Middletown, The Reverend Dudley Hughes, son of Trinity's former rector Stanley Hughes. Hughes remembered Norman Isham's Queen Anne coat of arms, which had caused such a row in 1930. Hughes recalled, "It must be around somewhere for my father often told about it and regretted that he had not insisted on its remaining in the church, since it was so bound up with the building's history."[32]

After an extensive search, sexton James Proudfoot found the coat of arms, crated and dusty, in a cellar. Ballard had the arms unpacked, repaired, cleaned, and installed where Isham had intended it, in the probable location of the original at the rear of the chancel and over the altarpiece, with its Ten Commandments. Unlike the arms of the Hanoverian kings who succeeded Anne, these contained a scroll with the motto, "*Semper Eadem.*" Freely translated, it means "Always the Same," a motto that Ballard thought particularly appropriate

*The royal arms of Queen Anne hanging over the altar, July 1956.
Norman Isham had designed and installed these royal arms in 1930, as the final
touch to his restoration plan. Patriotic sentiment forced Canon Hughes to remove
them in 1931, and they lay forgotten in storage until 1956, when Canon Ballard had
them hung again over the altar, at the time of the dedication of Honyman Hall. Another outcry of American patriotism forced Ballard to have them moved and hung
inside Honyman Hall.* Newport Daily News, 25 July 1956

for Trinity. In the early nineteenth century, Henry Bull had written of the altar-piece:

> However little the present generation may care for such baubles of this kind, still the antiquity of such ornaments and the propriety of them in the days they were put up, make them interesting—as indicating at first view, to the most perfect stranger, the antiquity of the structure which contained them—splendid for the days and country in which it was erected.[33]

Fully agreeing with Bull's sentiments, Ballard believed that parishioners would now have greater appreciation for the historical connections that he valued, and that the patriotic opposition that had arisen in 1930 would have dissipated. Ballard hoped that the parishioners would rejoice ro see their historic church once more honored with Anne's arms. They hung in place over the altar for the dedication of Honyman Hall, but Ballard immediately faced strong and vocal opposition. A number of parishioners strongly objected, as they had in 1930.[34] For a time, Ballard postponed "any immediate action and disposition of the coat of arms until the pulse of the Parish is determined"; it was eventually removed to Honyman Hall.[35]

In conjunction with the historical work at Trinity, Canon Ballard participated actively with other groups in restoration projects. In August 1956, Rabbi Theodore Lewis invited Ballard to give the main address at exercises in Touro Synagogue marking the 166th anniversary of George Washington's 1790 letter to the Hebrew congregation in Newport. In ceremonies to launch the first stage of a comprehensive restoration of the synagogue, actor Charlton Heston read the Washington letter. In his address, entitled "Freedom and Responsibility," Ballard declared, "War is far from the worst evil that can assail mankind, for slavery is worse."[36] Echoing widespread opinion within the parish during the Cold War, he pointed out that the Judeo-Christian religion is a fighting one. It has nothing to do with pacifism, he said, stressing that man must continually fight for freedom. "There is no room in God's creation for neutrality, pacifism or non-service," Ballard declared.[37]

Exemplifying this view, one of Trinity's regular parishioners, Claiborne Pell, dedicated his life of public service to the peaceful resolution of conflict and to furthering worldwide prosperity. Pell began his career as the longest-serving U.S. senator from Rhode Island with his election on the Democratic ticket in

1960; he remained in office, through five more elections, until his retirement in 1997. An honorary vice president of the American Bible Society, Pell, with his family, had a long connection with Trinity Church. Most famous for the creation of the "Pell Grant" in 1980 to reduce financial barriers to higher education, Pell served for many years as chairman of the Senate Foreign Relations Committee. In this position, he opposed U.S. involvement in the Vietnam War, helped secure ratification of the Intermediate-Range Nuclear Forces (INF) treaty to reduce nuclear weapons, and was the key figure behind the treaty to prohibit the use of environmental-modification techniques as weapons of war. During his first term in office, Pell arranged for Trinity's rector to deliver the opening prayer at two sessions of the U.S. Senate in 1961 and 1962.[38]

Listed among the U.S. presidents who visited Trinity Church is Dwight Eisenhower who had his summer White House in Newport for three of the four years in his second term. During his second summer in Newport, he visited Trinity on 15 September 1958. Canon Ballard gave him a tour of the church and he signed the church registry.

Through the years, Canon Ballard participated in many local civic and cultural activities in Newport. One of Ballard's main interests was to make the church more relevant to young people by creating links between religion and a variety of other cultural activities. In this connection, Ballard was a strong proponent of jazz music generally and of the Newport Jazz Festival in 1960, while at the same time condemning the disorder that accompanied the festival that summer in Newport. Over the years, Ballard became one of the major voices that led to general acceptance of the music festivals in Newport. By 1969, the parish was even offering the use of its Kay Street Parish House as a place of shelter for 150 young people who attended the festival and provided showers for five hundred that year.[39] Additionally, Ballard encouraged the use of Trinity's buildings for local drama groups, with performances ranging from *Murder in the Cathedral* to *Antigone*.[40]

Keenly interested in developing appreciation for the history of the parish, he not only led tours and researched its past but also encouraged others to follow his example. As part of his attempt to bring the parish's history to wider attention, he encouraged the loan of Daniel Russell's 1734 baptismal bowl for the English Speaking Union's exhibition of early American silver and art treasures at Christie's in London. Also at that time, the firm of Josiah Wedgwood & Sons of Staffordshire, England, selected Trinity Church as the first American building to depict on a Wedgwood medallion. The medallion, made of Wedg-

The Wedgwood medallion of Trinity Church.
The Josiah Wedgwood Company of Staffordshire, England, produced this medallion as part of its famous American buildings series in 1966.

wood jasper, showed the church in white relief on the famous Wedgwood blue background. Taken from a drawing of Trinity by William Hoyt, son of St. George's School faculty member Norris Hoyt, the oval medal measured three and a quarter inches by four and a quarter inches. Its production was limited to five hundred copies, of which one each was deposited with the Wedgwood Collections at the Smithsonian Institution, the Victoria and Albert Museum in London, and the Buten Museum of Wedgwood in Merion, Pennsylvania.[41]

Bringing attention to the historical importance of Trinity in another way, Ballard worked for Trinity's nomination as a National Historical Site, following the Department of the Interior's earlier designation of the Wanton-Lyman-Hazard House, the Colony House, Brick Market, the Vernon House, Touro Synagogue, and the Redwood Library in 1962. In July 1968, Interior Secretary Stuart Udall approved the designation for Trinity, along with the Hunter House and the Historical Society's Seventh-Day Meeting House, as well as the entire historic districts that the city had established in the Point and Hill sections.[42] Three years, later in 1971, another piece of Trinity's past was placed on the National Register of Historic Places, when Shiloh Church, built in 1799 by Trinity at the corner of School and Mary Streets as its school, was similarly listed.[43]

Ballard encouraged the use of music to attract young people to parish services. Mahalia Jackson sang the spiritual "Were You There?" at one service in 1957. In 1966, Trinity's Easter service included the first Rhode Island performance of The Reverend Ian Mitchell's *American Folk Mass*, written "to give parts of the liturgy a new and exciting sound without detracting from the real reason and purpose of this greatest and central act of Christian worship."[44] The Reverend John Cranston, headmaster of St. Michael's School, officiated at the service, the mass was sung by Trinity's choir, under the direction of Wesley J. Rooker, accompanied by three guitars and an autoharp.

After the service, Ballard observed that he was pleased when older members of the congregation encouraged him to initiate new programs to attract young people, but was perplexed when they disliked the results. Later that summer, the well-known folk singer Buffy Sainte-Marie sang at a folk mass. A year later, in December 1967, the composer, The Reverend Ian Mitchell, sang his folk mass as well as officiated and preached at a communion service. With his wife, Caroline, he also conducted workshops for choir leaders and church organists at Emmanuel Church.[45] For a time, Ballard conducted the folk mass as a regular feature of the eleven o'clock service. The *Providence Journal-Bulletin* quoted Ballard as saying, "Hit them with a bomb and pick up the pieces later. If you really believe in this thing, there is no sense in doing it on an obscure winter Sunday. So it worked. We survived."[46]

When Mrs. Alan T. Schumacher, of "Maplehurst" on Bellevue Avenue, sent the vestry a formal letter of complaint about the use of folk music during church services, she noted, "The great strength I feel of the catholic church of which we are a part is to teach the young people of today the traditions and moral principles of our Christian religion and not to make a mockery of our Religious ceremonies, when our congregation is on its knees praying to God and communing with the Lord."[47] In reply, clerk of the vestry Richard Wood reported that her letter had led to a lengthy and constructive meeting in which "the final consensus seems to be that the Church must welcome many innovations if it is to meet the extraordinary challenges of this dangerous world. We must, however, be certain that the innovations we adopt are well chosen, well timed, and well handled."[48]

Mitchell's *American Folk Mass* was repeated a number of times; one newspaper advertisement invited worshipers to "Another Swinging Service at Old Trinity Church." In an announcement that a combo would present songs by Bob Dylan and by Simon and Garfunkel, a parenthetical comment in small print noted, "It may not be dignified, but who wants a Church dying of dignity?"[49] On Sunday, 28 April 1968, in a variation on the approach, Trinity celebrated a

EAT HIS BODY, DRINK HIS BLOOD, AND WE'LL SING A SONG OF LOVE: ALLELU, ALLELU, ALLELU, ALLELUIA

Welcome to Another Swinging Sunday At OLD TRINITY CHURCH

The Liturgy Features Combo Music by the "SOMEWHAT HOLY SPIRITS"

This Contemporary Mass Starts At Eleven O'Clock

3/15/69

PRAISING THE LORD WITH A GROOVY SOUND

The American Folk Song Mass With Combo Mass

OFFERED IN

TRINITY CHURCH

Sunday, August 17th At Eleven O'Clock

YOU ARE INVITED TO SHARE IN THIS CONTEMPORARY SERVICE

Newport Daily News *advertisements for services at Trinity Church— top, 15 March 1960; bottom, 17 August 1969.*

choral Eucharist using the music of Geoffrey Beaumont's *Twentieth Century Folk Mass* and selected folk tunes. In July 1968, a record nine hundred parishioners and visitors attended a folk mass at which the folksinger Pete Seeger and the Hudson River Sloop Group sang, along with Ian Mitchell and his wife. Ballard, who called Seeger a "Christian missionary," announced that the loose plate collection of about five hundred dollars was to be donated to Seeger's antipollution campaign.[50]

Later that same year, during the July weekends of the Newport Jazz and Folk Festivals, two other Newport churches, St. John the Evangelist and Channing Memorial Unitarian Church, joined Trinity in using folk music at services. At Trinity, about three hundred parishioners attended a service in which Cranston led the choir.[51] In July 1970, in another musically innovative service at Trinity, Fr. Dick Blank presented his *Bossa Nova Mass*. A month later, drums were added to string combo for a jazz-rock anthem at the eleven o'clock service. In August 1972, another jazz-rock mass featured selections from *Godspell* and *Jesus Christ Superstar*, with accompaniment from electronic instruments.

In a newspaper article in 1970, Canon Ballard explained the challenge facing Trinity, as he saw it. The local Lutheran and Presbyterian churches were full every Sunday, but the Episcopalian churches were not. "The four Episcopal parishes in the little city of Newport continue an unhappy rivalry gradually degenerating into a struggle for the survival of the fittest."[52] Seeing himself as a lone voice crying in an unholy wilderness, Ballard suggested that the other Episcopal parishes in Newport close and join Trinity. The vital statistics of Trinity were similar to those of others, he said. The average age was fifty-eight, with sixty-three percent over the age of sixty and only seven percent under thirty. Over the past fifteen years, Trinity's Sunday school had steadily declined from 325 pupils to eighty-five. Other parishes reflected the same problem. With its strong finances and dynamic programs designed to attract the young, Ballard felt, Trinity represented the answer for the Episcopal Church in Newport. In his view, if the Episcopal Church was to survive, it needed to close ranks and branch into new ventures that would attract the coming generations.

Canon Ballard's period at Trinity Church was dominated by three major initiatives, all of which turned on issues of finance—relating to Queen Anne Square and Trinity Close, St. Michael's School, and Trinity Cemetery. Beyond these initiatives, the parish began considering the establishment of a nursing home.

Finances. In 1956 LeRoy King was elected for his thirty-fifth year as senior warden, marking 110 years since his grandfather, Edward King, had served as senior warden in 1847–49, followed in later years by his father, LeRoy King, and his uncle, George Gordon King. In 1956, Henry Wilkinson became junior warden and Reginald O'Neill treasurer. Along with this election, the parish adopted the largest budget in its history, at $81,997.

At the end of 1956, however, the treasurer's report indicated that there was an operating-budget deficit. Reacting strongly, the rector announced his complete dissatisfaction with the business and financial management of the parish. After consultation with the bishop, Ballard declared that he would exercise his right as rector to have a certified public accountant audit the parish's account; the bishop would select the firm. At a special meeting of the vestry in December, Ballard asked for the resignation of the senior warden, junior warden, and treasurer, and announced that he intended to appoint Rear Admiral Henry Eccles to be chairman of the finance committee for 1957.[53] Nonetheless, the parish officers not only did not resign but were reelected for an additional year at the annual meeting in January 1958.

Eccles, however assumed responsibility for the finance committee at this critical juncture, remaining the key figure in the financial affairs of the parish for more than a decade. The son of an Episcopal clergyman, Eccles was a highly decorated naval officer who had retired from active duty in 1952 but retained a close connection with the Naval War College, where he had become the U.S. Navy's foremost thinker on logistics as well as a prominent writer on the philosophy underlying military and operational concepts.[54]

With Eccles's assistance, the financial committee investigated the situation. The vestry was able to conclude that the parish's financial problem lay primarily in a bookkeeping system that did not account for all of its receipts and expenditures, particularly of collections from the Sunday school, the Family Service, and other miscellaneous sources of income.[55] Admiral Eccles presented a list of eight recommendations to place the parish's financial management on a sound base. In approving them, the vestry directed that the parish office take charge of all bookkeeping (following a procedure recommended by the National Council of the Church and approved by the diocese) and that all vestry members be kept fully informed of the parish's finances and financial plans. In further improvements, a system was worked out to count immediately all money collected and to make out slips for deposits in a locked bag in the bank's night deposit vault.[56] By 1958, these problems had been resolved. Eccles reported that

thankfulness, and
our trust in thee t
Jesus Christ our Lo

Rear Admiral Henry Eccles.
A highly decorated naval officer and the U.S. Navy's foremost thinker on logistics,
he was a prominent figure at the Naval War College, writing on the philosophy un-
derlying military and operational concepts. Eccles played a critical role for Trinity,
while serving, between 1952 and 1974, first as chairman of the parish's property
committee, and then the finance committee. He served as the treasurer, 1960—64,
and senior warden, 1964—65- He is shown here (left), attending General Conven-
tion at Miami in 1958, with The Right Reverend Arthur Lichtenberger (right) who
had just been elected presiding bishop of the United States.
Eccles Papers, Naval Historical Collection. Naval War College.

the investments had a market value of $1,040,653 and produced an income of
$42,552.[57]

The solidification of the parish's financial affairs gave rise to the need to
revise the charter. To accommodate rising values and future contingencies, the
new amendment increased the limit of the parish's holdings from $1,500,000 to
five million dollars.[58] In 1960, Eccles became treasurer, remaining in that
position until he became senior warden in 1964. At that point, Charles B.
McGowan became treasurer, and Vice Admiral Stuart H. Ingersoll, former president of the Naval War College, became chairman of the Finance Committee. In
1965, after serving as senior warden for a year, Eccles returned as a member of
the Finance Committee, where he was to be a key figure through 1974.

In 1964, the parish conducted an intensive every-member canvass, with guidance from professional fundraisers. Following this effort, the level of annual giving rose substantially. Still, while the parish's finances were generally sound, the budget characteristically operated with a deficit of up to twenty thousand dollars. For many years, this shortfall was balanced by the advancing market value of investments; in order to cover operating expenses, the parish found itself selling securities in its trust funds. After a number of years, a question arose as to the legality of this procedure under the church charter, which provided that "all donations made, or that may be made . . . shall be strictly used and applied according to intentions and directions of the donor."[59] Senior warden Eccles referred the matter to Richard B. Sheffield, of the law firm of Sheffield & Harvey, who reported that:

> We are of opinion that property given without restriction may be sold and the proceeds used for any purpose that the Corporation determines is in its best interests. Property that is restricted must be used in accordance with the terms of the gift. Property, intended to be "a permanent fund for the better support of said Corporation," is further explicitly restricted in its use as set forth.[60]

This opinion was clearly kept in mind when in 1966 the vestry faced many financial demands relating to St. Michael's School and Queen Anne Square, but it clearly began to match the uses of money with the sources of funds. To underscore the point, just at that point Miss Edith Wetmore left twenty-five thousand dollars to the parish as a permanent fund, the income of which was to be used strictly for repair, preservation, and renewal of the church, chapel, and Parish House.[61] The increasing complexity of parish finances and all the technical, fiscal, and legal issues they involved placed an increasing strain on the changing group of people who made up the vestry and had to manage parish affairs on a part-time basis.

With the financial affairs of the parish continuing to demand considerable effort, and after repeated suggestions that it do so, the vestry finally voted in 1970 to establish a permanent, full-time position of business manager for Trinity Church.[62] The vestry consulted with diocesan and national church administrators on the duties and responsibilities for the position. After running a nationwide advertisement in the *Wall Street Journal*, the vestry unanimously chose Capt. Curtis W. Bunting, USN (Ret.), a member of the vestry, to be the parish's first business manager. Bunting resigned from the vestry, with effect from 15 October 1970; from that point he attended vestry meetings but did not vote.

Queen Anne Square and Trinity Close. One of Ballard's indelible contributions to Newport was his vision for "Queen Anne Square," which he had begun to formulate and to discuss in general terms by 1958, building on the initial steps that his predecessor, MacColl, had taken. In August 1960, Ballard gleaned impressive support for his developing concept from the world-famous architect Eero Saarinen of Finland. On hearing of Ballard's early concept by which Trinity would become the principal building in a park area bounded by Thames, Mill, Spring and Church Streets after moving or demolishing the existing structures, Saarinen commented, "Such a move would revive the whole area. When one particular section is improved, as this would be, it would encourage nearby property owners to better their own. This has been the history elsewhere where similar steps have been taken."[63]

In the spring of 1962, the Redevelopment Agency presented its plan for urban renewal in Newport, including the first stage of its project to clear the west side of Thames Street from Marlborough Street to Market Square, demolish the buildings, and construct new roads and piers. In response the vestry formally voted its approval of the basic plan, promised the parish's cooperation, and agreed to consult with the Preservation Society and other agencies to make further specific plans.[64]

In November 1963, Robert Goelet wrote the parish that he planned to donate fifty thousand dollars to the church for landscaping Queen Anne Square. One of the vestrymen, Dr. Dotterer, reported that Goelet had told him in conversation that he would like the square to be completed in his lifetime and wanted something started immediately. A preliminary meeting was held with representatives of the Preservation Society. The vestry adopted a general statement to guide the work:

> The general purpose of the development to take place in the vicinity of Trinity Church . . . is to establish in the center of Newport an area which will be a living example (or representation) of Newport from its earliest days to the present. In order to accomplish this purpose there will be preservation, restoration and maintenance of a group of buildings. Trinity Church will landscape and maintain the areas and buildings it owns or acquires.[65]

Reminiscent of the flap over the royal arms in 1959, Ballard's proposed name for the square created immediate controversy. Mrs. Townsend Phillips wrote to the *Newport Daily News*, in support of Ballard's suggestion, but others were very critical. The donor, Robert Goelet himself, objected to the name in a letter to the newspaper: "Trinity Close would be my choice for a name yet I fear that many persons who have not graduated from Harvard might not understand the connection," Goelet wrote. Tongue in cheek, Howard Browne joined in the fray. "A local woman has fitly protested the name of a church development after a foreign queen," Browne wrote.

> In seconding the protest, I add that it is, while certainly a step in the right direction, far too timid. . . . I say carry this small beginning to its logical glorious conclusion. Cast off forever the foreign yoke: change the names of Portsmouth, Jamestown, Albion, Bristol, Charleston, Coventry, Cumberland, Greenwich, Exeter, Kingston and Warwick. And in our midst such shameful mementos as Barclay Square, Downing Street, Duke Street, Earl Avenue, Elizabeth Street, Harold Street, King Street, Marlborough Street, Prince Road, Richmond Street, Victoria Avenue, Wellington Avenue, Wesley Street, and William Street.[66]

In the summer of 1964, the parish had the opportunity to purchase the Atlantic gas station on the northwest corner of Spring and Mill Streets, a move that would complete the opening up of that block, which had earlier been dominated by Coddington School. In connection with the plan to demolish the gas station and landscape the area, local artist Felix de Weldon planned to provide a statue. Robert Goelet wrote to the parish that he was prepared to donate an additional $130,000 to landscape a new area to be called Trinity Close. However, the purchase of the gas station stalled over the owner's requirement to be given an alternative location for his business. Sites were located, but city zoning approval could not be obtained, delaying this aspect of the project.

In the meantime, Goelet arranged for plans from the landscape architects, Gilmore Clarke and Michael Rapuano of New York City, who were also involved with plans for Queen Anne Square to the west of the church and were then doing the landscaping for the 1964 New York World's Fair. By November 1964, though the gas station issue was still not solved, work was well under way on other parts of the plan to convert the newly purchased property and what had been the parking lot of Honyman Hall into a garden. The space was still known as Queen Anne Square, but Goelet continued to prefer "Trinity Close." Planted with a variety of flowering trees and shrubs, the garden was to feature an octagonal, green-granite fountain in its southwest corner near Mill Street. Initially, it had been planned to enclose the entire area in the same black iron fence that surrounded the north side of the church; the final landscaping was to feature a "multitude of paths leading through the garden and a number of park benches for the footsore and weary visitors' relief and enjoyment."[67]

The landscaping was completed and fountain installed the following summer, six months before Goelet's death in February 1966, but completion of the full project still lay in the future. Ballard continued to promote Queen Anne's name for the park, as well as the idea of extending it down the hill to the west. "Right now it is just Trinity Close to the laundry, but I can envisage a magnificent project here," said Canon Ballard, looking west from the fountain toward a laundry whose black smoke stack competes with Trinity Church.[68] Egan's Laundry still dominated the future site, and there was also a furniture store warehouse, several small apartment houses, and smaller buildings on the property.

Further plans were needed to develop the larger area between the church and Thames Street. In October 1966, in preparation for discussions with the administrators of Robert Goelet's estate concerning funding, Rear Admiral Eccles drafted a resolution, which the vestry approved, noting that accomplishment of the aim was dependent on three factors beyond the immediate control of the parish: acquisition of a large capital fund to purchase land and to landscape, the cooperation of the City Council, and the cooperation of the affected property owners. The vestry envisaged that "such a colonial square would be a residence area for Trinity clergy and for Church activities plus such other harmonious development that would be appropriate to this purpose."[69] The project moved ahead with the Goelet Foundation's grant of an additional twenty thousand dollars as matching funds to purchase the Tilley Plumbing Shop to the west of the church and the Alex Shea property on Frank Street, near the Rice House.

Even before the project was completed, it began to have an effect on the neighborhood, as Eero Saarinen had predicted seven years earlier. Nearby property owners began to contribute their own work to beautify the neighborhood. One of the first to do this was Trinity parishioner John Millar, who in March 1967 purchased an eighteenth-century house at the end of Cannon Street for five hundred dollars to save it from demolition as construction for Memorial

St. Michael's School.
The former Mason home on Rhode Island Avenue that became the home of St.
Michael's School. Founded in 1938, it was owned by Trinity Church from 1963
to 1971. P2713. Collection of the Newport Historical Society.

Boulevard consumed the street. Millar had the narrow rowhouse cut in half and moved in two parts to the site of an old garage at 35–39 Mill Street, where it could enhance the other side of the street from Honyman Hall and Trinity Close.[70]

St. Michael's School. On 22 November 1959, Canon Ballard preached a sermon in Trinity Church in which he drew attention to the precarious financial situation of St. Michael's Country Day School. Founded in 1938 and now located at the corner of Rhode Island Avenue and Memorial Boulevard, the school needed financial assistance if it was to survive; Ballard asked the parish to accept responsibility for it. He repeated similar views on 12 November 1961. Meanwhile, a joint Trinity Church-St. Michael's School committee had begun serious consideration of a merger plan. In October 1961, it presented a request for a legal opinion on the procedures necessary for Trinity Church to assume ownership of the school. The Reverend Canon William Shumaker, director of Christian Education for the diocese of Rhode Island, prepared a detailed plan for the merger. The matter raised widespread debate, both inside and outside the parish, but when it was brought to a vote at the annual meeting in January 1963, the corporation approved acquisition of the school by a vote of 117 to 35. Its corporate assets were transferred to the Corporation of Trinity Church.[71] Soon after the merger, Canon Ballard announced the selection of The Reverend John A. Cranston of St. Mark's Church, Mystic, Connecticut, as the new headmaster.

In order to deal efficiently with the administration of the school, the vestry altered the by-laws of the corporation. It created a new School Committee, of which Capt. John R. Wadleigh agreed to be the first member. In addition, the position of assistant treasurer was created to act, under the treasurer, as the treasurer of the School Committee.[72] Eccles, as Trinity's treasurer, also served as vice chairman of the St. Michael's board of trustees. In taking over St. Michael's and making it the "Parish Day School of Trinity Church, in Newport," the new school charter, approved by the Trinity corporation in 1963, stated:

> Believing that the education of children in the Christian Way
> of life is the responsibility of the Church, and the education
> of children is properly a part of the pastoral and educational
> ministry of the Church, and following the examples of our
> forefathers and contemporaries within the Episcopal Church,
> we do establish a school of good and Christian learning as
> part of the pastoral ministry of this Parish.[73]

In the summer of 1964, business connections involving the school created a major controversy. George Wein, the organizer of the Newport Jazz Festival, had hoped to use the Newport Casino as a site for one of the festival's workshops. Finding it unavailable, he approached city councilman and former senior warden Henry Wilkinson, who in turn telephoned the rector to ask about the availability of the St. Michael's School grounds. Wilkinson told Ballard of the city's concern about having a large number of festival attendees wandering around Newport with nothing to do in the daytime, and of his hope that the parish could assist by arranging for the use of its buildings. Wein assured Ballard that the plan could work as both the city and parish would want it to, and he agreed to donate one thousand dollars to the St. Michael's School scholarship fund. When vestry members learned of this arrangement, they formally complained to the bishop of Rhode Island, asking him to review the question of a rector's authority "to solely negotiate any contract or agreement with a third party for the use of Church property without the consent of the vestry."[74] Senior warden Eccles objected that the rector had erred in not consulting his vestry prior to committing the school property. The rector maintained that there was a conflict between the by-laws and the charter. On the advice of the chancellor of the diocese, Robert Jacobsen, Bishop Higgins reviewed the matter and agreed that

> when a use other than ecclesiastical purposes is concerned, there must be action and approval by the Vestry, under the provisions of Canon 13, Section 2. But in such cases the Vestry cannot act except with the concurrence of the Rector because of the powers reserved under Canon 45 to protect his use of the premises for ecclesiastical purposes.[75]

The rector disagreed with the chancellor's opinion. The bishop advised that further clarification would require the action of an ecclesiastical court. Pending further action in the matter, the vestry offered Canon Ballard a three-month sabbatical to write his proposed history of Trinity Church.[76]

Meanwhile, the vestry dealt with the school's financial situation. The student population had fallen from a high of 168 students in 1960–61 to a low of 113 in 1964–65. The loss of students had resulted from the change from a country day school to an Episcopal day school; students from other faiths were leaving, even though the school continued to be open to all faiths. Before Trinity acquired the school, the trustees had maintained a practice of accumulating deficits, beginning each school year with large payable accounts. Trinity eliminated this policy and also reduced the mortgage on the property, but there was still an operating deficit of eighty thousand dollars in 1966.[77]

Still, by 1966 it was clear that the school could be operated successfully, providing a high caliber of Christian education with a decreasing operating budget. In the light of that, the corporation voted to end the trial period of St. Michael's School and consider it a permanent part of the parish. The Corporation also decided to embark on a four-year endowment campaign, in 1966–70, starting among the parishioners of Trinity Church and the parents of St. Michael's students, supplemented by a further campaign to raise additional funds from other sources.[78]

On hearing of these plans, Bishop Higgins congratulated the rector:

> I am quite sure that Trinity Church is embarked on one of the
> most significant ventures in its long life. It is my hope that
> within the next decade St. Michael's School will become an
> increasingly valuable educational factor on the whole Island of
> New-port [sic] and that it will be a model parish Day School
> for the Diocese.[79]

At the annual meeting in 1970, Senior Warden Ray Barker stated that "St. Michael's School continues to be our most important mission." During that year, the parish gave St. Michael's $27,607, the majority of which was used to pay off debt principal.[80] In early 1970, Ballard declared that one of the chief strengths of Trinity Church was St. Michael's School. It was not the parish Sunday School that did the effective educational work, he wrote:

> The real work of religious education is being done at St.
> Michael's School, the Parish Day School of Trinity Church.
> For the past seven years Trinity Church has maintained this
> former Episcopal Charity at the cost of some $175,000 from
> its unrestricted capital funds. One hundred fifty boys and girls
> come under the influence of a Priest Headmaster and a fine
> faculty. This is genuine religious education.[81]

ST. MICHAEL'S
PARISH DAY SCHOOL
OF TRINITY CHURCH
Kindergarten Through Grade 9
NOW ACCEPTING REGISTRATIONS
FOR 1970 - 1971
(No Increase In Tuition This Year)
Office Open Monday-Friday 9-12 and 1-4:30
Dial 846-1068

THE REV. JOHN A. CRANSTON, M.A., S.T.M.
Headmaster

ALL DENOMINATIONS WELCOME

This school features small classes. A faculty of 17 assures
individual attention, discipline, good study habits.
ARTS-MUSIC-SPORTS

Newport Daily New advertisement for St. Michael's School, 1970

Plans for the school continued. In 1971, a foundation and nine friends of the school increased its endowment by $2,140, while the Rhode Island Foundation gave a matching grant of $2,500 to improve the library. But these healthy signs were interrupted by controversy.

At the 20 December 1970 vestry meeting, the headmaster, Father Cranston, reported that he was very unhappy with the school's music program and had, for that reason, canceled the Christmas service of lessons and carols, which was normally held at Trinity. Surprised by this announcement, Ballard called Cranston to his office and there, after some discussion, fired him as head-master, with effect from the school's graduation in June 1971.

During the previous summer the parish had hired John W. Ferreira as organist and choirmaster following the resignation of Wesley Rooker, who had been the organist for six years. After having played a key role at Trinity as one of the first church music directors on the East Coast to bring folk music into the field of religion, Rooker was about to begin graduate work at Rhode Island College. Ferreira, a 1965 graduate of Rogers High School, had begun his music career under Carroll W. J. Ball, organist of Emmanuel Church and director of the Swanhurst Choral Society. Just before entering on his new appointment at Trinity, Ferreira had received his Bachelor of Music degree at Westminster Choir College in Princeton, New Jersey.[82]

The rector had insisted that St Michael's employ Ferreira as its music teacher as well, believing that a closely coordinated music program was a good thing for both parish and school. At first the headmaster had refused, wanting to retain Rooker on the faculty, but he later agreed to accept the appointment. During this period, the Selective Service notified Ferreira that he would be called to active military duty, and Ballard asked Cranston to write an official letter to the draft board notifying it that Ferreira was an essential member of the school's faculty. When Ferreira appeared before the draft board, however, no letter was on file. The rector again asked Cranston to write on Ferreira's behalf, which he did, but apparently without making the case that Ferreira was an essential member of the faculty. Ballard was outraged, feeling that Cranston had deliberately sabotaged the lessons and carols service and "knifed" Ferreira. It was on these grounds that he justified Cranston's dismissal as headmaster.[83]

Cranston's dismissal created a huge protest at St. Michael's School, where he was widely respected. A large number of parents withdrew their children in protest against Ballard's action. In a series of meetings, the vestry examined its options. As its members collectively saw it, they could reinstate Cranston as rector; Ballard, however, adamantly refused to allow this. Alternatively, they could reestablish the school with a new headmaster, but the withdrawal of students would create an operating deficit of up to fifty thousand dollars. Finally, they considered a "turn the other cheek" plan of renting the school buildings to a parent-teachers-faculty group, for a token sum. However, as many saw it, the simplest way out of the dilemma was to "cut their losses and run." In the end, the vestry unanimously agreed to a motion presented by Capt. Herbert F. Rommel, USN (Ret.), as amended by Capt. Poyntell C. Staley, that the church close the school at the end of the 1970–71 academic year and offer the property and furnishings to an organized corporation formed by the school's parent-teacher-faculty association for one dollar per year.[84]

Further consideration of the legal and financial implications, and of the liability involved in leasing the school property, raised numerous issues. The vestry called a special meeting of the corporation and placed the matter before the parishioners, asking them to approve the vestry resolution to lease the school. The risk was that if the corporation defeated the motion, Trinity would continue to run the school, whereas a parent-teacher-faculty group supporting Cranston as headmaster had declared that if that occurred, it would open a competing school. The vestry saw that competition of this sort would substantially decrease the enrollment at St. Michael's and increase the deficit that Trinity would need to cover. After a long discussion, the consensus of the corporation

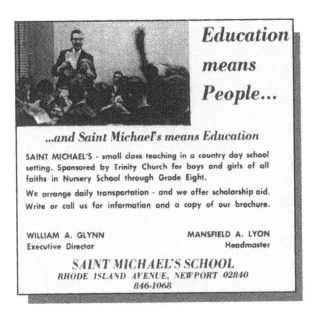

Newport Daily News *advertisement for St. Michael's School under its new direction, 1971.*

meeting was to call on the "rector and Father Cranston to sit down and resolve their differences as Christian gentlemen." With this hope in mind, the corporation defeated the motion to lease the school. As a result, the Trinity corporation continued to operate the school, despite the threat of split-up and a resulting operating deficit.[85]

In May 1971, William Glynn, a former St. Michael's headmaster and then director of schools in Foxboro, Massachusetts, became executive director of St. Michael's School. Father Cranston officially left the school on 3 June, and the parish discontinued paying his salary and rent from the end of that month.

Already plans for another school were being laid. When the vestry had preliminarily voted to close St. Michael's in March, a group of former St. Michael's parents, teachers, and faculty had immediately taken steps to form what they formally named the New School (renamed The Pennfield School in 1993), with Father Cranston as its first headmaster. In April the New School announced that seven of the twelve teachers at St. Michael's had joined the New School and that sixty-two of St. Michael's 130 students had applied for admission. At the same time, plans were laid for the New School to lease space at the Newport School for Girls on Ruggles Avenue.[86]

With the Trinity corporation's decision to reverse the vestry's decision and to continue operating St. Michael's School, a new headmaster was needed. Mansfield A. Lyon of Wallingford, Connecticut, became the new headmaster in June 1968. A graduate of Westminster School in Simsbury, Connecticut, and a 1954 graduate of Yale, he had taught at St. Michael's from 1956 to 1958 before joining the firm of Bunting and Lyon in Wallingford, where he had counseled families on schools and provided management advice to private schools.[87]

Trinity Cemetery. The first suggestion that the parish acquire a modern parish cemetery arose in January 1960, when Hugo J. Kay presented a proposal for Trinity Church to purchase a section of Aquidneck Memorial Park in Middletown to be used as a church cemetery. After consideration of the proposal, the church agreed to purchase twenty-two lots containing forty-four graves for $3,960, with a ten-year option on forty-four more lots.[88] Nearly four years later, at the end of 1963, Mrs. Robert R. Young donated to Trinity Church a forty-six-acre tract of land on the east side of East Main Road, directly across from the St. Mary's Episcopal Church cemetery. This land had originally been part of the

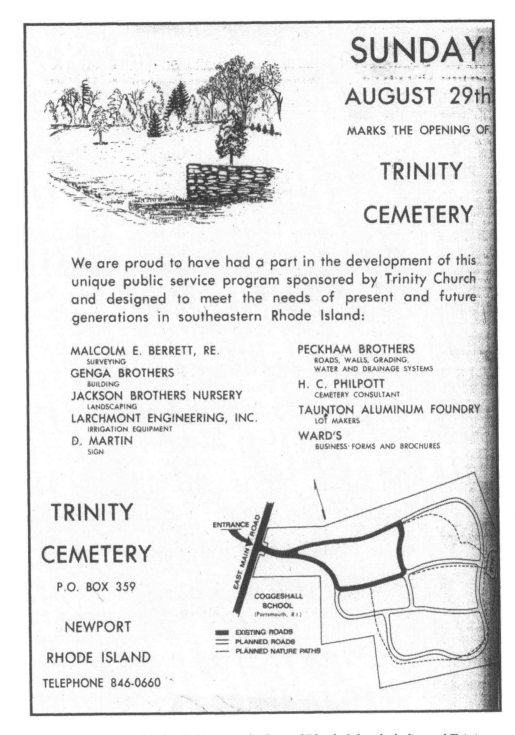

The Right Reverend John S. Higgins, bishop of Rhode Island, dedicated Trinity Cemetery in Portsmouth, 29 August 1971. Newport Daily News.

Anthony family farm, dating back to the first settlement.[89] In December 1964, the town of Portsmouth granted Trinity Church permission to operate a cemetery on the Young donation, but at this point the vestry discovered that there was no specific provision in the corporation charter that would allow it to operate a cemetery in Portsmouth or anywhere else.[90]

In June 1968, the parish commissioned a feasibility study to examine options available. At the January 1969 annual meeting, the corporation voted a recommendation to the vestry that it seriously consider during the forthcoming year the initial development of the proposed cemetery, at a funding level of fourteen thousand dollars. Immediately following the meeting, the vestry authorized undertaking a survey and initial planning.[91] The lapse of time and new zoning laws in Portsmouth required that the town's zoning board again approve the matter.

By 1970, the cemetery issue was becoming a problem. Local facilities were becoming increasingly scarce. The two nearby Episcopal churches with cemeteries, St. Mary's and the Berkeley Memorial, had limited them to their own parishes. No other Protestant cemeteries were available in the immediate area, and land for such uses was available only at increasing cost. Since, in this case, the land had been given on the specific condition that it be used as a parish cemetery, land cost was not an issue, although planners anticipated that an investment of about $220,000 would be required to develop the property. Interest derived from capital raised from site sales would provide income.[92]

The parish allocated an initial seventy thousand dollars in January 1970. After reviewing bids, the vestry hired Peckham Brothers Construction of Middletown to do the grading, rebuild stone walls, install drainage and water systems, and provide 2,800 feet of road on the site.[93] While this work was in progress, the vestry formally named the property "Trinity Cemetery."[94] Several hundred trees were planted in the park area, and plans called for the future construction of a pond and a nature walk at the east end of the wooded property. On 29 August 1971, a group of a hundred people gathered to witness the dedication of the cemetery by The Right Reverend John S. Higgins, bishop of Rhode Island. Seeing it as one of New England's most beautiful burial grounds, with its parklike atmosphere, Ballard envisaged that it would serve the needs of the parish and community for at least the next three centuries. Moreover, he believed, this project "promises to increase the endowments of the Church over the centuries."[95]

Trinity Nursing Home. In January 1971, the treasurer, Captain Rommel, presented a motion that the vestry recommend to the corporation a concept for the parish to operate a nursing home and that it appoint a committee for that purpose; the recommendation was approved.[96] By May 1971, however, several nursing homes were being planned for the area, and the vestry decided first to wait and observe what others were doing before further consideration of the plan.[97]

Impact on the Parish. By the middle of 1967, it had become clear that the financial burden on the parish involved in the range of projects to support St. Michael's School, to develop the land around the church, and create a new cemetery was making it increasingly difficult to maintain Kay Chapel and the High Street Parish House. At the same time, there was waning interest in both the traditional forms of parish activities and in the standard organization of Sunday school, using conventional grades.

The parish was declining in numbers, reflecting widespread trends within the national Episcopal Church. In the mid-1950s, the number of communicants in good standing had risen from the nine hundreds to 1,059, and there had been more than eight hundred families in the parish. In a typical year, baptized members had been listed as close to 2,300, with a total of 34,596 attending fifty-five services of all types. In 1958, communicants suddenly dropped to 640, the number of families to 425, and the number of baptized members to 844. In the mid-1960s, the parish had grown slightly, to 675, with the total number of baptized members at 1,100. Attendance at services dropped steadily from 35,459 in 1960 to 15,800 in 1972, and the number of services also declined precipitously, from an annual 577 in 1961 to 232 in 1963. While the number of townspeople and summer residents attending Trinity declined, this same period also saw an increase in the percentage of the congregation connected with the U.S. Navy; Ballard and others within the parish actively sought their participation. In numbers, however, service members did not fully replace the local families and summer residents that had previously attended.[98] The presence of a relatively large group of young, single service people changed the needs and the ministry of the parish.

In September 1967, the rector published his thoughts in *The Tower* on selling these two properties and asked for the opinions of members of the parish.[99] The issue raised widespread discussion. A number of people agreed with Margaret E. Carr, who wrote the senior warden expressing her concern at the vestry's lack of interest in neighborhood activities: "I am convinced that to abandon our parish house would be a major catastrophe, and to raze the chapels would be destructive not only of the many memorials given for them but also of confidence in the wisdom of our operations."[100]

In August 1969, the rector announced that the Sunday school program would be discontinued and that services would not be held in Kay Chapel or in its smaller Cavalry Chapel during the coming fall and winter, as a means of saving on heating bills. From that point onward the midweek services were held in Honyman Hall, and three Sunday services were held in Trinity. Considering another item on the vestry's agenda regarding the development of a cooperative venture in housing, Canon Ballard commented, "Can we keep buildings going that we don't need, when there is a desperate need for money for housing and the treatment of drug addiction?"[101] In subsequent years, Trinity remained a major supporter of the Church-Community Corporation that had emerged. Ballard, enthusiastically attempting to enlist the support of other Episcopal parishes in Newport, blatantly told their timorous rectors, "If you won't support CCC, it's spiritually dead."[102]

As a result of its discontinuing the use of Kay Chapel, the parish initiated the first 9 A.M. family service on Sunday, 14 September 1969. The vestry authorized the New England Black Pentecostal Church of Providence to use Kay

---

So the kids don't want to go to school on Sunday?

Well, Trinity Church doesn't have a Sunday School!

So why not come as a family to enjoy Sunday Worship? Tomorrow we feature the American Folk Song Mass. Great Combo and organ music at eleven o'clock. Enjoy being modern in a beautiful Colonial Church.

TRINITY CHURCH
25 Church Street, Newport

No Sunday school at Trinity!
Canon Ballard closed the Sunday school in 1969, as part of his plan to economize on expenses, to reinvigorate declining church attendance, and to attract young people to Trinity through modern popular music.
Newport Daily News, 1 October 1970.

Chapel for Sunday services for three months, and another Afro-American group, the Church of God in Christ, also used the building.

At the very end of the annual meeting in January 1960, Mrs. John Crosby had raised a question as to why no woman had ever been a member of the vestry. The rector pointed out that the charter forbade it but that this matter could be formally brought before the corporation.[103] It was another eight years before the parish's legal advisors, Sheffield & Harvey, raised the question again and advised the parish to alter the charter, deleting the word "male" in the five instances when it appeared in the charter and by-laws as a qualification for office. At a special corporation meeting on 14 January 1968, this change was made. At the annual meeting two weeks later, the corporation elected Mrs. Lyle A. Thompson as the first woman clerk of the vestry and Mrs. Powel H. Kazanjian the first vestrywoman of Trinity Church. A year later, in January 1969, the corporation elected the first black member of the vestry, O. William Hilton, Jr., who was the regional director for special education in Newport County.[104] In

THANKS

The Church Community Corporation

wishes to thank the following individuals and organizations who have contributed toward its financial goal of $60,000

Reverend George Behan
Francis A. Comstock
August B. Cordeiro
Marthe T. de Bethune
RADM Henry E. Eccles
Middletown United Methodist Church
Newport County Chamber of Commerce
Newport Daily News
Newport YMCA
Frederic E. Ossorio
Henry D. Phelps

The Point Association of Newport
Portsmouth Abbey
Robert Reimer
St. Mary's Church, Portsmouth
St. Paul's Church, Portsmouth
St. Spyridon's Church, Newport
Trinity Circle, Trinity Church
Trinity Church, Newport

The many anonymous donors who have contributed and persons who have given unselfishly of their time and effort in this endeavor.

Church - Community Corporation

Working for decent housing for families of low and moderate income on Aquidneck Island

The Church-Community Corporation was a major focus for Trinity's outreach from the time it was founded in 1969. Newport Daily News, c. 1970.

1970, the by-laws were further amended specifically to allow women as church-wardens.[105] In the following year, the vestry reflected the influence of the U.S. Navy at Trinity, as well as the welcome presence of women on the vestry. In 1971, vestry members included two retired naval officers, one active-duty officer, one petty officer, and a navy wife.[106]

After suffering several heart attacks between October 1971 and January 1972, Canon Ballard had attempted to return to his work part-time, but by August 1972 his physicians were advising him that he must retire, just short of nineteen years after coming to Trinity in 1953.[107] In September 1972, the pension board of the Episcopal Church accepted Ballard's request for a disability retirement; Ballard passed his parish responsibilities to The Reverend Thomas Wile, the curate, whom the vestry appointed priest in charge.

Immediately on his retirement to an eighteenth-century Newport Restoration Foundation house on Pelham Street, Ballard wrote a reflection on his ministry in Newport, entitling it *On the Agony of Being a Priest*, repeating much of what he said in his final annual report.[108] He was "certain that the changes directed by me have caused more uneasiness, even unreasoning resentments and cancellations of memberships, than the Prayer Book and service experimental changes made mandatory by our national and diocesan authorities."[109] Change, even revolutionary change, he believed, was the keynote of the final decades of the twentieth century as Trinity Church, the Episcopal communion, and the very institution of religion struggled to survive. Trinity Church, he said, was a wealthy church, whose assets had nearly doubled (to $1,925,000) during his years in Newport, though it spent three-quarters of a million on missionary support, the diocesan quota, St. Michael's School, Queen Anne Square and Trinity Close, Trinity Cemetery, the Church-Community Corporation, and other parish activities.

Yet money, he saw, only relieved poverty, not the other issues facing the church. His illness, he declared, had been caused by his "agony of frustration over what to do to save a dying Sunday School and youth work." He believed that these old-fashioned and ineffective programs had failed because young people increasingly preferred the drug and free-sex scene to the sort of activities that a church promoted. Almost three out of every four young people in America had lost interest in organized religion. In the face of this widespread trend away from traditional programs and approaches, "We hypocritically pretended we were promoting a splendid program of religious education and youth work—all the while knowing in the depths of our souls we were spiritual frauds."[110]

Notes

1. Newport Historical Society, Parish Records, Vestry Minutes 1926–1950, p. 489: "Report of the Rector. The Reverend James R. MacColl, III, to the Corporation of Trinity Church, January 9, 1950."
2. Vestry Minutes 1924–59, p. 493: letter from rector to John W. Rupp, 14 April 1950.
3. Trinity Church Scrapbook 1944–1951, clipping August 1950: "Trinity Church Letter Brings Truman Reply."
4. Ibid., inside back cover: "Trinity Church Left Surprise Bequest of $800,000 from Estate of Millionaire Eccentric Hetty Green Wilks," 16 February 1951; "Trinity Officials Slowly Recovering from Amazement at $800,000 Legacy," 17 February 1951.
5. Ibid., "Hamilton Fish Webster's $500,000 in Bequests Made in 1939 Released," 5 October 1951.
6. Vestry Minutes 1950–54, p. 155: minutes of the annual meeting, 14 January 1952.
7. Ibid., Minutes 10 February 1952, p. 177.
8. Annual Report of the Rector, 14 January 1952 [pp. 6–7].
9. Ibid.
10. Scrapbook, 1944–1951: "Men from *Superb* Attend Services," *Newport Daily News,* 3 September 1951.
11. Scrapbook, 1951–1955: "Trinity Holds Memorial Service: County Clergy Join in Honoring British King, 16 February 1952; *Order of Service in Memory of his Britannic Majesty King George VI, 1895 – 1952, Trinity Church, February 15, 1952 at 7:45 p.m.*
12. Ibid., "Trinity Receives Thanks of Canterbury Archbishop," *Newport Daily News,* 6 March 1952.
13. Vestry Minutes 1950–1954., p. 137: 4 December 1951.
14. Ibid., p. 171: letter from rector to city clerk, 15 January 1952.
15. Ibid., p. 205: letter from Stephen B. Luce to Industrial Trust Co, 5 May 1952; p. 250: Annual Report of the Rector, 12 January 1953.
16. Trinity Church Scrapbook, 1951–1955, "Trinity Church Landscaping Model," *Newport Daily News,* 6 September 1953. The building was later moved to 77 Bridge Street, in the Point area.
17. Vestry Minutes, 1950–1954: letter from the vestry to the corporation, 8 September 1953.
18. Ibid., special meeting of the vestry, 8 September 1953.
19. Trinity Scrapbook, 1951–1955, "Montgomery Speaks at War College: British Marshal Visits Trinity Church," *Newport Daily News,* 10 April 1953, pp. 1, 4.
20. Vestry Minutes, 1950–1954, Minutes, p. 287: letter from Rev. MacColl to John F. Tennant, secretary of the corporation and the vestry, 20 July 1953.
21. Ibid., p. 303: minutes, 12 October 1953.
22. Ibid., p. 338: minutes of the annual meeting, Recapitulation of Cash and Securities of Trinity Church as of December 31, 1953; Estimated Budget for 1954.
23. Ibid., p. 338: minutes of the annual meeting, report of the priest-in-charge, 10 January 1954, p. 3.
24. Ibid., p. 369: vestry minutes, 11 July 1954.
25. Ibid., p. 381: vestry minutes, 24 September 1954.
26. Letter from Rev. Alan P. Maynard to Hattendorf, 8 March 1996.
27. Vestry Minutes, 1954–1957, p. 34: letter from Deputy City Clerk Robert A. Shea to John F. Tennant, 28 February 1955.
28. Mason, *Annals of Trinity Church, 1698–1821* (Newport, RI: 1890), pp. 228, 233.

29. Vestry Minutes 1954–1957, p. 79: 8 January 1956; Letter from Charles W. Swartley, pastor, to vestryman, Trinity Church, 3 January 1956; Vestry Minutes 1957–59, p. 37: 10 August 1958.

30. *New York Times,* 19 June 1955.

31. Trinity Scrapbook, 1955–1957.

32. "Royal Arms Coat Returned to Trinity: Queen Anne's Emblem Removed in Revolution," *Providence Journal,* 29 July 1956.

33. Ibid.

34. Vestry Minutes 1954–57, p. 19: minutes, 12 August 1956.

35. Ibid., p. 124: minutes, 9 September 1956.

36. Trinity Scrapbook, 1955–57, "Touro Synagogue Restoration Work to Be Launched Soon, Finished by '58," *Newport Daily News,* 23 August 1956.

37. Ibid.

38. Ibid., *Congressional Record,* vol. 107, no. 65 (18 April 1961), p. 1, and vol. 108, no. 70 (3 May 1962), p. 1; "Claiborne deBorda Pell Biography," Salve Regina University, Pell Center for International Relations and Public Policy, http://www.salve.edu/pellbio.html (10/03/2000).

39. Trinity Scrapbook 1968–72: "Churches, Newport Agencies Provide Shelter for Visitors," *Newport Daily News,* no date.

40. Trinity Church Scrapbook, 1958–1962: "Canon Ballard Talks Sense about the Jazz Festival," *Rhode Island Churchman,* 22 July 1960; "Poignant Story of London Slums Told at Kay Chapel by Players," *Newport Daily News,* 20 April 1960;

41. Trinity Scrapbook, 1965–68, "Trinity Sketches Included in Wedgwood Medallion Display" and "Wedgwood Medallion of Trinity Produced," *Newport Daily News,* 26 September 1966.

42. Trinity Scrapbook, 1968–72, "Three Local Sites Designated," *Newport Daily News,* no date.

43. Trinity Scrapbook, 1968–72, "Church Here Put on U.S. Register," *Newport Daily News,* 10 February 1971.

44. Trinity Scrapbook, 1965–68, "U.S. Folk Music Mass Sung at Trinity Church," *Newport Daily News,* 11 April 1966.

45. Ibid., "Folk Mass Author Presents Episcopal Church Program," *Newport Daily News,* 11 December 1967; "Folk Music Rocks an Old Church," *Providence Journal-Bulletin,* 28 December 1967, p. 1.

46. Ibid.

47. Vestry Minutes, 1964–68: 17 April 1966. Letter from Phyllis G. Schumacher to Secretary of the vestry.

48. Ibid., Letter from the secretary of the vestry to Mrs. Alan T. Schumacher, 18 April 1968.

49. Trinity Scrapbook, 1965–68: clipping June 16 1968.

50. Trinity Scrapbook, 1968–72: "Folk Music's Modern Sound Fills Ancient Trinity Church," *Newport Daily News,* July 1969.

51. Trinity Scrapbook, 1965–68: "Folk Music Used in Three Churches," *Newport Daily News,* 25 July 1966.

52. Trinity Scrapbook, 1968–72; Lockett F. Ballard, "In Newport County: Common Sense or Suicide," *Rhode Island Churchman,* 19 February 1970, p. 11.

53. Vestry Minutes, 1954–57, p. 137: special meeting of the vestry, 16 December 1956; p. 145, amended, p. 145: 13 January 1957.

54. In 1985, the Naval War College named the Henry E. Eccles Library in honor of his many contributions to the college and to the U.S. Navy.

55. Vestry Minutes, 1954–1957, p. 149: 13 January 1957.

56. Ibid., p. 159: 10 March 1957.

57. Vestry Minutes, 1957–59, p. 15: 11 May 1958.

58. Ibid., p. 69: 8 March 1959.

59. Vestry Minutes, 1964–68: 16 November 1964: charter as amended 1947, Section II, quoted in letter from Richard Sheffield to Henry E. Eccles, 10 November 1964; see also minutes 10 December 1967 with letter of clarification from Sheffield to Eccles, 12 December 1967.

60. Ibid.

61. Vestry Minutes, 1968–65: 11 September 1966: letter from Charles McGowan to Eccles, 21 September 1966; 13 November 1966.

62. Vestry Minutes, 1969–72: 19 April 1970.

63. Trinity Scrapbook, 1963–65, "Noted Finnish Architect Urges City to Keep Heritage, Develop as Resort," *Newport Daily News* (no date).

64. Vestry Minutes 1959–63: 15 April 1962; "Queen Anne Square Proposal Aired by Trinity Vestryman," *Newport Daily News,* 16 April 1962.

65. Ibid., 10 November 1963.

66. Trinity Scrapbook, 1963–65: "A Clarion Call" letter to the editor, *Newport Daily News,* no date.

67. Ibid., "Trinity Garden Work Progressing," *Newport Daily News,* 28 November 1964.

68. Ibid., "Pleasant Mixture of Old and New," *Providence Journal-Bulletin,* 21 June 1965.

69. Vestry Minutes, 1964–68: 16 October 1966.

70. Trinity Scrapbook, 1965–68: "Address Change for Half a House," *Providence Journal-Bulletin* [misdated March 1967]; "Bit of Colonial Newport on Move," *Newport Daily News,* 6 April 1967.

71. Vestry Minutes, 1957–59, p. 113: 13 December 1959; Minutes 1959–63: 15 October 1961; annual meeting 28 January 1963.

72. Ibid., special meeting of the corporation, 21 July 1963.

73. Trinity Scrapbook, 1963–65: booklet, *St. Michael's School, Newport, Rhode Island* for academic year 1963–64.

74. Vestry Minutes, 1964–68: 9 August 1964.

75. Ibid: Senior warden's memo for the vestry of Trinity Church in Newport, 28 August 1964.

76. Ballard eventually wrote a history of the colonial era of the parish, but it was not published, because he cited no sources and the work did not attain the academic standards of professional historians. The typescript is in the Trinity Church Records at the Newport Historical Society.

77. Ibid., 10 December 1964; 16 October 1966: letter from Rear Adm. Henry Eccles to Sidney W. Davidson, 12 October 1966.

78. Ibid., special meeting of the corporation 7 March 1966.

79. Trinity Scrapbook, 1965–68: transcript of letter from Bishop John Seville Higgins to Rev. Canon Lockett F. Ballard, 16 March 1966.

80. Vestry Minutes, 1969–72: annual meeting 26 January 1970; Report of the Senior Warden Ray Barker; Report of Treasurer Herbert Rommel.

81. Trinity Scrapbook, 1968–72; Ballard, "Common Sense or Suicide," p. 11.

82. Trinity Scrapbook, 1968–72: "Trinity Church Names Organist, Choirmaster," *Newport Daily News,* I June 1970, p. 20.

83. Ibid., p. 473–74: 17 January 1971; p. 489, 611–13 special meeting 24 January.

84. Ibid., p. 491: special meeting, 11 February 1971.

85. Ibid., p. 465: special meeting of the corporation, 22 March 1971.

86. Trinity Scrapbook, 1968–72: "Church School Splits," *Providence Journal-Bulletin,* 30 March 1970; "New School Will Lease Space," *Newport Daily News,* 23 April 1971.

87. Trinity Scrapbook, 1968–72: "Headmaster Appointed," *Newport Daily News,* 29 June 1971.

88. Vestry Minutes, 1959–63, p. 135: 14 January 1960; p. 139: 13 March 1960; 12 June 1960.

89. Vestry Minutes, 1964–68: 12 January 1964.

90. Ibid., 10 January 1965.

91. Vestry Minutes, 1969–72: annual meeting, 19 January 1969; Vestry meeting, 16 February 1969.

92. Ibid., annual meeting, 26 January 1970: "Trinity Cemetery: Investment in the Future."

93. Ibid., Vestry Minutes, 15 August 1970.

94. Ibid., 20 December 1970.

95. "Review of 1971," *Trinity Tower,* 19 March 1972.

96. Vestry Minutes 1969–72., p. 597: 17 January 1971.

97. Ibid., p. 463: 23 May 1971. Study of Feasibility of Trinity Church to Construct and Establish a Nursing Home in the Newport Area. 19 December 1971, rev. 24 January 1972.

98. Capt. Charles K. Moore, USN (Ret.), "Trinity Church Demographics, 1726–1992."

99. Ibid., Minutes, 13 August 1967.

100. Ibid., 11 February 1968: Letter from Margaret Carr to Ray Barker, 30 November 1967.

101. Vestry Minutes, 1969–72: 17 August 1969.

102. Recollection of B. Mitchell Simpson III.

103. Vestry Minutes, 1959–63. Unpaginated at end of volume: annual meeting, 25 January 1960.

104. Trinity Scrapbook, 1968–72: "Trinity Church Picks Black Vestryman," New*port Daily News,* 29 January 1969.

105. Vestry Minutes 1969–72: 21 December 1969.

106. Moore, "Demographics."

107. Ibid., Letter of resignation: Ballard to Church Wardens and Vestry, 17 August 1972.

108. Lockett F. Ballard, "On the Agony of Being a Priest," *Trinity Tower*, 27 February 1972, 5 March 1972 and *The Rhode Island Churchman*, 21 September 1972, pp. 13–14.

109. Ibid.

110. Ibid.

The Trinity Church neighborhood, c. 1973.
To the south of the church, the Atlantic Richfield gas station stands on the corner of
Spring and Mill Streets. West of it stands Honyman Hall. Further to the west stands
the chimney of Egan's Laundry and other commercial buildings leading down to
Thames Street. The Alexander Hamilton Rice House stands on the south side of
Church Street. John Hopf photo.

12

Divestment and Consolidation, 1973–2000

The new ventures that had begun during the past quarter-century remained in place on Ballard's retirement, but that would quickly change as his successors moved to divest both new and old acquisitions, while trying to consolidate the parish anew. Wile remained as priest in charge, from September 1972 until February 1973, when he was called to be a canon at the American Cathedral in Paris. In the meantime, guest preachers—quite often it was the former naval chaplain and canon of the archdiocese of Jerusalem, The Reverend Dr. John D. Zimmerman, who lived in retirement nearby—filled Trinity's pulpit, until a new rector was named.

In the interim period between rectors, the corporation conducted some important business by approving changes and modifications to the charter. At a special meeting in January 1973, the corporation voted to increase the limit of property owned by Trinity Church from five million to ten million dollars. The assistant treasurer of the church was made an official member of the vestry and given the right to vote, and the procedures concerning the election of a rector were updated. Among the updates was removal of the charter provision that the appointment of a rector be of life tenure.[1]

In this interim period, a major change for the city occurred when the U.S. Navy announced that it would soon discontinue using Newport as a fleet base and that its ships and sailors, with their families, would move to other homeports. The Cruiser-Destroyer Force, U.S. Atlantic Fleet was no longer to be based in Newport, and other fleet-related activities were also scheduled to close throughout Narragansett Bay, as would the naval shipyard in Boston. Local lore attributed the base closure to political vindictiveness resulting from the fact that Massachusetts and Rhode Island had been the only two states in the Union to vote against Richard Nixon in the 1972 presidential election. The real reason was that the nation had far more bases than it could afford. In choosing which were to be closed, more important factors dominated. In the case of Newport, the skies over southern New England were dominated by the main air traffic routes between Europe and New York; it was no longer safe for the navy to use the waters off the New England coast for naval exercises that involved a combination of missiles, aircraft, and ships.[2] Nevertheless, the departure of the ships and sailors that had been so prominent a feature of the city for so many years brought a dramatic economic and social change. Some despaired of the future of Newport. Property values fell, and local clergy braced for a decline in congregations and looked for new orientations for their ministries, focusing on closer cooperation between churches and on long-term residents.[3]

This local trend combined with a wider national trend, exemplified in the anti-Vietnam War sentiment of the 1960s. While this issue had divided the membership of the Episcopal Church at large, Episcopalians in 1971 made up one of the largest groups of conscientious objectors in the country.[4] In previous eras, the Anglican and Episcopal Churches had been noted for strong connections to national public service. As institutions they had avoided social criticism and even tended to blunt challenges of the status quo. Much of that changed in the 1960s and 1970s, when the national Episcopal Church, the clergy, and the seminaries began to show a much more active interest in promoting social change and developing social values.

Meanwhile, after considering twenty-three candidates, the corporation, on the advice of the calling committee and the vestry, elected The Reverend Charles J. Minifie as the new rector, with the specific goal of increasing the Christian Education Program, getting lay members involved in the parish's work, and developing outreach programs in the community.[5] The thirty-two-year-old Minifie, known to many as "Chad," had been born in Providence and was the third generation of his family to enter the Episcopal ministry. At the time of his appointment to Newport, his father, The Reverend Benjamin Minifie, was the rector of Grace Church, New York. The young Minifie had attended the Lenox School and graduated from Trinity College, Hartford, Connecticut, in 1963, before going onto the Episcopal Theological College in Cambridge, Massachusetts. At the time of his appointment, he was assistant rector of Trinity Church, Portland, Oregon. During the summer of 1967 he had been priest in charge of St. Olave's Church in London and since 1968 had served as rector of St. Andrews-by-the-Sea, a summer chapel in Hyannisport, Massachusetts. Before going to Oregon, he had been in charge of the Sunday school program (which had doubled in size under his leadership) at St. Thomas's Church, New York City. In the church at Portland, he had been in charge of a religious education program with 223 children and two hundred adults.[6]

As a young clergyman who had been trained in the 1960s, Minifie naturally reflected many of the values and views of his generation. At Trinity, he was the first rector of the parish in thirty years who did not have a personal connection with military service. Although the parish continued to have a significant naval element, Minifie was an obviously attractive candidate, married and with a family, and whose experience in parish education brought the hope that he could revive the Sunday school and a family-oriented parish.

His arrival at Trinity coincided with a number of trends within the national church in terms of liturgical practice. Very quietly, the national flag was removed for a time from display within the church; the traditional national hymns were no longer heard; and old favorites of the previous generation, such as "Onward Christian Soldiers, Marching as to War," disappeared from use.

As far back as the 1930s, a seminary liturgical movement had experimented with the idea of celebrating the Eucharist with the priest facing the congregation; in the late 1940s, this practice had begun to move to the parish level, particularly when new churches were constructed. The idea was allow the congregation to see what was going on and also to emphasize and to make vivid the corporate nature of Communion. It took a long time for older parishes to make this transition, as altars in Episcopal churches were traditionally fixed against the east wall of the chancel.[7]

In Trinity's case, the colonial altar table had always stood against the wall, and since 1875 the large brass cross dedicated to the memory of its beloved rector The Reverend Isaac P. White had been centered above it, where the brass complemented the gold-painted letters of the inscriptions on the eighteenth-century altarpiece. In January 1967, the parish received a thousand-dollar bequest from the estate of Mrs. Eva Hietman Panunzio to commission a modern silver cross for the altar.[8] Eventually, that cross, with its smaller base, would sit on the ledge beneath the altarpiece alongside the single silver candlesticks and silver vases. Thus, Trinity could accommodate the liturgical changes that were included in the experimental services and in the 1979 Book of Common Prayer, without fundamentally damaging the original colonial design.

The most divisive sign of redirection in the church was the move to revise the Book of Common Prayer, replacing its stately but antique language with modern American speech. A number of prominent clergyman thought that the 1928 book, being comfortable and familiar, did not encourage the activism many now sought in the church. Beginning with the 1953 Prayer Book Studies IV, a number of new innovations and approaches had been laid out, which slowly made their way into practice. From 1964, the Church's General Conventions began to approve a series of trial services, with the 1967 *Liturgy of the Lord's Supper* and, in 1970, *Services for Trial Use*, known because of the color of its binding as the "Green Book."[9]

Canon Ballard had begun to use a variety of experimental services, and even before taking up his duties at Trinity, Minifie made it clear that he was not among those who opposed revision of the Book of Common Prayer. On his first visit to Newport, he commented that he preferred the Green Book. However, on learning that most parishioners did not yet accept the Green Book, he assured the vestry that he would educate the parish on the issues before making any further or permanent changes.[10]

Shortly after The Reverend Gordon Stenning, of St. Mary's Church, Portsmouth, dean of the Aquidneck deanery, presided at Minifie's formal installation as rector on 9 September 1973, Minifie announced the appointment of a new organist and choir director to succeed John Ferreira. The appointment of Marian Van Slyke was significant in the parish's history. A widely loved and respected person, she was thought at the time to be the first woman to hold the position.[11] The longtime director of the Navy Choristers in Newport, she had also been director of the Salve Regina College Glee Club and of the Naval Officer Candidate School in Newport, and accompanist for the Swanhurst Choral Society. She had been music director of the First Baptist Church in Fall River for eight years and for thirteen years before that of the First Presbyterian Church in Newport. When she had first come to Newport, in 1946, she had spent two years as organist at the Christian Science church.[12]

One of the early musical innovations of her tenure was a candlelight evensong service in honor of St. Cecilia, the patron saint of music. Held on 18 November 1973, it was the first evensong that any parishioner could recall at Trinity. The senior warden, Charles S. Dotterer, thought it the first ever held in the church in honor of St. Cecilia, although as Mrs. Van Slyke recalled, the church's first organist, Charles Pachelbel, had founded the St. Cecilia Society, America's oldest musical society, after he had left Newport for Charleston. (William Selby, who had been appointed Trinity's organist in 1773, later formed the Handel and Haydn Society in Boston in honor of St. Cecilia.)[13]

In his address during the St. Cecilia's Day evensong, Minifie underscored his belief in the importance of good music in the worship life of the church. Shortly thereafter, the parish installed its new Wicks organ, and a series of Sunday afternoon concerts began, inaugurated by the Barrington College

Brass Trio in February 1974. The Brown University Chamber Choir sang at an evensong in March, and Polish pianist Marguerite Szapinalska gave a recital in July. Not to forget the earlier musical innovations at Trinity, The Reverend Ian Mitchell returned with his folk mass that same year.

Among other early changes, Minifie purchased his own home, at 29 John Street, allowing the vestry to sell 81 Rhode Island Avenue, which had been the rectory since 1945. In October 1973, the vestry approved the sale of the property to parishioners Mansfield and Mary Lyon; the proceeds of the sale were subsequently deposited in the Church Endowment Fund.[14]

At the annual corporation meeting in January 1974, the new rector and the parish could assess the condition of the parish and begin to lay out the direction it would now take. For nearly a year, between 1 November 1972 and 1 October 1973, the parish had not had a full-time rector or assistant. In this period, Capt. Curtis Bunting, as business manager, had been the continuity for the parish. The value of the church's capital endowment had eroded by 15 percent during the previous year, due a combination of a decline in stock market values and the parish's continuing deficit spending of the principal.

Meanwhile, a number of the long-time members of the parish passed on their parish responsibilities to a new generation. Among the longest-serving who retired at this point were senior warden Dr. Charles Dotterer, who had completed twenty years of service, and Margaret E. Carr, who had served sixty-three years in the Altar Society. With research assistance and text by former vestryman John F. Millar, the parish published a new color brochure in August 1973, with photos by John T. Hopf, entitled *A Visit to Historic Trinity Church.*

Under Minifie's leadership, the Sunday school reopened with an average attendance of forty children at the High Street parish house, and an adult group of about fifteen also began to meet. At the same time, a Youth Group, which had been started two years before, began to grow and become more active. The Queen Anne Square and Trinity Close projects, however, were at a momentary standstill. Trinity Cemetery was developing slowly, but only eighty lots had been sold, and only nineteen burials had taken place, requiring seven thousand dollars from the parish to cover more than half of its operating expenses. At St. Michael's School, under the cooperation of headmaster Mansfield Lyon and executive director William Glynn, enrollment had increased from eighty-one students in September 1971 to 165 in 1974, while the operating deficit had fallen from twenty-five thousand dollars to a projected eight thousand dollars. During these years, Lyons instituted a "St. Michael's Day" at Trinity, a joint service for St. Michael's School families and Trinity parishioners that typically included morning prayer and a musical presentation by St. Michael's pupils.

In his first report to the corporation, The Reverend Minifie said, "Trinity Church is blessed with a glorious building and thanks to the generosity of people in the past, we have a moderately large endowment. But we can not rest on the labors of those who came before."[15] Across the nation, Minifie observed, the church was in serious trouble, but he saw that Trinity had all the ingredients of becoming a great parish—"a parish which is a living, viable Christian community which serves all sorts and conditions and which is an inspiration and source of strength."[16]

In October 1974, there was threat of arson in Newport, and Newport police placed a guard around the church on 20 and 21 October. The senior warden worked out a watch list with sixty-four volunteers, including many young officers from the Naval War College. The rector believed that Trinity remained an arson threat "for unique Freudian reasons."[17] On advice of the police chief, volunteers maintained the watch, with some difficulty, until late February 1975.

With Minifie's second year, new changes were seen in a variety of areas. At St. Michael's, Mansfield Lyon added the responsibilities of executive director to those of headmaster, and the corporation moved to designate the school a regional one that served all of Aquidneck Island.[18] Shortly thereafter, the parish and the school jointly established a five-year plan to make St. Michael's eventually independent from the parish. On another front, Atlantic Richfield, the national corporation that owned the ARCO gas station at the northeast corner of Spring and Mill Streets, offered to sell the property to Trinity for thirty-seven thousand dollars. Accepting the offer quickly, the parish immediately demolished the red-brick, neocolonial building and had the site landscaped, using the twenty-thousand-dollar fund that the Goelet Foundation had provided to carry out the 1965 concept.

January 1971 the Hill Association, a recently established neighborhood homeowners' and residents' group headed by its founder and first president, Capt. J. C. Myers, persuaded the City Council to cancel the Redevelopment Agency's plan to demolish the Vanderbilt Memorial YMCA Building on Mary Street, extend Clarke Street to Church Street, and leave open space for modern residential development under the shadow of Trinity Church. Myers argued that the agency's plan made no sense when the basic idea was to preserve the historic environment and to promote the aesthetic beauty of the city. At this point, all the buildings on the waterfront side of Thames Street had been torn down, and on the west side of Thames Street, just below the church, Egan's Laundry remained with its large smokestack still obscuring the view. Parishioner and founder of Christmas in Newport, Mrs. Ruth Myers commented, "Egan's is a blight on the waterfront."[19]

As the *Providence Journal-Bulletin* noted, the key figure who brought about the transformation of Newport from an urban version of "Cinderella" or "The Ugly Duckling" was Doris Duke. Between 1968 and 1973, through her Newport Restoration Foundation, she had already put more than five million dollars of her reported $300 million into restoring Newport's colonial heritage. By 1973, she had completed the restoration of twenty-five buildings in the city and had acquired another forty-five.[20] One was the YMCA on Mary Street, which for a time became the foundation's carpentry shop.

As part of her concept for Newport, Doris Duke was committed to expanding and bringing to fruition the concept for Queen Anne Square that Canon Ballard had envisaged. In February 1974, the Redevelopment Agency and the City Planning Board formally approved the combined Trinity Church-Restoration Foundation Plan. To further this, Duke and officials from the Newport Restoration Foundation met with the rector in July 1974. During that meeting Miss Duke expressed her desire to have the park around the church extended all the way to Thames Street, commenting, "Trinity Church was Newport's most important building."[21] Following up on this idea in March 1975, the vestry strongly endorsed another plan that the Newport Restoration Foundation had put forward to modify the Redevelopment Agency's plan for commercial development around Queen Anne Square. In its place, the Restoration Foundation and the Trinity Church Corporation planned to create a park-like atmosphere that would enhance the church's setting in the neighborhood. In March 1975, the vestry unanimously and formally agreed to join with the Newport Restoration Foundation, Inc., in co-developing Queen Anne Square.[22]

In the course of subsequent discussions, Minifie indicated that Trinity wished to use the land just west of Honyman Hall to erect a building for parish education. Miss Duke was not happy with this suggestion, but in later meetings the idea surfaced of using what was thought to be the seventeenth-century Governor Caleb Carr House, then part of the Egan Laundry complex, as the shell for Trinity's new building. It quickly became clear that funding could be found to incorporate the old fabric in the proposed building, but not to build an entirely new structure.

In the following years, Trinity and its colonial heritage repeatedly came into the public spotlight. In March 1974, the diocese of Rhode Island revived an old custom of making the rectors of the first Rhode Island parishes founded in the colonial period honorary canons of St. John's Cathedral in Providence. The appointment carried few rights or responsibilities, but from that point Minifie was entitled to add "Canon" to his formal title and to wear a purple rather than black cassock.[23]

In December 1975, Christmas in Newport's candlelight and choral service at Trinity Church was broadcast nationwide on ABC Television, and on 11 January 1976, the archbishop of Canterbury, The Most Reverend F. Donald Coggan, preached at a 4 P.M. service that was carried live by local television. It was the 101st archbishop of Canterbury's first public appearance in the United States since his consecration in 1974. Invited to Trinity to mark the 250th anniversary of the building, Dr. Coggan noted in his sermon that he regularly visited

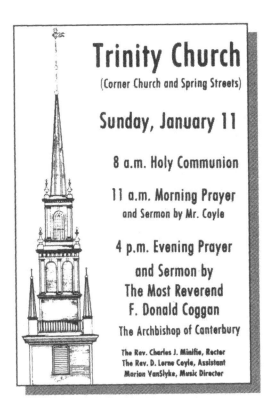

Newport Daily News *notice of the evening prayer service, 11 January 1975, with a sermon by the archbishop of Canterbury*

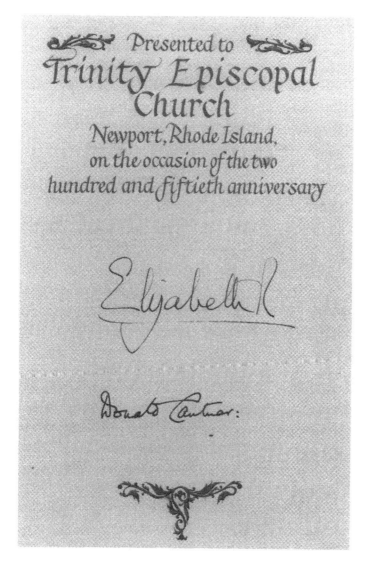

Presentation page from the New English Bible, *signed by Her Majesty the Queen and the archbishop of Canterbury.*

churches in England that were celebrating their thousandth or 1,300th anniversaries. "A danger of historical churches is to become a museum," he said; establishing discussion groups on what a church was for was one method to keep a church alive. He outlined the three things that, he believed, were the specific purposes of any church: worship, holiness, and outreach to preach Christ, as the Good News for man. "A Church," he said, "is not a private club, but rather is a training ground for Christian commandos."[24]

Leaving Rhode Island proved to be an adventure for the archbishop. The assistant rector, The Reverend D. Lorne Coyle, and his wife Jane were assigned to take him and his chaplain to the Providence airport, so that Dr. Coggan could address the United Nations. As Coyle would remember,

> Getting to the airport in our little Toyota Corolla was harder than I had expected. The car was sliding all over. On the access road to the airport, which had not been plowed, I slid into the soft shoulder of snow. I got out and asked Jane and the chaplain to help me push while His Grace drove. "Nonsense," he said, "I am not that old. I'll push while Mrs. Coyle drives!" We got the car back on the road and got to the little plane. The Archbishop seemed dismayed when he saw the size of the plane. He was not comforted when the pilot asked him how much he weighed. "Sixteen stone," he replied. Now it was the pilot's turn to look uncomfortable, not having any idea what a stone weighed. But they made it to the UN safely.[25]

A few weeks after the archbishop of Canterbury's visit, the attention of the parish was drawn back again to the long-gestating plans for Queen Anne Square. After much discussion the Redevelopment Agency and the city's Planning Board approved the joint plan that Trinity Church and the Newport Restoration Foundation had submitted. The nationally televised Christmas service, the visit of the archbishop, and the fact that an estimated twenty thousand visitors a year came to see the church underscored the importance of the church building to the community.

The new plans differed significantly from the plans laid three years before. A fire in the Egan Laundry buildings along Thames Street opened up the entire area from Thames Street to the church. The projected removal of the Governor Carr House to become the shell of the parish's new education building was projected to be the costliest item on the budget, at $325,000. Other houses that would have to be moved for the project were the Cotton House, moved from Cotton's Court to Mill Street, and the Patykewich House at 22 Frank Street. The Langley House at 21 Church Street was turned around and moved from the south to the north side of Church Street, and the parish's Alexander Hamilton Rice House was moved from the south side of Church Street and turned around to sit on the north side of Mill. In addition, the new plan called for the restoration of Frank Street with Belgian paving blocks and blue-stone borders, and for the installation of gas fixtures to light the street and the square.[26]

Implementation of these plans for Queen Anne Square ran immediately into difficulty. The Egan family, who had constructed the laundry buildings in 1950 and owned them, objected. Unable to find a suitable place to relocate their business, they proposed a three-story modern structure for the site, which some critics likened to "a contemporary ski lodge in Aspen."[27] The Redevelopment Agency voted to begin proceedings in Superior Court against the Egans; the family entered a petition of their own, questioning the legality of the city's plans.

In the end, the Superior Court declined to issue a restraining order to a legislative body, an equal branch of government, and the City Council gave its

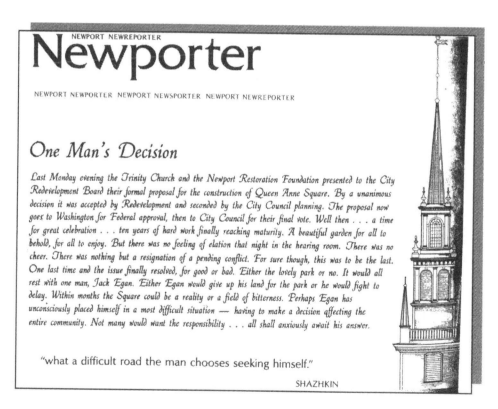

Newporter

NEWPORT NEWREPORTER

NEWPORT NEWSPORTER NEWPORT NEWSPORTER NEWPORT NEWREPORTER

One Man's Decision

Last Monday evening the Trinity Church and the Newport Restoration Foundation presented to the City Redevelopment Board their formal proposal for the construction of Queen Anne Square. By a unanimous decision it was accepted by Redevelopment and seconded by the City Council planning. The proposal now goes to Washington for Federal approval, then to City Council for their final vote. Well then . . . a time for great celebration . . . ten years of hard work finally reaching maturity. A beautiful garden for all to behold, for all to enjoy. But there was no feeling of elation that night in the hearing room. There was no cheer. There was nothing but a resignation of a pending conflict. For sure though, this was to be the last. One last time and the issue finally resolved, for good or bad. Either the lovely park or no. It would all rest with one man, Jack Egan. Either Egan would give up his land for the park or he would fight to delay. Within months the Square could be a reality or a field of bitterness. Perhaps Egan has unconsciously placed himself in a most difficult situation — having to make a decision affecting the entire community. Not many would want the responsibility . . . all shall anxiously await his answer.

"what a difficult road the man chooses seeking himself."

SHAZHKIN

This 1973 notice in the Newport New Reporter *called attention to the critical decision that the owners of Egan's Laundry faced in regard to the proposed Queen Anne Square.*

final approval on 26 May 1976 to the plan that Trinity and the Newport Restoration Foundation proposed.[28] To implement its portion of the plan, the Trinity corporation approved the adaptive reuse of the Carr House as well as the simultaneous sale of the High Street parish house and Kay Chapel to help fund the necessary construction. The Church of God in Christ was then using these buildings; Trinity terminated its lease so that the plan could proceed.[29]

In the period between May and July 1976, a number of events took place to mark the bicentennial of the United States as well as the 250th anniversary of Trinity Church. The visit of the archbishop of Canterbury had begun the parish's celebration, and it was followed on 2 May by Rhode Island Independence Day, for which President Gerald Ford had been invited to speak from Trinity's pulpit and in Touro Synagogue. The president's appearance was canceled, reportedly due to the presidential primary elections that were then taking place. James M. Cannon, President Ford's assistant for domestic affairs and director of the Domestic Council, spoke in his place. On 20 June, the presiding bishop of the United States, The Right Reverend John M. Allin, preached at Trinity, and on the following Sunday, the dean of the Washington National Cathedral, The Very Reverend Francis B. Sayre, was the preacher.

Sayre's visit to Trinity coincided with the parish's ecumenical service for the captains and crews of the square-rigged sail training vessels that were also visiting Newport. In his Sunday sermon at Trinity on 27 June 1976, published on the same day in the New York Sunday Times, Sayre declared:

> We are grateful on this Sunday of national remembrance, to
> all these captains and their crews who have sailed across the
> rolling main, and come to this ancient port to remind us of our
> youth and to refresh our hope. They man a fleet of beautiful and
> stately grace, built like ships before them of the skill of careful
> artisans; and sailed by courage in the tops, and discipline upon
> the deck below, by those who have striven to embody the plain
> and precious blessing with which this continent came to be
> endowed.[30]

Skillfully linking the seaman's craft to the nation and to faith, Sayre declared, "Their word to us this morning, and to all America, is simply that the landfall is the same as it was 200 years ago. The course is constant: the goal unchanged: 'Steady as you go.' "[31]

TRINITY CHURCH
POST OFFICE BOX 359

NEWPORT, RHODE ISLAND 02840

THE REVEREND CHARLES J. MINIFIE
Rector

THE REVEREND D. LORNE COYLE
Assistant

Parish Office
27 CHURCH STREET
TEL. 401-846-0660

November 15, 1975

Her Majesty The Queen
Buckingham Palace
London SW 7, England

Your Majesty:

My good friend and former Bishop, the Rt. Rev. Horace
W. B. Donegan, the retired Bishop of New York, suggested that
I write to you directly. We desire that you come to Newport,
Rhode Island, on Wednesday, June 30, 1976, to dedicate Queen
Anne Square, a two acre park lying directly west of this his-
toric church and named in honor of Queen Anne. Queen Anne
Square has been six years in the discussion and planning stages.
Next June it will have become a reality and will be presented
to the citizens of Newport.

Your consort, Prince Philip, has been invited to Newport
on June 30, 1976 to present the prizes on the occasion of the
Tall Ships which will be in Newport at that time. It is therefore most fitting and appropriate that you be invited to dedicate Queen Anne Square to a monarch who meant so much to Trinity
Church.

Trinity Church's historic building was completed 250 years
ago and Queen Anne made many important contributions to the life
of this parish including the gift of a bell in 1709. To celebrate this 250th Anniversary in 1976, we have planned a number
of events including a visit on January 11th of His Grace, The
Archbishop of Canterbury. I am enclosing a copy of a recently
published booklet which in pictures and words tells Trinity's
history far better than this brief letter.

Trinity Church has had and continues to have a distinguished history and your coming here on June 30th would mean a
great deal to us and to the citizens of Newport.

This letter comes to you with my warm best wishes and
greetings!

Sincerely yours,

Charles J. Minifie

*The rector's first letter of invitation to the queen. Several subsequent letters
followed before the invitation was accepted.*

Parish Records. Collection of the Newport Historical Society.

Her Majesty Queen Elizabeth II and The Reverend Charles J. Minifie, rector of Trinity Church, with the Queen Anne Square stone behind them. Mrs. Minifie and their daughter, Rachel, are facing the queen.

The final visit of the celebration came on Saturday, 10 July 1976, nearly a week after the nation's two-hundredth anniversary celebration. At the conclusion of a state visit to the United States, Queen Elizabeth II and Prince Philip arrived by air at Theodore F. Green Airport in Providence in the late afternoon. Gov. Philip Noel greeted them. They traveled in a motorcade directly to Newport. From the Newport Bridge, the motorcade passed down Washington Street, Long Wharf, America's Cup Avenue, and Memorial Boulevard before turning north on Spring Street to Trinity Church, where some three thousand spectators were gathered around Trinity and in the still-incomplete Queen Anne Square. Getting out of the limousine on Mill Street at the Goelet Fountain, the queen reviewed members of the Newport Artillery Company, dressed in red uniforms, as she and Prince Philip walked to the south side of the church to unveil the plaque dedicating Queen Anne Square. Escorted to the entrance of the church, they were shown by Minifie a model of what the completed square would look like and presented with one of the Wedgwood medallions of Trinity. John J. Slocum, president of the local branch of the English Speaking Union, then presented the queen and Prince Philip with a bas-relief bust by Felix de Weldon of King George VI, with an inscription carved in stone by John Benson. Mayor Humphrey J. Donnelly III presented the queen with a Newport flag and an oil painting by artist Jay Killians of the completed Queen Anne Square. In addition, he presented two "theorem paintings" on velvet by local folk artist Margaret Wood.

Following the presentations, Minifie escorted the royal couple into the church to show them the historic structure. Passing the 1702 bell on its stand at the entrance, Mayor Donnelly drew attention to it by asking, "Aren't you going to show Her Majesty the bell?" When Minifie mentioned that recent research questioned the long-held belief that it had been the personal gift of Queen Anne, the queen replied, "You have been doing your homework. That is what the Bicentennial has done. It has sent us back to the history books."[32] Minifie pointed out the royal crown atop the old organ case given by Dean Berkeley, the wine-glass pulpit still in its original position, and the pew George Washington is said to have used. There the queen sat for a few moments to read the plaque commemorating Washington's visit. Then she went to the altar, where the rector showed her the parish silver. Pointing out the 1704 S.P.G. chalice and patten, Minifie explained that it was used only at Christmas and Easter. The royal couple showed particular interest in the Kay baptismal bowl, which had been used to baptize two of the country's naval heroes, Oliver Hazard Perry and Matthew Perry. At the end of the visit, the queen presented Minifie with a copy of the New English Bible, which both she and the archbishop of Canterbury had inscribed to Trinity Church.

Leaving by the door through the sacristy at the east end of the building after a twenty-five-minute visit, the royal party returned to their vehicles and proceeded to the Destroyer Pier One, where later that evening President Ford, Secretary of State Henry Kissinger, Foreign Secretary Anthony Crosland, Sen. Claiborne Pell, and the British and American ambassadors joined the queen on board the royal yacht *Britannia* for dinner.

Later that same summer, on 29 August, for the first time since the 1960s, folksinger Pete Seeger returned to Trinity to sing at the Sunday morning service. Reverting to historical themes just four weeks later, the Founder's

Festival on 25–26 September marked the weekend closest to the actual 250th anniversary of the building and of the first recorded service in the building on 28 September 1726. On Saturday, booths set up on the church grounds offered gifts and homemade baked goods for sale, and the choir, dressed in eighteenth-century costumes, sang hymns. On Sunday, in an attempt to duplicate early eighteenth-century practice, there were no flowers or candles on the altar, and instead of organ music Marian Van Slyke played the harpsichord. The morning prayer service was conducted from an original 1766 edition of the Book of Common Prayer, from the parish's book collection. Both Minifie and the assistant rector, Lorne Coyle, wore white wigs and black cassocks with white bands. John F. Millar, also dressed in a colonial costume, stood in the clerk's desk at the bottom of the triple-tiered pulpit and led the congregation in reading the psalm and singing the canticles, as the parish clerk would have done in that period. In preparation for the sermon, the churchwardens took their nodding wands in hand to keep the congregation attentive, using the sharp end for gentlemen or an attached feather for the ladies. Typical of colonial practice, Minifie, in wig and surplice, fortified himself with a shot of rum just before mounting the long staircase to the high pulpit. In the end, however, he did not attempt to make his sermon as long as the typical seventy-five minutes that his predecessor, James Honyman, had taken, but his sermon did use many quotes from an original Honyman sermon.

The Founders' Fair and the eighteenth-century-style service marked the last of the large events in the parish's year-long 250th anniversary celebration. Shortly after they were completed, the issues surrounding Queen Anne Square once again surfaced in the local news. Progress had been halted by court order, pending a resolution of the disputes in court. However, in mid-July, on the eve of the queen's visit to Newport, two unidentified men had climbed to the top of the Egan's Laundry smokestack in the pouring rain and cut a guy wire and pulled the stack so that it leaned five or ten degrees. A danger to public safety, it was immediately demolished despite the court order; a newspaper headline declared, "Robin [Hood] slays city's 'eyesore.' "[33] In early September, the court began to hear arguments to halt the plans for Queen Anne Square in Superior Court. By the middle of the month, the Egans had dropped their legal objections, allowing the plans to proceed; they received $428,549 from the Redevelopment Agency in a relocation payment.[34]

Meanwhile, there were changes taking place in the worship services. In January 1977, five hundred of the new *Draft Proposed Book of Common Prayer* books arrived, and more were on the way. From March 1977, Minifie planned to use Rite I, which was closer to the 1928 prayer book, during Lent and Advent, but use Rite II, which had already been in use for fifteen months in the parish, for the remainder of the year during the eleven o'clock service. At the eight o'clock service and in Wednesday services, the old Book of Common Prayer would be used. On the first Sunday and on possible Thursday services, the new prayer book would be used.[35]

Ground had been broken for the parish's new Carr House on 10 July 1977; construction was completed in June 1978 at the cost of $530,000, toward which donations of $260,000 had been received or pledged by the spring of 1978. Shortly afterwards Mr. Lawrence Allen purchased the High Street parish house and Kay Chapel for $127,500. The proceeds from this sale were put toward the construction of Carr House. The sale of Kay Chapel raised much concern about the monuments remaining in it, particularly the stained-glass window given by the King family. Kay and Cavalry Chapels were formally deconsecrated in 14 April 1979, and the property was divided into two lots for sale. To relieve concern about many of the memorials and furnishings, the parish planned to include a small chapel In Carr House.[36]

In the end, the new building, which retained the name Carr House, was not the refurbished colonial house that had been originally envisaged in the early stages of the project, but a new building that was a blend of colonial style and modern construction techniques. The building around which earlier plans had turned had been largely destroyed in the demolition of Egan's Laundry. In October 1977, Brown University's Public Archaeology Laboratory conducted an investigation of the remains and found that the old Carr House that had stood on Mill Street was not Gov. Caleb Carr's seventeenth-century "mansion house" but that of his son, John Carr.[37] In a deep basement area of the new building there was a large kitchen, meeting rooms for the parish and the community, and toilets; an elevator led to the first floor, where classrooms and a chapel would be located. The second floor was designed for classes and for the music department, and there was third-floor apartment. Minifie and Bishop Belden formally dedicated Carr House on 9 July 1978. During the morning prayer service that immediately preceded the dedication, Minifie noted, "Our cultural, educational and fellowship needs are just as important as our spiritual, and indeed are an integral part of the whole person. It is in this new parish house that the solid foundations will be laid and built upon for all who use it."[38]

These words marked Minifie's final sermon and final day as rector of Trinity Church. In February 1978, the senior warden, John Hatch, and the officers of the vestry had recommended that the contract with the rector not be renewed, as it had specified goals for increasing the Christian education program, increasing lay involvement in the parish, and developing community outreach. At the March vestry meeting, the rector apologized for his misinterpretation of the vestry's intention, he having thought that the vestry required the conclusion of the rector's association with Trinity Church, rather than the development of new goals in a new contract.[39] Despite clearing up that misunderstanding, and in light of a series of personal, marital, and family problems, Minifie announced that he would leave Trinity Church at the termination of his current contract, without negotiating a new one.

Minifie told the vestry that he had been going through the time of life where many face confusion about who they are and where they are going, and that this had caused stress both at home and within the parish. Advising the vestry to be alert for such situations in a new rector, he told the bishop that he supported Trinity's concept of a five-year contract between rector and parish. Senior warden John Hatch underscored Minifie's contribution to uplifting the parish spiritually, and vestryman Terry Schrubb wondered if the parish was requiring something of its rector that it should not. Minifie had been expected to deal with in political problems and architectural planning, to act as an executive as well as a priest, Schrubb pointed out.

Minifie agreed and noted that while some of this had been his own doing, aspects over which he had had no control had certainly caused frustration. "A priest is an administrator," Minifie told the vestry, "but being a priest in an historic church such as Trinity involves additional responsibilities." Through all of it, however, "he believed that he had developed a considerably stronger faith in God than when he came here."[40] Not long after making public his announcement that he would leave Trinity, Minifie also made public his interest in going into politics and becoming a Republican candidate for the U.S. Senate seat held by parishioner Claiborne Pell.[41] It was late in the political year for a serious campaign, and these plans quickly fizzled.

Upon notification of Minifie's resignation, Bishop Belden approved the vestry's nomination of the assistant rector, The Reverend D. Lorne Coyle, as priest in charge from 19 August 1978, on the basis of a letter of understanding concerning his duties and responsibilities.[42] Coyle had come to Trinity as assistant rector in July 1974, shortly after graduating with distinction from the

Senior warden John F. Hatch presents the Trinity Church key to The Reverend D. Lorne Coyle on 15 January 1979, following his installation as rector. Between them is The Reverend Dr. George I. Hunter, Jr., Lawrence Professor at the Episcopal Divinity School and Coyle's mentor, along with The Reverend Gordon Stenning.

Episcopal Divinity School in Cambridge, Massachusetts. Ordained a deacon in his home parish of St. Elizabeth's Church, Ridgewood, New Jersey, in June 1975, Coyle had graduated from Ridgewood High School and Amherst College. Ordained a priest as recently as 7 December 1975 at Trinity, Coyle specifically asked for an experienced assistant during his period as priest in charge; the bishop appointed The Reverend Daniel Quinby Williams, the retired rector of Emmanuel Church, Newport, to fill this position.

In discussing the selection of a new rector with the Trinity vestry, the bishop and the diocesan staff made it clear that it was not appropriate to short-circuit the elaborate computer search and consultation system that the diocese had in place by selecting a young priest in charge. "The young chap never grows into the image of the Rector in the eyes of many members of the parish," Canon Westhorp of the diocesan staff advised.[43]

A search committee for a new rector was appointed. It sent out questionnaires to five hundred members of the congregation. Of the 188 returned, 113 indicated that they wished to have Coyle called as the next rector.[44] Immediately advising the bishop, senior warden John Hatch reported back that Bishop Belden had given his blessing to calling Coyle as rector but cautioned the vestry to draw up a contract that would safeguard Coyle from being "burned out" by overwork. A month later, on 19 November 1978, a special meeting of the corporation elected The Reverend D. Lome Coyle the rector of Trinity Church.[45]

One of Coyle's first problems was to deal with the uncertainty surrounding Doris Duke's commitment to continuing the plan for Queen Anne Square when the funding for the Redevelopment Agency expired in June 1978. Before receiving her assurances on this matter, however, the vestry reconfirmed its own determination to develop a park, whether or not she was able to participate and to move houses as she had planned.

In early October 1978, the Newport Restoration Foundation had threatened to abandon the project unless it was left "unhindered to enjoy complete artistic as well as financial control" as well as "sole and exclusive discretion" over the project. The Redevelopment Agency gave Doris Duke a free hand to develop Queen Anne Square as she and Trinity Church had proposed in 1975. Immediately a team of archaeologists from Brown University's Public Archaeology Laboratory began a survey to prevent inadvertent destruction of historic artifacts. Shortly thereafter, Metropolitan Movers began the long-planned move of the colonial homes.[46]

The parish also wanted to have a parking lot for church use worked into the plan; Coyle and vestryman Herbert A. Lawton, Jr., met with Miss Duke to discuss the parking issue on several occasions.[47] Coyle later recalled,

> She agreed to come to my office. She sat down and began to tat. Without looking up from her tatting, she listened to my presentation about the parking lot we were going to establish on our property. When done, I asked her if she had any concerns or questions. She smiled, thanked me, and left.
>
> I was jubilant. It had gone far easier than I could have imagined.
>
> The next Sunday, as we were lining up for the procession that starts the 10 a.m. service, John Hatch, one of the ushers and then senior warden, grabbed my arm and said, "You'd better come and see this." What I saw was Miss Duke out in Queen Anne Square, scarf on her blond head, riding in the bucket of a bulldozer directing a flatbed truck. On the truck was a large pine tree. She proceeded to plant that tree right square in the center of the proposed entrance to the parking lot, blocking all access. That was her answer to my proposal. I grew to love that tree.[48]

The final legal step for Queen Anne Square occurred in 1981, when the Redevelopment Agency of Newport formally recorded the deed to the property in perpetuity, allowing a shed for Trinity to store its lawn maintenance equipment, otherwise:

> Subject, however, to the restriction that said park, while always being open for public enjoyment, shall not be used for commercial activity of any kind and that no building or structures temporary or permanent, shall be erected thereon. The preceding restriction shall include tents, booths, stages and display stands but shall not prohibit the erection or installation of statues, monuments, fountains, park benches, drinking fountains, trash receptacles or other street furniture normally found in public parks.[49]

Several other property and finance-related issues arose early in the Coyle years. In 1979, the market value of the endowment fund stood at $1,256,356, and under the management of the Finance Committee, chaired by Curtis Bunting and the treasurer, Jeffrey L. Gordon, the parish budget for 1980 was balanced for the first time in twenty-one years. Endowment income and pledges had increased and were coupled to both fiscal restraint and improved financial planning. A curator of the parish was appointed, and a careful inventory of Trinity's valuable antiques was made to determine their appropriateness to the parish. As a result, all documents were transferred to the Newport Historical Society for "perpetual care," and the vestry agreed to sell at auction an original Rembrandt print, some books unrelated to the parish, and several chairs.[50] This, combined with the theft of some antiques from Honyman Hall, reduced the parish's liability.

Trinity's new emphasis on a balanced budget and increased fiscal restraint was noticed very early by the diocese. Not for the first time in its history, Trinity had declined to pay the full amount of the apportionment that the diocese demanded. Trinity had been very generous to the diocese in the past, but some on the vestry were beginning to think that the diocese was expecting too much and depending excessively on Trinity's endowment income. In June 1980, the new bishop of Rhode Island, The Right Reverend George Hunt III, asked to attend a meeting of the vestry in order to introduce himself and, particularly, find out why the vestry had voted not to meet its quota for the year.

During the meeting, the bishop explained the diocese's needs for funds and asked that Trinity pay the amount requested, noting that no parish in his diocese had more income than Trinity. Several vestry members put pressing questions to the bishop as to why several different accounting systems and criteria were used to compute a parish's quota, and why Trinity's quota, using any measure of fair apportionment, was 20 percent higher than that of any other parish. The treasurer pointed out that Trinity could not meet the quota without eliminating some of its programs and asked that the bishop explore those programs before making the demands that he did. The meeting resulted in a momentary impasse when the bishop declared that Trinity should pay its full quota and let him explain his reasons for asking, rather than requiring him to explain beforehand.[51]

The parish's new approach to fiscal matters involved a number of other changes as well. With the opening of the new Carr House, there was little practical need for the parish to retain the Alexander Hamilton Rice House, which the Rice family had presented to the parish in 1955, restored at the cost of approximately thirty-three thousand dollars, and for which Mrs. Rice had left a fund of $100,000, the income of which was to be used for maintenance. Selling the building raised serious legal and moral questions about the church's handling of gifts, and its disposal of property that the city and the Restoration Foundation had moved to its present location as part of the Queen Anne Square project. For the moment, the parish decided to renovate the building and rent it as a single-family dwelling.[52]

Trinity Cemetery in Portsmouth also continued to be a financial drain on the parish. The parish's cemetery management committee recommended that the parish seek a buyer for the property, pursuing interest that had been expressed, but no action was taken at this time.[53]

St. Michael's School had since 1976 been renting its property from the parish with an option to buy the land and buildings. In November 1980, the board of trustees of St. Michael's voted to proceed with that option, to purchase the property for $160,000 and to take title on 15 June 1981.[54] On 22 June 1981, following the five-year plan that the parish and the school had established in 1976, Trinity Church sold St. Michael's School, allowing it to become an independent entity as St. Michael's Country Day School.[55] One of the issues involved with this transfer was St. Michael's Endowment Fund. Since the separation of the two institutions in 1976, the church had been obligated to manage this fund and provide at least three thousand dollars annually in scholarships; this arrangement continued.[56]

Less than a month later, on 13 July 1981, a fire occurred in Honyman Hall, destroying the financial secretary's office. The reconstruction of much data was required. Repair and restoration of the building was completed by January 1982, with the installation of a new fire alarm system.

After the Book of Common Prayer 1979 was introduced at Trinity, Senior Warden J. Christian Myers and his wife Elizabeth formally requested that Trinity have Holy Communion at every service instead of the alternating pattern of morning prayer and Holy Communion that had been used at Trinity for so long. The rector formed a committee of parishioners to advise him on the matter.[57] A survey of parishioners showed a strong feeling for retaining the morning prayer service; as a result, the rector instituted a composite morning prayer and Communion. Also, in 1982 the General Convention had approved a new hymnal to replace the 1940 edition. This change was implemented at Trinity in February 1986.[58]

In early 1982, the vestry made plans to fill the staff position of property manager. Several candidates had expressed an interest, but Herbert A. Lawton, Jr., who had long served on the Property Committee and as a vestryman, was the logical candidate. The rector chose him, with the vestry's full approval for this position.[59] In other areas relating to the staff, the vestry examined the issues involving the rector's appointment as specified in 1978. That agreement required a review four years after appointment, but since no criteria had been established, the vestry delayed consideration until the following year. In August 1983, senior warden B. Mitchell Simpson III presented the issues to the vestry. He explained that The Reverend Coyle had signed a covenant with Trinity for a five-year term as rector beginning in 1978, and that his agreement to serve was now to be renewed without a terminal date but with provision for a quinquennial review of his performance and an explanation as to justifiable grounds that either the vestry or the rector might employ to dissolve the agreement.[60] Simpson facetiously noted that they were dealing with a covenant that put the rector and the corporation in roles analogous to "labor" and "management." The idea had been to seek a healthy combination of flexibility, in order to adjust to anticipated and unanticipated changes and stability, so that both the parish and the rector could have some confidence in long-range anticipations. On the basis of this agreement, the vestry renewed Coyle's covenant as rector.[61]

In early 1984, Coyle invited Bishop Desmond Tutu to preach at Trinity in connection with the bicentennial of the consecration of Bishop Seabury as the first bishop in the United States. Described as "one of South Africa's most articulate Christians," he was bishop of Lesotho and, at the time that he came to Trinity, was the first black person to serve as General Secretary of the South African Council of Churches.[62] The week before he planned to preach at Trinity, the Nobel Committee in Oslo announced Tutu's selection as the Nobel Peace Prize laureate for 1984, recognizing his work for justice and racial harmony and against the policy of apartheid in South Africa. Despite the selection, Tutu kept his commitment to come to Trinity, where he preached at a diocesan evening prayer service on Friday, 2 November, and at the Sunday service on 4 November. The press gave his visit to Newport much attention. "After the first long press conference on Friday, the Bishop had about two hours before the diocesan Evening Prayer service at Trinity," Coyle later recalled.

> Several reporters wanted exclusive interviews. However, the Bishop said he needed some space alone and time to pray. Several women of our parish, led by Jean Gorham, had prepared some hot tea and scones for him upstairs in Honyman Hall. He was most grateful for their ministrations, and took his tea and scones to my office. He asked me to call him in one hour. I figured he was tired and would nap. When I came back in an hour, I knocked and found him on his knees on my oak floor, in deep prayer. He had chosen communion with our Lord over a nap and public relations.[63]

Tutu's visit also had its mischievous side. The Coyles hosted a small dinner for him at the Clarke Cooke House, whose owner, David Ray, reserved an entire floor out of his concern for the bishop's security. For the dinner, Mrs. Coyle selected a fixed menu with an exquisite French dessert. As the rector remembered,

> When it came time for dessert, however, Bishop Tutu innocently asked the server if he might have a banana split, instead? Despite the fact that the Clarke Cooke House never had such a dessert item on its menu, the server said yes. Some time later, the desserts arrived, with the Bishop's banana split. I heard later that the sous-chef had had to go home to find bananas for the Bishop.[64]

As early as October 1978, parishioner John F. Millar had written to the rector reporting that based on conversations he had had with the Rhode Island State Preservation Officer, Mrs. Antoinette Downing, he believed that favorable attention would be given to an application from Trinity to refurbish the interior of the building. This, however, would require a panel of experts to make recommendations and then applications for two grants, one to defray the costs of the experts and another to carry out their recommendations.[65] The initial prospect was that this would be a long process. A Trinity Church Preservation Commission was established to examine the issue of historic preservation for the building. In 1982, a pilot project was inaugurated for the tower, with a $3,100 loan from the endowment funds to stimulate interest and contributions toward a full-scale restoration both inside and outside.

In April 1984, the parish commissioned Irving B. Haynes and Associates of Providence to survey the fabric of the building and make a study of the archival record. Their study determined that there had been significant distortion of the building frame and that certain connections in the structure were in imminent danger of failure. The interior framing, particularly the ceiling, had come free from its original anchorage, and the south gallery was only precariously supported on its entire length. The building as a whole was leaning to the north by approximately six inches from sill to plate, and the tip of the spire was out of plumb by eighteen inches. The ceiling joists had dropped approximately six inches from their original positions. Lacking the stone and brick walls of Wren's London churches, the original builders had had to rely on heavy wooden timbers with mortise-and-tenon connections, providing little north-south support. This condition had been made worse when the building was lengthened by twenty-six feet in 1762. "That the Church has survived as well as it has is great testimony to Mr. Munday and the builders," the report noted. [66]

In another problem, the tower was acting as a rigid structure, without an integrated connection to the church building. Originally inadequate, it had been rebuilt in the 1760's, leaving by 1980 "a confusing marriage of two tower structures; the later being built into and around the earlier structure at certain levels."[65]

In August 1984, Daniel Paquette, chairman of the Preservation Commission, presented the results of "The Trinity Church Study" by Haynes and Associates, specifying the structural deficiencies of the church building and the areas that required further exploration in detail. On hearing Paquette's report and after a flashlight tour of remote parts of the building, the corporation authorized a fifteen-thousand-dollar loan from the endowment to implement Phase I of the project.[68] Shortly afterward the Department of the Interior placed Trinity on its list of endangered national historic sites.

To facilitate the plans, in August 1985 treasurer Jeffrey L. Gordon proposed that the parish establish a Trinity Preservation Fund in the form of a separate corporation, following the model of the Cathedral of St. John the Divine, with a board that included the rector, senior warden, and treasurer.[69]

During a portion of the restoration work, the regular services in the church had to be relocated. Consideration was given to using the Congregational church and obtaining the use of the parish's former Kay Chapel, but in the end services were moved to the Carr House basement, renamed for the purpose "The Great Hall." At the outset, its basement area was not a beautiful space. As the rector noted, "Right now, it is about as worshipful as an airplane hangar."[70] The associate rector, The Reverend Marston Price, oversaw the arrangements for the new temporary worship space, designed by Ade Bethune as liturgical consultant.[71] In the meantime, the rector wished to maintain the tradition of unbroken Sunday worship services in the building during reconstruction. As work progressed, small groups of selected volunteers met in the construction area to maintain the tradition, while after July 1986 the main services were moved to the new worship space in Carr House.

The $2.9 million restoration project took fifteen months to complete. Using the plans of Haynes and Associates, the Dimeo Corporation carried out the rehabilitation work. A new tubular steel frame was inserted between the interior plaster and the outer wall, so that it was not noticeable. Tied to piers that anchored the building to the ledge rock, the new structure took the stress away from the original wood beams and gave the building the structural support it had lacked. The four windows in the east and west ends that had been sealed off more than a century before were reopened. A new reproduction of the original brass chandelier was hung in the chancel. The bells were restored, and the old red carpet and red curtain at the east window were removed. The building was repainted inside and out. The blue ceiling was replaced by white, and the white woodwork was painted a muted colonial grayish green. Outside, the pristine white was altered to an antique white that surprised many and created much local comment.[72]

With the work complete, the church reopened on the 261st anniversary of the first service held in the building, 27 September 1987. For the opening, the vestry and choir moved in procession from Carr House, circled the building, and entered the restored church as the bells rang out from the steeple. As the

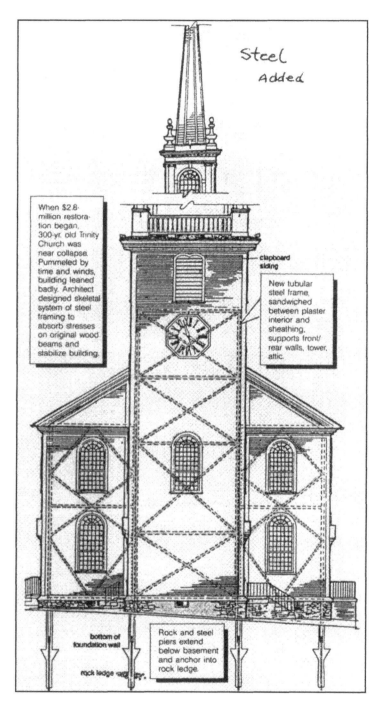

Renovation, 1986–87.
Over a fifteen month period, the church building was entirely renovated. Steel
girders were inserted to support the building.

procession entered the church, bagpiper Alexander Gair, dressed in a kilt, was "piping a jubilant but stately 'Amazing Grace.' "[73] Nearly four months later, on 24 January 1988, the building was formally rededicated; the presiding bishop, The Right Reverend Edmond L. Browning, preached.

The completion of the building restoration required a new historical brochure to replace the one issued in 1973, which was now outdated. Bobbi Wright prepared the text around new photographs taken by John Corbett. The publication was designed by graphic designer Dorothy Sanschagrin.[74]

With the completion of the restoration, a number of other issues also were brought to conclusion. By 1989, the income from rental and endowment for the Alexander Hamilton Rice House could no longer sustain current expenses, and the building met no current need. The parish sold the property, then located at 24 Mill Street. However, in memory of the Rice family's contributions to the parish, the parish modified the name of the neighboring parish building to the Carr-Rice House.[73] In 1991, the endowment was substantially increased by Seth DeBlois's unrestricted gift of seventy thousand dollars.[76]

At the same time, however, the continuing deficits in the operation of Trinity Cemetery were increasing concern about its financial viability. A number of proposals were made, but in 1989 the cemetery recorded a loss of $40,719. At this point the vestry discovered that cemetery administrator, Michael Lynch, had taken approximately sixteen thousand dollars of cemetery funds, whereupon the corporation took action to prosecute him.[77]

As part of the restoration, the new steel supporting structure was skillfully hidden from view and could only be seen behind closed doors.

By 1991, the cemetery had its first positive cash flow of $2,990, and interest in buying it began to grow again.[78] Finally, on 4 March 1992, the parish sold the cemetery to Fred Donnell, owner of Newport Memorial Park, for $232,000. As part of this sale, the church made every effort to honor the moral and legal obligations it had toward cemetery lot holders; a Cemetery Perpetual Care Trust Fund was established.[79]

Over the period between 1980 and 1992, average yearly attendance at all services was 23,300, and an average of 328 people made annual pledges. There were still four Episcopal churches within the city of Newport, two in Middletown, two in Portsmouth, and one in Jamestown. Of Trinity's congregation, 64 percent lived in Newport, 24 percent in Middletown, and 7 percent in Portsmouth, with nine members from Jamestown. About 36 percent of Trinity's congregation were lifelong Episcopalians, the larger percentage of these attending the eight o'clock service, with its Rite I liturgy. In the 1992–93 period, the parish declined in numbers again. By 1993, it had the names of 733 people on the books, of whom about 260 regularly attended church on Sunday, sixty-two at the eight o'clock service and 198 at 11 A.M.; of that number twenty were in the senior choir, twelve in the junior choir, and approximately ten were children in the pews, with another eleven in the nursery or children's hour.[80]

In August 1992, Coyle announced that he had received a call from Holy Trinity Church, Vero Beach, the largest parish in central Florida, and that he would leave Trinity on 27 September 1992. The Reverend Mary B. Johnstone, the associate rector, was selected as priest in charge. In June 1993, the vestry selected her as interim rector, making the appointment retroactive to 1 January 1993. Trinity's first woman priest, Johnstone had arrived as a deacon in training in 1984 and then gradually moved up, becoming deacon in 1985, priest and curate in 1989, and associate rector in 1990. Coinciding with her appointment as priest in charge, the parish received its second woman priest, The Reverend Mary Carson, a graduate of Kenyon College; she was ordained on 29 December 1992.

At the annual meeting in January 1993, the treasurer reported on the financial health of the parish. The previous year had seen a slight ($1,726) deficit, but the budget for the coming year was balanced. The parish had received thirty-five thousand dollars in bequests; pledge income had been $220,000 in the previous year. The market value of the endowment stood at $1,758,076. Jeffrey Gordon advised that the parish should invest endowment income in order to grow the total amount to meet future needs; he recommended paying out only 3 to 5 percent of the market value in any given year. During 1992, the Trinity

Landmark Preservation Fund, Inc., received donations of one hundred thousand dollars, bringing its total value to $572,677. In an analysis of worship attendance between 1986 and 1992, the parish found that numbers had remained fairly constant at fifty people attending the 8 a.m. Sunday morning service, and two hundred the 11 A.M. service.

Looking back on her years at Trinity, The Reverend Johnstone later recalled the important events and trends that she had observed during her tenure, stressing in particular the parish's commitment to four particular areas: historic preservation and the organization of a guides program for the church in both summer and winter; biblical literacy, through the Bethel Bible Series program that began in 1985 and the *Kerygma* program; a first-quality music program involving the organist, choirs, recitals, and concerts; and small-group ministry via *Koinonia* groups and the singles program.[81]

In January 1994, Johnstone departed the parish to become rector of St. Columba's Church, Boothbay Maine; the corporation had not yet chosen a new rector. At the suggestion of the diocese, The Very Reverend James Annand, recently retired dean of the Berkeley Divinity School at Yale University, became the interim rector.

In this general period, several people joined the Trinity parish staff who were with the parish at the point this volume ends or nearly so. In January 1994, Marie Maguire, who had been filling in on a part-time basis for the parish secretary, Eleanor Munro, who had herself served the parish for fourteen years, became the full-time parish secretary. A native of Ireland, she had been trained at the Public Relations Institute of Ireland and had worked in that field for seven years, becoming an account executive for a Dublin-based public relations firm. Following the example of several members of her family, she immigrated to the United States, coming to Newport in December 1993.

About the same time the organist, Donald Ingram, resigned to join Coyle in Vero Beach, Florida, and the parish hired J. Frederick Jodry as organist and choirmaster. A 1984 graduate of the New England Conservatory of Music in organ performance (with distinction in performance and in academics), he had also earned a master of music in early music performance. After studying languages and organ in Germany, he had served as acting director of choral activities and instructor in music theory and history at Brown University as well as director of the Scola Cantorum of Boston. He remained the organist and choir director until September 2000.

The Reverend Canon Roy D. Green, rector of Trinity Church, 1994—98.

Having begun their work in April 1993, the rector search committee reviewed 170 resumes and by August narrowed the list to fifty. Candidates were sent three key questions to answer, and members of the committee traveled in groups of three to Michigan, Tennessee, New Jersey, Virginia, Connecticut, Pennsylvania, and Washington. Three candidates were each invited to Trinity for a weekend, to participate in a Eucharist, three-hour interview, homily, tours, and social occasions. After this process the search committee recommended The Reverend Dr. Roy Green. Returning to Newport, Dr. Green met with the vestry on 12 April, and the corporation voted to appoint him on 24 April.[82]

A 1968 graduate of Florida State University, Green had earned a master of divinity degree in parish ministry from the Virginia Theological Seminary in 1971 and a doctorate of ministry in ethics in 1984. Ordained in 1972, he had served as curate at St. Michael's Church, Orlando, Florida, and assistant rector and priest in charge of the Falls Church, in Falls Church, Virginia, after which he had spent nine years as rector of St. Mark's Church, Orchard Park, New York. He came to Newport from Emmanuel Church, Mercer Island, Washington, where he had been rector since 1987. In October 1993, he had been one of four final candidates for the bishopric of Ohio.

Green began his ministry in Newport on 3 July 1994, ending a nineteen-month gap since Reverend Coyle's departure. Bishop Hunt formally installed him on 23 October, in a service called "A Celebration of a New Ministry," with a bagpipe-accompanied "festival procession' and "concluding procession."[83] In December 1995, The Reverend Marshall Shelly, a 1989 graduate of Kenyon College and a 1994 graduate of the General Theological Seminary, became assistant rector.

Among the prominent events in the immediate area, film director Stephen Spielberg and his film company, Dreamworks, began filming *Amistad* in mid-March 1997. The filming dominated much of Newport for more than a month. Newport, along with Mystic Seaport's waterfront, played the role of New Haven for the film, which dramatized the 1839 mutiny on board the Spanish slave ship *Amistad*, the involvement of the U.S. Navy in apprehending the vessel off Long Island, and the subsequent landmark court case concerning slave rights. For the film, the lower part of Queen Anne Square became the site of a theatrical replica of the New London jail, although this structure contravened the specific deed restriction against the construction of temporary buildings.[84] Trinity's tower was prominent in the opening moments of the film and in several shots involving the prison, as well as some momentary scenes within the church. Just before filming began, however, an arsonist once again threatened both the city and Trinity. On the advice of city officials, a team of volunteers stood watches to protect the building, as in 1974–75.

For a ten-week period in 1997, the parish returned to conducting temporary Sunday worship in the Great Hall of the Carr-Rice House, as it had in 1987–88. This time, the move was caused by the need to repaint the ceiling in the church with a special acoustical paint as part of the preparations for the parish's three-hundredth anniversary. For many years the parish had planned to mark the three-hundredth anniversary of the parish in 1998, and in 1996 the vestry formally established the Tercentenary Commission, cochaired by Cora Lee Gibbs and Jean E. Gorham, with subcommittees to deal with worship, history, events, and fund-raising.[85] The commission chose to mark the celebrations over an entire year, from September 1998 to September 1999. This appropriately recognized the fact that there is no firm, datable, surviving evidence for the 1698 date for the first gathering of the congregation before the formal request for a minister was made to Lord Bellomont on 26 September 1699.

The year of celebration began with a Holy Eucharist for the tercentenary, celebrated on 27 September 1998 by The Right Reverend Geralyn Wolf,

The Right Reverend Geralyn Wolf, bishop of Rhode Island, at the Trinity Church Tercentenary Service, 27 September 1998.

bishop of Rhode Island. For this occasion, the presiding bishop of the United States, The Most Reverend Frank T. Griswold, sent the letter that appears as the frontispiece of this volume. The tercentenary celebration involved a variety of other activities, including a lecture series presented in conjunction with the Newport Historical Society and the International Berkeley Society, an exhibition of paintings of Trinity by local artists, a photographic exhibition, a display of items about Trinity history at the Newport Historical Society, a display of Bishop Berkeley's books at the Redwood Library, a display and lecture on the parish's historic silver, and a planned series of guided tours to other historic churches. A stone plaque honoring the founders of Trinity as named in the 1699 document was laid at the foot of the steps at the south entrance to the tower, and along the north side of Frank Street, leading to the Queen Anne Square dedication plaque, a "Founders' Walk of Bricks" was laid with the names of current Trinity supporters inscribed on the bricks.

The year-long anniversary celebration had only just begun when, on 19 October 1998, The Reverend Canon Roy Green tendered his resignation to the vestry, after only four and a half years as rector. Effective immediately after Christmas, he became Canon for Christian Formation in the diocese, building youth ministries.[86] In his penultimate sermon on 13 December 1998, Green reflected on the things that he had learned in his period at Trinity and confided how they might serve Trinity in its future. "I know that I have let you down," he said. "I have not measured up to everyone's expectations. I have not always done what you wished, and in some cases, I have not provided the pastoral support you required."[87] He told the congregation that when it comes to a new rector,

> tell your rector how you expect her or his spouse to be visible and active in the congregation. You don't quite expect an unpaid parish assistant, but you do have expectations. Tell the Rector you expect a "crackerjack" administrator, who knows everybody's responsibilities to the letter and can manage every detail. Tell the new Rector you expect a full church, every Sunday, both services. Tell the Rector you want a deep spirituality to flow from him and spread to all the congregation—and realize so far I have described three full-time jobs. Tell your rector about what traditions are sacred and not surprise him. Say that you want ordinary persons to feel welcome here, and the wealthy to attend regularly. Learn to bless and affirm, friends, as well as correct. Love the one you chose, and commit your prayer support.[88]

At a special meeting of the vestry on 2 December 1998, with Geralyn Wolf, to discuss the process of searching for a new rector, The Reverend Marshall T. Rice was selected as interim rector.[89]

Between 1992 and 1998, the number of people making pledges had dropped from 366 to 209, and parish officials considered that only about three hundred to 330 people were active members in a parish of seven hundred nominal members. The parish endowment fund stood at a market value of $2,262,597 on 1 January 1999, while the Trinity Landmark Preservation Fund stood at $1,134, 269.[87]

Under Rice's leadership, the parish carried out all the planned events of the tercentennial celebration, which included a 30 May 1999 worship service using the 1662 Book of Common Prayer, with liturgy and music, as used in the early days of the parish. During this period, the number of parishioners pledging increased to 240, and the average amount increased to an average seventeen to nineteen dollars weekly. Additionally, the parish exceeded its goals in donations to Episcopal charities. In a major contribution, the three brothers of parishioner Paul A. Giffen each donated thirty thousand dollars to support the music program. In recognition of Paul Giffen's long service to the parish and in the choir, the music room in Carr-Rice House was renamed for him.[91]

The rector search committee reviewed thirty-seven names and then narrowed this list down to eight and then five final candidates.[92] As a result of this work, on 17 July 2000 the vestry met and recommended The Reverend Canon John Lawrence to the corporation as the next rector; the corporation approved his selection on 30 July 2000. Canon Lawrence arrived in Newport on 17 September 2000 to begin his ministry as the twenty-ninth rector of Trinity Church.

A native New Englander, Canon Lawrence had graduated from George Washington University and the General Theological Seminary. Immediately before coming to Newport, he had been canon to the ordinary—that is, the chief executive assistant—to Bishop Herbert Thompson in the diocese of Southern Ohio. Before that he had been rector of three parishes in New York and in Ohio. As rector of these parishes, he had revitalized an urban church with declining membership, managed a successful capital campaign, and helped a suburban parish develop a new focus and new outreach programs.[93]

In just over a quarter of a century, Trinity Church had gone through a period of divestment and consolidation, becoming not only smaller in terms of

The Reverend Canon John E. Lawrence was formally instituted as rector of Trinity Church on 9 December 2000. Photo *Newport Daily News*, Travis Hartman.

the properties it owned but also dramatically smaller in the number of parishioners. This short period had seen three rectors, two of whom stayed for only four and five years, and there had been two long interim periods without a rector. The parish had divested itself of major components of the parish: the High Street parish house, Kay Chapel, St. Michael's School, and Trinity Cemetery. Compared to the first half of the twentieth century, there had been dramatic volatility in the clergy, the size of the congregation, and the very liturgy of the church.

Yet as difficult and frustrating as this period had been for many, in the perspective of three centuries of parish history, the parish remained what it always has been—an active place for worship, evangelism, parish life, outreach, and stewardship within the historic Anglican and Episcopalian tradition. The distinctive beauty of its 1726 building, along with its tradition of fine music, are the distinctive features that weave the heritage of town and church into the fabric of modern-day church life. Trinity serves primarily as a focal point of a spirit-filled, Christ-centered congregation that is very conscious of its Anglican tradition. It is also a place of rare architectural and historic beauty that complements that basic mission. With its long history combining the features of active worship, glorious music, great architecture, and fascinating historical tradition, Trinity has remained "always the same." The unchanging devotion that Trinity Church has shown over the past three centuries, in exercising the principles of the Anglican tradition within its historic building, and linking the historical nature of the church at large with those of the town and parish, exemplifies the words that Queen Anne took as her motto: *Semper Eadem.*

Notes

1. Vestry minutes 1973–77: Special Meeting of the Corporation, 7 January 1973.
2. John B. Hattendorf, "The Decision to Close Rhode Island Bases in 1973," in Rhode Island Historical Society, *What a Difference a Bay Makes* (Providence, RI: 1993), pp. 104–106.
3. Scrapbook 1972–77: "Navy Cut to Hurt Island Churches," *Newport Daily News,* 15 June 1973.
4. Pritchard, *A History of the Episcopal Church* (Harrisburg, PA: 1993), pp. 260–61.
5. Vestry minutes 1973–77: Special Meeting of the Corporation, 1 April 1973; Vestry minutes 1978–82: 19 February 1978.
6. Trinity Scrapbook 1972–77: "Trinity Church Appoints Oregonian as New Rector," *Newport Daily News*, 2 April 1973.
7. Pritchard, pp. 239^12.
8. Vestry minutes 1964–68: 8 January 1967.
9. Pritchard, pp. 251–54.
10. Vestry minutes 1973–77: Special meeting 6 May 1973.
11. In fact, Floride Towle had been the first woman organist in 1810–17. In succession to her in the period 1817–27, three rival women had alternated in the job: Elizabeth Davis (later, she married Robert P. Lee), Mary Easton, and Maria Burdick.
12. Ibid., "Trinity Names Woman," *Newport Daily News,* no date.
13. Ibid., "Choir Evensong Truly Inspiring," *Newport Daily News,* 21 November 1973; "Concert Honors St. Cecilia in Newport," *Rhode Island Churchman,* 13 December 1973.
14. Vestry minutes, 1973–77: Special meeting of the vestry, 23 October 1973; annual meeting, report of the business manager, 28 January 1974.
15. Ibid., annual meeting: Report of Charles J. Minifie, p. 4.
16. Ibid.
17. Ibid., 19 January 1975.
18. Ibid., Resolution passed at annual meeting, 19 January 1975.
19. Trinity Scrapbook 1972–73: "For Residents of Historic Hill, it's YMCA vs. Egan's Laundry," *Newport Daily News,* 16 January 1973.
20. Ibid., "Newport, Before and After: Exhibit Shows Restoration of 18th Century Houses," *Providence Sunday Journal,* 14 January 1974.
21. Vestry minutes 1973–77, 18 August 1974.
22. Ibid., resolution, 16 March 1975.
23. Scrapbook 1972–77: "Minifie Elected Honorary Canon," *Rhode Island,* March 1974.
24. Ibid., "Different Perspective: The Archbishop of Canterbury Speaks at Trinity Church in Newport," *Rhode Island Churchman,* February 1976, p. 1.
25. Rector's memorandum to Prof. John Hattendorf, 30 July 1996, re "Scintillating and Breezy Anecdotes to Liven Up Your Scholarship."
26. Ibid., "Queen Anne Square Gets Nod at $1 Million," *Newport Daily News,* 24 February 1976.
27. Ibid., "Egan Building Threatens Queen Anne Square," *Newport Daily News,* no date.
28. Ibid., *Newport Daily News* clippings: "City Would Evict Egan," "Egans enter New Contest," "Queen Anne Square May Face Legal Delay," "Suit Fails to Halt Action of Queen Anne Square."
29. Ibid., special corporation meeting, 7 March 1977.
30. Scrapbook 1972–77: Francis B. Sayre, Jr., "The Tall Ships," *New York Times,* 27 June 1976.
31. Ibid.
32. Ibid., "Thousands Welcome Queen, Prince Philip to Newport."
33. "'Robin' Slays City's 'Eyesore,'" *Providence Journal-Bulletin,* 12 July 1976, p. B-1.

34. Ibid., clippings: "Court Vetoes Egans"; *Newport Daily News,* 3 September 1976; "Egan Asks $428,549," *Newport Daily News,* 11 August 1976, and "Egans Drop Court Fight to Stop Queen Anne Sq.," 14 September 1976.

35. Vestry minutes 1972–77: 27 February 1977.

36. Vestry minutes 1978–82: 18 February 1979; 21 April 1979.

37. Nain Anderson et al., *Archaeological Investigations in Queen Anne Square, Newport, Rhode Island (1979), p. 42.*

38. "'Ordinary people' cited for Parish House Work," *Newport Daily News,* 10 July 1978, p. 6.

39. Vestry minutes 1978–82: 19 February 1978; 1 March 1978.

40. Ibid., 1 March 1978.

41. "Minifie Will Give Final Sermon," *Newport Daily News,* 8 July 1978, p. 7.

42. Vestry minutes, special vestry meeting with Bishop Frederick Belden, 23 April 1979; letter from the senior and junior warden to D. Lorne Coyle, 12 April 1978.

43. Vestry minutes 1978–82: Special vestry meeting 23 April 1978.

44. Ibid., vestry meeting, 15 October 1978; meeting of the corporation, 19 November 1978.

45. Ibid., special meeting of the vestry, 5 November 1978.

46. "Moving of Colonial Houses at Square Begins–Gently," *Providence Journal–Bulletin, East Bay Journal,* 4 October 1978, p. B-l.

47. Vestry minutes 1978–82: vestry meeting, 21 May 1978; 17 September 1978.

48. Rector's memorandum to Prof. John Hattendorf, 30 July 1996.

49. City Hall, City of Newport Land Evidence Records, vol. 304, pp.944–45.

50. Vestry minutes 1978–82, 17 February 1981; 17 November 1981. This arrangement was reconfirmed in 1996.

51. Ibid., 17 June 1980.

52. Ibid., 18 March 1979.

53. Ibid., 24 June 1979; 19 August 1979.

54. Ibid., 21 October 1980.

55. Ibid., 16 June 1981.

56. Ibid., 16 February 1982.

57. Ibid., 18 August 1981.

58. *Trinity Tower,* 23 February 1986.

59. Vestry minutes 1978–82: 16 February 1982.

60. "Covenant between Trinity Church in Newport and Donald Lorne Coyle; with Particular Terms and Conditions of the Rector's Tenure, both with Effect from 20 November 1983."

61. Vestry minutes 1983–1985, special meeting of the vestry, 24 August 1983.

62. Jan Webster, introduction to Desmond Tutu, *Voice of One Crying in the Wilderness* (1982).

63. Rector's memorandum to Prof. John Hattendorf, 30 July 1996.

64. Ibid.

65. Vestry minutes, 1977–82: Vestry meeting 15 October 1978.

66. Irving Hayes and Associates, *Trinity Church Study,* Abstract, July 1984, p. 2.

67. Ibid.

68. Vestry minutes, 1983–85: Special vestry meeting, 21 August 1984; special corporation meeting, 5 September 1984.

69. Ibid., 20 August 1985.

70. "Trinity Outlines Restoration," *Newport Daily News,* 28 January 1986.

71. Vestry minutes, 1985–89: 10 June 1986; Ad Hoc Worship Committee Report, 20 January 1986.

72. "Congregation Returns to Historic Home," *Newport Daily News,* 28 September 1987, p. 1; "Restoration Done, Trinity Reopens on 261st Anniversary," *Providence Sunday Journal,* 27 September 1987, p. C-l.

73. "Congregation Returns to Historic Home," p. 1.

74. Ibid., 10 April 1990

75. Vestry minutes, 1989–1993: 22 January 1989; special corporation meeting, 12 February 1989.

76. Ibid., 14 May 1991.

77. Ibid., 12 September 1989; annual meeting, 28 January 1990.

78. Ibid., 13 August 1991.

79. Ibid., 9 June 1992.

80. Capt. Charles K. Moore, "Trinity Church Demographics, 1726–1992."

81. Letter from Rev. Mary Johnstone to Hattendorf, 23 February 1996.

82. Vestry minutes 1994–98: 5 April, 12 April, 13 April, 24 April 1994.

83. "Trinity 29th Rector Installed," *Clarion,* November 1994.

84. City Hall, City of Newport Land Evidence Records, vol. 304, pp. 944–45.

85. Vestry minutes, 9 April 1996.

86. Vestry minutes, 1997–2000: Special vestry meeting, 19 October 1998.

87. Revd Canon Roy D. Green, remarks to the Congregation of Trinity Church, Advent III, 13 December 1998.

88. Ibid.

89. Ibid., special vestry meeting, 2 December 1998.

90. Parish profile, November 1999.

91. Vestry minutes, 1997–2000, 14 December 1999; 8 February 2000.

92. Ibid., 14 March 2000; 9 May 2000.

93. *Trinity Voice,* July 2000.

Bibliography

MANUSCRIPTS

Bodleian Library, University of Oxford, England::
    Duke Humfrey's Library:
        Mss Rawlinson
        Mss Clarendon

Rhodes House Library:
    Records of the United Society for the Propagation of the Gospel
    Records of The Associates of Dr. Bray

Episcopal Diocese of Massachusetts, Diocesan Library and Archives, Boston:
    Parish Records, Christ Church, Boston

Holy Trinity Church, Marylebone Road, London, England:
    Records of the Society for Promoting Christian Knowledge
        [moved in 1999 to Cambridge University Library]

Lambeth Palace Library, London, England:
    Fulham Papers
    Papers of the Society for the Propagation of the Gospel

Massachusetts Historical Society, Boston, Massachusetts
    Papers of Christ Church, Boston

Naval Historical Collection, Naval War College, Newport, RI:
    Ms Coll. 52: Papers of Rear Admiral Henry E. Eccles
    Trinity Church Correspondence: Box 13, file 3; Box 27, file 34; Box 89, file 3

New Haven Colony Historical Society, New Haven, CT:
    Mss 7: Ezra Stiles Papers, Box I, Folder S: Meeting of the Company of the
    Redwood Library, 28 December 1750. [Xerox copy at Redwood Library,
    Newport.]

Newport Historical Society, Newport, RI:
    Parish Records of Trinity Church
    Norman Morrison Isham Trinity Church restoration notes and drawings:
    Mss Boxes A-11, A-12
    Misc. Church Records, Box 39, files 2–5

Public Record Office, Kew, London, England:
    Admiralty
    Colonial Office

Rhode Island Historical Society, Providence, RI:
    Mss 294: Papers of Gabriel Bernon

Society for the Preservation of New England Antiquities, Boston, Massachusetts
    S.P.N.E.A. Correspondence File: Newport - Trinity Church
    Newport, Rhode Island, Files and Photographs

University of Rhode Island, Kingston, RI:
    Special Collections, Manuscript Collection 41: Records of the Diocese of
    Rhode Island
    Box 12
        folder 124: Anna Brophy, "The Swedish Episcopal Church in Rhode
        Island, 1888–1903"
        folder 136: Letters from Rev. Vinton as Diocesan secretary, 1840s
    Box 31
        folders 210–223: Papers relating to Trinity Church, 1750–1841
        including establishment of diocese, election of Seabury as Bishop,
        Eulogy on death of Honyman, excommunication of Rev. James Sayre,
        establishment of Diocese, Rev. William Smith.
    Box 95
        folders 64–67: Administration and reports regarding Trinity Church
        c. 1951–1988

PUBLISHED DOCUMENTS

John Russell Bartlett, ed. *The Records of the Colony of Rhode Island and Providence Plantations in New England*. 7 volumes. Providence, RI: A. Crawford Greene and Brothers State Printers, 1856–62.

"Memoir of Trinity Church, Newport, R.I.," compiled by Henry Bull, Esq., at the request of the Rector, Rev. Francis Vinton. Recorded by John Sterne, Esq. in 1841–42." [Copied by Charles L. Stanhope for publication] in the *Newport Mercury*, 28 October 1882. Also reprinted in Wilkins Updike, *A History of the Episcopal Church in Narragansett, Rhode Island*. Second Edition, edited, enlarged, and annotated by Rev. David Goodwin. Boston: Merrymount Press, 1907, vol. 2, pp. 150–77.

John S. Ezell, ed. *The New Democracy in America: Travels of Francisco de Miranda in the United States, 1783–84*. Translated by Judson P. Wood. Norman: University of Oklahoma Press, 1963.

Franklin Bowditch Dexter, ed. *The Literary Diary of Ezra Stiles, D.D., L.L.D.* New York: Scribner, 1901.

H. W. Foote, ed. *Annals of King's Chapel from the Puritan Age of New England to the Present Day.* Boston: Little, Brown, 1882.

Rev. Daniel Goodwin, ed. *A Letter Book and Abstract of Out Services. Written during the Years 1743, 1751, by the Rev. James MacSparran, Doctor in Divinity and sometime Rector of Saint Paul's Church, Narragansett, Rhode Island.* Boston: Merrymount Press, 1899.

Ira D. Gruber, ed. *John Pebbles' American War: The Diary of a Scottish Grenadier, 1776–1782.* Army Records Society, vol. 13. Phoenix Mill: Sutton Publishing for the Army Records Society, 1998.

George Keith. "A Journal of the Travels and Ministry of the Reverend George Keith, AM," *Collections of the Protestant Episcopal Historical Society for the Year 1851.* New York: Stratford & Swords, 1851, pp. 13–26.

George Champlin Mason, comp. *Annals of Trinity Church, Newport, Rhode Island, 1698–1821.* Newport, RI: George C. Mason, 1890.

———. *Annals of Trinity Church, Newport, Rhode Island, 1821–1892.* Second Series. Newport, RI: V. Francis Mott, M.D., 1894.

Howard C. Rice, Jr., and Anne S. K. Brown, eds. *The American Campaigns of Rochambeau's Army, 1780, 1781, 1782, 1783.* Providence, RI: Brown University Press; and Princeton: Princeton University Press, 1972.

Unpublished Theses and Articles

Ron Potvin. "The Christmas Explosion of 1934," unpublished draft article.

Edward Bruce Tucker. "The Founders Remembered: The Anglicanization of the Puritan Tradition in New England, 1690–1760." Ph.D. Thesis, Brown University, 1978.

Contemporary Sermons, and Pamphlets

George Bisset. *A Sermon Preached in Trinity Church, Newport, Rhode-Island on Monday 3 June 1771; At the Funeral of Mrs. Abigail Wanton, late consort of the Hon. Joseph Wanton, Esq., who died on the 31st of May in the thirty-sixth year of her Age.* Newport, RI: Solomon Southwick, 1771.

————. *The Trial of a False Apostle. A Sermon Preached in Trinity Church, Newport, Rhode Island, on Sunday, October 24, 1773.* Newport, RI: Solomon Southwick, 1773.

————. *Honesty the Best Policy in the Worst of Times, Illustrated and proved from the Exemplary Conduct of Joseph of Arimathea, and its consequent Rewards with an application to the case of suffering loyalists. A Sermon intended to have been preached at Newport, Rhode-Island, on the Sunday, preceding the evacuation of that Garrison by his Majesty's Troops, and afterwards preached at St. Paul's and St. George's Chapels, New York, on Sunday, October 8, 1780.* London: W. Richardson, 1784.

[John Bours]. *An Appeal to the Public; in which the Misrepresentations and Calumnies contained in a pamphlet entitled "A Narrative of Certain Matters relative to Trinity Church, in Newport, in the State of Rhode Island," by a very extraordinary man, the Rev. James Sayre, A.M., late Minister of said Church, are pointed out and his very strange conduct during the time of his ministration at Newport, faithfully related. By John Bours, Merchant, and one of the Vestry of said Church.* Newport, RI: Peter Eades at the office of the *Newport Herald*, 1789.

[Theodore Dehon]. *A Discourse delivered in Newport, Rhode Island, before the Congregation of Trinity Church, the Masonic Society, and the Newport Guards, the Sunday Following the Intelligence of the Death of General George Washington. By Theodore Dehon, A.M., Rector of Trinity Church.* Newport, RI: Henry Barber, 1800.

[James Honyman]. *Faults on All Sides. The Case of Religion Consider'd: Shewing the Substance of True Godliness: wherein are also particulariz'd, Sundry Errors, Maxims and Corruptions of Men and Sects of this present Age, with Suitable Observations and Reflections thereon. With Some conclusive Reasons to perswade to Unity, Moderation and Charity. Presented to the Inhabitants (especially) of the Colony of Rhode Island; and all others who make Possession of the Gospel of our Lord Jesus Christ.* Newport, RI: Printed for the author, and sold by E. Nearegreas and J. Franklin, 1728.

————. *A Sermon Preached at the King's-Chapel.* (Boston: 1733).

Thomas Pollen. *A Sermon Preached in Trinity Church, Newport, Rhode Island, on Thursday, May 29, 1755. Upon occasion of the Embarkation of some of the Colony's Troops, in Order to go against the Enemy. Published at the Desire of the Council of War, at Newport.* Newport, RI: 1757.

————. *The Principal Marks of True Patriotism. A Sermon Preached in Trinity Church, at Newport, in Rhode Island, on the 5th day of March 1758 By Thomas Pollen, M.A., and humbly dedicated to His Excellency, John Earl of Loudon.* Newport, RI: 1758.

O[liver] S[herman] Prescott. *The Power of the Resurrection: A Sermon Preached in Trinity Church, Newport, R.I. on the Seventh Sunday after Trinity, 1863, being the Sunday following the Funeral of Clement Clark Moore, L.L.D.* Newport, RI: Charles E. Hammett, Jr., 1863.

[James Sayre]. *A Candid Narrative of Certain Matters Relating to Trinity-Church in New Port, in the State of Rhode Island, by James Sayre, A.M., late Minister of Said Church: With a view of correcting the egregious misrepresentations of Mr. John Bours, contained in a Letter Addressed to the Author in the Newport Herald of October 9th 1788.* Fairfield, CT: Forgue and Bulkeley, 1788.

[William Smith]. *A Discourse at the Opening of the Convention of Clerical and Lay Delegates of the Church, in the State of Rhode Island, delivered in Trinity Church, Newport, Thursday, the 18th of November 1790. Psalm cxxii., 7–9. By William Smith, A.M., Rector.* Newport, RI: 1790.

———. *The Convict's Visitor: or, Penitential offices (in the antient way of liturgy) consisting of prayers, lessons and meditations, with suitable devotions before, and at the time of execution.* Newport, RI: Peter Edes, 1791.

———. *A Discourse delivered in St. John's Church, Providence on Wednesday, the 31st day of July 1793 at the ordination of Rev. John Usher of Bristol.* Providence, RI: 1793.

———. *A Discourse delivered Before the Grand Lodge of the Most Ancient and honorable Fraternity of Free and Accepted Masons of the State of Rhode Island and Providence Plantations in Trinity Church, Newport, on the 27th day of June 1791, celebrating the Festival of St. John the Baptist.* Providence, RI: 1794.

Francis Vinton. *The Destinies of Our Country: A Sermon Preached on the National Fast Day, March 15, 1841 and by request, on the Fifth Sunday after Trinity, in Trinity Church, Newport, R.I.* Boston: J. B. Dow, 1841.

———. "The Reception of the Newport Artillery by their townsmen, Thursday, May 19, 1842, 3 o'clock, p.m.," *Herald of the Times.* Extra. Newport, RI: James Atkinson, 1842.

———. *Loyalty and Piety: or the Christian's civil obligations defined; a discourse preached in Trinity Church, Newport, R.I., on Thursday, July 21, 1842, the day of public thanks giving.* Providence, RI: Burnett & King, 1842.

———. *The Church, her Lord's almoner to the world, a sermon preached in Grace Church, Providence, before the missionary convocation of the church in Rhode Island on Jan. 10, 1844.* Providence, RI: n.p., 1844.

———. *A Remembrance of the Former Days: Being the farewell discourse to Trinity Church, Newport, R.I., preached on the fifth Sunday after Trinity, July 7th, 1844.* Providence, RI: Samuel C. Blodget, 1844.

BOOKS AND ARTICLES

Nain Anderson, et al. *Archaeological Investigation in Queen Anne Square, Newport, Rhode Island, 1979.* Providence, RI: Public Archaeology Laboratory, Brown University, 1979.

Maurice Linÿer de la Barbée, *Chevalier de Ternay: Vie de Charles Henry Louis d'Arsac de Ternay. Chef d'escadre des armées navales (1723–1780).* Grenoble: Editions des 4 Seigneurs, 1972.

Richard M. Bayles, ed. *History of Newport County, Rhode Island, From the Year 1638 to the Year 1887.* New York: L. E. Preston & Co., 1888.

F. Edward Beardslee. *Life and Correspondence of the Rt. Rev. Samuel Seabury, D.D.* Boston: Houghton-Mifflin, 1881.

Clifton Hartwell Brewer. *A History of Religious Education in the Episcopal Church to 1835.* New Haven, CT: Yale University Press, 1924.

Carl Bridenbaugh, *Cities in the Wilderness: The First Century of Urban Life in America, 1625–1742.* New York: Alfred A. Knopf, 1964.

———. *Mitre and Sceptre: Transatlantic Faiths, Ideas, Personalities and Politics, 1689–1725.* New York: Oxford University Press, 1964.

Kenneth Walter Cameron. *The Younger Doctor William Smith 1754–1821: The Role of Seabury's Brilliant Scottish Presbyter in the Formative Period of the Diocese of Connecticut: A Divinity Story.* Hartford, CT: Transcendental Books, 1980.

Ralph E. Carpenter, Jr. *The Arts and Crafts of Newport, Rhode Island, 1640–1820.* Newport, RI: Preservation Society of Newport County, 1954.

Mrs. French E. Chadwick. "The Visit of General Washington to Newport in 1781." *Special Bulletin of the Newport Historical Society*, Number Six Extra Number (February 1913), pp. 1–18. [Ref to Trinity on pp. 10–12.]

Wm. King Covell. *The Organs of Trinity Church Newport, R.I.* London: "Musical Opinion, 1935; Article reprinted as a pamphlet from *The Organ*, vol. XIV, no. 56 (April 1935).

366

Elaine Forman Crane. *A Dependent People: Newport, Rhode Island, in the Revolutionary Era.* New York: Fordham University Press, 1985.

———. "Uneasy Coexistence: Religious Tensions in Eighteenth Century Newport," *Newport History*, vol. 53 No. 3 (Summer 1980), pp. 101–11.

Arthur Lyon Cross. "The Anglican Episcopate and the American Colonies." *Harvard Historical Studies*, vol. 9. New York: Longman's Green & Co., 1902.

Lorraine Le H. Dexter. "Steps from Trinity Church to the Point," *Newport History*, vol. 49, part 4, no. 160 (Fall 1975), pp. 329–46.

Antoinette F. Downing and Vincent J. Scully, Jr. *The Architectural Heritage of Newport, Rhode Island, 1640–1915.* Second Edition, Revised. New York: Bramhall House, 1967.

[Willard Eddy]. *History of the Free Chapel of St. John the Evangelist, Newport, R.I., 1875–83.* Newport, RI: 1935.

Allan Forbes and Paul F. Cadman. *France and New England.* 3 volumes. Boston: State Street Trust Company, 1925–29.

John William Haley. *George Washington and Rhode Island.* Providence: State of Rhode Island Commission of Education, 1932.

Sydney V. James. *Colonial Rhode Island: A History.* New York: Scribner, 1975.

———. *John Clarke and His Legacies: Religion and Law in Colonial Rhode Island, 1638–1750.* Edited by Theodore Dwight Bozeman. University Park: Pennsylvania State University, 1999.

Edwin S. Gaustad. *George Berkeley in America.* New Haven, CT: Yale University Press, 1979.

Philip S. Haffenden. *New England in the English Nation, 1689–1713.* Oxford: Clarendon Press, 1974.

Adam Hodgson. *Letters from North America, Written during a Tour in the United States and Canada.* London: 1824.

Norman Morrison Isham. *Trinity Church in Newport, Rhode Island: A History of the Fabric.* Boston: Printed for the Subscribers, 1936.

A. Luce and T. E. Jessop, eds. *The Works of George Berkeley, Bishop of Cloyne.* London: Thomas Nelson and Sons, Ltd., 1979.

Charles T. Laugler. *Thomas Bray's Grand Design: Libraries of the Church of England in America, 1695–1785.* ACRI. Publications in Librarianship, no. 35. Chicago: American Library Association, 1973.

Samuel Eliot Morison. *The European Discovery of America: The Northern Voyage, AD 500–1600.* New York: Oxford University Press, 1971.

Arthur Howard Nichols. "The Bells of Trinity Church, Newport, R.I.," *The New England Historical and Genealogical Register,* vol.70 (April 1916), pp. 147–49.

Edgar Legare Pennington. *The First Hundred Years of the Church of England in Rhode Island.* Hartford, CT: Church Mission Publishing, 1935.

Robert Prichard. *A History of the Episcopal Church.* Harrisburg, PA: Morehouse Publishing, 1991.

K. Steele. *Politics of Colonial Policy: The Board of Trade in Colonial Administration, 1696–1720.* Oxford: Clarendon Press, 1968.

Bruce Steiner. *Samuel Seabury, 1729–1796: A Study in the High Church Tradition.* Athens: Ohio University Press, 1971.

Erich Taylor. *Charles Theodore Pachelbel and the Berkeley Organ at Trinity Church, Newport, Rhode Island.* Newport, RI, 1939.

H. P. Thompson. *Into All Lands: The History of the Society for the Propagation of the Gospel in Foreign Parts, 1701–1950.* London: S.P.C.K., 1951.

Delbert W. Tildesley. *St. Michael's Church in Bristol, Rhode Island, 1718–1983.* Bristol, RI: St. Michael's Church, 1989.

Henry G. Turnbull, ed. *A Century on the Point: Notes from the History of the Zabriskie Memorial Church of St. John the Evangelist.* Newport: St. John's Church Centennial Committee, 1975

Dudley Tyng. *Rhode Island Episcopalians, 1635–1953.* Providence, RI: Little Rhody Press, 1954.

Wilkins Updike. *A History of the Episcopal Church in Narragansett, Rhode Island.* Second edition, edited, enlarged and annotated by Rev. David Goodwin. Boston: Merrymount Press, 1907.

Eileen Warburton. *In Living Memory: A Chronicle of Newport, Rhode Island, 1888–1988.* Newport, RI: Newport Savings and Loan/Island Trust Company, 1988.

Frederick Lawes Weis. *The Colonial Clergy and the Colonial Churches of New England.* Lancaster, MA: Society of the Descendants of Colonial Clergy, 1936.

John Frederick Woolverton. *Colonial Anglicanism in North America.* Detroit: Wayne State University Press, 1984.

Bibliography on the Church Silver

MANUSCRIPTS

Caroline Tennant [Kaull]. "The Trinity Church Silver," Mss. c. 1964, in files of the Trinity Altar Guild.

ARTICLES AND BOOKS

C. Louis Avery. *Early American Silver.* New York and London: Century Company, 1930.

Margaret Ballard. "Early Silver in Trinity Church, Newport, Rhode Island," *Antiques Magazine*, vol. 120, no. 4 (1981), pp. 922–25.

Kathryn C. Buhler. *American Silver, 1655–1825, in the Museum of Fine Arts, Boston.* Boston: New York Graphic Society for the Museum of Fine Arts, 1972.

Ralph E. Carpenter, Jr. *The Arts and Crafts of Newport, Rhode Island, 1640–1820.* Newport, RI: Preservation Society of Newport County, 1954.

Edward Alfred Jones. *The Old Silver of American Churches.* Letchworth, England: privately printed at the Arden Press for the National Society of Colonial Dames in America, 1913.

Henry N. Flynt and Martha Gandy Fales. *The Heritage Foundation Collection of Silver with Biographical Sketches of New England Silversmiths, 1625–1825.* Old Deerfield, MA: Heritage Foundation, 1968.

Katherine Morrison McClinton. *Collecting American 19th Century Silver.* New York: Scribner, 1968.

Jessie McNab. *Silver: The Smithsonian Illustrated Library of Antiques.* New York: The Cooper Hewitt Museum, 1981.

Museum of Fine Arts, Boston. *American Church Silver of the Seventeenth and Eighteenth Centuries, with a few pieces of domestic plate, exhibited July to December 1911.* Boston: Museum of Fine Arts, 1911.

Providence College. *American Silver, 1670–1830: The Cornelius C. Moore Collection at Providence College.* Providence: R.I. Rhode Island Bicentennial Foundation, for Providence College 1980. See also, Sotheby's (Firm). *The Cornelius C. Moore Collection auction, January 31, 1986 and exhibition, 25–30 January 1986.* Sotheby's Sale 5430. New York: Sotheby's 1986.

Barbara McLean Ward, ed. *Silver in American Life: Selections from the Mabel Brady Garvan and Other Collections at Yale University.* Boston: David R. Godine, Publisher, 1979.

David B. Warren. *Marks of Achievement: Four Centuries of American Presentation Silver.* New York: The Museum of Fine Arts, Houston, in association with Harry Abrahms, Inc., 1987, pp. 38–9.

Edward Wenham. *The Practical Book of American Silver.* Philadelphia and New York: J. B. Lippincott Co., 1949.

Index

A

Adair, Bill, 260

African-Americans, 55, 60, 66-67, 77, 80, 95, 98, 100, 101, 109, 120, 171, 174, 216, 237, 313-314, 344; parish school for slaves, 95, 98, 100, 101, 109-10, 118, 120, 135 note 39

Alexander Hamilton Rice House, 288, 302, 320, 330, 342, 348

All Saints Chapel, Newport, 185-187, 189, 191-192, 193, 194-196, 198-199

Allen, Lawrence, 337

Allin, Rt. Rev. John M., 332

Almy, Joshua, 116

Almy, Mary, 116

Altar, 29, 32, 35, 47, 58, 209, 215, 218, 240, 242, 246, 250, 254, 287, 323. See also, Chancel

Altar Society, 272, 325

Altarpiece, x, 47, 128, 251, 290, 291

American Cathedral in Paris, 321

American Church in Rome, 236

Amherst College, 339

Amistad, Film, 352

Andrews, Christine, 269

Andrews, Harry, 260

Andros, Gov. Edmund, 7-9

Anglican Church. Beliefs, 6, 7, 30, 48, 52-53, 78; established church, 6, 8

Anketell, Rev. John, 203, 206

Annand, Very Rev. James, 350

Anne, Queen, x, 40-42, 52-53, 220; portrait 20; royal arms, x, 47, 256, 257, 289-291, 301. See also, Queen Anne Square

Anniversary celebrations. (1898-99) 200th of parish, 231; (1926) 200th of building, 249, 254-255; (1934) Lafayette Centenary, 260; (1948) 250th of parish, 270-271; (1955) 175th Washington-

Rochambeau, 289; (1976) 250th of building, 328-329; (1984) Seabury Centenary, 343-344; (1998-1999) 300th of parish, 352-353, 354

Annual Meeting. See Corporation, meetings

Anthony family, 311

Apostle's Creed, 47, 169,

Appleton, William Sumner, 251

Aquidneck House, Newport, 195

Aquidneck Island, 2, 3, 121, 128, 326

Aquidneck Memorial Park, 309

Arbuthnot, Adm. Marion, 130

ARCO gas station. See Atlantic Rich-field Oil Co.

Army. American, 128, 286; British, 127-128; French, 130-133

Arson threats. See, Fire and arson

Associates of Dr. Bray, 95, 96, 100, 109, 120

Astor, John J., 279

Astor, (Mrs.) John J., 223-224

Astor, William B., 279

Atherton, Sarah, 154

Atlantic Richfield Oil Co., 301, 320, 326

Auchincloss, Anne Burr, 255

Auchincloss, (Mrs.) Hugh D., 254

Auchincloss, (Mrs.) Hugh D., Jr., 255

Auchmuty, Robert Nichol (d. 1813), 150, 152, 154

Ayrault, Daniel, 53, 55, 79

Ayrault, Daniel, Jr., 120

Ayrault family, 61, 120

Ayrault House, 55

Ayrault, Pierre, 21

Azores, 64

B

Babcock, Rev. Luke, 117

Badger, Rev. Moses, 143

Ball, Carol W. J., 307

Ballard, Rev. Canon Lockett Ford, x, 286-315, 318 note 76, 324, 327

Bankes, Capt. W. J., 281

Bannister family, 61

Bannister, John, 82, 100

Baptist Church and Baptists, 5, 17, 30, 52, 53, 60, 66, 75, 81, 83, 102, 104, 110, 112, 128, 130, 262, 270, 324; Sabbatarian Meeting House, 55, 189, 293

Baptismal bowls, 49, 57, 74. See also, Font

Barbados, 64

Barclay, Robert, 61

Bardeen, Maxwell D., Jr., xi

Bardin, Capt. Charles, 73, 92, 93, 115, 116

Barjot, Vice-Adm. Pierre, 284

Barker, Capt. and Mrs. Frank H., xi

Barker, Ray, 306

Barker, S. M. C., x

Barrington College Brass Trio, 325

Basement. See Cellar

Baskerville, Mary S., xi

Bass, Rt. Rev. Edward, 156, 158

Beach, Rev. John, 90

Beadle's Pew, 252-253

Beale, Richard, 123

Behan, Reverend George, 314

Belden, Bishop, 337, 338, 339

Bell, church, 37, 38-39, 47, 75, 117, 161, 168, 220, 221, 257, 272, 284, 335, 346-347

Bellomont, earl of. See Coote, Richard

Belmont, Oliver Hazard Perry, 231

Bennett, Chaplain D. S., 281

Bennett, Cornelius, 78, 80

Benson, John Howard, 254, 335

Berkeley, Agnes, 66

Berkeley, Anne, 64

Berkeley, Anthony, 66

Berkeley, Rt. Rev. George, 61-72, 78, 81, 92, 127, 255, 335, 353; *Alciphron*, 68-69; portrait, 62

Berkeley, Lucia, 70

Berkeley Memorial Chapel. See St. Columba's Church, Middletown, R.I.

Berkeley, Philip, 66

Bermuda, 11, 63, 64

Bernon, Gabriel, 21, 140

About the Author

John B. Hattendorf first became a member of Trinity Church in 1964 while attending the Naval Officer Candidate School in Newport. Earlier in that year, he received his bachelor's degree in history from Kenyon College, which subsequently awarded him an honorary doctorate of humane letters (LHD) in 1997. He served as an officer in the U.S. Navy on board three destroyers during the Vietnam War era, at the Naval Historical Center in Washington, D.C., and at the Naval War College in Newport. He went on to earn a master's degree in history at Brown University in 1971, and his doctorate (DPhil) in modern history in 1979 from the University of Oxford in England, where he wrote his thesis on the reign of Queen Anne. He returned to the Naval War College in 1977, where he coauthored the centennial history of the College in 1984. He served as the Ernest J. King Professor of Maritime History for thirty-two years from 1984 to 2016 as well as being the first director of the College's Maritime History Department and the director of the Naval War College Museum, 2003-2016. He has been visiting professor of naval and military history at the National University of Singapore in 1981–83 and has served on a year-long exchange with the German Armed Forces Military History Research Office in 1990–91, which included a term as visiting professor at the University of Freiburg.

He is the author, coauthor, or editor of more than forty books as well as numerous articles in the fields of maritime and early modern European history. Widely recognized for his scholarship, he has earned the University of Oxford's higher doctorate—the Doctor of Letters degree (DLitt)—and the U.S. Navy's Distinguished Civilian Service Award. Among his works, three touch on Anglican and Episcopal Church history: *A Dusty Path: A Pictorial History of Kenyon College* (Gambier, Ohio: 1964), *The Two Beginnings: A History of St. George's Church, Tanglin* (Singapore: 1984), and *John Robinson's Account of Sweden, 1688* (Stockholm: 1998). The last is a study of Sweden by the legation chaplain in Stockholm, who later rose to negotiate the Peace of Utrecht for Britain and to become bishop of London and, in that role, the bishop for Anglican churches in America, 1713–23. He is a member of the Historical Society of the Episcopal Church and National Episcopal Historians and Archivists.

John and his wife, Berit, were married at Trinity Church. They have three daughters, Kristina, Ingrid, and Anna, all of whom were members of the Trinity Church children's choir. In addition to serving as an historical guide and parish historian at Trinity, John has twice been a delegate to the diocesan convention.

October, 2018

Made in the USA
Middletown, DE
06 September 2024

59806951R00221